T0145222

Advances in Information Security

Volume 63

Series editor

Sushil Jajodia, George Mason University, Fairfax, VA, USA

More information about this series at http://www.springer.com/series/5576

Edward J.M. Colbert • Alexander Kott
Editors

Cyber-security of SCADA and Other Industrial Control Systems

 Springer

Editors
Edward J.M. Colbert
US Army Research Laboratory
Adelphi, MD, USA

Alexander Kott
US Army Research Laboratory
Adelphi, MD, USA

ISSN 1568-2633
Advances in Information Security
ISBN 978-3-319-81203-8   ISBN 978-3-319-32125-7   (eBook)
DOI 10.1007/978-3-319-32125-7

Printed on acid-free paper

This Springer imprint is published by Springer Nature
The registered company is Springer International Publishing AG Switzerland

Acknowledgements

The authors of Chap. 4 would like to thank Aaron Sneary and Chris Sistrunk for their insightful comments on the chapter.

The authors of Chap. 9 would like to state that permission was granted by the USACE Chief of Engineers to publish the material for Chap. 9. The views and opinions expressed in this chapter are those of the individual authors and not those of the US Army, or other sponsor organizations.

The authors of Chap. 13 would like to state that Sandia National Laboratories is a multi-program laboratory managed and operated by Sandia Corporation, a wholly owned subsidiary of Lockheed Martin Corporation, for the U.S. Department of Energy's National Nuclear Security Administration under contract DE-AC04-94AL85000.

Contents

About the Authors

Kemal Akkaya (Chap. 3) is an associate professor in the Department of Electrical and Computer Engineering at Florida International University (FIU). He received his Ph.D. in computer science from the University of Maryland in Baltimore County in 2005, after which he held assistant and associate professorships at the Department of Computer Science at Southern Illinois University (SIU) and a visiting professorship at the George Washington University. Dr. Akkaya currently leads the Advanced Wireless and Security Lab (ADWISE) in the ECE Department at FIU. His current research interests include security and privacy, energy-aware routing, topology control, and quality-of-service issues in a variety of wireless networks such as sensor networks, multimedia sensor networks, smart grid communication networks, and vehicular networks. Dr. Akkaya is a senior member of the IEEE. He is the area editor of Elsevier *Ad Hoc Network* journal and serves on the editorial board of IEEE Communications Surveys and Tutorials. He has served as the guest editor for the *Journal of High Speed Networks*, *Computer Communications* journal, and Elsevier *Ad Hoc Networks* journal and is in the TPC of many leading wireless networking conferences. He has published over 100 papers in peer-reviewed journal and conferences. He has received the "Top Cited" article award from Elsevier in 2010.

Misty Blowers (Chap. 16) is the lead for in-house research in cyber operations at the US Air Force Research Laboratory, Information Directorate. She obtained her Ph.D. from the SUNY College of Environmental Science and Forestry in applied science and engineering and an M.S. in computer science from Syracuse University. She has extensive research experience in the fields of machine learning, big data analytics, industrial process design, systems engineering, cybersecurity, modeling, and simulation. She has authored over 50 publications and provided plenary talks on behavior analysis of manufacturing processes. She led a team of young engineers to launch a new start company which won the top award by a panel of new venture capitalist and local scientific leaders. Her patented technology has resulted in AFRL licenses across four different domains with potential for numerous more applications and licenses currently being pursued. Dr. Blowers was named the 2014 Technologist of the Year by the Technical Association of Central New York.

Norbou Buchler (Chap. 10) is a cognitive scientist in the Human Research and Engineering Directorate of the Army Research Laboratory. His basic research interests are to understand human cognition and decision-making at network levels of interaction using multidisciplinary approaches including social network analysis, cognitive modeling, multi-agent systems, and behavioral laboratory experimentation. His applied research focuses on human system integration and developing agent-based decision-support technologies for application in both cybersecurity and Mission Command environments. Norbou received his Ph.D. in experimental psychology from Syracuse University, and did two postdoctoral fellowships, first at Carnegie Mellon University examining computational modeling and behavioral approaches to cognition and second at the Center for Cognitive Neuroscience at Duke University using functional magnetic resonance imaging (fMRI) and diffusion tensor imaging approaches to elucidate the neural correlates of memory retrieval.

Hasan Cam (Chap. 10) is a computer scientist at the US Army Research Lab. He currently works on the projects involved with metrics, models, and data analytics for assessing cyber vulnerability, risk, resilience, agility, and mission assurance over wired, mobile, and tactical networks. He serves as the government lead for the risk area in Cyber Collaborative Research Alliance. His research interests include cybersecurity, networks, algorithms, and parallel processing. He has served as an editorial member of two journals, namely, *Computer Communications* and *International Journal of Communications Systems*, a guest editor of two special issues of journals, an organizer of symposiums and workshops, and a technical program committee member in numerous conferences. He received the Ph.D. degree in electrical and computer engineering from Purdue University in 1992 and the M.S. degree in computer science from Polytechnic University, New York, in 1986. He is a senior member of the IEEE.

J. Ryan Carr (Chap. 8) received his Ph.D. in computer science from the University of Maryland in 2013. His research on artificial intelligence, game theory, and social learning has been published in highly competitive venues such as the Proceedings of the Royal Society, AAAI, and AAMAS. He is currently a researcher at the Johns Hopkins University Applied Physics Laboratory, where he develops large-scale data analytics and cloud computing systems.

Mehmet H. Cintuglu (Chap. 3) received the B.S. and M.S. degrees in electrical engineering from Gazi University, Ankara, Turkey, in 2008 and 2011, respectively. He is currently pursuing the Ph.D. degree in electrical engineering. He is currently a research assistant at the Energy Systems Research Laboratory, Electrical and Computer Engineering Department, College of Engineering and Computing, Florida International University, Miami, FL, USA. From 2009 to 2011, he was a power systems project engineer at an electric utility company in Turkey. His current research interests include active distribution networks and wide-area monitoring, protection, and control.

Edward J.M. Colbert (Editor, Chaps. 1, 2, 11, and 16) currently performs computer security research for the Army Research Laboratory (ARL) in Adelphi, Maryland. At ARL, Dr. Colbert leads research on methods for defending Army SCADA and ICS systems. Before working at ARL, Dr. Colbert performed telecommunications research for the Department of Defense, Verizon, and the Johns Hopkins University Applied Physics Laboratory. Dr. Colbert received the bachelor of science degree in engineering physics from the University of Illinois (1987), the master of science in physics from the University of Illinois (1988), the master of science in astronomy from the University of Maryland (1993), and the Ph.D. in astronomy from the University of Maryland (1997). Dr. Colbert holds a research professorship at the Catholic University of America in Washington, DC, and has over 50 publications in refereed journals.

Zachary A. Collier (Chap. 9) is a Ph.D. student in the Department of Systems and Information Engineering at the University of Virginia. He is a member of the Society for Risk Analysis. Prior to joining UVa, he worked for the US Army Engineer Research and Development Center on the Risk and Decision Science Team. Mr. Collier has a master of engineering management from Duke University and a B.S. in mechanical engineering from Florida State University. His research interests include the application of decision analysis, risk analysis, and other systems-modeling techniques across the life cycles of technological, infrastructure, and other socio-technical systems. Applications include the management of logistics, business, environmental, and other emerging risks during the development, acquisition, and use of novel products, processes, and technologies.

Bharat Doshi (Chap. 10) is senior research scientist (cybersecurity) in the US Army. Prior to joining the US Army, Dr. Doshi worked at Johns Hopkins University Applied Physics Laboratory for 10 years, Bell Labs for 24 years, and academia for 6 years. His research spans the whole gamut of commercial communications and networking technologies as well as major communications, networking, and cybersecurity programs in the Department of Defense and the Department of Homeland Security. He is a fellow of Bell Labs and a fellow of the IEEE. He has published over 125 papers and holds 46 US patents.

Nick Evancich (Chap. 6) holds bachelor's and master's degrees in electrical engineering from Purdue University. His area of research is in cybersecurity focusing on network security. Specifically his research centers on automated exploitation generation. His work at Intelligent Automation Inc. covers a wide variety of cyber topics: process introspection, anonymization, and situational awareness. Prior to joining Intelligent Automation Inc., he worked at JHU/APL where he worked on anti-submarine warfare, chem/bio detection systems, and unattended ground sensors; additionally he worked on DARPA's TIGR program which improved tactical situational awareness. His academic interests include malware detection, mobile security, and compiler design.

Angelyn S. Flowers (Chap. 7), a computational social scientist, is coordinator of the graduate program in homeland security and a professor of criminal justice at the University of the District of Columbia, where she also serves as co-director of the Institute for Public Safety and Justice. Her recent publications on cybersecurity have appeared in IEEE journals and in the *Journal of Homeland Security and Emergency Management*, with book chapters in upcoming publications as diverse as privacy and digital devices, to homeland security and emergency management. Dr. Flowers served on the academic advisory board for *Weapons of Mass Destruction and Terrorism* for McGraw-Hill Publishing Company's Contemporary Learning Series. She earned a Ph.D. in interdisciplinary studies from Commonwealth Open University (British Virgin Islands) stemming from her work in developing a multi-agent model simulating the effect of enforcement mechanisms on risk taking behavior, a juris doctorate from Georgetown University Law Center, and a bachelor's degree from Howard University. She is admitted to practice law before several courts in the USA, including the US Supreme Court. Research interests include cybersecurity, multi-agent modeling, complex systems analysis, and critical infrastructure protection.

Alexander A. Ganin (Chap. 9) is a contractor at the Risk and Decision Science Team within the Environmental Laboratory of the US Army Engineer Research and Development Center. He is also a research scientist at the Department of Systems and Information Engineering at the University of Virginia. Dr. Ganin received his Ph.D. in physics for studies of electronic properties of carbon nanotubes in 2013 from the Voronezh State University in Russia. Before that, he worked in the software development industry. Currently Alexander Ganin is involved in multiple risk assessment, cybersecurity, resilience, and multi-criteria decision analysis projects. His research interests include nanotechnology, software development, and metricization of resilience as a property of systems represented as complex networks. Dr. Ganin is a Society for Risk Analysis student member.

Carlos Aguayo Gonzalez (Chap. 12) is a founder and chief technology officer of PFP Cybersecurity, which develops unique physics-based cybersecurity solutions for critical infrastructure, including industrial control systems and supply-chain risk management. He received his Ph.D. and M.S. degrees from Virginia Tech both in electrical engineering. The PFP Cybersecurity approach has its foundation on Dr. Aguayo Gonzalez's doctoral work. He has extensive research and development (R&D) experience in cybersecurity, critical infrastructure protection, side-channel analysis, machine learning, and signal processing. Dr. Aguayo Gonzalez has served as principal investigator in multiple R&D projects in cybersecurity protection of critical infrastructure. Key sponsors of this research include the following: the National Science Foundation, Army, Air Force, Defense Advanced Research Projects Agency, and Department of Homeland Security.

J. Daniel Gordon (Chap. 8) is a cyber engineer in the asymmetric operations sector at Johns Hopkins APL. He previously worked as a mathematician and software developer for the US Department of Defense from 2008 to 2014. He received his bachelor of science in discrete mathematics and bachelor of science in psychology from Georgia Tech in 2008 and is currently pursuing his master of science in applied and computational mathematics from Johns Hopkins University.

Daryl Haegley, OCP, CCO (Chap. 14) leads control systems cybersecurity efforts from the Office of the Assistant Secretary of Defense for Energy, Installations, and Environment. He has 25+ years of military and federal civilian experience, currently overseeing the cybersecurity and information risk management effort to modernize and integrate real property, geospatial, and energy systems for the DoD. He leads DoD policy development, cyber infrastructure terrain assessments and analysis, and technical working groups evaluating and standardizing DoD's cybersecurity control systems security baseline and overlay specifics for control systems (CS)/ platform information technology (I-PIT) systems, such as electronic (smart) meters and other embedded electronic control systems. Additionally, he leads the development of the cybersecurity of Facility Control Systems Unified Facilities Guide (UFC) and Enterprise Energy Information Management (EEIM) Capability initiative to standardize DoD processes and integrate systems needed to systematically track, analyze, and report facility energy and related costs. He maintains four certifications, three master's degrees, and one patent. Mr. Haegley's chapter is written in his personal capacity, and the views expressed do not necessarily reflect those of the DoD or the USA.

Matthew H. Henry (Chap. 8) is a principal system scientist at the Johns Hopkins Applied Physics Laboratory (APL) and a member of the adjunct faculty of the JHU Whiting School of Engineering. Matt's recent work has focused on model-based analysis of cyber, cyber-physical, and tactical systems. His methodological and applied research contributions in the areas of systems modeling, risk analysis, and multi-objective optimization have been published widely in a variety of journals, conference proceedings, and technical volumes. He received his Ph.D. in 2007 from the University of Virginia in systems and information engineering, and he holds M.S.E. and B.S. degrees in electrical and aerospace engineering, respectively. Prior to his career in research, Matt practiced as a control systems engineer in the automotive and aerospace industries.

Blaine Hoffman (Chap. 10) is an ORAU postdoctoral research fellow in the Human Research and Engineering Directorate of the US Army Research Laboratory. He currently is involved in research concerning the workflow and tasks of cybersecurity analysts and exploring how tools can aid and support cyber defense. His research interests span user experience and usability using user-centered practices to explore community interactions, decision-support scenarios, mobile computing, and better integration of technology with activities and tasks encountered daily. He dual majored in computer science and communication while earning his B.S. from Denison University. His interest in combining the study and development of technology with social sciences and research led him to Pennsylvania State University, where he earned his Ph.D. in the College of Information Sciences and Technology.

Frank Honkus III (Chap. 15) supports USCYBERCOM J5 on the Joint Base Architecture for Secure Industrial Control Systems (J-BASICS) Joint Test, developing defensive tactics, techniques, and procedures to detect, mitigate, and recover from cyber attacks against industrial control systems (ICS). He has supported USCYBERCOM J2, conducting intelligence analysis and briefing senior leadership on ICS cybersecurity and mission assurance. Mr. Honkus has also supported the Department of Homeland Security's Office of Infrastructure Protection, producing daily and monthly reports and providing briefings to the financial services, telecommunications, and information technology sectors. He earned his master's degree from the University of Pittsburgh, Pennsylvania, with a major in security and intelligence and minor in human security.

Steve Hutchinson (Chap. 11) is a cybersecurity researcher at ICF International and contracted to the US Army Research Laboratory (ARL) in Adelphi, MD. His principal research interests are the cognitive aspects of cybersecurity decision-making and the use of computation and human-machine interface techniques to augment analyst capabilities. He has an M.S. in instruction science, graduate studies in computer science, and B.S. in electrical engineering and was initially employed at the Eastman Kodak Company as a manufacturing/process control engineer.

Jose Iribarne (Chap. 16) is the director of Mill Strategic Projects and Technology at WestRock, a global packaging company with 42,000 employees in 275 locations across 30 countries. He received a B.S. in mechanical engineering from the University of Chile in 1985 and M.S. and Ph.D. degrees from the State University of New York, College of Environmental Science and Forestry, in 1995 and 1999, respectively. Dr. Iribarne is a former Fulbright scholar with 6 years in R&D and more than 30 publications, from energy efficiency to Kraft pulp strength, oxygen delignification, and recycling. He has another 24 years of experience in facilities and engineering projects at all levels, from feasibility studies to managing a $15-million annual capital expenditure program. He has worked in Energy Efficiency and Pulp and Paper since 1985 with direct experience in sustainability, cleaner production, pulping, recycling, and papermaking.

Alexander Kott (Editor, Chaps. 1, 9, and 16) serves as the chief of the Network Science Division of the Army Research Laboratory headquartered in Adelphi, MD. In this position, he is responsible for fundamental research and applied development in performance and security of both tactical mobile and strategic networks. He oversees projects in network performance and security, intrusion detection, and network emulation. Between 2003 and 2008, Dr. Kott served as a Defense Advanced

Research Projects Agency (DARPA) program manager responsible for a number of large-scale advanced technology research programs. His earlier positions included technical director at BBN Technologies, Cambridge, MA; director of R&D at Logica Carnegie Group, Pittsburgh, PA; and IT research department manager at AlliedSignal, Inc., Morristown, NJ. Dr. Kott received the Secretary of Defense Exceptional Public Service Award and accompanying Exceptional Public Service Medal, in October 2008. He earned his Ph.D. from the University of Pittsburgh, Pittsburgh, PA, in 1989, published over 70 technical papers, and co-authored and edited six technical books.

Ryan M. Layer (Chap. 8) received B.S. and M.S. degrees in computer science from Texas A&M University, College Station, USA, in 2003 and 2005. From 2005 to 2009, he researched network attack modeling techniques at the Johns Hopkins Applied Physics Laboratory in Laurel, MD, USA. In 2014, he received his Ph.D. in computer science from the University of Virginia, Charlottesville, USA, and is now a postdoctoral researcher at the University of Utah, Salt Lake City, USA, where he develops algorithms for analyzing large-scale genetic data sets.

Brian Van Leeuwen (Chap. 13) is a distinguished technical staff member at Sandia National Laboratories. He is a member of the Critical Systems Security Department where he performs analysis of secure information systems. For 15 years, he has been involved in the analysis of secure information systems using modeling and simulation methods. He received his master of science degree in electrical engineering in 1989 from Arizona State University, Tempe, Arizona.

Jason Li (Chap. 6) received his Ph.D. degree from the University of Maryland at College Park. He is currently a vice president and senior director at Intelligent Automation Inc., where he has been working on research and development programs in the area of networks and cybersecurity. Over the years, he has initiated and worked on numerous R&D programs related to protocol design and development for satellite networks, mobile code technology and its applications in security, realistic and repeatable wireless networks test and evaluation, moving target defense, cyber situational awareness, attack impact analysis, airborne networks, complex networks, ad hoc and sensor networks, efficient network management, and software agents. Dr. Li has led the effort of architecting the networks and security programs at IAI, establishing enduring trust relationship with various customers, and working with the IAI team and the collaborators to deliver quality results that meet the customer's needs.

Igor Linkov (Chap. 9) is the Risk and Decision Science Focus Area lead at the US Army Engineer Research and Development Center. He is an adjunct professor of engineering and public policy at Carnegie Mellon University and professor of practice in electrical and computer engineering at the University of Connecticut. Dr. Linkov has managed multiple risk assessments and risk management projects in the areas of environmental management, cybersecurity, critical infrastructure, climate change, and systems vulnerability. He is currently developing resilience assessment and management approaches for infrastructure and cyber systems. As one of the leaders of the USACE Resilience PDT, he is working on developing the USACE Resilience Roadmap and is part of several interagency committees and working groups tasked with developing resilience metrics and resilience management approaches. He has published widely on environmental policy, environmental modeling, and risk analysis, including fourteen books and over 250 peer-reviewed papers and book chapters. Dr. Linkov is a Society for Risk Analysis fellow and recipient of the 2005 Chauncey Starr Award for exceptional contribution to risk analysis and 2014 Outstanding Professional Award.

Eric Luiijf, M.Sc. (Eng)Delft (Chaps. 2 and 5), a former officer in the Royal Netherlands Navy, is a principal consultant for Cyber Operations and Critical (Information) Infrastructure Protection at the Netherlands Organisation for Applied Scientific Research (TNO), the Hague, the Netherlands. He supports the Dutch government in the area of cybersecurity and takes part in European Union critical infrastructure resilience and smart grid projects. He was member of the core team which developed the second Dutch national cybersecurity strategy. In 2005, Eric analyzed the risk of SCADA systems and the need for governance by the Dutch government. As part of the National Infrastructure Against Cybercrime (NICC) program, he developed a SCADA security benchmark which has been applied to the Dutch drinking water, energy, and wastewater management sectors. He developed SCADA security good practices for the Dutch drinking water sector which were published in Dutch and have been translated into English, Italian, and Japanese.

Osama Mohammed (Chap. 3) is a professor of electrical engineering and is the director of the Energy Systems Research Laboratory at Florida International University (FIU), Miami, Florida, USA. Professor Mohammed is world renowned in the power and energy systems field. He performed multiple research projects for federal agencies and industries over the past 35 years and has active research programs from the US Department of Defense and Department of Energy. He has published more than 400 articles in refereed journals and other IEEE refereed international conferences. He also authored a book and several book chapters. He is a fellow of the IEEE and the Applied Computational Electromagnetics Society. Professor Mohammed is a recipient of the IEEE Power and Energy Society Cyril Veinott Electromechanical Energy Conversion Award and the 2012 Outstanding Research Award from FIU. Professor Mohammed holds M.S. and Ph.D. degrees from Virginia Tech, Blacksburg, Virginia, USA. A complete list of publications is available at http://www.energy.fiu.edu/contact.

Apurva Mohan (Chap. 3) is a senior research scientist and technical program manager at Honeywell ACS Labs, Golden Valley, MN. His research interests are in the areas of cybersecurity and privacy applications to the Internet of Things, industrial control systems, smart grid security, cloud computing, and sensitive data protection. He serves as principal investigator and program manager for various research projects funded by the US government and Honeywell International. One of his current research focuses include cybersecurity for energy control systems, where he is leading cybersecurity initiatives for securing microgrids at US Department of Defense installations. He has also made contributions to several standard bodies including the OpenADR alliance to strengthen the security of smart grid protocols. In the past, he has made contributions to protection against unauthorized access of sensitive healthcare data in highly distributed and federated healthcare environments. He holds a master's degree and Ph.D. focusing on cybersecurity from the Georgia Institute of Technology, where he was a TI:GER scholar.

Alessandro Oltramari (Chap. 7) is a postdoctoral research associate at Carnegie Mellon University, CyLab. He received his Ph.D. from University of Trento (Italy) in cognitive science and education, in co-tutorship with the Institute of Cognitive Sciences and Technologies of the Italian National Research Council (ISTC-CNR). He has held a research position at the Laboratory for Applied Ontology (ISTC-CNR) in Trento from 2000 to 2010. He has been a visiting research associate at Princeton University (Cognitive Science Laboratory) in 2005 and 2006. His research activity at Carnegie Mellon University mainly deals with integrating ontologies and cognitive architectures for high-level reasoning in knowledge-intensive tasks. In particular, he develops computational models of decision-making in cybersecurity, focusing on the interaction between defenders, attackers, and users.

Mahesh Panwar (Chap. 9) is a contractor to the US Army Engineer Research and Development Center. His research interests include decision analysis and cybersecurity. Panwar received a master of science from the George Washington University and a bachelor of arts in physics and philosophy from the University of Virginia.

Jeffrey Reed (Chap. 12) is the founder of *Wireless @ Virginia Tech* and served as its director until 2014. He is the founding faculty member of the Ted and Karyn Hume Center for National Security and Technology and served as its interim director when founded in 2010. His book *Software Radio: A Modern Approach to Radio Design* was published by Prentice Hall, and his latest textbook *Cellular Communications: A Comprehensive and Practical Guide* was published by Wiley-IEEE in 2014. He is co-founder of Cognitive Radio Technologies (CRT), a company commercializing of the cognitive radio technologies; Allied Communications, a company developing spectrum sharing technologies; and Power Fingerprinting, a company specializing in security for embedded systems. In 2005, Dr. Reed became fellow to the IEEE for contributions to software radio and communications signal processing and for leadership in engineering education. He is also a distinguished lecturer for the IEEE Vehicular Technology Society. In 2013, he was awarded the International Achievement Award by the Wireless Innovations Forum. In 2012, he served on the President's Council of Advisors of Science and Technology Working Group that examine ways to transition federal spectrum to allow commercial use and improve economic activity. Dr. Reed is a member of CSMAC, a group that provides advice to the NTIA on spectrum issues.

Sidney C. Smith (Chap. 7) graduated from Towson State University with a bachelor's degree in computer science in January of 1990. In 2013, he earned his master's degree in computer science at Towson University (TU) where his thesis was on the impact of packet loss on network intrusion detection. He is current working on his doctorate at TU. He began his career in information assurance in April of 1990 when he was hired by the US Army as a systems administrator. Since that time, he has served as an information systems security officer, information assurance security officer, an information assurance network manager, and an information assurance program manager. In addition, he has served as an agent of the certification authority and privacy officer. In January 2010, he was hired as the team leader for the Army Research Laboratory Product Integration and Test Team. He has been a Certified Information System Security Professional since 2006, certified in the National Security Agency INFOSEC Assessment Methodology and INFOSEC Evaluation Methodology since 2006, Security+ Certified since 2008, a Certified Authorization Professional since 2008, and a Certified Information Systems Auditor since 2010.

Daniel Sullivan (Chaps. 2 and 3) is a senior principal software engineer at the Raytheon Company and is a member of the ICF International team supporting the Army Research Laboratory conducting research in protecting industrial control systems from cyber threats. He served 10 years as a naval officer and then held positions in system integration and information assurance for Department of Defense programs. He earned a master of science degree in electrical engineering from the Naval Postgraduate School and a bachelor of science degree in electrical engineering from the University of Illinois at Urbana-Champaign, IL. His certifications include Global Industrial Cyber Security Professional (GICSP), Certified Information Systems Security Professional (CISSP), and Certified Ethical Hacker (CEH). He is co-inventor of one patent.

Selcuk Uluagac (Chap. 3) is currently an assistant professor in the Department of Electrical and Computer Engineering (ECE) at Florida International University (FIU). Before joining FIU, he was a senior research engineer in the School of ECE at Georgia Institute of Technology. Prior to Georgia Tech, he was a senior research engineer at Symantec. He earned his Ph.D. from the School of ECE, Georgia Tech, in 2010 and an M.Sc. in information security from the School of Computer Science, Georgia Tech, and an M.Sc. in ECE from Carnegie Mellon University in 2009 and 2002, respectively. The focus of his research is on cybersecurity topics with an emphasis on its practical and applied aspects. In 2015, he received a Faculty Early Career Development (CAREER) Award from the US National Science Foundation (NSF) and the US Air Force Office of Sponsored Research (AFOSR)'s 2015 Summer Faculty Fellowship Award.

Vincent Urias (Chap. 13) is a principal member of technical staff at Sandia National Laboratories, where he has spent the last twelve years conducting cybersecurity research and development. His research areas include cyber test bedding, cyber modeling and simulation, as well as cyber analytics, cloud computing, and networking.

Tarek Youssef (Chap. 3) was born in Cairo, Egypt. He received the B.S. and M.S. degrees in electrical engineering from Helwan University, Cairo. Tarek has more than 10 years of experience in the communication and security field. In 2012, he worked as researcher in the Université Libre de Bruxelles, Belgium, and then moved to the Energy Systems Research Laboratory at Florida International University where he is currently a Ph.D. candidate. His Ph.D. topic is entitled "Co-Design of Security Aware Power System Distribution Architecture as Cyber Physical System." His research interests include cyber physical systems, communications, wide-area measurements, smart grid security, and real-time monitoring of power systems. He also has interest in artificial intelligence and signal processing applications in the power and energy systems area.

David R. Zaret (Chap. 8) is a computer scientist at the Johns Hopkins Applied Physics Laboratory and a member of the part-time computer science faculty in the Johns Hopkins Whiting School of Engineering. He was formerly a lead operations research analyst at United Parcel Service. He received a B.A. in mathematics from the University of Wisconsin, master's degrees in mathematics from the University of Michigan and computer science from Johns Hopkins University, and Ph.D. in philosophy from Brown University. The focus of his work at APL has been on formal methods, cryptographic protocols, and cyber attack and risk modeling. He is currently working on the development of partially observable stochastic game models for network attack and mitigation analysis and on algorithmic techniques for mission-based cyber risk analysis.

Chapter 1
Introduction and Preview

Alexander Kott, Carlos Aguayo Gonzalez, and Edward J.M. Colbert

The term Industrial Control System (ICS) refers to a variety of systems comprised of computers, electrical and mechanical devices, and manual processes overseen by humans; they perform automated or partially automated control of equipment in manufacturing and chemical plants, electric utilities, distribution and transportation systems and many other industries.

While strong concerns about security of ICSs, particularly in the context of critical national infrastructure, were expressed even in early 2000s (Lüders 2005; US Department of Energy 2002), it was not until the legendary 2010 Stuxnet episode (Langner 2011) that security of ICSs entered public and government discourse and acquired today's saliency (Executive Order 2013; Stouffer et al 2015).

This book takes a broad-ranging look at cyber security of ICS: from exploring types of components, layers, zones and sub-systems of ICS, to threats and attacks on ICS, to intrusion detection specific to ICS, to risk assessment and governance of ICS, to future of ICS.

Edward J.M. Colbert - Also ICF International, Inc.

A. Kott (✉) • E.J.M. Colbert
US Army Research Laboratory, Adelphi, MD, USA
e-mail: alexander.kott1.civ@mail.mil; edward.j.colbert2.civ@mail.mil

C. Aguayo Gonzalez
PFP Cybersecurity, Vienna, VA, USA

© Springer International Publishing Switzerland 2016
E.J.M. Colbert, A. Kott (eds.), *Cyber-security of SCADA and Other Industrial Control Systems*, Advances in Information Security 66,
DOI 10.1007/978-3-319-32125-7_1

In this introductory chapter we begin by exploring basic concepts and segments of the general class of Cyber-Physical Systems (CPSs), which include ICSs and SCADA[1] systems. This helps understand the differences between cyber security of ICSs and that of conventional IT systems. Then, we provide a preview of the entire book.

1.1 The Structure and Functions of an ICS

A key difference between ICSs and traditional Information Technology (IT) systems is that ICSs interact strongly with the physical environment. ICSs and all CPSs are cybersystems and are therefore vulnerable to cyber attacks. This connection with the physical world, however, presents unique challenges and opportunities.

CPSs integrate computational resources, communication capabilities, sensing, and actuation in effort to monitor and control physical processes. CPSs are found in critical infrastructure such as transportation networks, Unmanned Aerial Vehicle Systems (UASs), nuclear power generation, electric power distribution networks, water and gas distribution networks, and advanced communication systems.

In traditional critical infrastructure systems great efforts are committed to address concerns about safety and reliability, and to develop the appropriate techniques for fault detection, isolation, and recovery. In CPSs, however, the additional "cyber" element introduces specific vulnerabilities which are not directly addressed in traditional fault tolerance and reliable computing practices. Addressing the cyber element in CPS safety and reliability is of utmost importance, since the introduction of highly integrated CPS into critical infrastructures and emerging systems could lead to situations where cyber based attacks against CPSs could adversely affect widespread public safety (Cardenas 2008).

1.1.1 Key Segments of an ICS

In general, ICSs can be very complex systems. They can involve thousands of different components distributed across geographical regions and controlling complex processes at real-time. Most of the time, the large scale of these systems, as well as the diversity of devices and requirements, requires ICS systems to be segmented into multiple operational zones. Each operational zone has unique characteristics and requirements. In order to cope with the complexity, different models have been developed to represent ICS systems (IEC TS 62443-1-1 2009; NIST 2014). From a cyber security perspective, ICS systems can be broadly segmented into three different zones:

- Enterprise zone,
- Control zone, and
- Field zone.

---

[1] Supervisory Control and Data Acquisition (SCADA) systems are a sub-class of ICSs in which control is performed over multiple, distributed individual lower-level control systems (hence the word "supervisory"). See Chap. 2 for a more detailed discussion of the different types of ICSs.

Having this segmentation is extremely useful in determining relevant security controls. The three-zone model has been used (IEC TS 62443-1-1 2009; Knapp 2012), although different names are often used to refer to similar concepts. The general components and characteristics of each zone are shown in Fig. 1.1 and described below.

The Enterprise zone includes business networks and enterprise systems; it includes diverse endpoint devices that evolve rapidly and are upgraded continuously. This zone includes business networks, commonly based on the IP protocol and very often connected to external networks and the Internet. These networks are most of the time kept separate from the operational networks used in the other zones. The enterprise zone is very similar to traditional IT environments found outside the realm of ICSs. Therefore, many cybersecurity solutions from the IT world can be directly applied.

The Control zone includes the distributed control elements in SCADA systems. These zones include the control room environments. The Control zone shares a few similarities with the Enterprise zone, such as networks based on the IP protocol. The requirements of the Control zone, however, shift drastically to emphasize safety and reliability. The devices in this zone may not be updated as often and the networks may be subject to strict timing constraints. Therefore, few cybersecurity solutions from the IT world can be directly used in this zone.

The Field zone, also known as the plant, process, or operations zone, includes the devices and networks in charge of control and automation. The field zone is the one that hosts the CPSs. The devices in this zone often include single-purpose embedded

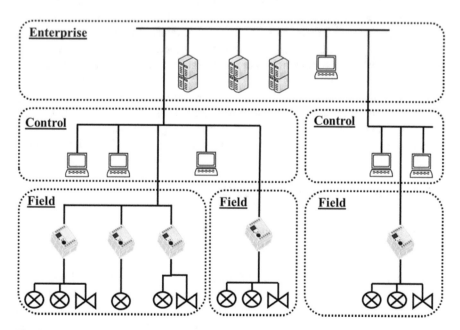

Fig. 1.1 ICS three-tiered security model

devices, such as Programmable Logic Controllers (PLCs), which have constrained computational resources. The communication networks in this zone are much more diverse and go beyond IP networks, employing a large variety of industrial protocols and physical interfaces. Devices and networks in the field zone are subject to strict safety, reliability, and timing requirements. Therefore, the cybersecurity solutions from the IT world rarely if ever apply.

This three-tiered model is admittedly oversimplified. However, it is very useful to differentiate the unique technical aspects that shape security requirements. Each zone has different security requirements and it is important to establish strong boundaries and abstractions between zones. The consequences of cyber attacks on the different zones are also very different.

A good example of different operational zones in ICSs is found in the modern electrical smart grid. At the same time it exemplifies how modern ICSs are very complex systems that often do not fit a general network models for cybersecurity. For instance, the smart grid is a sophisticated architecture of communication, control, monitoring, and automation with a goal of improving the way electricity is generated, distributed, and consumed. The smart grid is distributed across vast geographical regions and includes multiple zones, including multiple field zones, each one very complex in itself.

As shown in Fig. 1.2, the smart grid is separated into four major areas: generation, transmission, and distribution of energy, as well as the advanced metering at the end-user premises. Each one of the major areas is a vast and a very complex system on its own, with multiple field and control zones that need to interact with one another. The smart grid also highlights the complexity and diversity at the enterprise levels. The smart grid requires a variety of energy services and back-office services that while included in the enterprise zone, could be considered their own zone.

It can be argued that current cybersecurity approaches for the smart grid adequately protect higher zones (such as IT networks), since they share many commonalities with other enterprise level systems. The energy generation, transmission and distribution areas, however, rely heavily on CPSs and include vast distributed field zones made up of ICSs with dedicated and limited functionality. Protecting such complex systems from cyber attack is a daunting challenge which designers need to meet along with additional constraints, such as safety and reliability requirements.

1.1.2 Safety and Reliability in ICS

One of the main operational distinctions on the Field zone as compared with the Enterprise zone is the strict requirements for reliability and safety, especially for control of critical infrastructure. For example, Field devices in critical infrastructure are designed as safety-critical, fault-tolerant systems. These safety and reliability requirements have a profound impact in multiple aspects of ICSs, from design (e.g., redundant systems) to maintenance (e.g., upgrading and patches). Because of this, we give special attention to describing the specific requirements that arise as results of safety and reliability requirements in field devices and networks.

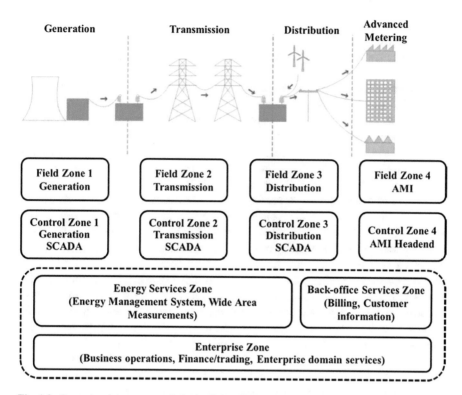

Fig. 1.2 Operational zones example in the Smart Grid

Field systems in critical infrastructure are required to provide very high levels of availability, on-demand reliability, and in some cases safety under a wide range of operating conditions. Because of the potential consequences of a critical system's failure, these systems must reduce the likelihood of even low-probability fault events. Systems where the consequences of failure are high must be dependable systems, which have the ability to avoid service failures that are more frequent and more severe than is acceptable to the user(s) and also have the ability to deliver service that can be justifiably trusted. Dependable systems often use the following approaches to enhance the reliability and safety of the systems in the presence of faults:

- Fault avoidance—avoid faults by design, i.e., build the system correctly from the beginning
- Fault removal—reduce, by verification and testing the presence of faults
- Fault tolerance—provide correct function despite presence of faults

Fault tolerance is the only one active in the operational phase. Thus, for the fault tolerance techniques to work effectively, it is important to understand the types of faults the system may experience. Traditionally, fault tolerance methods and techniques have been used for two classes of faults/failures. The first is hardware faults that could be permanent or transient in nature. The second is software faults that become active when unusual inputs and state conditions occur. Both hardware and software fault tolerance techniques make use of redundancy to overcome the effects of faults.

Hardware fault tolerance methods use techniques like voting, masking, EDC codes, duplication and comparison to detect and correct the effects of faults. These techniques work for hardware faults because hardware faults are assumed to occur randomly, independently of one another. Software faults usually do not occur randomly or independently from one another, they occur when input/state conditions arise that trigger a software bug. As such, merely replication and redundancy do not work.

Software fault tolerance techniques often employ diversity and defense-in-depth techniques to detect and correct software faults at runtime. These include: diverse forms of the software running on different processors, N-version programming where different versions of the program are written by diverse programming teams, runtime monitors where a "safety monitor" checks the outputs for reasonableness or a property violation. In general, fault-tolerant systems relay on resilient designs and continuous state awareness or monitoring. In these systems, self-monitoring and self-testing features are prominent such as cyclic hardware testing, timing analysis to detect processes that hang, independent watchdog timers, hardwired shutdown in the case of failure, data integrity checks, and in case of failure, faulty messages and signals are used by application level error detection to enforce fail-safe operation.

Another important characteristic of dependable systems is that they are often real-time. A real-time system is characterized by its ongoing interaction with its environment, continuously accepting requests from the environment and continuously producing reactions. In real time systems, correctness or safeness of the reactive system is related to its behavior over time as it interacts with its environment. Thus, correctness of the result also depends on timeliness of delivery.

While hardware and software fault tolerant methods are sufficient for randomly occurring or design faults, they are not sufficient when the faults are malicious and intentional in nature—faults caused by cyber attacks. In the context of CPSs, true resiliency must consider what represents the proper operation of the process application in the face of many adverse conditions, including those attributable to threats from undesirable human interactions, such as those of malicious cyber actors. Cyber faults in CPSs fall into two classes.

- Non-malicious failures, introduced without malicious objectives
- Malicious failures or cyber-attacks, introduced during either system development with the intent to cause harm to the system during its use, or directly during use

While non-malicious faults and failures are mostly introduced by inadvertent mistakes and bad operator decisions, malicious failures or cyber-attacks are introduced by an intelligent human adversary or threat agent with the malicious objective to alter the functioning of the system. For instance, an adversary could launch an external attack in which the attacker intercepts messages, injects false data, or denies access to certain modules. While these actions can certainly disrupt the operation of the system, they can be detected and mitigated with current technologies, such as firewalls, encryption, and authentication. In other cases, an attacker could compromise and completely control some system components. In this scenario, the attacker could modify or drop critical messages, inject false reporting and monitoring information, generate false events, disable critical safety measures, coordinate attacks involving multiple components, and much more.

1.1.3 Security of ICS Field Network Components

The Field Zone in ICSs epitomizes the differences between traditional cybersecurity in IT systems and ICSs. Systems in the field zones, including the endpoints (such as controllers) and its networks (conduits), are often the ones with the most stringent requirements in terms of reliability and safety, and the most sensitivity to timing disruptions. They are often implemented with severe resources constraints, often relying on legacy platforms that are not updated or patched, and using proprietary communication protocols.

Current approaches are limited to monitoring the conduits (access networks) to the field zones that attempt to create protected "islands", but can still leave Field elements unprotected and unmonitored. Existing cyber security approaches typically cannot be applied to the field elements due to the limited computational capabilities of the field elements. Current approaches for protecting the Field zone from cyber attack are traditionally limited to physical security, while network security (e.g., intrusion prevention and intrusion detection) is often limited to the conduits, and end-point protection to a limited extent. In terms of endpoint protection for Field devices, current cyber security solutions do not meet the field requirements adequately. For instance, there is lack of adequate antivirus software for the embedded systems in CPSs, and monitoring techniques that rely in virtual machine hypervisors are difficult to deploy in resource-constrained, legacy embedded platforms common in field devices.

While the Field zone highlights the difficulty in protecting ICSs from cyber attacks, the challenges presented by the Field zone operational environment also impact the attacker's ability to achieve their malicious objectives without being detected or triggering safety events. In a way, the Field zone is the most difficult to attack, since attackers need to have intimate knowledge of the process and systems in order to achieve the malicious objectives without being discovered, and without triggering any of the safety and security mechanisms (Krotofil 2015).

The interaction with the physical world, therefore, presents unique opportunities to protect field systems. Researchers have explored measuring the physical process to validate that the cyber element has not been compromised. For instance, electricity theft detectors where data analytics software is used by the utility on the collected meter data to identify possible electricity theft situations and abnormal consumption trends. This approach leverages the information provided by physical sensors to detect potential cyber attacks (Nizar 2009).

1.2 Preview of this Book

Having introduced some key features, characteristics and challenges of ICSs, let us offer the reader a preview of this book. We (here "we" refers collectively to all co-authors of this book) begin the discussion of ICS security with the Chap. 2 by introducing the basic components of ICSs, their functions, variety, and ways in which they connect and interact to produce the intended effects. The scope of an ICS may vary enormously. It ranges from a single PLC controlling a motor, to an ICS controlling a utility company's power generation plant or an ICS that control a nation's power transmission system. ICS configurations also differ greatly. Such configurations may range from a single component to wide area networks spanning a whole continent with many thousands of ICS components. In spite of such diversity, the basic building blocks of an ICS can be assigned to only a few classes. These include for example PLCs, Remote Terminal Units, Communication Gateways, and a few others which we discuss in this chapter. Unlike an IT system, an ICS monitors or interacts with something physical in the real world, and therefore an ICS includes field devices. ICSs are normally controlled by a human operator and Human Machine Interfaces (HMIs) are important components of an ICS.

All these diverse components must communicate with other components of the ICS. To do so, they are often connected within "wired" communication architecture. Although wired connections render valuable reliable services to the infrastructure elements, nature or man-made disasters can damage the ICS wired communication infrastructure. It is just one of the reasons why wireless technologies—which we discuss in the Chap. 3—are gradually gaining popularity in ICS architectures, especially as ICS systems undergoing extensive upgrade efforts in the last few years. Still, replacement of wired communications with wireless is likely to continue at an accelerated pace. This is because incorporating wireless technologies into existing ICSs can bring many benefits including: (1) lowering installation costs and maintenance, (2) providing ad hoc on-demand deployment architecture that is robust and agile in responding to cyber and physical threats, and (3) providing redundancy, which is critically important in ICSs. In this chapter, as a case study, we discuss how an existing Smart Grid system could be integrated with the wireless technologies, focusing on the implementation of a real Smart Grid hardware/software testbed.

A modern ICS is a complex system that depends on many different components and technologies to monitor and control physical processes; along with many of the managerial, administrative, and regulatory responsibilities associated with this task. The computation and communication components within an ICS are often categorized into Operations Technology (OT) and IT based on the system functions they support. We discuss this categorization in the Chap. 4. Clearly, the key difference is that OT focuses on the monitoring and control of the physical process. This introduces substantial differences in how OT systems—as contrasted with IT systems—are operated and managed, along with the technologies used to support them.

After we explored the general nature of ICS and SCADA systems, in Chap. 5 we take a broad look at threats to these systems, i.e., the causes of cyber incidents. This chapter defines an ICS threat as "potential cause of an unwanted incident through the use of one of more ICSs, which may result in harm to individuals, a system, an organization, critical infrastructure and vital societal services, the environment or the society at large". Related to threat is vulnerability, which is defined as "weakness of an asset or control that can be exploited by one or more threats." The combination of ICS threats and vulnerabilities lead to the ICS risk and to a possibility of a successful attack.

Therefore in Chap. 6 we explore how threats enable specific attacks, and the classes and examples of attacks on such systems. The nature and efficacy of attacks are largely determined by a complex mix of security deficiencies in ICS systems that aggregate architectures and approaches from several epochs of technological history. For example, SCADA systems of the second generation were distributed, but used non-standard protocols. This enabled centralized supervisory servers and remote PLCs and RTUs. Security was often overlooked in this generation. The third generation of SCADA systems used common network protocols such as TCP/IP. This generation added the concept of Process Control Network (PCN), which allowed SCADA enclaves to connect to the Internet at large. The connection enabled operators to remotely manage the SCADA ecosystem but also introduced malware to the enclaves. To provide a more concrete sample context for discussion of such attacks, the chapter presents a notional system that captures key features of many SCADA systems. Finally, the chapter discusses Stuxnet — a well-studied and documented rootkit used on a SCADA system — in detail.

With many types of systems, elements, threats, attacks, vulnerabilities, threat actors and so on, it is natural to wonder whether some conceptual order could be imposed on the complex and seemingly chaotic space of ICS security. Taxonomies and ontologies are among means by which humans bring order, meaning and knowledge management to broad domains of things, concepts and principles. For this reason, in Chap. 7 we offer an overview of selected ICS security taxonomies and elements of emerging ontologies. Ontologies are already used in a variety of applications, from Search Engine Optimization, Knowledge Discovery (e.g., elicitation of patterns of interactions within genomic data), and traditional AI and common-sense reasoning. The use of ontologies to complement ICS security taxonomies is a logical extension.

To enhance the security of any system, and to defend it effectively, one must know the risks associated with failures of the system's security. Common definitions of risk typically talk about the likelihood of an undesirable event, and a measure of the impact of the event. Therefore, Chap. 8 focuses on the problems of cyber risk assessment and management, with emphasis on application to ICS analysis. There are important benefits in such quantifications of risks and risk mitigations. They open doors to comprehensive risk management decision-making, potentially highly rigorous and insightful. Quantification of risks can also contribute to rapid, automated or semi-automated implementation of remediation plans. The chapter includes a detailed example Petri net analysis of a hazardous liquid loading system process, its failure modes and costs associated with the failure modes.

Risk is the best known and perhaps the best studied example within a much broader class of cyber security metrics. However, risk is not the only possible cyber security metrics. Other metrics can exist and could be potentially very valuable to defenders of ICS systems. When used effectively, metrics can help to clarify one's understanding of the processes of a particular area of a system, and from there, provide information for external review and assist towards further improvement. In terms of cyber security metrics, ICSs tend to have unique features: in many cases, these systems are older technologies that were designed for functionality rather than security. Therefore, metrics for ICSs must be tailored to a diverse group of systems with have many features which were not necessarily built with connectivity and security in mind. For this reason, in Chap. 9, we first outline the general theory of performance metrics, and highlight examples from the cyber security domain and ICS in particular. We then focus on a particular example of a class of metrics—metrics of resilience. The chapter presents two approaches for the generation of metrics based on the concept of resilience using a matrix-based approach and a network-based approach. Finally, a discussion of the benefits and drawbacks of different methods is presented along with a process and tips intended to aid in devising effective metrics.

The next chapter—Chap. 10—explores the science, technology and practice of human perception, comprehension and projection of events and entities in cyber defense of ICS. The chapter delves into the scope of situational awareness (SA), and its roles in the success of the mission carried out by ICS or SCADA system support. Such control systems provide the cyber-physical-human couplings needed to collect information from various sensors and devices and provide a reporting and control interface for effective human-in-the-loop involvement in managing and securing the physical elements of production and critical infrastructure. The characteristics of ICS environments add additional considerations and challenges for human defenders. Cybersecurity operations typically require a human analyst to understand the network environment and the attackers. In defending ICS environment, however, an analyst must also understand the physical dimension of the ICS environment. This poses serious challenges to maintaining cybersecurity and SA as it spans the human, cyber, and physical dimensions and a myriad of possible interactions and exploits. Maintaining SA is critical to the cybersecurity of an ICS. This chapter addresses the specific challenges posed by the physical, cyber, and human dimensions that must be considered and understood in order for human analysts to best assess and understand the requirements to successfully defend against potential attacks.

Even if the threats, risk factors and other security metrics are well understood and effectively mitigated, a determined adversary will have non-negligible probability of successful penetration of the ICS. In the Chap. 11 we use the word "intrusion" to refer to a broad range of processes and effects associated with the presence and actions of malicious software in an ICS. Once an intrusion has occurred, the first and necessary step for defeat and remediation of the intrusion is to detect the existence of the intrusion. Much of the chapter's attention is on the difficult question of whether insights and approaches developed for IDS intended for ICT can be adapted for ICS. To answer this question, the chapter explores the modern intrusion detection techniques in ICT such as host-based techniques and network-based techniques, and the differences and relative advantages of signature-based and non-signature methods. We also introduce approaches based on an appreciable degree of knowledge about the process controlled by the ICS. These methods focus on monitoring the underlying process in the control system rather than monitoring network traffic. One of the methods presented in the chapter attempts to model process variable excursions beyond their appropriate ranges using machine-learning techniques. The second method requires plant personnel input to define critical process variable limits. Semantic modeling of plant control variables is used in both methods. The chapter concludes with a detailed case study of IDS in the context of a sample plant and its ICS.

In the following chapter—Chap. 12—we continue to explore the topic introduced in the previous chapter, but with a special focus on use of physical measurements for intrusion detection. We explain that monitoring the physical environment in the Field zone can get very valuable information, not only about the physical process (control), but also about the execution status of controllers and digital devices. Since field controllers ultimately determine the physical process, it is possible to obtain an indirect assessment of the integrity of the field devices my monitoring the process itself. This concept can be extended to the monitoring of the physical processes happening inside the controllers themselves, and in this way assess directly the execution status of the controllers. The chapter concludes with the case study of an implemented IDS system for a commonly used PLC. The IDS determines the baseline. Then, we introduce a malicious modification, similar in structure and operation to Stuxnet, into the PLC logic and the IDS uses the baseline to detect the intrusion.

Chapter 13 points out that the need for experimental approaches is particularly acute with respect to ICS cyber security. The ability to assess cyber posture, effectiveness, and impact for predictive analysis is predicated on the assumption that operators, users, and others have prior and complete understanding of the effects and impacts caused by cyber adversaries. Obviously, this is often not the case. When compared to the physical world, cyber is quite different, in that it does not follow physical scientific laws; rather, cyber is unbounded because it is a human-made science. As a result, understanding and quantifying effects are still an immature science. Many systems do not lend themselves to closed form mathematical solutions. Thus experimentation becomes a key method of performing analysis of these systems. In order to develop a foundation for identifying and bounding the issues, one approach to this problem is empirically through experimentation, much like physical sciences such as chemistry and physics.

In spite of decision support technologies, such as experimentation and simulation discussed in the previous chapter, it remains challenging for ICS stakeholders (leaders, managers, operators, etc.) to make informed decisions regarding formulating guidance, assigning responsibilities, balancing security and efficiency, allocating funding, determining return on investment, and measuring performance. Formulating and establishing an overarching plan that supports and guides such decisions is often called governance. This is the subject of Chap. 14.

Generally the term governance refers to processes of interaction and decision-making among the actors who collectively solve the problem such as ensuring and maintaining security of an ICSs. Governance includes actions and processes that engender and support stable practices and organizations. In the context of ICSs, such processes ensure that benefits of ICSs are delivered in a well controlled manner and are aligned with long-term goals and success of the enterprise. This chapter begins with an illustrative story, inspired by real-life experiences, which help the reader to appreciate some of the practical reasons for good governance of ICSs. Then the chapter describes the definitions, purposes and sources of governance. Because governance is particularly important for the purposes of ICS security assessments, the chapter continues by focusing on frameworks and methodologies that govern ICS assessments.

The next chapter—Chap. 15—reaches to a subject of potential active and military response to an attack on ICS performed by a nation state. A subject like this rarely if ever enters the purview of a typical ICS stakeholder. However, because ICS attacks are so likely to be perpetuated by a nation state, and because any response to an ICS attacks may touch on issues related to a hostile nation state, we feel that this book benefits from exploring this unusual topic. Evidence exists that nation-state actors have realized the utility of holding ICSs at risk; they have also demonstrated intent to gain and retain access to ICS networks, and a willingness to use such an access when deemed necessary. The chapter considers three case studies. The first case, made public in 2015, concerns the alleged episodes in which the Chinese government hacked into the computer networks of the U.S. Congress, Department of Defense, State Department, and major American corporations. The second is the Operation Cleaver in which Iranian state sponsored cyber actors have allegedly conducted several attacks against critical infrastructure. The third case explores the Havex malware, first reported in June 2014, which was presumably developed and distributed by a nation-state actor.

We chose to conclude this book with a look into the future of ICS cyber security. As best as we can see, much of this future unfolds in the context of the Internet of Things (IoT). In fact, we envision that all industrial and infrastructure environments, and CPSs in general, will take the form reminiscent of what today is referred to as the IoT. Therefore, the final chapter of the book is called *In Conclusion: The Future Internet of Things and Security of its Control Systems* (Chap. 16). IoT is envisioned as multitude of heterogeneous devices densely interconnected and communicating with the objective of accomplishing a diverse range of objectives, often collaboratively. One can argue that in the relatively near future, the IoT construct will subsume industrial plants, infrastructures, housing and other systems that today are controlled by ICS and SCADA systems. In the IoT environments, cybersecurity will derive largely from system agility, moving-target defenses, cybermaneuvering, and other autonomous or semi-autonomous behaviors. Cyber security of IoT may also benefit from new design methods for mixed-trusted systems; and from big data analytics—predictive and autonomous.

References

Cardenas, A.A. (2008). Secure control: Towards survivable cyber-physical systems. In *The 28th International Conference on Distributed Computing Systems Workshops* (pp. 495–500). IEEE.

Executive Order No. 13636. (2013). *Improving critical infrastructure cybersecurity.* Retrieved from http://www.gpo.gov/fdsys/pkg/FR-2013-02-19/pdf/2013-03915.pdf.

IEC TS 62443-1-1. (2009). *Security for industrial automation and control systems—Models and concepts.* IEC, International Electrotechnical Commission.

Stouffer, K., Lightman, S., Pillitteri, V., Abrams, M., & Hahn, A. (2015). *Guide to industrial control systems (ICS) security.* NIST Special Publication 800-82 Revision 2.

Knapp, E. D. (2012). Industrial control systems cybersecurity proof of concept. In *Department of Homeland Security Industrial Control Systems Joint Working Group Spring Conference, Savannah, GA.*

Krotofil, M. (2015). Rocking the pocket book: Hacking chemical plants. In *DefCon Conference, DEFCON.*

Langner, R. (2011). Stuxnet: Dissecting a cyberwarfare weapon. *IEEE Security & Privacy, 9*(3), 49–51.

Lüders, S. (2005). *Control systems under attack?* 10th ICALEPCS international conference on accelerator and large experimental physics control systems (pp. FR2.4–6O). Geneva: CERN. Retrieved November 8, 2015, from https://accelconf.web.cern.ch/accelconf/ica05/proceedings/pdf/O5_008.pdf.

NIST. (2014). *Framework for improving critical infrastructure cybersecurity.* NIST, National Institute of Standards and Technology.

Nizar, A.H. (2009). Identification and detection of electricity customer behaviour irregularities. In Nizar, A.H., & Dong, Z.Y. (Eds.), *Power systems conference and exposition. PSCE'09. IEEE/PES* (pp. 1–10). IEEE.

US Department of Energy. (2002). *21 steps to improve cyber security of SCADA networks.* Washington, DC: US Department of Energy. Retrieved from http://energy.gov/sites/prod/files/oeprod/DocumentsandMedia/21_Steps_-_SCADA.pdf.

Chapter 2
Components of Industrial Control Systems

Daniel Sullivan, Eric Luiijf, and Edward J.M. Colbert

2.1   Introduction

A cyber attack on an ICS must begin at an ICS element, and influence some of the other elements. For this reason, we begin the discussion of ICS security by introducing the basic components of ICSs, their functions, variety, and ways in which they connect and interact to produce the intended effects.

As we started to discuss in the previous chapter, ICSs monitor and control industrial processes across a myriad of industries and critical infrastructures on a global scale (Weiss 2010). Examples of critical infrastructure domains that depend on ICSs include transportation, energy production, transmission and distribution, drinking water production and wastewater treatment processes, agriculture, food and chemical processing, water flow control (dams, pumps), and manufacturing. ICSs also influence our every day personal lives, e.g., by maintaining a comfortable temperature in our homes and controlling our automobiles.

The scope of an ICS may vary enormously. It ranges from a single PLC controlling a motor to an ICS controlling a utility company's power generation plant or an ICS that control a nation's power transmission system. ICS configurations also differ greatly. Such configurations may range from a single component to wide area networks (WANs) spanning a whole continent with many thousands of ICS components.

D. Sullivan (✉) • E.J.M. Colbert
US Army Research Laboratory, Adelphi, MD, USA
e-mail: daniel.sullivan@raytheon.com; edward.j.colbert2.civ@mail.mil

E. Luiijf
Networked Organisations, Netherlands Organisation for Applied Scientific Research,
Rijswijk, The Netherlands
e-mail: eric.luiijf@tno.nl

© Springer International Publishing Switzerland 2016
E.J.M. Colbert, A. Kott (eds.), *Cyber-security of SCADA and Other Industrial Control Systems*, Advances in Information Security 66,
DOI 10.1007/978-3-319-32125-7_2

In spite of such diversity, the basic building blocks of an ICS can be assigned to only a few classes. These include for example Programmable Logic Controllers (PLCs), Remote Terminal Units (RTUs), Communication Gateways, and a few others which we discuss in this chapter. Unlike an information technology (IT) system, an ICS monitors or interacts with something physical in the real world, and therefore an ICS includes field devices. An ICS may be completely automated, but normally is controlled or at least supervised by a human operator. Therefore, human machine interfaces (HMIs) are important components of an ICS.

2.2 Industrial Control System Functional Components

ICS components include controllers, software applications, field devices, and communications devices. This section describes the three types of ICS controllers as well as the other component types and their general use.

2.2.1 Programmable Logic Controller

Some decades ago, the first PLC was comprised of discrete logic components and amplifiers. Nowadays, a PLC is a microprocessor-controlled electronic device which reads input signals from sensors, executes programmed instructions using these inputs as well as orders from supervisory controllers, and creates output signals which may change switch settings or move actuators (see Sect. 2.2.9). A PLC is the first type of ICS controller and is the boundary between the cyber world and the "real-world." A PLC is often rugged to operate in remote locations under harsh environmental (e.g., temperature, heat, vibration, electromagnetic fields) conditions. PLCs as well as other industrial components may be deployed for 10–15 years and sometimes longer (NIST SP800-82 2015), often operating continuously.

A PLC operates a real-time operating system (RTOS) which is very different from desktop operating systems such as Microsoft Windows. The control loop which the PLC manages requires a non-blocking deterministic scan and execution cycle. The time to read all inputs, execute logic, and write outputs only lasts a few milliseconds. The cycle is then continuously repeated. See Fig. 2.1 for an illustration of the PLC scan cycle (Knapp 2011). Modern PLCs may use a UNIX-derived micro-kernel and present a built-in web interface.

Modern PLCs may be programmed in a proprietary or an industry-standard language. Five standardized ICS programming languages exist: function block diagram (FBD), ladder diagram (LD), structured text (ST), instruction list (IL), and sequential function chart (SFC) (International Electrotechnical Commission [IEC] 61131-3 2003).

A PLC has a power supply, central processing unit (CPU), communications interface, and input/output (I/O) module(s). An I/O module can either be digital or

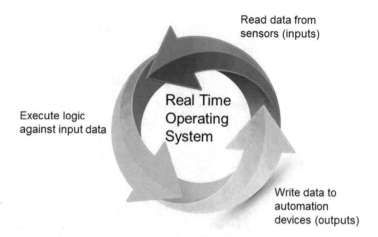

Fig. 2.1 PLC scan cycle

analog. A digital input module measures a "1" or "0" according to the input voltage. An analog input module receives a current or voltage measurement from a sensor corresponding to the physical parameter being measured. Sensors such as thermometers, pressure gauges, flow meters, and speedometers may deliver analog input signals.

Two types of digital output modules exist. The first type produces a voltage which corresponds to a "1" or "0". The second type of digital output module is an electronic relay which opens or closes its contacts. In contrast to a digital output module, the PLC analog output module delivers a varying current or voltage which is set by the PLC's program during each scan cycle.

Figure 2.2 illustrates a Siemens S7-300 with a power supply, CPU, digital I/O module and analog I/O modules. The model depicted has a built-in communications interface in the CPU module. Moreover, modern modular packaging of PLC components allows for modular configuring of the set of I/O modules, fast replacement in case of a failing module, and optionally support redundant CPU and backup battery modules.

PLCs are found in multiple types of ICSs (see Sect. 2.3) and typically use a local network to communicate with supervisory processes using, for instance, serial, fiber optic, or Ethernet links.

2.2.2 Remote Terminal Unit

A RTU is a microprocessor-controlled electronic device and is designed for harsh environments (e.g., temperature, heat, vibration, electromagnetic fields). Two types of RTUs are common—station and field RTUs. Field RTUs receive input signals

Fig. 2.2 Siemens S7-300
PLC

Fig. 2.3 Gemini model
RTU 2.5 monitoring
voltage switchgear
(courtesy Lucy Electric
Limited)

from field devices and sensors and then execute programmed logic with these inputs. An example of a field RTU is portrayed in Fig. 2.3. The field RTU gathers data by polling the field devices/sensors at a predefined interval. Field RTUs are interfaces between field devices/sensors and the station RTU.

Station RTUs are also found at remote sites and receive data from field RTUs as well as orders from supervisory controllers. The station RTU then creates output values to control physical devices and through them physical processes. A control center communicates with a station RTU. These two types of RTUs, field and station, may be combined in a single physical RTU.

The RTU is the second type of ICS controller and has a power supply, CPU, as well as digital and analog I/O modules. Likewise, the RTU is the boundary between the cyber world and the real-world controlling physical processes. RTUs are being developed with similar capabilities as typically possessed by PLCs. Originally, RTUs had proprietary programming tools but are starting to incorporate the same programming languages used by PLCs. A RTU may communicate with the control center using WAN technologies such as satellite, microwave, unlicensed radio, cellular backhaul, General Packet Radio Service (GPRS), Terrestrial Trunked Radio (TETRA), dial-up across the plain old telephone system (POTS), Integrated Services Digital Network (ISDN), or Internet-based links.

Control center automation, such as a supervisory controller or a custom-developed application server, communicates with the RTU. The RTU collects input signals from machinery or other infrastructure and stores this data until the control center automation polls the RTU. After polling the RTU, either the control center automation or a human operator may direct the RTU in how to control the physical processes. In addition to polling, the RTU communication with the control center may be event-based. Also, the RTU can be programmed to take control actions independently of the control center.

2.2.3 Intelligent Electronic Device

In the ICS domain, an Intelligent Electronic Device (IED) is "any device incorporating one or more processors with the capability to receive or send data/control from or to an external source (e.g., electronic multi-function meters, digital relays, controllers)" (McDonald 2003, p. 23). An IED is the third type of ICS controller. Utility companies are deploying IEDs to their substations to improve automation and information flow to their enterprise networks, see Fig. 2.4 for a photograph of an IED. An

Fig. 2.4 IED to protect capacitor banks (courtesy Schweitzer Engineering Laboratories)

IED can be polled either by an automation process (controller or a custom-developed application server) in the control center or by a RTU at a field site via serial, Ethernet or even a wireless link.

An IED is also known as a digital protective relay or a microprocessor-based relay. An IED performs five functions: protection, control, monitoring, metering, and communications (Hewitson et al. 2005). Some IEDs may have more advanced capabilities than other IEDs.

Examples of an IED protection functions are detecting faults at a substation such as over-current, earth faults, phase discontinuity, as well as over and under voltage conditions. An IED control function may include local and remote control of up to twelve switching objects and provide a visual display and operator controls on the device front panel. The monitoring capability may report on the circuit breaker condition and record events. An IED metering function may track three-phase currents, neutral current, active power, and other current, voltage, or power metrics. The communications function consists of the network technologies available for the IED to communicate with supervisory components (Hewitson et al. 2005).

2.2.4   Engineering Workstation

The Engineering Workstation is typically a desktop computer or server running a standard operating system such as Microsoft Windows or Linux. This machine hosts the programming software for controllers (i.e., PLC, RTU, IED) and applications. Engineers use this platform to make changes to controller logic and industrial applications. They can also deploy firmware changes using a memory card. The automation process logic and data are stored in project files hosted on the Engineering Workstation.

2.2.5   Human Machine Interface

The HMI is a software application which provides situational awareness of the automation processes to a plant operator such as process values, alarms, and data trends. An HMI can operate on various platforms, including desktop computers, tablets, smart phones, or dedicated flat panel screens.

The HMI can monitor multiple process networks. It can be programmed with the capability for the operator to send commands to a controller. An example of when an operator would send a manual command is to direct an automation process to change ingredients to produce a new food product. The HMI typically displays a model of the manufacturing or plant process with status information such as temperature, flow information and tank levels (see Fig. 2.5 for an example HMI dis-

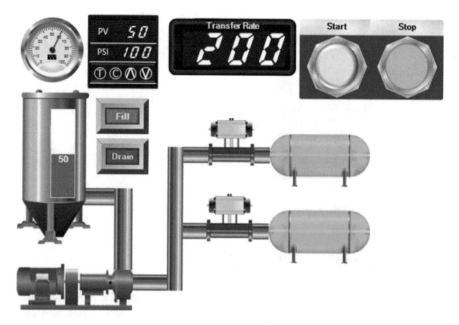

Fig. 2.5 Example of a HMI

play). The HMI can also offer controls which the plant operator can use to manually control plant components such as opening or closing valves and starting or stopping pumps. HMI functions are programmed by engineers on the Engineering Workstation and deployed as software modules to the HMI platform.

2.2.6 Data Historian

A Data Historian (also called an "Operational Historian") is a software application which collects real-time process data from automation processes and aggregates the data in a database for concurrent and later analysis. The same data which is displayed by a HMI is stored in the Data Historian and each data point is timestamped. A Data Historian is usually a desktop workstation or server running a standard operating system such as Microsoft Windows or Linux. Some Data Historians use a relational database for the storage of such data. However, the Data Historian is not the same as an IT database system. A Data Historian is designed for a very fast ingest of data without dropping data, does not support referential integrity in tables, and uses industrial interface protocols. The Data Historian may have interfaces with industrial protocols such as Modbus or Open Platform Communications (OPC) to directly connect to a HMI, PLC, or RTU to retrieve data (Chardin, Lacombe, & Petit 2013).

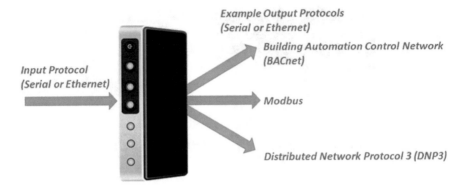

Fig. 2.6 Communications gateway

2.2.7 Communications Gateways

A Communications Gateway enables two devices with dissimilar protocols or transport to communicate. As depicted in Fig. 2.6, this device transforms data from a
sending system to match the protocol and transmission medium of a destination
host. An example of this transformation is the translation from Modbus messages
on a serial link (Recommended Standard-232 [RS-232]/RS-485) to OPC messages
on Ethernet.

2.2.8 Front End Processor

A Front End Processor (FEP) is a dedicated communications processor. A FEP is
used when a HMI or control center server needs to poll status information from
multiple RTUs or IEDs. Figure 2.7 illustrates one deployment of a FEP. By using a
FEP, the processing time and latencies due to WAN links will not interfere with a
plant operator executing control functions on a HMI (Sharma 2011). A FEP may
include Communications Gateway functions such as converting from vendor proprietary protocols to open standard ones.

2.2.9 ICS Field Devices

Field devices are the sensors, transducers, actuators, and machinery which directly
interface with a controller (i.e., PLC, RTU, or IED) via the digital or analog I/O
module. A field device may also use an industrial protocol such as Modbus or

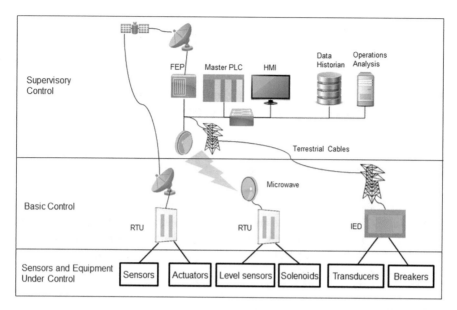

Fig. 2.7   Use of a FEP for WAN communications

Voltage Transducer   Stepper Motor and Driver   Valve and Motorized Drive

Fig. 2.8   Examples of Field Devices (courtesy of Aim Dynamic (www.aimdynamics.com) and Advanced Micro Controls, Inc. (AMCI))

PROFIBUS to communicate with the controller. Figure 2.8 presents photographs of a few ICS field devices. Sensors measure characteristics of the "real world" and represent this information in digital or analog signals for the controller's input. Sensors are available to measure temperature, humidity, pressure, sound, vibration, voltage, and current as well as other physical characteristics. Examples of the actuators are valve controllers, motor controllers, frequency converters, and solenoids which are controlling motors, pumps, valves, turbines, agitators, burners and compressors. In turn, the electrically operated actuators may for instance pressurize hydraulic circuits to amplify the controlled physical forces.

2.3   Types of ICS

ICSs are characterized according to their use as well as according to the geographic separation between the controller (i.e., PLC, RTU, IED) and the supervisory components such as the HMI and Data Historian. Some terms in the ICS domain as outlined in this section have a similar meaning and are frequently used interchangeably.

2.3.1   *Process Control System*

A Process Control System (PCS) controls an automation process in a manufacturing environment. Examples of PCSs are ICSs which monitor and control processes to create discrete parts (e.g., stamping metal parts), or to produce medicines or adhesives in a batch process, or fuels or chemicals in a continuous process. A PCS is commonly found in a factory.

2.3.2   *Safety Instrumented System*

The objective of a Safety Instrumented System (SIS) is to monitor an automation process and take actions to prevent an unsafe plant state or operation. A SIS has sensors sending input signals to a controller which is programmed to actuate equipment to prevent an unsafe state or mitigate the impact of unsafe operations. (Functional Safety: Safety Instrumented Systems for Process Industry 2004). The SIS is a process separate from a PCS. When an unsafe state exists which risks plant personnel, the general public, or the environment, the SIS drives the system towards a safe state. A simple example of an unsafe plant state is the flame-out of an incinerator which could result in accumulation of fuel gas. The SIS detects the flame-out and closes the main fuel gas supply valve (Mostia 2003).

2.3.3   *Distributed Control System*

A Distributed Control System (DCS) controls multiple automation processes at a single site (or plant). A DCS may monitor and supervise several PCSs at a plant, or, as Fig. 2.9 depicts, a DCS may control all factory automation. DCS examples include the control processes at oil refineries, drinking water and wastewater treatment plants, and car assembly lines (NIST SP800-82 2015). DCS communications can be characterized as process-driven polling between a HMI and PLC within a small geographic area (Galloway & Hancke 2012).

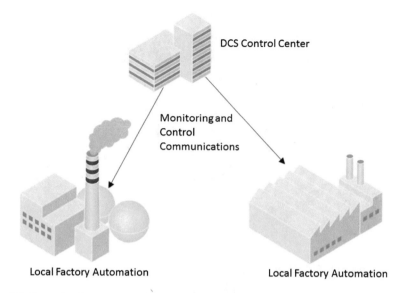

Fig. 2.9 Example of a DCS control center managing two factory sites

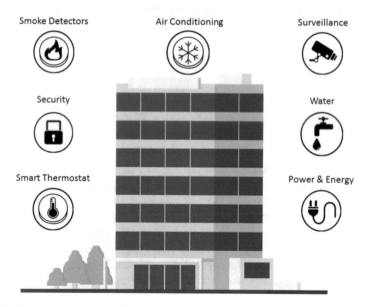

Fig. 2.10 Typical systems controlled by a BAS

2.3.4   Building Automation System

A Building Automation System (BAS) is a type of ICS which monitors and controls a building's infrastructure services such as heating, ventilation, air conditioning and cooling (HVAC), lighting, sunshields, elevators, fire protection, energy management

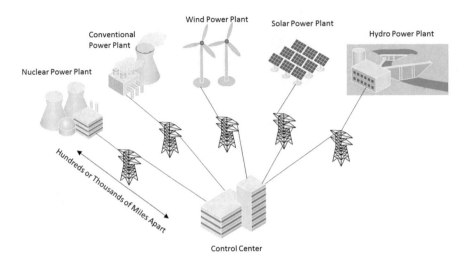

Fig. 2.11 Example of a SCADA system

and security (National Joint Apprenticeship & Training Committee [NJATC] 2009). Figure 2.10 illustrates examples of building services controlled by a BAS. A BAS was once a set of separate and independent systems within a building. Nowadays, with the transition of ICSs to the Internet Protocol (IP) and Ethernet, a BAS may share the same transport fabric as the IT backbone.

2.3.5 Supervisory Control and Data Acquisition

Supervisory Control and Data Acquisition (SCADA) is a type of ICS which collects data and monitors automation across geographic areas which can be thousands of miles apart (Bailey & Wright 2003). Figure 2.11 illustrates an example SCADA system. In this diagram, the SCADA control center monitors and manages remote field controllers such as RTUs and IEDs at several energy production plants. The status information is presented to human operators on a HMI. The human operators can use the HMI software or a supervisory control application to take control of the ICS. Examples of operator's manual actions include changing the set point of a process temperature, open/close valves when filling a reservoir, or start/stop pumps along a pipeline.

A SCADA system may supervise one or more DCSs or PCSs at distant geographic locations. As a result, a SCADA system may use different communications methods than a DCS or PCS. Since DCSs and PCSs are near the machinery under control, they will frequently poll the PLCs such as one poll of all status information each second. The SCADA control center could be separated from RTUs by thousands of miles, and as a result, latency, bandwidth, jitter, and reliability of the communications channels influence what information the SCADA applications receive. The SCADA control center may poll the controllers less frequently than a DCS or

PCS and may only want status information such as when an alarm or event occurs (Galloway & Hancke 2012)

2.3.6 Energy Management System

An Energy Management System (EMS) monitors and controls the generation and transmission of electricity. An EMS is a type of SCADA implemented to manage the power grid within national boundaries as well as between nations (Weiss 2010, p. 15). The Midcontinent Independent System Operator (MISO) is an EMS covering 65,800 miles of transmission lines between a set of US states and one Canadian province (MISO 2015).

2.3.7 Other Type of ICSs

Compact forms of ICSs are increasingly embedded in less obvious platforms as trucks, trains, cars, and autonomous systems such as robots. A modern car has an engine control unit supported by an increasing number of other control units and control modules under the hood which react to a multitude of input sensors and leverage a wide range of actuators to increase the safety of the driver and passenger(s) (Smith 2014). Some embedded functions controlled by these electronic control units (ECUs) are lane deviation detection and haptic feedback, engine performance, traction control, the firing of airbags, distance control assistance, adaptive cruise control and parking assistance. The amount of ECUs in a modern car increases by the day (Arthur D. Little, Inc 2006). Presently, a new car has 70 to 100 ECUs. The control modules and units make use of similar technologies and protocols as are used by PLCs.

References

Arthur D. Little, Inc. (2006). *Market and technology study automotive power electronics 2015*, USA. Retrieved September 12, 2015, from http://www.adl.com/uploads/tx_extthoughtleadership/ADL_Study_Power_Electronics_2015.pdf.

Bailey, D., & Wright, E. (2003). *Practical SCADA for industry*. Vancouver: IDC Technologies.

Chardin, B., Lacombe, J., & Petit, J. (2013). Data historians in the data management landscape. In R. Nambiar & M. Poess (Eds.), *Selected topics in performance evaluation and benchmarking* (pp. 124–139). New York: Springer.

Galloway, B., & Hancke, G. (2012). Introduction to industrial control networks. *Institute of Electrical and Electronic Engineers (IEEE) Communications Surveys & Tutorials, 15*(2), 860–880. Retrieved September 8, 2015, from http://ieeexplore.ieee.org/stamp/stamp.jsp?arnumber=6248648.

Hewitson, L., Brown, M., & Balakrishnan, R. (2005). *Practical power system protection*. Amsterdam, The Netherlands: Newnes.

Instrumentation, Systems, & Automation (ISA) Society. (2004). *Functional safety: Instrumented systems for the process industry sector—Part 1: Framework, definitions, system, hardware and software requirements*. Research Triangle Park, NC: Instrumentation, Systems, & Automation (ISA)Society.RetrievedJune16,2015,fromhttps://www.isa.org/pdfs/microsites267/s-840001-pt1/.

International Electrotechnical Commission (IEC). (2003). *IEC 61131-3 Programmable controllers—Part 3: Programming languages*. Geneva, CH. Retrieved June 16, 2015, from http://d1.amobbs.com/bbs_upload782111/files_31/ourdev_569653.pdf.

Knapp, E. (2011). *Industrial network security: Securing critical infrastructure networks for smart grid, SCADA, and other industrial control systems*. Waltham, MA: Elsevier.

McDonald, J. (2003). Substation automation: IED integration and availability of information. *Institute of Electrical and Electronic Engineers (IEEE) Power & Energy Magazine, 16*(2), 181–188. doi:10.1109/MPAE.2003.1192023.

MISO. (2015). *Corporate information*. Retrieved June 8, 2015, from https://www.misoenergy.org/Library/Repository/Communication%20Material/Corporate/Corporate%20Fact%20Sheet.pdf.

Mostia Jr., B. (2003). *The safety instrumented function: An s-word worth knowing*. Retrieved September 11, 2015, from http://www2.emersonprocess.com/siteadmincenter/PM%20DeltaV%20Documents/Articles/ControlMagazine/The-Safety-Instrumented-Function-An-S-Word-Worth-Knowing.pdf.

National Institute of Standards and Technology. (2015). *Guide to industrial control system (ICS) security (NIST SP 800-82 Rev 2)*. Gaithersburg, MD. Retrieved from http://dx.doi.org/10.6028/NIST.SP.800-82r2.

National Joint Apprenticeship & Training Committee (NJATC). (2009). *Building automation system integration with open protocols*. Orland Park, IL: American Technical Publishers.

Sharma, K. (2011). *Overview of industrial process automation*. Waltham, MA: Elsevier.

Smith, C. (2014). *2014 car hackers handbook*. Open Garages, USA. http://opengarages.org/handbook/2014_car_hackers_handbook_compressed.pdf.

Weiss, J. (2010). *Protecting industrial control systems from electronic threats*. New York: Momentum Press.

Chapter 3
Wireless Infrastructure in Industrial Control Systems

**Selcuk Uluagac, Kemal Akkaya, Apurva Mohan, Mehmet H. Cintuglu,
Tarek Youssef, Osama Mohammed, and Daniel Sullivan**

3.1   Introduction

The diverse components of an ICS discussed in the previous chapter must communicate
with other components of the ICS. To do so, they are often connected within a "wired"
communication architecture. Although wired connections render valuable reliable services to the infrastructure elements, nature or man-made disasters can damage the ICS
wired communication infrastructure. It is just one of the reasons why wireless technologies are gradually gaining popularity in ICS architectures, especially as ICS systems
undergoing extensive upgrade efforts in the last few years. Nevertheless, although
wireless technologies (e.g., Wireless Local Area Network [WLAN]) are maturing and
standardizing (NIST 2009) as viable solutions, they are not yet fully exploited as part of
upgrade efforts.

   Still, replacement of wired communications with wireless is likely to continue at
an accelerated pace. This is because incorporating wireless technologies into existing ICSs can bring many benefits including: (1) lowering installation costs and
maintenance, (2) providing ad-hoc on-demand deployment architecture that is
robust and agile in responding to cyber and physical threats, and (3) providing
redundancy, which is critically important in ICSs.

S. Uluagac (✉) • K. Akkaya • M.H. Cintuglu • T. Youssef • O. Mohammed
Department of Electrical & Computer Engineering, Florida International University,
Miami, FL, USA
e-mail: suluagac@fiu.edu

A. Mohan
Honeywell ACS Labs, Integrated Security Technology, Golden Valley, MN, USA

D. Sullivan
Adelphi Laboratory Center, US Army Research Laboratory, Adelphi, MD, USA

© Springer International Publishing Switzerland 2016   29
E.J.M. Colbert, A. Kott (eds.), *Cyber-security of SCADA and Other Industrial
Control Systems*, Advances in Information Security 66,
DOI 10.1007/978-3-319-32125-7_3

In this chapter, we explore how current state-of-the art wireless communications technologies could be utilized in ICSs with a goal to protect these systems against malicious cyber and physical activities. To provide a more concrete context for this discussion, we focus on an ICS as applied to smart grid systems. We first provide a general overview of the wireless technologies that can be used by ICSs, exploring the suitability of current wireless technologies with ICSs. Then, we discuss the pertinent cyber and physical threats to the ICSs. Next, as a case study, we discuss how an existing smart grid system could be integrated with the wireless technologies, focusing on the implementation of a real smart grid hardware/software testbed developed at the Electrical and Computer Engineering Department at the Florida International University.

3.2 Wireless Technologies for ICSs

In this section, we first discuss the benefits of including wireless technologies into ICSs. Then, we explore different wireless technologies for the ICSs.

A typical wired ICS infrastructure considering a multi-tier Smart-Grid architecture is given in Fig. 3.1 as an example. In the architecture, the data is collected by the field devices including, phasor measurement units [PMUs], PLCs, IEDs during the different phases of the smart grid (i.e., power generation, transmission, and distribution). Moreover, the customer side with smart meters and electrical vehicles is also included in this ICS infrastructure.

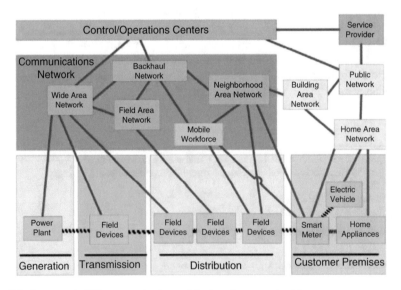

Fig. 3.1 An example ICS communication architecture (e.g., smart grid)

All these devices at different phases are normally connected with wires to the communication architecture. Although wired connections render valuable reliable services to the infrastructure elements, nature or man-made disasters can damage the ICS communication infrastructure. In fact, deploying wireless-enabled equipment (e.g., PMUs, PLCs, IEDs, smart meters) in lieu of wired ones in an ICS infrastructure brings several benefits. The equipment can be easily deployed without redundant cables. In this way, the cost of cabling and installation for the infrastructure can be further decreased with the integration of wireless equipment. There are numerous wireless technologies that can offer different communication ranges. This provides a flexible deployment strategy where even redundancy, which is a desired feature in an ICS architecture against failures, can be achieved. Even in disaster conditions, the wireless equipment can be easily integrated into the ICS architecture and operations can be recovered faster than a fully wired ICS infrastructure. This type of infrastructure-independent integration of wireless equipment can provide a self-healing feature to the damaged ICS infrastructure. Finally, the impact on the higher layer protocols that are used in the ICS network (e.g., IEC 61850, DNP3) to carry the collected data would be minimum because only the physical layer (wireless medium) will be changed in the protocol stack.

As ICSs collect mostly sensor data from devices, the need for bandwidth and speed may not be as stringent as other technologies. Instead, the primary design objectives are reliability, adaptability, availability, safety, and scalability. To this end, several wireless technologies have been designed and are being used in ICS infrastructures for a number of years now. According to a recent report (Moore 2013) about wireless use in industry, the protocols in significant use are IEEE 802.11x (23 %), Bluetooth (21 %), and cellular (15 %). IEEE 802.11x and cellular systems are technologies that are also adopted broadly outside the ICS environment and are well-understood. The newest version for low energy Bluetooth Low Energy (BLE) is gaining wide adoption in ICS systems. Moreover, about a third of the wireless protocols used in ICS such as Wireless HART, ISA 100.11a, Z-Wave, and Zigbee are proprietary. Microwave and satellite technologies are also used for accessing the RTUs within and beyond line-of-sight, respectively. These wireless protocols are briefly introduced in the rest of this section. Note that pertinent security threats will be articulated in Sect. 3.3.

3.2.1   WirelessHART

WirelessHART is a technology from the Highway Addressable Remote Transducer (HART) Communication Foundation, which is one of the widely used industrial standard for real-time applications (Song et al. 2008; Yang et al. 2010). It is a centralized wireless network that uses a central network manager to provide static routing and communications schedules. WirelessHART builds its physical layer based on IEEE 802.15.4-2006 and specifies the Data Link, Network, Transport, and Application layers as seen in Table. 3.1.

The network manager in WirelessHART maintains a complete list of all devices and has full knowledge of the network topology. It gets this information by pulling the neighbor tables from each network device. This neighbor table contains a list of all devices that a network device can connect to. Each node can act as a router on behalf of others. The network manager is also responsible for network configuration and network monitoring. Within this network manager, there is a security manager, which will be responsible for key generation. These devices are shown in Fig. 3.2.

Table 3.1 Wireless HART protocol stack	TCP/IP layer	Wireless HART layer
	Application	Predefined data types
	TCP/UDP	Reliable stream transport
	IP	Graph-based redundant mesh routing
	MAC	IEEE 802.15.4 compliant TDMA
	Physical	IEEE 802.15.4 2.4 GHz

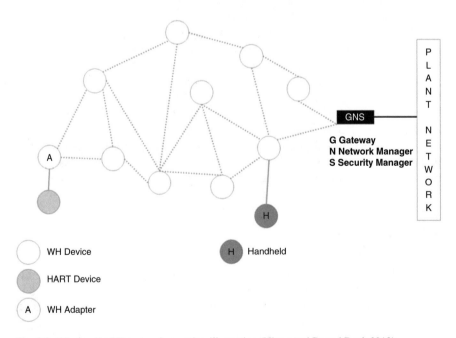

Fig. 3.2 WirelessHART protocol operation illustration (Nixon and Round Rock 2012)

3.2.2   ISA 100.11a Standard

Similar to WirelessHART, ISA 100.11a is suitable for applications in the electric power system such as a substation or a generation plant (Akyol et al. 2010). It describes a mesh network designed to provide secure wireless communication to process control. It builds the Data Link Layer, Network Layer, Transport Layer, and Application layer; on top of the Physical layer of IEEE 802.15.4-2006 as shown in Table 3.2.

ISA100.11a supports two types of network topology: star and mesh. ISA100.11a has routing mechanisms at two different levels: (1) subnet-level mesh routing, and (2) back-bone-level routing. While subnet-level mesh routing is performed at the data link layer, backbone-level routing is performed at the network layer. At the subnet-level, graph routing and source routing are used. Different from Wireless HART, it is based on User Datagram Protocol (UDP) and can work with Ipv6 through the use of Ipv6 over Low power Wireless Personal Area Network (6LowPAN), which is an adaptation layer to support 128 bit IP addresses.

The network architecture for ISA 100.11a is very similar to that of Wireless HART in terms of meshing among the involved nodes such as sensors, actuators and portable devices. It also uses a gateway that is capable of providing security and network management as shown in Fig. 3.3.

Table 3.2 ISO 100.11a protocol stack

TCP/IP layer	ISO 100.11a layer
Application	ISA native protocols
TCP/UDP	UDP
IP	6LowPAN
MAC	IEEE 802.15.4
Physical	IEEE 802.15.4 2.4 GHz

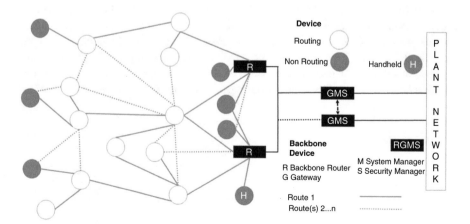

Fig. 3.3 ISA 100.11a (Nixon and Round Rock 2012)

3.2.3   Z-Wave

Z-Wave is a proprietary technology developed by Zen-Sys (Z-wave 2015) and is intended for home control and automation (Gomez and Paradells 2010). Z-Wave has two basic types of devices: controller and slave. A controller device can issue control commands while a slave is an end device that executes commands from the controller. Controllers are differentiated further based on their functions in the network. A primary controller is the only controller in the Z-Wave mesh network that has the ability to include or exclude devices in the network and hence it has the latest network topology in its routing table. Other controllers copy their information from the primary controller when they join the network. Typical primary controllers are portable (e.g., a battery-operated remote control) while secondary controllers are typically static and connected to a power source. Slave devices may also forward a message if the received command message requested them to do so. A special slave, called a routing slave, is allowed to send messages to other nodes without being requested to do so. A routing slave has predefined static routes to some nodes when it joins the network.

Z-Wave employs a source routing mechanism at the routing layer. The controller that initiates the message stores a complete route of up to four hops to the destination in the frame. Every intermediate node forwards the message according to this route.

3.2.4   Zigbee

ZigBee is the specification of a low-cost, low-power wireless communications solution, meant to be integrated as the main building block of ubiquitous networks (Zigbee Alliance, 2009). It is maintained by the ZigBee Alliance, which develops the specification and certifies its proper implementation. ZigBee defines a communication layer at layer 3 and above in the Open System Interconnection (OSI) model. Zigbee transmits at 868 MHz, 915 MHz, and 2.4 GHz in the Industrial, Scientific, Medical (ISM) radio band at 250 kbps with a range up to 10 m. However, the distance to send data is much greater when multiple radios form a mesh network. It builds on the foundation of the IEEE 802.15.4 standard at the MAC and physical layers. These layers are shown in Table 3.3. There are three kinds of nodes in a ZigBee network: coordinator, end device, and router. These nodes can organize in a mesh or tree-based architecture

Table 3.3 Zigbee protocol stack

TCP/IP layer	Zigbee
Application	Application objects
TCP/UDP	Application support sublayer
IP	Zigbee tree or mesh
MAC	IEEE 802.15.4
Physical	IEEE 802.15.4 2.4 GHz

to communicate the collected data from sensors to a root node. Zigbee is an open standard and has been used for many other applications such as Internet of Things. Hence, it can be easily adapted to use in a wireless-enabled ICS infrastructure.

3.2.5 Bluetooth

Bluetooth is based on the open IEEE 802.15.1 standard and operates in the 2.4 GHz ISM band. The Bluetooth Special Interest Group (SIG) maintains the standard. Bluetooth is susceptible to interference from other devices, which emit radio frequencies (RF) in this band such as Zigbee, Wi-Fi, microwave ovens, baby monitors, welding machines, and high voltage lines. Bluetooth is available in two versions: Classic Bluetooth and Bluetooth low-energy (BLE). Accelerometers, temperature and pressure sensors are available with Bluetooth, and vendors can offer new features (called profiles) for an ICS such as RS-232 or RS-485 emulation in order to replace serial wires (Nilsson 2013). One use of Bluetooth is in pole-mounted RTUs for the electrical grid. A technician can drive close to a utility pole and access the RTU remotely with a laptop computer without de-energizing the transmission lines or placing personnel at risk (connectBlue 2011). Bluetooth operates in a master-slave paradigm. One master node can communicate with 7 slave nodes in a piconet. The role of master and slave can be changed between nodes. Bluetooth has 128 bit authentication and encryption. Prior to Bluetooth version 4.1, the Secure and Fast Encryption Routine + (SAFER+) block cipher provided the cryptographic algorithms. In BLE, Advanced Encryption Standard-Counter with Cipher Block Chaining Media Authentication Code (AES-CCM) is the cipher. See NIST Special Publication 800-121 Rev 1 for guidelines to secure Bluetooth links (NIST 2012). Devices can be up to 10 meters apart, and longer range modules can extend the range to 1 km line of sight (Publitek European Editors 2013). Bluetooth currently does not have a mesh capability, however, the SIG formed a Bluetooth Smart Mesh Working Group to design an architecture for mesh networks (Bluetooth SIG 2015).

3.2.6 Microwave

Microwave links are used in SCADA and EMS to connect the control center with remote RTUs, which are in line-of-sight. Utilities are replacing microwave towers with fiber optic cables along their pipeline or transmission tower right-of-ways, however, microwave relays can be useful when crossing rivers. Microwave is ultra-high frequency (UHF) radio operating between 1 GHz to 300 GHz. Microwave can be deployed in point-to-point links or point-to-multipoint. Point-to-point links have transceivers at each site and directional antennas. Point-to-multipoint networks will have a master station with an omni-directional antenna (Marihart 2001). Microwave is vulnerable to interception and the frequencies of licensed carriers are available from the Federal Communications Commission (FCC). While legacy microwave towers may not encrypt their links, today's microwave radios are available with built-in encryptors, which are certified as Federal Information Processing Standard 140-2 compliant.

3.2.7 Satellite

Very small aperture satellites (VSAT) link the control centers with remote sites which are beyond line of sight, and therefore, unsuitable for microwave. Examples of VSAT use in ICS are communications with offshore oil platforms or electrical substations, which do not have telephone service. Also, VSAT can enable an EMS to monitor substations separated by forests and mountain ranges. The remote VSAT sites operate in a star topology by exchanging messages with a central satellite hub. Two technologies are available for VSAT service and they have their own strengths. One technology is Time Division Multiple Access (TDMA) and the second is Single Channel Per Carrier (SCPC). With TDMA, each VSAT terminal has a time slot to exchange messages the satellite operations center. Multiple customers can share the satellite link bandwidth, which can result in cost savings. However with SCPC, a dedicated link exists between the satellite hub and each VSAT terminal. SCPC may have a greater cost of ownership than TDMA for a large number of VSAT sites (EMC Satcom Technologies 2015).

3.3 Cyber and Physical Threats to Wireless ICSs

In this section, we discuss the security of the wireless-enabled ICS infrastructure. First, we introduce a generic threat model, and then articulate specific threats for the wireless ICS technologies. Finally, we list the desired security services for the wireless ICS.

3.3.1 Generic Threat Model

Conceptually, the threats to the wireless-enabled smart grid could be listed from four different complementary perspectives: (1) Method-specific, (2) target-specific, (3) protocol-specific, and (4) identity-specific.

Method-specific threats define how the threats are executed. The method-specific threats can be either passive or active. In the passive method, the attacker only monitors (or eavesdrops), records the communication data occurring in the wireless medium, and analyzes the collected ICS data to gain meaningful information. In the active one, the attacker tries to send fake authentication messages, malformed packets, or replay a past communication to the components of the ICS infrastructure. As passive threats are surreptitious, it is harder to catch their existence. However, it is easier to catch the existence of an active attacker, but its damage to the smart grid can be relatively higher than the passive threats.

Target-specific threats classify the attacks according to which device the threats target. Any device such as IEDs, PMUs, PLCs, and smart meters could be valuable targets for potential malicious activities.

In *protocol-specific threats*, the attackers aim to exploit the vulnerabilities associated with the networking protocols, software suits (DNP3, IEC 61850, IEEE C37.118 Syncrophasor Protocol, Modbus, etc.) that run in the smart grid. Finally, depending on the identity of the attacker, i.e., whether an attacker is a legitimate member of the network during an attack or not, she can be defined as insider or outsider attacker. Insiders are more dangerous than the outsiders as they have more knowledge about the internal architecture of the wireless-enabled ICS infrastructure.

In reality, there is no hard line between these attacking models and they complement each other because an insider could be a passive attacker trying to exploit IEC 61850 on an IED in the ICS infrastructure. The threat model for the wireless-enabled ICS infrastructure is presented in Fig. 3.4.

3.3.2   Specific Threats for Wireless ICS Technologies

In this sub-section, we present specific threats to wireless technologies in ICS. These specific threats are based on the proprietary protocols (e.g., WirelessHART, ISA 100.11.a, ZigBee, etc.) introduced in the previous section.

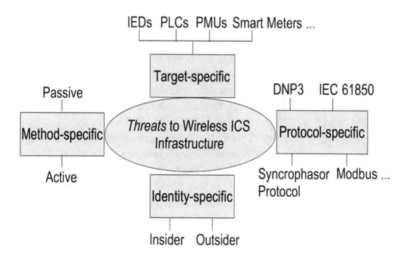

Fig. 3.4 Threats to wireless ICS infrastructure

Those proprietary protocols are typically not well-vetted and often times rely on the fact that their design and implementation are not known to the general public. This is partly true because hackers find it easiest to attack protocols with well-known and published vulnerabilities, but this fact alone does not provide enough security to proprietary protocols.

Key Generation, Distribution, and Management—Secure key generation, distribution, and management are one of the biggest challenges in securing industrial wireless systems. Proprietary systems face this challenge even more because proprietary key management schemes to build trust could become a big impediment to interoperability. One of the security threats in proprietary systems arise with key generation using protocols that are non-compliant to NIST 140-2 standard (NIST 2011). Also maintaining a secure out of band channel for distributing keys, and their management aspects like revocation, refresh, providing desirable properties like forward and backward secrecy are non-trivial challenges. Adding to the complexity is the fact that deployed systems have unique environmental and deployment characteristics which constrain the solution set available for designing secure mechanisms. Standardized protocols like ZigBee, WirelessHART, or ISA 100.11a use specific key management mechanisms. Although standardized protocols have a well-vetted key management mechanisms, vulnerabilities in the systems typically stem from faulty design or weaker implementation. Sometimes when new constraints are added to well-vetted protocols, it leads to lowering the security. BLE is an example of this where additional constraints to energy usage led to a redesign of the existing security mechanisms making them weaker and vulnerable to many attacks (La Polla et al. 2013). The current version of BLE is 4.0 which has a number of well-known vulnerabilities like eavesdropping, secret key brute force leading to integrity and confidentiality compromise, vulnerable key exchange, guessable pseudo random number sequence for frequency hopping, etc. most of which were not present in the parent Bluetooth protocol.

Jamming—Jamming is a common problem in personal area network wireless technologies. Jamming can occur inadvertently due to high levels of noise especially for protocols in the ISM band, but such jamming is temporary and does not have a huge negative consequence. On the other hand, jamming can be used as an effective tool by an attacker to create availability issues in wireless systems. This becomes especially concerning if the wireless device is a control device and making it unavailable could enable a hacker to gain unauthorized access to resources or removing control of an ICS process leading to a disaster.

Battery exhaustion attacks—This attack is executed when an attacker engages a wireless device to perform some computation while being anonymous. The attacker continues the operation until the battery of the device is completely exhausted, leading to availability issues. An example of this could be an attacker trying to authenticate to a wireless device using an automated script. This becomes a larger problem in remote unmanned areas where replacing the battery at regular intervals could be a problem.

Resource-constrained end devices—Resource constrained end devices using wireless technologies have fewer resources like processing and memory to dedicate to the security functions. An example would be a device with an 8 or 16 bit microcontroller with limited memory. Often, these devices are not capable of implementing security best practices and are forced to compromise with weaker implementations. However, with cheaper memory and faster processors this risk is become a lesser concern.

Protection on the device—Lack of advanced protection technologies on wireless end devices is another specific attack vector. Protecting security secrets like crypto keys, certificates, credentials, etc. on end devices is a challenge that opens up avenues for attackers. Newer devices are using more advanced mechanisms that block access to them in the field post-deployment, however, this problem still plagues legacy devices.

3.3.3 Desired Security Mechanisms

Desired security mechanisms are usually defined by the national and international standardization bodies (e.g., National Institute of Standards and Technology [NIST], International Telecommunication Union [ITU]) and are used by many researchers and practitioners who aim to develop secure systems. In this sub-section, we use the security architecture suggested by the ITU's Recommendation X.800 (ITU 1991) documentation, which is referred to as the Security Architecture for Open Systems Interconnect (OSI) as our guideline in addressing the threats discussed in the previous sub-section.

Confidentiality: Confidentiality refers to the protection of the exchanged content (e.g., gathered data, reports, commands) among the components of the ICS infrastructure devices such as IEDs, PMUs, PLCs, Smart Meters. A malicious entity, which has the privilege to access the content, should not be able to decode the exchanged messages in the network. Confidentially also entails the protection against any unintended information leakage from the applications, controllers, and devices within the ICS infrastructure. This is particularly important because the data generated and collected by any ICS equipment, e.g., PMUs, IEDs are usually very periodic. Data collection policies associated with the collected data may be discovered with simple timing or side-channel analysis. Similarly, an increased delay in the traffic can inform a potential attacker about the behavior of the ICS infrastructure. This unintended information disclosure from data devices, applications, and ICS controllers should also be considered as part of any confidentiality service.

Traditionally, confidentiality can be provided by adopting either symmetric or asymmetric key-based encryption schemes (Stallings and Brown 2015). In symmetric encryption, one key is utilized among the PMUs, PLCs, smart meters, IEDs, applications, and other networking equipment and controllers. Examples of symmetric encryption that can be utilized for the smart grid include AES, Rivest Cipher 4 (RC4). On the other hand, in asymmetric encryption, a pair of two keys (aka public and private) are utilized among the communicating components of the ICS infrastructure. RSA and elliptic curve cryptography (ECC) are the two most important examples of asymmetric encryption that could be deployed. Moreover, the maturing state-of-the art encryption mechanisms based on fully-homomorphic-encryption (FHE) (Gentry 2009) could be utilized for specifically preserving the privacy of the traffic. FHE ensures that a user's personal information is not leaked to servers or a third party.

Specifically, the FHE encryption scheme, ε, has an algorithm, *Evaluate$_\varepsilon$* that, given plaintext, $\neq_1, \neq_2, \ldots, \neq_t$, for any valid ε, private, public key pair (sk, pk), any circuit C, and any ciphertext $\psi_i \leftarrow Encrypt(pk, \pi_i)$, yields

$$\psi \leftarrow Evaluate_\varepsilon\left(pk, C, \psi_1, \psi_2, \ldots, \psi_t\right) \tag{3.1}$$

such that $Decrypt_\varepsilon\left(sk, \psi\right) = C\left(\pi_1,,,\pi_2,,,\ldots,,,\pi_t\right)$

A typical scenario of FHE is illustrated in Fig. 3.5. The user sends the information encrypted with public key, *pk*, by function *Encrypt* to the server. The server does operations on the encrypted numbers with function *Evaluate* with *pk* and outputs ψ. The server sends ψ back to the user. The user, then, decrypts with function *Decrypt* using her private key *sk* and obtains the result of $C\left(\pi_1,,,\pi_2,,,\ldots,,,\pi_t\right)$. In this way, the server conducts the desired operation for the user without acquiring any plaintext.

Authentication: Authentication involves guaranteeing the genuineness of the communication among the ICS infrastructure devices. An authentication mechanism verifies if the exchanged information stems from the legitimate participants of the infrastructure because a malicious entity (e.g., a compromised IED) may be able to inject counterfeit content or resend the same content into the ICS. More specifically, an adversarial ICS application may attempt to insert fake application data that may circumvent policies imposed by other applications. Adversaries may also insert malicious data to damage the system by influencing the state estimation, which is crucial to evaluate the system demand.

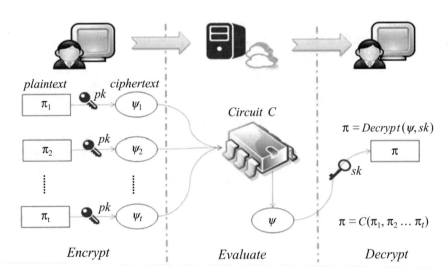

Fig. 3.5 Illustration of fully homomorphic encryption

Authentication can fundamentally be provided based on three factors (Stallings and Brown 2015): (1) *Knowledge factor*: the proof of the knowledge of some secret (e.g., passwords) is provided to the authenticator. Symmetric, asymmetric key-based encryption schemes, and hashing algorithms can all be utilized as part of the authentication mechanism with the knowledge factor. (2) *Possession factor*: authenticator verifies the claimant using the credentials provided by a specialized hardware. Electronic cards, smart cards, smart tokens physically owned by the claimant can be utilized and integrated with the wireless-enabled ICS infrastructure devices and applications. (3) *Identity factor*: the authenticator utilizes features uniquely identifying in the verification of the claimant. Both static or dynamic patterns that can identify the devices and applications can be utilized. For instance, behavioral information from the devices and applications such as communication patterns, timing patterns, delays can all be utilized (Liu et al. 2014) as part of this authentication method. Within the wireless-enabled ICS infrastructure, all of these authentication techniques can be individually or a combination of one or more of the techniques could be adopted. If more than one factor is utilized, the authentication is called multi-factor authentication.

Integrity: Integrity refers to the capability to detect if the exchanged content between the communicating devices of the ICS infrastructure have been altered or not. Moreover, the integrity service involves ensuring that the exchanged content is not deleted, replication of old data, counterfeit, or stale because the nature of the messages in the wireless-enabled ICS infrastructure is very time-sensitive.

Integrity is usually provided by appending the cryptographic digest of the message content to the message itself (Stallings and Brown 2015). When the PMUs, PLCs, IEDs, applications, networking equipment and controllers receive the message, they can check to see if the digest of the content matches the digest they compute on their end. If the digests match each other, then the message is deemed legitimate and not to have changed from its original content. Content digests in integrity are usually created with the usage of hashing algorithms. There are several hashing algorithms such (e.g., MD5, Secure Hash Algorithm-2 [SHA-2]) in use today, which do not require the presence of keys unless they are specifically designed to work with keys like keyed- hashing (e.g., hash message authentication code [HMAC], cipher-based authentication code [CMAC]). Alternatively, integrity can be provided as part of a digital authentication mechanism utilizing symmetric and asymmetric encryption techniques. For instance, the last block of the encrypted data in AES can be appended to the message that would be sent as the integrity code. In a similar fashion, a private key in the asymmetric encryption techniques (e.g., RSA, ECC) can be used to pro-vide the integrity code appended to the message.

Access Control: With access control, unauthorized use of a resource in the wireless-enabled ICS infrastructure is prevented. Access control addresses permissible actions that an entity of the ICS infrastructure has with content or a service. For instance, IEDs should not be allowed to have the privileges on PMUs. Proper security measures must prevent any unauthorized access. An unauthenticated application might try to access resources for which it does not have authorized privileges. Or, an authenticated application, IED, PMU, or PLC may abuse its privileges.

Access control is usually achieved through four different methods (Stallings and Brown 2015): (1) *discretionary access control (DAC)*; (2) *mandatory access control (MAC)*; (3) *role-based access control (RBAC)*; and (4) *attribute-based access control (ABAC)*. In DAC, access control decisions are made based on the exclusive rights that are set for the applications, IEDs, PMUs, and PLCs. An entity in DAC can enable another entity to access its resources. In MAC, access control function considers the criticality of the resources, rights of the applications, and the ICS devices dependent on the resources. In MAC, an entity can not enable another entity for to access its resources. In RBAC, access control decisions are based on the roles created within the ICS infrastructure. A role can include more than one entity e.g., IEDs. Moreover, a role defines the capabilities of an entity with a certain role. Finally, in ABAC, the access control decisions are based on the features of the applications, IEDs, PMUs, and PLCs, resources to be accessed, and environmental conditions.

Availability: Due to the threats to wireless-enabled ICS infrastructure, some portion of the infrastructure or some of the functionalities or services provided by the ICSs could be damaged and unavailable to the participants of the infrastructure. For instance, some PLCs could be compromised and they could cease functioning. A Denial-of-Service (DoS) type attack can overwhelm the communication links. In a similar fashion, an ICS device can be a single point of failure. Moreover, adversaries may jam the wireless medium, effectively hampering all the communications. Thus, high availability ensures that the necessary functionalities or the services provided by the wireless-enabled ICS infrastructure are always carried out, even in the case of attacks.

Usually, an ICS infrastructure usually includes redundant components to ensure the continuous operation during failures. In a similar fashion, the wireless-enabled ICS infrastructure can be designed with such redundancy to achieve high availability.

Accountability: With accountability (aka non-repudiation (Stallings and Brown 2015)) wireless-enabled ICS infrastructure ensures that a device or a software component (e.g., applications, IEDs, PMUs, and PLCs) can not refute the reception of a message from the other device or application or the sending of a message to the other device or application in the communication.

Accountability can be provided as a service bundled inside authentication and integrity. For instance, a digital signature scheme (DSS) (Stallings and Brown 2015), which is based on utilizing encryption methods would address accountability. Additionally, proper auditing mechanisms and logs should be utilized to provide accountability in the wireless-enabled ICS infrastructure.

3.3.4   Additional Security Mechanisms

In this sub-section, we will present some security mechanisms to address the cyber threats identified in the threat model in Sect. 3.3.2.

Key Generation, Distribution, and Management—The threats in key generation, distribution, and management are typically addressed by conforming to standards and implementing best practices in wireless systems. For example, secure key related process standards like NIST 140-2 provide guidance. Protocols also leverage deployment specific characteristics for leveraging infra-structural support. For example, in advanced metering infrastructure (AMI), the metering infrastructure is used as a secure out of band mechanism to exchange shared secret keys. Key generation can be done using software libraries that are compliant with NIST 140-2 making it easier for systems to main compliance.

Jamming—Jamming of wireless channels is a hard problem to counter directly as it exploits the physical properties of wireless systems by drastically reducing the SNR on the wireless channel. As such, jamming risks are mitigated by a number of compensating controls in wireless systems. Traditional mechanisms like frequency hopping are deployed. Additionally, heartbeat signals, acknowledgements, anomaly detection (high SNR for some periods of time), etc. are used to detect and mitigate jamming in wireless systems.

Battery Exhaustion Attacks—Battery exhaustion attacks may not be completely avoidable, but their impact can be minimized in most cases. Techniques such as prolonging the sleep time for devices, rapid message filtering before more interactive processing of messages, etc. are mechanisms to minimize their impact.

Resource constrained devices could use hardware based security provided by cryptographic chips to secure cryptographic information on the devices. Hardware based protection can provide strong protection for cryptographic keys, certificates, etc. as well as provide on chip support for cryptographic algorithms like SHA-256 and AES-256.

3.4 Integration of Wireless Technologies to an Existing ICS Infrastructure: Smart Grid and Micro-Grid Case

In this section, we study how wireless technologies can be integrated into an existing testbed. For this, we utilize the Smart Grid Testbed located within the Electrical and Computer Engineering Department at Florida International University (FIU) as a case study as part of our ongoing work (Salehi et al. 2012a, b)

3.4.1 FIU Smart Grid Testbed

The FIU Smart Grid Testbed is shown in Fig. 3.6. The FIU testbed provides an excellent environment for implementation and validation of the wireless communication infrastructure and providing security against the threats. It consists of a small scale AC/DC hybrid power system, which includes reconfigurable transmission lines and bus bars, several microgrids, storage devices, and a variety of renewable energy emulators for wind turbines, photovoltaic (PV) solar panels, and fuel cells. All these devices are inter-connected for control purposes and serves as a research and education laboratory for real-time, real-world smart grid applications (Youssef et al. 2015).

Fig. 3.6 A view of the Smart Grid testbed at Florida International University (FIU)

In a smart grid, wide-area monitoring and protection aims to provide protection and control for globally interconnected transmission networks. One or several Phasor Data Concentrators (PDC) are operated as central controller which collects substation measurements from the deployed phasor measurement units (PMUs) on transmission level (Cintuglu et al. 2015a, b; Cintuglu and Mohammed 2013a, b; Mazloomzadeh et al. 2013a, b, 2015; Mohamed et al. 2013). Measurements from dispersed substations are collected in a central controller to monitor system status in very precise synchronization. The time synchronization is generally established using Inter-Range Instrument Group-B (IRIG-B) code by a satellite clock to have a proper time reference value from a global positioning system (GPS) clock to accomplish reliable synchronized measurements from the whole network. In a wide-area protection and control scheme, central control units may force local substations to carry out mandatory emergency and remedial actions such as controlled islanding in case of blackout. Under-frequency load shedding schemes and aggregated distributed generation control can be adopted according to global monitoring feedback.

As part of our ongoing work to upgrade the FIU Smart Grid testbed, a wireless-enabled (PMU)/IED and PLC components are shown in Fig. 3.7 a and b, respectively. In these devices, the current and voltage analog measurements are converted to digital values via with analog/digital converters. The sampling rate defines the frequency response of the anti-aliasing filters. The sampling clock is phase-locked with the GPS clock pulse. The microprocessor calculates the positive sequence of the current and voltage measurement values. The time-stamp is created identifying the universal time coordinated (UTC). PMU time-stamped measurements are transferred over the wireless medium to the PDC using one of the technologies discussed earlier. PLCs are used as wireless power system field actuators for load switching, governor control, and automatic voltage regulator (AVR) control.

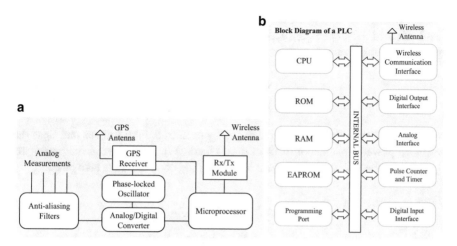

Fig. 3.7 (**a**) PMU/IED components, (**b**) PLC block diagram

3.4.2 Test Case: Handling Islanding Situation via Wireless Communication

Power systems would result in instability when exposed to severe abnormal contingencies, natural disasters, and man-made attacks. Depending on generation and load balance, this spurs an islanding condition. When the power import is terminated by an islanding situation, the initial generation and load imbalance causes a frequency drop (Cintuglu and Mohammed 2013a, b; Mazloomzadeh et al. 2015). Spinning reserve of the generators is utilized to respond to the frequency fall in accordance with droop adjustments. The recovery can continue until all generator valves are fully open. Beyond this point, load shedding and the stored energy reserve of microgrids should be initiated to enable continuous recovery. A wireless-enabled infrastructure can allow for optimal efficiency in the integrated operation of the entire system during recovery in an islanding situation (Cintuglu et al. 2015a, b; Cintuglu and Mohammed 2013a, b).

Specifically, we first formulate the problem as an optimization problem, which involves the minimization of the sum of all generation and distributions costs over the islanded network, subject to generation capacity constraints, load balance requirements, and any other limitations that need to be taken into account. The decisions involve the selection of loads to shed at the disruption instance, the amount of power to be generated at each of the sources, e.g., microgrids, and the allocation of the generated power over the local loads. This is a complex nonlinear optimization problem due to the dependence between load shedding decisions and subsequent generation and resource allocation decisions, which introduce integer variables and non-convexities in standard formulations of the problem. Hence, development of special solution procedures is required to address this initial deterministic decision problem.

To demonstrate the basics of this problem setup, we provide the following general description involving a sample cost structure. Without loss of generality, assume that the islanded area consists of a set M of microgrids only, where each microgrid m∈M corresponds to a generation source. Moreover, let L refer to the set of local loads. In the recovery stage, depending on the aggregated microgrid capacity, local generation must match local loads:

$$\sum_{i=1}^{N} S_{Gi} - \sum_{j=1}^{M} S_{Lj} \geq 0 \qquad (3.2)$$

where S_G is the complex power generated by each of the |M| sources and S_L is the complex power consumed by each of the |L| loads. Whenever the load surpasses the generation, the following intelligent load-shedding conditions are take place:

$$P_{ILS} = P_{island} - \sum_{i=1}^{M} P_{triplist} \qquad (3.3)$$

$$Q_{ILS} = Q_{island} - \sum_{i=1}^{M} Q_{triplist} \qquad (3.4)$$

$P_{triplist}$ and $Q_{triplist}$ are respectively a list of the active and reactive power needs of the loads ordered by priority. P_{island} and Q_{island} are respectively the total active and reactive power of the substation in islanded mode. Thus, P_{ILS} and Q_{ILS} determine if the substation has enough active and reactive power resources to meet the loads. The synchronous generator will have the typical quadratic cost function given:

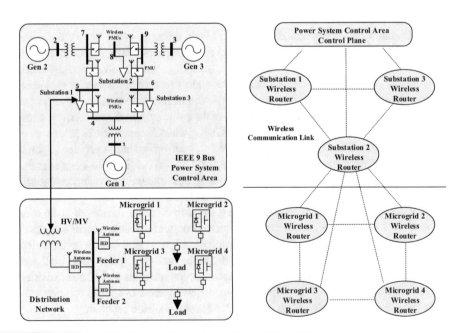

Fig. 3.8 Physical power system and wireless communication links

$$F_i\left(P_{Gi}\right) = \sum_{i=1}^{n} a_i + b_i P_i + c_i P_i^2 \tag{3.5}$$

A high level view of this communication and the control infrastructure model with wireless equipment is given in Fig. 3.8. Wireless communication links between substation and microgrid wireless-enabled PMUs are established along with the power system physical infrastructure.

3.5   Summary and Conclusions

Deploying wireless-enabled equipment in an ICS infrastructure brings several benefits.

The equipment can be deployed more easily, the deployment strategy is more flexible, deployment costs are typical smaller, and operations can be recovered faster in the case of system failure. A wireless deployment only involves changing the physical layer for ICS communication protocols. ICSs can have a much lower bandwidth requirement and transmission speeds may not be as stringent. Some examples of wireless communication protocols used in ICSs are given in the chapter.

The security of the wireless-enabled ICS infrastructure can be accomplished by combating threats in the following four perspectives: (1) Method-specific, (2) target-specific, (3) protocol-specific, and (4) identity-specific. Some examples of specific security issues are key generation, key distribution, key management, jamming (intentional and noise), battery resource exhaustion attacks, and the lack of security features in wireless end devices. Security architectures from NIST and the ITU are available to improve confidentiality, authentication, integrity, access control, availability, and accountability in wireless infrastructure.

Integrating wireless technologies into ICS infrastructure presents ample unique research challenges in security and networking to engineers and scientists. As a case study, we discussed how an existing smart grid with several micro-grids could be integrated using wireless technologies. Security research of wireless ICS infrastructure is ongoing in the smart grid hardware/software testbed at the Florida International University.

References

Akyol, B., Kirkham, H., Clements, S., & Hadley, M. (2010). *A survey of wireless communications for the electric power system.* Prepared for the US Department of Energy.
Bluetooth Special Interest Group. (2015). *Bluetooth technology adding mesh networking to spur new wave of innovation.* Retrieved June 24, 2015, from http://www.bluetooth.com/Pages/Press-Releases-Detail.aspx?ItemID=224.

Cintuglu, M.H., Elsayed, A., & Mohammed, O.A. (2015). Microgrid automation assisted by synchrophasors. *6th Innovative Smart Grid Technologies Conference (ISGT North America), Washington, DC.*

Cintuglu, M.H., Ma, T., & Mohammed, O.A. (2015). Aggregated active distribution networks for secondary control of islanded power systems. *IEEE Power & Energy Society General Meeting.*

Cintuglu, M. H., & Mohammed, O. A. (2013). Islanding detection in microgrids. *Power and Energy Society General Meeting (PES).*

Cintuglu, M. H., & Mohammed, O. A. (2013). Simulation of digitalized power systems using PMU and intelligent control. *48th IEEE IAS Annual Meeting, Orlando, USA.*

connectBlue. (2011). *Wireless access to pole mounted RTUs.* Retrieved June 12, 2015, from http://www.connectblue.com/fileadmin/Connectblue/Web2006/Documents/References/Schneider_Electric_RTU.pdf.

Gentry, C. (2009). *A fully homomorphic encryption scheme.* Ph.D. thesis, Stanford University.

Gomez, C., & Paradells, J. (2010). Wireless home automation networks: A survey of architectures and technologies. *IEEE Communications Magazine, 48,* 92–101.

ITU Recommendation X.800. (1991). *Security architecture for open systems interconnection for CCITT applications.* International Telecommunications Union.

La Polla, M., Martinelli, F., & Sgandurra, D. (2013). A survey on security for mobile devices. *IEEE Communications Surveys & Tutorials, 15*(1), 446–471.

Liu, W., Uluagac, A., & Beyah, R. (2014). Maca: A privacy-preserving multi-factor cloud authentication system utilizing big data. *IEEE INFOCOM Big Data Workshop,* pp. 518–523.

Marihart, D. (2001). Communications technology guidelines for EMS/SCADA systems. *Institute of Electrical and Electronic Engineers (IEEE) Transactions on Power Delivery, 16*(2), 181–1188. Retrieved June 24, 2015, from http://ieeexplore.ieee.org/stamp/stamp.jsp?arnumber=915480.

Mazloomzadeh, A., Cintuglu, M. H., & Mohammed, O. A. (2013). Islanding detection using synchronized measurement in smart microgrids. *IEEE PES Conference on Innovative Smart Grid Technologies Latin America (ISGT LA), Sao Paulo, Brazil,* pp. 1–7.

Mazloomzadeh, A., Cintuglu, M. H., & Mohammed, O. A. (2015). Development and evaluation of a laboratory based phasor measurement devices. *Accepted for Presentation and Publication at the 6th Innovative Smart Grid Technologies Conference (ISGT North America), Washington, DC, USA.*

Mazloomzadeh, A., Mohammed, O., & Zonouz, S. (2013). TSB: Trusted sensing base for the power grid. *IEEE SmartGridComm symposium, Vancouver, Canada.*

Mohamed, A. G., Youssef, T., & Mohammed, O. A. (2013). Wide area monitoring and control for voltage assessment in smart grids with distributed generation. *Proceedings of the 2013 PES Innovative Smart Grid Technologies Conference (ISGT North America), Washington, DC, USA.*

Moore, T. (2013). *The world market for wireless technology by share of units in industrial applications.* Retrieved from http://www.controleng.com/single-article/research-wireless-use-in-industry/5b97f5d429813c649a05240ad5efd280.html.

National Institute of Standards and Technology. (2012). *Guide to Bluetooth security (NIST SP 800-121 Rev 1).* Gaithersburg, MD. Retrieved June 24, 2012, from http://csrc.nist.gov/publications/drafts/800-121r1/Draft-SP800-121_Rev1.pdf.

Nilsson, R. (2013). *Industrial wireless: Bluetooth can be robust, easy to use.* Retrieved June 12, 2015, from http://www.controleng.com/single-article/industrial-wireless-bluetooth-can-be--robust-easy-to-use/cbd481b6e65b08d2e743f8e09fb95528.html.

Nixon, M., & Round Rock, T.X. (2012). *A comparison of WirelessHART™ and ISA100. 11a.* Whitepaper, Emerson Process Management.

Publitek European Editors. (2013). *Using Bluetooth for data communications in industrial automation.* Retrieved June 12, 2015, from http://www.controleng.com/single-article/industrial-wireless-bluetooth-can-be-robust-easy-to-use/cbd481b6e65b08d2e743f8e09fb95528.html.

Salehi, V., Mohamed, A., Mazloomzadeh, A., & Mohammed, O. A. (2012a). Laboratory-based smart power system, part I: Design and system development. *IEEE Transactions on Smart Grid, 3*(3), 1394–1404.

Salehi, V., Mohamed, A., Mazloomzadeh, A., & Mohammed, O. A. (2012b). Laboratory-based smart power system, part II: Control, monitoring, and protection. *IEEE Transactions on Smart Grid, 3*(3), 1405–1417.

EMC Satcom Technologies. (2015). *TDMA vs. SCPC*. Retrieved June 24, 2015, from http://www.emcsatcom.com/component/docman/doc_download/26-tdma-vs-scpc-in-satellite-networks%3 FItemid%3D&ei=l7GKVda3KMO4ggTOg4CwDA&usg=AFQjCNHi_RE2U7Yt4s7L7kYx6 0zBbcEbFg&bvm=bv.96339352,d.eXY.

Song, J., Han, S., Mok, A., Chen, D., Lucas, M. & Nixon, M. (2008). WirelessHart: Applying wireless technology in real-time industrial process control. *IEEE Real-Time and Embedded Technology and Applications Symposium (RTAS)*, pp. 377–386.

Stallings, W., & Brown, L. (2015). *Computer security: Principles and practice* (3rd ed.). Prentice Hall.

The US National Institute of Standards and Technology (NIST) (2009). *The smart grid interoperability standards roadmap*. Electric Power Research Institute (EPRI). Tech. Rep.

The US National Institute of Standards and Technology (NIST). (2011). *FIPS PUB 140-2, Security requirements for cryptographic modules*.

Yang, D., Xu, Y., & Gidlund, M. (2010). Coexistence of ieee802.15.4 based networks: A survey. *IECON 2010—36th Annual Conference on IEEE Industrial Electronics Society*, pp. 2107–2113.

Youssef, T. A., Elsayed, A., & Mohammed, O. A. (2015). DDS based interoperability framework for smart grid testbed infrastructure. *15th IEEE International Conference on Environments and Electrical Engineering*.

Zigbee Alliance. (2009). *IEEE 802.15. 4, ZigBee standard*. On http://www.zigbee.org.

Z-Wave Alliance. (2015). On http://z-wavealliance.org.

Chapter 4
Operational Technology and Information Technology in Industrial Control Systems

Adam Hahn

4.1 Introduction

A modern ICS is a complex system that depends on many different components and technologies to monitor and control physical processes; along with many of the managerial, administrative, and regulatory responsibilities associated with this task. The heart of ICSs are *operational technology (OT)* which supports availability and safety of critical processes. Modern-day ICSs have incorporated *information technology (IT)* based on the system functions desired in the overall system. For reference, definitions of each are as follows:

- OT—is hardware and software that detects or causes a change through the direct monitoring and/or control of physical devices, processes and events in the enterprise (Gartner 2015).
- IT—the technology involving the development, maintenance, and use of computer systems, software, and networks for the processing and distribution of data (Merriam-Webster 2015).

Clearly, the key difference is that OT focuses on the monitoring and control of the physical process. OT's focus on supporting some physical process introduces substantial differences in how the OT systems—as contrasted with IT systems—are operated and managed, along with the technologies used to support them.

Identifying the key differences between IT and OT is vitally important in order to understand the challenges in securing an ICS, especially since security methodsorginally designed for IT technology are now being applied to ICSs. The OT often has additional managerial, operational, and technological constraints that provide a more challenging security environment. This chapter explores fundamental

A. Hahn (✉)
Washington State University
e-mail: ahahn@eecs.wsu.edu

© Springer International Publishing Switzerland 2016
E.J.M. Colbert, A. Kott (eds.), *Cyber-security of SCADA and Other Industrial Control Systems*, Advances in Information Security 66,
DOI 10.1007/978-3-319-32125-7_4

issues ICS operators face when securing when OT systems and compares these issues with those of IT security managers. The idea of security for OT and IT is not the same, as OT security focuses almost exclusively on availability and safety.

Although many differences between IT and OT have historic roots, emerging technologies are causing a convergence of IT and OT domains. For this reason, the chapter discusses the technologies driving the convergence and then identifies cybersecurity related implications of this convergence.

4.2 Difference Between IT and OT

IT and OT differences are found across the operational, technical, and managerial domains of the system. The differences in each domain introduce unique challenges and constraints on the security posture of the ICS. Figure 4.1 presents a high level categorization of cybersecurity challenges found within each domain. This section will explore each area by providing examples where cybersecurity procedures, technologies, and investments differ from traditional IT environments.

4.2.1 Operational

The primarily goal of the ICS is to control and monitor some physical process (e.g., power grid, gas pipeline, manufacturing system). This is typically performed through some combination of sensors, actuators, controllers, and human operators.

Fig. 4.1 Factors that influence differences between OT and IT

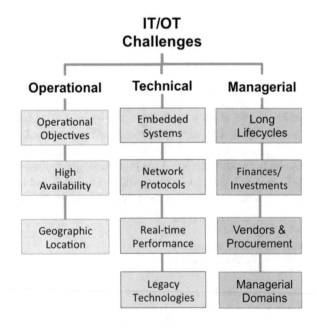

This creates unique operational requirements for the system, which are substantially different from traditional IT environments. Within an IT system, the engineer's and operator's primarily objective is to control and manage the data on their systems. Therefore security is generally focused on maintaining the confidentiality, integrity and availability of that data. However, within an ICS, security must also focus on the safety, environmental factors, regulation, interdependencies, and profitability of a physical process, as demonstrated in Fig. 4.2. Additionally, because the ICS monitors a physical process, the system must operate in near real-time and often very high availability demands are present. The ICS operator must also be concerned with regulatory requirements, environmental impacts, and interdependencies that the ICS has on other systems and infrastructures. This section will explore these operational challenges in greater detail.

4.2.1.1 Operational Objectives

An ICS often has multiple objectives that must be balanced during its operations. Examples of foundational ICS objectives include:

- maintaining profitable margins,
- minimizing the safety or environmental impacts,
- limiting damage or wear to physical assets,
- managing broader society dependences on the ICS.

Cybersecurity is an important property to support many of these objectives; however, it is usually not a main operational objective. Therefore, the organization must balance the importance of cybersecurity with respect to many other operational challenges.

Safety

An ICS malfunction often has the ability to negatively impact the safety of its employees and neighboring communities. Safety concerns could result from kinetic forces (e.g., explosions, crashes), electrocution, radiation, or toxic chemical releases.

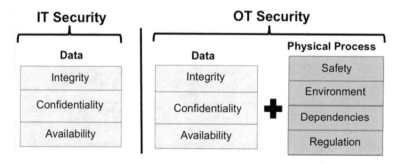

Fig. 4.2 Operational requirements of OT versus IT

Therefore, safety is often a top priority for ICS operators. The ICS will often provision dedicated systems specifically to monitor safety parameters. Additionally, many of the procedures and policies within the ICS are predicated on a safety-first focus.

Multiple fatalities have occurred due to the incorrect operation of an ICS. An example of a safety-related ICS failure occurred in 1999, when a gasoline pipe began leaking in Bellingham, WA and eventually ignited causing a large explosion (Abrams and Weiss 2007). The explosion killed three people, caused eight injuries, and provided further damage to local property and the environment. The event was attributed to a malfunction of the SCADA system, which was unavailable at the time of the event.

Environmental

An ICS failure could also negatively impact the environment due to the release of dangerous chemicals, radiation, or other materials. There are many facets of the ecosystem that could be damaged by an ICS, including plants, wildlife, air quality, and water sources.

An example of how an ICS failure can damage the environment occurred at the Maroochy Shire sewage plant in Australia in 2000 (Abrams and Weiss 2008). A disgruntled employee, that was recently terminated, was able to remotely access the plant's wireless networks on multiple occasions and used that access to dump sewage into nearby rivers. This eventually resulted in hundreds of thousands of gallons of sewage being released into the local waterways.

Societal Dependencies

Often the physical components of the system comprise much of our Nation's Critical Infrastructure (CI). Therefore, a failure in the ICS may either directly or indirectly impact interdependent infrastructures. The White House Presidential Policy Directive (PPD) 21 Security has identified key critical infrastructure sector, many of which are heavily dependent on ICS to ensure the health of the system (The White House 2013). The following list identifies key CI sectors with a strong dependence on ICS.

• Chemical	• Energy
• Critical manufacturing	• Food and agriculture
• Dams	• Nuclear reactors, materials, and waste
• Transportation	• Water and wastewater systems

The impact of an ICS failure on societal interdependencies can be clearly viewed in the 2003 Northeastern U.S. power outage. While there were many different physical system and procedural failures during the outage, a key failure was within a

SCADA system operated by the Midwest Independent Transmission System Operators (MISO). The failed SCADA system could not provide operators with an accurate state estimation of the grid. This likely contributed to a cascading failure that eventually resulted in a loss of over 61,800 MW of load. The broader impact to society included 50 million people without power and an estimated economic loss of $4–$10 billion (U.S.-Canada Power System Outage Task Force 2004).

Physical Infrastructure

ICS failures also have the potential to cause damage to expensive physical system components of the ICS (e.g., boilers, motors, transformers, storage tanks, generators, pipelines). These items have extremely high capital costs and cannot be easily repaired or replaced. This also often requires a long system outage and substantial costs to the ICS.

Multiple examples are available where a cyber attack against an ICS has caused physical damage to the system. A staged event by Idaho National Laboratory (INL) demonstrated how an attack on the electric grid could physically damage generators. In the event, a protection relay was attacked and was then used to continually trip and open a circuit breaker connecting the generator to the grid (Zeller 2011). Continually reclosing the breaker when the generator was out of sync with the grid caused the destruction of the generator. Additionally, the Stuxnet malware demonstrates another example where physical infrastructure was destroyed by a cyber attack. In this scenario, the PLCs were infected to eventually cause damage uranium enrichment centrifuges (Kushner 2013).

4.2.1.2 High Availability Requirements

ICS often must operate with very high availability, presenting multiple constraints on the implementation of cybersecurity protections. Examples of ICS with high availability requirements include electric power grid, water/gas systems, and manufacturing systems. These systems are often required to have 4–5 9's of uptimes (i.e., 99.99 %, 99.999 %), meaning they can only be down for 5 to 50 min during a year. This downtime must be scheduled to also incorporate unforeseen outages along with many system maintenance functions for the systems. Frequently, all system maintenance must be performed during one outage period scheduled annually or semi-annually.

This requirement introduces many negative implications on the design and deployment of the security mechanisms necessary to protect the system. Specific examples of security functions that are constrained by high-availability needs are explored in the following list.

- *Security updates/patching*—Adding a security patch or update typically requires that a system to be rebooted which degrades availability. Installing a patch will reduce the risk to cyber attack, but could also increased other operational ICS risks from the outage. For example, the patch may not be adequately tested and could cause the system to operate unreliably (National Institute of Standards and Technology [NIST] 2015). Therefore, the operator must carefully calculate and weigh the various risks associated the installation of the patch. Often the ICS is forced to wait until the scheduled maintenance/outage period.

- *Security assessment*—The system's security posture should be regularly validated through various assessment and auditing activities (e.g., penetration testing, vulnerability assessments) to ensure the system is free from known vulnerabilities, misconfigurations, and attacker footprints. Unfortunately, many of the techniques used to perform these assessments, such as port scans and vulnerability scans, can degrade the performance of the system or cause a complete system crash. Numerous examples off system damage from security assessment activities exist, including a failed SCADA server that locked up an oil pipeline and another where a system scan caused the destruction of a batch of integrated circuits in a chip fabrication plant (NIST 2015).

- *"Fail-closed" security mechanisms*—Many security mechanisms (e.g., authentication, firewall) will "fail-closed", meaning that they default to a state where they deny access in order to block unauthorized individuals. However, such techniques could also negatively impact ICS operations if they incorrectly block authorized operations. For example, a firewall misconfiguration could block critical messages (e.g., actuator signal, sensor reading) or an operator that incorrectly enters a password might be unable to perform some critical system operation.

Because the introduction of a security mechanism could impact the correct operation of the ICS, these concerns often introduce conflicting objectives between safety and security.

4.2.1.3 Geographic Location

An ICS often must operate across geographically distributed locations. For example, electric power grids, oil pipelines, and transportation systems can span hundreds, or even thousands, of miles. Other systems such as damns and waste water plants must operate across land and bodies of water.

This geographic dispersion creates problems implementing physical system protections, leaving the system vulnerable to physical tampering. If an attacker can tamper with a remote device, they could manipulate the control of that device, spoof measurement data originating from the device, or gain access to system data. If the attacker can gain physical system access, they can often obtain data important to accessing other system resources, including passwords and cryptographic keys, providing them with greater access to other systems within the ICS.

Additionally, distributed systems also present system management challenges since operators and engineers cannot always physically access the system. They must implement remote administration interfaces to perform these functions from a central location. However, attackers could also use these remote administration interfaces to gain system access.

4.2.2 Technological

In addition to the operational differences, an ICS also has many unique technical requirements for the software and communication platforms used to support its operations. Key differences include:

- Unique communication protocols and architectures,
- Real-time performance demands,
- Dependence on resource constrained embedded devices,
- Domains specific device manufactures and integrators,
- Complex integration of digital, analog, and mechanical controls.

Each property will be explained in further detail, including the unique impact that property has on the system's security.

4.2.2.1 Limited Support for Security Mechanisms

OT systems often lack the technical security mechanisms necessary to protect the ICS. Designing a comprehensive ICS security strategy requires a strong understanding of the technical capabilities of each system. NIST 800-82 overviews the technical security controls necessary to protect an ICS, along with many of the challenges faced when implementing these controls due to the lack of supported security features in many OT systems (NIST 2015). Table 4.1 explores various categorizes of technical security controls and then identifies key security mechanisms that are often unsupported within OT environments.

4.2.2.2 Embedded Systems

ICS environments heavily depend on embedded systems that have resource constraints, such as, limited processing power, storage, and bandwidth. These resource constraints often directly influence the ability to implement important security features. Systems with limited memory and processing power often cannot support certain security mechanisms, such as intrusion detection or anti-virus software as these systems often depend on computational expensive searching algorithms across the storage and memory used in a systems. Additionally, to performing real-time system operations complicate the scheduling of system processes, leaving very little time to schedule security related tasks. The additional computation and communication required to support many of the security mechanisms also increase the power consumption, thereby, directly reducing the lifespan of devices depending on battery power.

Table 4.1 OT limitations inhibiting common information security controls

Control category	Common OT limitations
Access control	Many OT platforms fail to provide capabilities to enforce access controls on users and therefore cannot provide granular control over information access or system capabilities
Auditing and accountability	OT systems often do not have the ability to collect and store security related events, which may be necessary to verify the integrity of the system and to detect potential security violations
Configuration management	OT systems may not provide the owner with sufficient control over the system's configurations. Examples could include not allowing the disabling of unused network servers or hard-coded system credentials
Identity and authentication	OT systems may not support strong techniques to identify and authenticate users. They may support weak identifiers, such as short passwords instead of multifactor authentication. Additionally, they cannot be configured to use authentication servers (e.g., LDAP) or authentication protocols (e.g., RADIUS)
System and communications protection	OT systems often have limited mechanisms to protect data during communications. Examples of common limitations include the lack of strong cryptography algorithms and protocols, and an insufficient ability to withstand denial of service attacks
System and information integrity	OT systems often cannot sufficiently enforce or verify the integrity of a system. Examples of insufficient capabilities include (i) mechanisms to support system patching, (ii) support for malware detection capabilities, and (iii) mechanisms to verify the integrity of the system and information

4.2.2.3   Network Protocols

An ICS depends on a very broad set of network protocols, including those commonly used in traditional IT, along with many specifically designed to support OT requirements. Table 4.2 identifies some protocols unique to OT and IT, along with some of the differences between the two domains.

Specific security-related differences between IT and OT are included below.

- *Security capabilities*: While both IT and OT protocols were often designed without security, many IT protocols have updated version that add security features. Examples of secure IT protocols include HTTPS, DNSSEC, and IPv6. OT protocols are often designed to provide increased reliability from communication errors, such as bit flips, through heavy use of Cyclic Redundancy Check (CRCs). However this does not provide any additional security to cyber attack. While OT protocols have begun adding security features (e.g., DNP3 SA, IEC 62351), these are still emerging and are not as widespread as those in IT.
- *Limited support of security devices*: Because OT often utilizes many of their own protocols; there is often insufficient support of the protocols in many of the network security devices (e.g., firewall, IDS) used to protect the ICS. For example, firewalls

Table 4.2 Network protocols for IT and OT

	IT	OT
Protocols	HTTP, DNS, SSH, SMTP, SNMP, NTP	DNP3, Modbus, IEC 61850, IEC 608705, EtherCat, BACnet
Data	Large payloads	Analog, binary values
Operations	Stochastic	Deterministic
Security	Recently developed	Still emerging

might often have limited ability to develop rules for the unique parameters within the OT protocols (e.g., DNP3 function codes). Additionally, IDS rules also need to be tailored toward the specific protocols uses.

4.2.2.4   Real-Time Performance

ICS systems often need to operate in real-time in order to manage some physical process. This has a strong impact on both the design of controllers and the system communications. Communication latency and jitter become extremely important properties to ensure the system operates in real-time. Communication latency is defined as the time it takes for a message to traverse the network, including the delays in router queues and the signal propagation time across the physical network. Jitter, which is the variance in the latency, must also be limited. These constraints create challenges implementing many security mechanisms, such as the encryption and authentication of messages, which depend on computationally expensive cryptographic operations.

Many ICS domains have identified challenges implementing cryptographic protections on system communications. In power systems, many concerns have been raised over the ability to perform computationally expensive public-key cryptography in available time. For example, the IEC 61850 standard has identified acceptable latency for various substation operations (Mohagheghi et al. 2009), which are identified in Table 4.3. Additionally, the American Gas Association (AGA) Task Group 12 explores many latency challenges of adding cryptographic protections for communications (American Gas Association 2006).

Researchers have identified performance overhead from expensive public-key cryptography applications (Hauser et al. 2012). While many ICS applications have strong bounds on acceptable communication latency, these times many still be acceptable for many uses. Table 4.4 explores the time required to perform of standard cryptographic operations computed on a 2.8 GHz AMD processor in a publisher/subscriber architecture. Notice that RSA and DSA algorithms may introduce excessive delay for any control application that requires millisecond level latencies. This provides evidence that certain ICS operations cannot be performed while still implementing important security protections.

Table 4.3 IEC 61850 communication latency requirements

Functions	Message type	Delay (ms)
Fault isolation and protection	Type 1A/P1	3
	Type 1A/P2	10
Routine automation functions	Type 1B/P1	100
	Type 1B/P1	20
Measurement readings	Type 2	100
	Type3	500

Table 4.4 Performance overhead for cryptographic operations

Algorithm	Pub (ms)	Sub (ms)	Total (ms)
128 bit AES	0.04	0.03	0.07
SHA-256	0.01	0.01	0.02
2048 bit RSA	59.00	2.04	61.04
1024 bit DSA	4.10	9.80	14.90

4.2.2.5 Legacy and Esoteric Technologies

There is often a heavy dependence on legacy technologies in an ICS due to long system lifespans, which is further discussed in Sect. 4.2.3.1. Additionally, many of the technologies, platforms, and devices used may be specific to general ICS, or even specific ICS domains. Both occurrences introduce challenges when trying to implement strong security.

Legacy systems traditionally do not have sufficient security mechanisms to protect against many modern threats. For example, legacy network protocols typically lack support for encryption and authentication of messages sent across untrusted networks. On the software side, these systems often lack user authentication, access control, and auditing capabilities. Additionally, the devices often have not undergone rigorous security testing during their design to verify they don't have security vulnerabilities or backdoors (Department of Homeland Security [DHS] 2011). Protecting these legacy systems requires that the ICS deploy additional technologies, such as VPNs and firewalls that can encapsulate the legacy devices and implement required security functions.

In addition to the legacy nature of ICS technologies, many technologies are also esoteric because they are often not broadly used outside of ICS. Generally the security posture of the technologies is not well understood. Additionally, it creates challenges finding skilled professionals to administer the system and to perform necessary security assessments.

4.2.2.6 Cyber-Physical Risk Analysis

In addition to the previously identified issues that differentiate IT and OT environments, the complexity of the cyber-physical system properties further complicates the risk management function. A modern ICS will traditionally have a broad range of control and monitoring systems to ensure the safety and appropriate operation of the system. While this book focuses heavily on digital control systems; many other mechanical, electromagnetic, and analog systems are also used to monitor and control the system. These systems are not directly vulnerable to cyber attack unless they can be controlled by or influenced by some other digital controller or communication. Therefore, these systems provide additional levels for protection from cyber attack as they present limitations in how they system can be manipulated.

This combination of the complex cyber components, physical system properties, and non-digital control (e.g., analog, electromagnetic) complicates the analysis of how an attacker could manipulate system control. Often the risk to the system from a cyber attack is not well understood, and often may be understated due to these additional safeguards. This complicates an already complex process of analyzing risk from cyber attack.

4.2.3 Managerial

The management of the OT systems also differs from their IT counterparts. For example, ICS capital investments are often greater because they incorporate a complex physical infrastructure. Therefore, the ICS must operate for many decades in order to recuperate the infrastructure's cost. Additionally, the ICS may also have more constrained revenue streams that the organizations cybersecurity budget. This section will explore many of these issues and their security implications.

4.2.3.1 Long Lifecycle

An ICS often has larger costs to procure, deploy, and integrate the various systems. The system must stay in production for a long timeframe in order to recoup the cost from this investment. For example, relays in power system are typically expected to operate for over 20 years (Bradley et al. 2007), while system lifecycles in this traditional IT environments are typically 3–5 years. This long lifecycle introduces many cybersecurity challenges, specifically from (i) evolving cyber threats and (ii) dependencies on unsupported systems.

The short lifecycles in traditional IT environments makes them more maneuverable to address evolving cyber threats. Because ICS systems have long lifecycles they often have difficulty addressing many new threats. For example, many popular cryptographic mechanisms (e.g., DES, MD5) no longer provide adequate security, while many commonly used cryptographic protocols (e.g., SSLv2) are no longer secure. Additionally, most editions of Windows XP reached their end of life on April 8th 2014, which means that Microsoft no longer provides patches for vulnerabilities discovered within that system (Microsoft 2015a, b). While many of these platforms are commonly deployed in ICS environments, they will not receive patches from new vulnerabilities.

Table 4.5 provides an overview of popular software platforms, cryptographic protocols, and cryptographic algorithms used within both IT and OT environments. The table identifies when the technology was released, how long it is either supported by the developer, or when it was no longer considered able to provide adequate security based on analysis of security experts. The total lifespans are often over 10 years, and occasionally over 20 years. However, often the technologies are not adopted immediately after their release, so the actual lifespan of the deployed technology is much shorter.

4.2.3.2 Financial Investments

The revenue structure of an ICS is often based on fixed service rates, such as public utilities, that have limited control over their budget for cybersecurity. For example, utilities within the United States are commonly governed by a public utilities commission (PUC). The PUC ensures that the utilities offer a reasonable service rate to their customers, ensuring the utility's revenue is tied to their operating costs and capital investments. Often the utility's cybersecurity investments (e.g., technology, employees, and processes) must be directly approved by the PUC, therefore the utility does not directly control their budget for cybersecurity investment.

The cost to protect the utility from cyber attack directly increases the utilities operating cost, unfortunately, often the utility's rate has not been adjusted to incorporate this cost increase. In many cases the PUC may lack the expertise to adequately judge the risk from cyber attack, preventing the utility from collecting adequate funding. This creates a gap between when critical cybersecurity investment needs are identified and when the utility can recuperate the cost of the investment (Keogh and Cody 2013).

Table 4.5 Lifespan of software platforms and cryptographic technologies

	Technology	Released year	End of support	Total lifespan (years)
Software platforms	Windows XP	2015	Microsoft (2015b)	13
	OpenSSL 1.0.0	2015	OpenSSL (2015)	5
	Linux Kernel v2.4	2012	Tarreau (2012)	11
Cryptographic protocols	SSL v 2.0	2011	Turner and Polk (2011a)	16
	SSL v 3.0	2015	Barnes et al. (2015)	19
Cryptographic algorithms	DES	2004	Kelly (2006)	29
	RC4	2015	Popov (2015)	28
	MD5	2011	Turner and Polk (2011b)	19

4.2.3.3   Vendors & Procurement

ICS domains also have product vendors and system procurement processes that different from IT environments. This can have broad impacts on how security is management throughout the system's lifecycle. For example, most IT vendors have well defined polices stating how they prefer to handle vulnerability disclosures and when patches are released (e.g., Microsoft Patch Tuesday, Oracle Quarterly Patches) (Microsoft 2011; Oracle 2015). Additionally, many IT platforms develop tools to help with the management and installment of patches (e.g., Microsoft Windows Server Update Services) (Microsoft 2015a).

ICS vendors typically do not have similar procedures. Reported vulnerabilities often go unpatched; and in the case that a patch is available, it often cannot be applied due to concerns that it will impact system availability (Tom et al. 2008). System updates often have to undergo additional testing to verify the work reliability the unique configurations and other OT software platforms. Also, the ICS may not have a test network/environment where the patches can be validated before moving to production systems.

Often the ICS will contract a third-party company, or integrator, to deploy and configure systems. This means that the ICS operator may not have deep technical knowledge about the configuration and technologies used to enable the communication and control. This presents numerous security challenges throughout system lifecycles. First, without a strong understanding of system technologies and configurations, the ICS operator cannot effectively monitor their system for attack or intrusions. Second, the ICS may have limited ability to perform contingency planning and recovery activities unless the integrators are directly involved. Also, the ICS may have a limited ability to perform future system changes, such as implementing security patches or updates on these systems. Often the ICS depends on the integrator to both test and install the patches, which can increase the system's period of vulnerability.

4.2.3.4   Managerial Domains

In addition to the previously identified ICS operational challenges, these systems also face cultural challenges in their management and administration. An ICS must simultaneously manage an array of both IT and OT technologies, generally having unique staff focusing on each domain. This can create conflict over who has managerial responsibility over the different systems and software deployed in the ICS.

One approach is that each domain manage the systems that fall within their expertise. IT staff have expertise in the technologies/vendors commonly used in IT environments (e.g., Microsoft, Cisco, HTTP, IP networks), and therefore should manage them; while OT people should manage devices from traditionally OT technologies and vendors (e.g., Siemens, GE, DNP3, RS-232). However, because the OT components will often also include some commodity IT technologies, the IT staff could negatively impact the operation of the ICS by performing an incorrect configuration or adding a potentially problematic patch.

The opposite approach would be that IT staff only work to support office automation system and servers, which don't store or manage operational ICS data, while OT staff manage all SCADA and control systems. This approach should provide improved support of ICS operations, but may also increase the vulnerability of the system since the OT staff may not possess the in-depth knowledge of the IT technologies. Additionally, there may often be unclear bounds where a system falls in regards to their categorization as OT or IT. Examples may include historian systems that engineering workstations that do not directly manage the process operations, but may contain operational data.

There's a growing trend towards convergence of OT and IT systems in modern ICS, which is addressed more in Sect. 4.3. This convergence will further blend the differences between the IT and OT domains by clouding administrative and managerial boundaries over the components of the ICS.

4.3   Convergence of IT Technologies into ICSs

The previous section explored a range of differences between IT and OT; however, current trends are creating a convergence of these domains (Gartner 2011). There are many initiatives driving this convergence, including technological advances, pressure to reduce operating cost, and increasingly ubiquitous communications.

Many ICS protocols, such as DNP3, originally operated over serial networks (i.e., RS-232), but are now commonly based on IP. Historical ICS technologies often used time division multiplexing (TDM) due to its deterministic nature. However, modern protocols, such as IEC 61850, are heavily based on non-deterministic, statistical multiplexed networks, such as Ethernet. These changes allow OT devices to operate many networks services commonly found within IT (e.g., web servers, SSH servers).

While these trends provide a number of advantages, they also introduce an undetermined amount of risk to the ICS. This section will introduce some initiatives in the convergence of IT and OT, along with some discussion about the security implications.

4.3.1   Mobile Computing

Mobile devices are being increasingly considered for adoption within ICS. These devices will provide engineers and maintenance personal with ubiquitous access to system information and control functions. While this provides the ICS with more control over the ICS, it also introduces additional risk and creates a further overlap between OT and IT domains. Mobile devices could be used to support multiple different functions (e.g., check email, view corporate or public Internet websites, ICS operations). This presents an opportunity for an attack on the IT side to propagate to the OT side.

While the ICS may provide and control the mobile device, there are also increasing "bring your own device" (BYOD) trends. With BYOD, employees can utilize their personal mobile devices rather than simultaneously carrying multiple devices around. While BYOD may be more convenient for users and cheaper for the organization, they also present significant risk as organization has little control over the security posture of personally owned devices. The ICS has little ability to control or enforce the security policies and mechanisms implemented on an employee owned mobile devices. Therefore, the ICS can have little confidence in the device's integrity.

4.3.2   Cloud Computing

Cloud computing infrastructures are also gaining some interest within ICS. Many researchers are exploring the benefits of cloud computing in ICS to reduce cost or increase reliability (Givehchi et al. 2013). Multiple ICS sectors have already begun exploring or adopting cloud computing. For example, recent trends for the manufacturing sector suggest almost half of the manufacturing and distribution applications will move to the cloud within 10 years (Columbus 2013). Additionally, researchers have been exploring how the power grid can leverage the Amazon EC2 cloud to improve data sharing, consistency across computing infrastructures, and create more accurate grid state estimators (Maheshwari et al. 2013).

Cloud-based systems provide a unique system management challenges. The cloud operator is generally responsible for the control and management of most their infrastructure, which varies depending on whether the cloud provides Infrastructure-, Platform-, or Software-as-a-Services (e.g., IaaS, PaaS, SaaS). In these cases the ICS will have little influence over the operation of the cloud platforms. To alleviate these concerns, private clouds could be used to either to provide the ICS with direct control of the infrastructure, or at least provide them with greater influence over the infrastructure. For example similar private clouds are used in the U.S. federal government and many businesses (U.S. Government Accountability Office [GAO] 2014).

4.3.3   Internet of Things and Smart Cities

The Internet of Things (IOT) and Smart Cities are two emerging trends that will likely drive an increased IT and OT convergence. We discuss this in more detail in Chap. 16.

As an example, power utilities are increasingly adopting smart meters and Advanced Metering Infrastructures (AMI). These systems expand distribution networks throughout entire cities; with the smart meters often reaching into consumer's homes and often directly connecting to consumer devices (e.g., thermostat). Additionally, the smart meters commonly use the same wireless communication technologies and networks as other IT systems. For example, 3G/4G cell data is commonly used to support smart meter readings, while many other meters transmit over an IEEE 802.15.4 networks which maybe be co-occupied by many other consumer devices for non-ICS functions.

Similar trends are identified across many other sectors. Many different utilities are also exploring AMI infrastructures to provide customers with near real-time awareness of their consumption. Water utilities have also been deploying AMI networks to provide consumers with water consumption information; this is especially popular in areas that have limited water supply. For example, the city of San Francisco's water utility has already deployed an AMI to curb consumption (San Francisco Public Utilities Commission [SFPUC] 2010). Leak detection is another key benefit that AMIs can provide to water utilities.

Trends like AMIs for electricity, water, and gas are evolving into the design of smart cities, which explore methods to improve quality of life and efficiency of cities through increased usage of communication and computation. With multiple domains evolving to smart technology (e.g., water, gas, electricity, transportation, emergency response), many of the emerging applications require ubiquitous network to support the required communications. The high cost of deploying such a network is creating initiatives for "city-wide" networks, which would be leveraged by many different infrastructures. Examples of city-wide networks are proposed by many current vendors. For example, CISCO is marketing "City-Wifi" technologies, while wireless companies envision 4G technologies as a converged network platform (Cisco 2015; Verizon 2015).

4.4 Summary and Conclusions

ICSs are traditionally OT systems, where process control is priority for the human operators and availability and safety dominate security concerns. IT systems, on the other hand, have grossly different hardware and network infrastructure, human usage policies, performance requirements, and security defense methods. IT security methods typically focus on protecting user confidentiality and integrity as they execute a large variety of "processes." As IT system technologies begin to converge into ICSs, it becomes more critical to understand and analyze these differences in order to manage expectations of future ICS security. This is especially important if IT security methods are considered for defending ICSs from attack.

References

Abrams, M., & Weiss, J. (2007, September). *Bellingham, Washington, control system cyber security case study*. National Institute of Standards and Technology (NIST). Retrieved from http://csrc.nist.gov/groups/SMA/fisma/ics/documents/Bellingham_Case_Study_report%20 20Sep071.pdf.

Abrams, M., & Weiss, J. (2008). *Malicious control system cyber security attack case study–Maroochy water services.* Australia: National Institute of Standards and Technology (NIST). Retrieved from http://csrc.nist.gov/groups/SMA/fisma/ics/documents/Maroochy-Water-Services-Case-Study_report.pdf.

American Gas Association (AGA). (2006, March 14). Report No. 12. *Cryptographic protection of SCADA communications part 1: Background, policies and test plan.*

Barnes, R., Thomson, M., Pironti, A., Langley, A. (2015, June). *Deprecating secure sockets layer version 3.0.* Internet Engineering Task Force (IETF). Retrieved from https://tools.ietf.org/html/rfc7568.

Bradley, I., Ciufo, J., Cooperberg, A., Tavener, C. (2007, June). *Life-cycle management for system protection.* Transmission & Distribution World Magazine.

Cisco. (2015). *Cisco smart + connected city Wi-Fi: The foundation of urban services.* Retrieved from http://www.cisco.com/web/strategy/docs/smart-connected-city-network-aag.pdf.

Columbus, L. (2013, May 6). *10 ways cloud computing is revolutionizing manufacturing.* Forbes. Retrievedfromhttp://www.forbes.com/sites/louiscolumbus/2013/05/06/ten-ways-cloud-computing-is-revolutionizing-manufacturing/.

Department of Homeland Security (DHS) (2011, May). *Common cybersecurity vulnerabilities in industrial control systems.*

Gartner. (2011, March) *Gartner says the worlds of IT and operational technology are converging.* Retrieved from http://www.gartner.com/newsroom/id/1590814.

Gartner IT Glossary. (2015, August 15). *Operational technology.* Retrieved from http://www.gartner.com/it-glossary/operational-technology-ot.

Givehchi, O., Trsek, H., Jasperneite, J. (2013, September). Cloud computing for industrial automation systems—A comprehensive overview. *IEEE 18th conference on emerging technologies & factory automation (ETFA), September 10–13.*

Hauser, C., Manivannan, T., & Bakken, D. (2012, Janaury). Evaluating multicast message authentication protocols for use in wide area power grid data delivery services. *45th Hawaii International Conference on System Science (HICSS),* pp. 2151–2158.

Kelly, S. (2006, December). *Security implications of using the data encryption standard (DES).* Internet Engineering Task Force (IETF). Retrieved from https://tools.ietf.org/html/rfc4772.

Keogh, M., & Cody, C. (2013, February). *Cybersecurity for state regulators 2.0.* The National Association of Regulatory Utility Commissioners. Retrieved from http://www.naruc.org/Grants/Documents/NARUC%20Cybersecurity%20Primer%202.0.pdf.

Kushner, D. (2013, February 26). *The real story of Stuxnet.* IEEE spectrum. Retrieved from http://spectrum.ieee.org/telecom/security/the-real-story-of-stuxnet.

Maheshwari, K., Lim, M., Wang, L., Birman, K., & van Renesse, R., (2013, February). Toward a reliable, secure and fault tolerant smart grid state estimation in the cloud. *IEEE PES Innovative Smart Grid Technologies (ISGT),* 2013.

Merriam-Webster. (2015, August 15). *Information technology.* Retrieved from http://www.merriam-webster.com/dictionary/information%20technology.

Microsoft. (2011). *Coordinated vulnerability disclosure at Microsoft.* Retrieved from http://go.microsoft.com/?linkid=9770197.

Microsoft. (2015a, August 15). *Windows server update services.* Retrieved from https://technet.microsoft.com/en-us/security/bulletin/dn602597.aspx.

Microsoft. (2015b, June 22). *Microsoft support lifecycle.* Retrieved from https://support.microsoft.com/en-us/lifecycle/search?alpha=Windows%20Server.

Mohagheghi, S., Stoupis, J., & Wang, Z. (2009). Communication protocols and networks for power systems—Current status and future trends. *Proceedings of Power Systems Conference and Exposition (PES '09).*

National Institute of Standards and Technology (NIST). (2015). *Guide to industrial control system security.* Revision 2. Special Publication 800–82.

OpenSSL Release Strategy. (2015, August 9). *OpenSSL software foundation.* Retrieved from https://www.openssl.org/policies/releasestrat.html.

Oracle. (2015, August 15). *Critical patch updates, security alerts and third party bulletin.* Retrieved from http://www.oracle.com/technetwork/topics/security/alerts-086861.html.

Popov, A. (2015, February). *Prohibiting RC4 cipher suites.* Internet Engineering Task Force (IETF). Retrieved from https://tools.ietf.org/html/rfc7465.

San Francisco Public Utilities Commission (SFPUC). (2010, April). *SFPUC automated water meter program.* Retrieved from http://www.sfwater.org/modules/showdocument.aspx?documentid=13.

Tarreau, W. (2012, April 9). *Linux Kernel mailing list.* Retrieved from https://lkml.org/lkml/2012/4/9/127.

The White House. (2013, February 12). *Presidential policy directive (PPD) 21, Critical infrastructure security and resilience.*

Tom, S., Christiansen, D., & Berrett, D. (2008, December). *Recommended practice for patch management of control systems.* Department of Homeland Security (DHS).

Turner S., & Polk T. (2011a, March). *Prohibiting secure sockets layer (SSL) version 2.0.* Internet Engineering Task Force (IETF). Retrieved from https://tools.ietf.org/html/rfc6176.

Turner, S., & Polk, T. (2011b, March). *RFC 6151, updated security considerations for the MD5 message-digest and the HMAC-MD5 algorithms.* Internet Engineering Task Force (IETF). Retrieved from https://tools.ietf.org/html/rfc6151.

U.S. Government Accountability Office (GAO). (2014, September). *Cloud computing: Additional opportunities and savings need to be pursued.* GA-14-753.

U.S.-Canada Power System Outage Task Force. (2004, April). *Final report on the August 14, 2003 blackout in the United State and Canada, causes and recommendations.*

Verizon. (2015). *Helping the city of Charlotte envision a more sustainable future.* Retrieved from http://www.verizonenterprise.com/resources/casestudies/cs_helping-the-city-of-charlotte_en_xg.pdf.

Zeller, M. (2011). *Myth or reality—Does Aurora vulnerability pose a risk to my generator?* Schweitzer Engineering Laboratories. Texas A&M Conference for Protection Relay Engineers.

Chapter 5
Threats in Industrial Control Systems

Eric Luiijf

5.1 Introduction

Having explored the general nature of ICS and SCADA systems, it is time to take a broad look at threats to these systems, i.e., the causes of cyber incidents. An ISO standard (ISO27000 2014) for information and communication technology (ICT) defines threat as *potential cause of an unwanted incident, which may result in harm to a system or organization*. The former (ISO22399 2007) standard, which stems from the incident preparedness and operational continuity management domain, defines a threat as *potential cause of an unwanted incident, which may result in harm to individuals, a system or organization, the environment or the community*.

ICSs bridge the ICT world with the physical world of organizations, critical infrastructure and vital societal services.[1] For that reason this chapter defines an ICS threat as *potential cause of an unwanted incident through the use of one of more ICSs, which may result in harm to individuals, a system, an organization, critical infrastructure and vital societal services, the environment or the society at large*. The viewpoint is that of the (potential) organizational and business impact by cyber-insecure ICSs rather than from the viewpoint of technological threats to individual ICS components only. While some others would take the latter viewpoint for discussing the ICS threats, we deliberately have chosen for this approach as it helps to cover many of the important aspects regarding the insecurity of ICSs which would otherwise be overlooked.

Related to threat is vulnerability, which is defined by the (ISO22399 2007) standard *as weakness of an asset or control that can be exploited by one or more threats*. The combination of ICS threats and vulnerabilities lead to the ICS risk.

E. Luiijf (✉)
Networked Organisations, Netherlands Organisation for Applied Scientific Research,
Rijswijk, the Netherlands
e-mail: eric.luiijf@tno.nl

[1] A number of national definitions of critical infrastructure and vital societal services can be found on CIPedia(c) (2015).

© Springer International Publishing Switzerland 2016
E.J.M. Colbert, A. Kott (eds.), *Cyber-security of SCADA and Other Industrial Control Systems*, Advances in Information Security 66,
DOI 10.1007/978-3-319-32125-7_5

5.2   The ICS Threat Landscape: A Paradigm Shifted

The ICS threat landscape comprises a wide set of threats. Although most ICS threats were always present in a latent way, it was only since the early 2000s that these threats come to the fore. Since the early 2000s, some ICS engineers like Joe Weiss and Eric Byers as well as cyber security experts warned about the insecurity of ICSs and the related risk to critical infrastructures (Averill and Luiijf 2010; Dubowski 2004; Frontline 2003; Luiijf and Lassche 2006; Weiss 2009). They recognized the paradigm shift that took place at the inside and the outside of the ICS domain which opened a new 'can of threats' to ICSs.

ICSs were traditionally designed around reliability and safety (Russel 2015). For a long time, cyber security and mutual authentication of components were not a design and operational consideration for ICSs because:

- ICSs were based on specialized hardware, proprietary code and protocol standards. Only specialists knew about how to use them, and anyway, nobody else, including hackers, could be interested in the ICS domain, protocols and communications.
- ICSs operate in a closed environment without any connectivity with other domains; just some physical security.
- ICSs operate only in a benign environment. Therefore, there was no reason for creating secure and robust ICS protocols, apply any cryptographic protection other than a cyclic redundancy check on packets, and to stress test the ICS protocol implementations.

The aforementioned paradigm shift took place due to the take up of the fast innovation cycles in IT hardware, IT software and networking by the ICS domain. All basic assumptions about the cyber security context of ICSs have been flawed by those developments (Luiijf and Te Paske 2015, pp. 23–24):

- ICS applications, MES, HMI and crucial ICS services increasingly operate on and make use of commercial off-the-shelf hardware, common operating systems (e.g., Windows and Unix), the TCP/IP protocol suite, and open source environments. The new trend is SCADA applications on smart phones; soon they will appear on smart watches as well.
- ICS knowledge and documentation on ICS services, ICS protocols and their weaknesses is widely available on the internet.
- ICS networks are either directly or indirectly connected to public networks such as the internet. ICSs are sometimes even controlled by a HMI interface running on a tablet from home locations, and Trojans and worms found holes in the network connections to infect ICS servers, services and HMI. Hackers can locate internet-accessible and vulnerable ICS by service and manufacturer very efficiently with the Shodan search engine (Shodan 2015).
- ICSs have fallen victim to disgruntled insiders and hackers have become very interested in ICSs as shown by the number of ICS-related talks at hacker conventions such as Black Hat and DEF CON® in the USA and their European and

Asia-Pacific pendants. ICS security testing frameworks for the MetaSploit toolset are publically available, not only for system and process engineers but also for the malicious hacking communities. See for instance (SCADAhacker.com 2015).

Moreover, ICSs are not only found in the primary processes of an organization. ICSs embed and hide themselves in upgrades of well-known 'functionality' which one experience on a daily basis without realizing that it contains and is operated by one or more ICSs. For example, a building automation system (BAS), fire control system, air conditioning or access control. Often, neither the IT department, nor the ICS department is responsible for their cyber security. This is ICS threat which creeps into organizations via the backdoor as has been explained in Luiijf (2013) and GAO (2015). That hacking of such ICSs may impact the primary operations as well has been demonstrated when hackers switched of the air-condition system of a computer center of a large bank. At the same time, these unsecured ICSs can be a hackers' entry point to ICT systems as was demonstrated by the hack of Target's points of sales using HVAC systems as entry (Krebs 2014).

Although important, these ICS threats represent only a single and mainly technological aspect of the ICS threat landscape. Other ICS domain specific threats need to be understood well by the organization before the various risk factors to the business including those stemming from ICT and ICS systems and networks can be addressed in a balanced way keeping in mind the set of threat actors. Threat actors involuntary or deliberately explore the threats. If vulnerabilities are around in the organizational structure, ICS systems and networks, procedures and so on, threat actors like incapable management, operators, ICS users, process control engineers, third party engineers, maintenance engineers, (former) insiders (e.g., disgruntled employees), hackers, hacktivists, organized crime, foreign intelligence, and foreign state-sponsored and state actors may cause an unwanted event to happen. The event may cause impact to business, critical infrastructure operations, and safety.

The various sets of ICS threats spanning the ICS threat landscape can be decomposed into threats stemming from:

1. Organizational aspects related to the organization and its subcontractors involved in the deployment, use, and maintenance of ICS (5.3);
2. ICS architecture and ICS technology (5.4);
3. Networking and telecommunications (5.5);
4. Human factors (5.6);
5. Operational maintenance (5.7);
6. The environment of ICS systems and communications (5.8).

5.3 Organizational Threats

In this section we will discuss various aspects of the threat to the business objectives due to organizational aspects related to ICSs.

5.3.1   The Executive Level

In many organizations deploying ICSs a lack of understanding of the cyber security threat for ICSs at all organization levels can be found. It starts at the executive level which manages the risk to the business objectives of the organization and protects the public and private shareholder interests. The executive level understands the primary production objectives of the organization such as the transmission of power, railway passenger transport, provision of drinking water, and airport baggage handling. The focus on the business side causes a lack of interest by the executive level in the underlying technological aspects of the processes that lie beyond optimal production performance and safety. That the primary business processes are monitored and controlled by ICSs, which introduce a set of new technology-related threats, does not appeal to the executive level as it concerns a functional domain, not (directly) the business and profits to be made.

It turns out hard for most ICS departments to convey their needs to the executive level. The latter may remark that cyber security has been assigned to the IT department and that that department may help to address the cyber threats to ICSs. Problem solved; no costs. As a result, amongst other policy and policy implementation elements no ICS security policy is present, no risk analysis takes place, no security auditing of the ICS domain takes place, no analysis of firewall/DMZ logging takes place, and it is unclear who is in charge when an ICS security incident happens. Moreover, when a cyber-security incident happens in the ICS-domain, there are no transparent reporting lines to the executive level presumed that the process responsible is willing to admit and report a cyber-security incident in the ICS domain. These ICS security elements are factors that contribute to the threat of long disruptions of crucial business processes due to ICS security incidents.

5.3.2   The Chief Information Security Officer

At the next organizational level, Chief Information Security Officers (CISOs) or equivalent responsibilities are often unaware about ICS threats; they concentrate on the ICT side challenges only. Other CISOs which extended their responsibility to the ICS domain may think that they understand the issues as they seem to be the same as those in the ICT domain. Applying the same (ISO27000 2014)-series or NIST (Stouffler et al. 2015) controls for the systems in the ICS domain would do the trick, isn't it? For those CISOs, the ICS domain may bring a set of threat surprises to the foreground as is shown later in this chapter. And even though a CISO understands the threats to the ICS well, he/she will only be focused on the ICSs which monitor and control the primary (business) processes. ICSs which are hidden in 'functionality' are connected to public networks such as the internet while their cyber security is unmanaged. CISOs may use ICSs on a daily basis in their organizations, e.g., a BAS, but never realize and thus govern the related cyber threat until a major cyber security incident happens in their ICSs (Luiijf 2013). An example of the risk was shown when a Jesse William McGraw (a.k.a. "GhostExodus") posted pictures on the Internet of the compromised Heating, Ventilating, and Air Conditioning (HVAC) system of a Texas hospital. Luckily he was caught before causing the serious damages he planned to occur (FBI 2009). However, when asked, most CISOs have no answer to the question "who is responsible and secures the BAS of your organization?".

5.3.3 Cultural Differences

The cultures of both the IT/ICT department and the ICS department often largely differ. The ICS domain first focuses on the availability, visibility, operability of the ICS-controlled processes, the process efficiency, and safety. Cyber security, including the integrity and confidentiality aspects, is of a lesser concern. Contrary to the ICS domain, the ICT domain puts the preservation of confidentiality first, followed by integrity and availability. Ad hoc reconfiguring and rebooting ICT services to remove a cyber security vulnerability is not uncommon whereas the continuity of the 24 h per day, 7 days a week processes does not allow any touching of the ICSs. Beyond combined ICS–ICT technical threats, the lack of understanding of those differences creates misunderstandings and frictions between the ICT and ICS departments. Addressing this organizational threat requires bridging the gap between both the ICS and ICT cultures. A first step might be to draw network diagrams from the left (internet), via ICT to ICS at the right. The 'normal' top to bottom network figure unintentionally suggests a dominance of ICT over the ICS domain. Then have both staffs explain the operational and security challenges for their domains while being seated intermingled. After a while, the gap in understanding between both departments may close.

5.3.4 Education and Training

Many lessons about cyber threats have been learned by organizations in their ICT domain. Moreover, legislation and regulation may nowadays require proper risk governance of the ICT risk. Examples are the mandated reporting of cyber security breaches by organizations to regulatory agencies and public authorities in for instance EU Member States and a number of US states. In general, personnel of organizations are made aware of and trained to recognize cyber threats to ICT.

On the other hand, ICS operators and engineers as well as external support to the ICS domain such as ICS vendors, system integrators, and maintenance personnel, are not well educated and trained—if at all—in cyber security of ICSs. A number of ICS hack incidents worldwide stem from this ICS threat as shown by Luiijf (2013). Good practices and work force development approaches which include ICS security topics try to remedy this threat (MSB 2014, p. 60).

5.3.5 *Depreciation Cycle*

Organizations replace their ICT equipment each 3–4 years. The financial depreciation cycle aligns with the fast technical advancements of ICT and the need to have more processing and networking power on the desk to run the latest applications. In contrast to the ICT domain, a technical and financial depreciation cycle for ICSs may be very long. Washington's Metrorail uses RTUs that "some of them have been in place as long as 35 years" (National Transportation Safety Board 2010, p. 25), a situation that is not uncommon in various other critical infrastructure sectors around the globe. Twenty to thirty years was not uncommon in some sectors: "When an ICS works, do not touch it, let alone replace it." A case in point for those believing in this approach is the breakdown of Heathrow's Terminal 4 baggage system after a software upgrade (Computerwoche 2008). Whether that is the right strategy needs discussion.

Technological aging ICSs, however, shall be nowadays considered as a threat as old technology with limited processing and memory capacities are not able to run (more) secure ICS applications (compare the capabilities of a Commodore-64 with that of your current laptop). With the introduction of commercial off-the-shelf ICT in the ICS domain, this type of threat comes even more to the fore. One can find 486-based systems as well as configurations with unpatched Windows XP SP1 systems in water purification installations, in the control of X-ray and Positron Emission Tomography (PET) systems in hospitals, in Automated Teller Machines and in the control system of bridges. Hardware systems and operating systems which you have replaced at home quite a long time ago are still 24/7 in operation in the ICS domain. An issue is that their increasingly becoming shorter technological lifetime does not match the technological lifetime of the process equipment which is being monitored and controlled. Moreover, compatibility with legacy ICSs may require newer ICSs not to enable security capabilities. How the ICS legacy threat can be addressed is discussed in (Oosterink 2012) who defined legacy systems as "systems which cannot be secured completely by regular measures and technologies and therefore pose a larger risk to the continuity, integrity and confidentiality of the controlled process(es)". It will anyway be hard to convince executive management to budget for a replacement and upgrade of the legacy ICSs as the major overhaul of the ICS-controlled production system or industrial plant is still years away. As (Anderson and Moore 2006) and (Moore 2010) pointed out, there exists a rife misalignment of incentives between those responsible for (ICS) cyber security and those who benefit from protection. The ICS department, as a functional domain, is therefore often last in line when handing out investment budgets.

These organizational ICS threats need to be addressed by:

- Leadership and cyber security awareness by the executive management level following for instance the principles outlined by the World Economic Forum (World Economic Forum 2014).
- Realistic investment levels for keeping ICS technology current taking into account the total cost of ownership in balance with the risk related to the cyber risk to ICSs and the potential impact on the business, image and stakeholder value.

5.3.6 ICT Security Standards

Sticking to a strict implementation of ICT-based security standards to the ICS domain may be a threat to the business objectives, a not so obvious threat which we explain hereafter. The ISO27001 (2013) standard is a widely established standard for information security management. This standard is accompanied by the ISO27002 (2013) standard which contains a set of information security controls, categorized into topics such as access control, communication security, physical security, human resource security, etc. These standards were originally developed for the office environment, but the ISO/IEC 27001:2013 standard could be applied across both the ICT and ICS domains. The organizational threat, however, is that the ICT department mandates a strict application of the full set of ICT controls to the ICS domain. Although the security controls of the ISO/IEC 27002:2013 are generic and applicable to all types of information systems and application domains, it is not trivial and even may be counterproductive to implement certain controls in the ICS domain. Hurdles are the 24/7 operational requirements, legacy ICSs and limited resource capabilities of ICSs as have been discussed before. Consider for instance the security control which states that a user access needs to be blocked after three subsequent failed login attempts. When that occurs on the main console (HMI) of an ICS plant in the mid of the night, the operational view and ability to control is lost for hours. It will be clear that some deviations of the strict application of the ICT security controls are required in the ICS domain. Moreover, a mismatch exists between the safety critical ICS domain and the ISO/IEC 27002 controls, as already was outlined by the European Workshop on Industrial Computer Systems Reliability, Safety and Security (EWICS 2015) in 2003. Currently, the International Society of Automation (ISA) works on international standards for the ICS domain to close this gap between standards and practical applicability in the ICS domain (Luiijf and Te Paske 2015, pp. 43–45).

5.3.7 Procurement

When new ICSs and ICS-related services (e.g., maintenance, support, outsourcing) are procured, it would be the right moment to enhance the cyber security. However, business-related pressure on investment and recurring cost levels is a business-related threat that may cause the relaxation or even complete removal of the cyber security requirements. Also during a contract renewal, the chance to include ICS security topics in the contract may be lost due to the lack of appropriate business drivers. This organizational ICS threat is a result of a skewed return on security investment (ROSI): security benefits are taken by departments that differ from the ones that are billed for the costs (MSB 2014, pp. 21, 42–43; Sonnenreich et al. 2006).

5.4 Architecture and Technology Threats

We will see that in larger ICS-controlled environments, for example a refinery, a set of threats stems from the need to make old ICS technologies compatible with new technologies, the aging and legacy aspects, and the unknowingly use of unconfigured new functionality. Smaller ICS environments may encounter some of these challenges. Mitigating most of the technology-related threats, however, do not require technological changes but a change in organizational leadership (internal issue) and a change of culture of manufacturers and system integrators (control of external acquired services) (BSI 2014) shows a first step in this direction.

5.4.1 Old Technology

As ICS components have a long life-time, their processing and memory capacities may be too limited to run newer ICS applications. Dealing with such components withholds the implementation and or activation of cryptographic security modules that require processor power and memory both of which are needed for the control of processes. Moreover, many ICS components and application software were developed in the period of deployment in a benign environment where only a limited set of people understood the inside of ICSs. Factory default passwords were embedded deep in the hardware and software. It was not common practice to replace such factory default passwords if the option was offered at all. Stuxnet (see Sect. 6.3) abused such a hard-wired password in the Siemens WinCC SCADA product that controlled the uranium enrichment centrifuges at Naţanz, Iran (Nicolas Falliere 2011). It took long before Siemens allowed other users of the products to change the factory default password as they could not assess the impact to the operational systems when the password was changed (Espiner 2010).

Aging of ICS components brings another threat: manufacturers cease to exist or for other reasons are unable to supply spare parts. The author came across organizations with maintenance engineers that are expert in soldering and replacing faulty transistors, capacitors and discrete logic chips in PLCs and related components. When repair becomes infeasible, it may take long before the ICS-controlled processes operate again normally. Management of such organizations states that manual control of the controlled processes is an alternative when a breakdown occurs. They seem to overlook the fact that the work force was reduced years ago because of the automation of processes. Those that are around now have lost all practical experience with manual operations.

5.4.2 Insecurity by Design

Another ICS threat is that components are packaged with factory default passwords. Security options are disabled by default. Installing components in the ICS domain is therefore easy, but inherently insecure. A rule of thumb is that thirty percent of utilities do not make the effort, are technically unable to change, or are contractually not allowed to change factory default password(s).

It is hard to convince ICS manufacturers to move to components that are secure out of the box. Only recently, some of the ICS manufacturers have started to change their products to have a default secure state which requires password changes during installation.

A strongly related threat is that authentication information including passwords are often not encrypted and can be found by cyber attackers in clear text in memory or in eavesdropped communication.

An example of this set of threats is a PLC of a well-known manufacturer which is wrapped in a sheet of paper. The sheet shows a drill hole template and posturizes where to connect the power plug and a UTP cable. A CD and a double page installation guide show that one should start the CD in a PC on the network where the PLC is connected to. The executable on the network then tries to discover the PLC. A web based interface assists in configuring the PLC. It is only on page 52 of the manual, which is a pdf (on the CD) that one can read how to set or remove (four spaces) a password. As most people do not read manuals, this type of PLCs is installed without any password protection and they will be directly connected to the internet. Using the Shodan tool (Shodan 2015), hackers found such PLCs without any authentication protection or just id=owner, password=owner in Belgium and The Netherlands. The PLCs controlled the pumps of a tropical swimming paradise, the heating system of the Salvation Army headquarters in Amsterdam, a wind power generator, waste water pumps and other functionalities (Luiijf 2013).

5.4.3   New functionality for Old Packaging

A lot of ICSs were developed in the sixties as proprietary hardware based on transistor board technology (Russel 2015). Replacement components for ten years or older installations will internally be based on more modern technology but still have field compatible interfaces. Manufacturers may have added new functionality to the component which is only documented deep down in the manual. For example, PLCs may nowadays contain a web server 'on a chip' which offers a user friendly access to the functionality of the PLC, an embedded email client and an SNMP agent. Engineers may not recognize the change. They replace a defective component as soon as possible by a new one in the mid of the night. The new functionality will be waiting in a not configured out-of-the box state for the first unauthorized person to connect.

5.4.4   Protocols

As discussed previously in this volume, a lot of ICSs and their protocols were designed in the period of proprietary products and benign closed environments. When discussing the threat of ICS protocols, we need to distinguish between hard to correct errors in the ICS protocol specification and weaknesses in the protocol implementation (Igure et al. 2006, p. 502).

With respect to the protocol specification, the ICS architectures and designs assumed a security posture of security by obscurity, lack of knowledge about ICS technology, and no actors interested in and willing to attack and disrupt ICSs. Therefore, the variety of ICS protocols do not protect the content of protocol messages, do not protect against man-in-the-middle attacks, and do not prescribe what to do when an illogical protocol element is detected. Recent studies have analyzed the security of protocols such as Modbus and Modbus over TCP (Fovino 2014, p. 460; Huitsing et al. 2008; Shayto et al. 2008), KNX/IP and KNX/EIB (Judmayer et al. 2014), and other ICS protocols. From those studies it is clear that the ICS protocols are not secure and resilient against cyber-attacks. These insecure ICS protocols form an ICS threat vector that is exploited by hackers (SCADAhacker.com 2015) and Trojan software.

Apart from fundamental protocol errors and weaknesses, ICS protocol implementations are not made robust. According to manufacturers and system integrators, end-users of ICSs are often only interested in new ICS functionalities and not in security and robustness of protocol implementations. The internet-world has learned its lessons in a hard way over time, e.g., with the ping-of-death attack and DNS BIND weaknesses. Lessons that have not found their way into ICS protocol implementations yet. Network sniffers are often used by network managers in the ICT world to scan for active systems and ports in their network. However, when ICSs receives an unexpected packet sent by such a tool or a packet which does not conform to the ICS protocol, the ICSs either may ignore the packet, may stop communicating or even stop functioning (crash).

Tests by CERN[2] performed on 25 ICS devices from seven different manufacturers at their TOCSSiC test stand showed that 32% of the ICS devices crashed when experiencing a denial-of-service attack: "The devices had to be restarted by power-cycling the device." "In 21% of the Nessus tests, the device crashed during the scan. After power-cycling the device, the scan was repeated without the corresponding plug-in. In the remaining 18%, Nessus reported significant security holes {..}" (Lüders 2005). For example, a Modbus server crashed when the Modbus port 502 was scanned and longer than expected input to various other protocols on ICS equipment caused ICS crashes alike a ping-of-death.

Similarly, penetration testing has caused an industrial robot to make an unexpected rotation (Duggan 2005), city lighting go dark and more.

Despite the safety-related aspects of processes controlled by ICS, this threat of lack of input validation, a lesson identified long ago (Luiijf 2014), and the lack of

---

[2] CERN operates the Large Hadron Collider (LHC) in Geneva, Switzerland where a high-energy beam with an energy equivalent to 85 kg of TNT is steered 10,000 times a second through a 3-mm hole in a 27-km wide circle. A complex set of ICSs steer this beam and monitors and controls many aspects of this unique and complex machine. The LHC is used to discover the Higgs particle and understand other building blocks of nature.

robustness of ICS protocol implementations still exists in most current ICS components and applications as demonstrated by a number of the (ICS-CERT 2015) alerts and advisories.

5.5   Networking and Telecommunications

This section discusses specific ICS threats related to networking and telecommunications. We will not discuss the general risk of using networking technologies such as TCP/IP and WiFi; for those security aspects we refer you to existing books on networking security. Most ICS threats in this area stem from weak protocols and protocol implementations and the too optimistic use of insecure functionalities which use wireless communication (see Chap. 3).

5.5.1   Operational Environment

One of the architectural assumptions about the operational environment of ICSs a number of years ago was that the ICS domain was a benign closed environment completely disconnected from other networks. Gradually, long distance connections for wide area operations and modem sets for remote maintenance were added. Those communication needs were driven by process engineering requirements to improve the reliability and the process quality.

Currently there exists a business need to move operational data from the inside of the ICS domain to business applications. For example, based on laws and regulations, bulk power generator companies need to supply momentary information about state, available reserve capacities, and available black-start capacity to their transmission system operator (TSO) in order to manage the N-1 criterion and reduce the risk of a blackout. This information can be used for trading energy at the spot market as well. Such communication flows require the opening of firewalls and or the Demilitarized Zone (DMZ) for the information flow from the ICS domain to the business domain. The ICS threat is that such an opening, when incorrectly configured or weakly monitored and maintained, opens the access for unauthorized outsiders and malware to the ICS domain. Managing the interconnection is less easy than it may look as not all firewalls support the ICS-specific protocols (Igure et al. 2006, p. 502). At the same time, audits in larger ICS-networks often reveal the existence of multiple unauthorized connections between both domains and with public networks.

The use of short-range wireless communications in ICSs opens another can of threats (Reaves and Morris 2012). Once again protocol weaknesses and weak implementations, this time at the lower levels of the ISO/OSI Basic Reference Model. The main threat is that one installs a wireless connection, e.g., to connect field devices avoiding hard to maintain "Christmas trees" of wires, without any planning and guarantees to maintain it thereafter. When it works, it is forgotten that cryptographic keys need to be replaced with a certain frequency, that a crypto-graphic algorithm may require replacement or strengthening after a number of years, etcetera. The practice of install and forget of wireless connectivity is a threat in an increasing number of ICS-controlled installations while the hacker communi-ties acquire increasingly sophisticated and powerful toolsets to, for instance, derive keys from wireless traffic. Examples of such tools are software defined radio and rainbow tables.

5.5.2   Remote Network Access

Operators, maintenance engineers and third parties require remote access to the ICS domain to ensure 24/7 operations and optimal processing conditions. Ageing ICS domains still use POTS dial-in modems although they are quickly being replaced by internet-based access methods. Most organizations make use of virtual private network (VPN) technology to connect to the corporate ICT network from remote locations. From the inside organization network, authorized users may connect to the ICS domain. Some organizations allow a direct 'dial-up' connection to their ICS domain.

Other organizations offer a direct remote VPN-based connection to the ICS domain. A proper access control from outside the internal premises requires at least a two-factor authentication and strict control of authorizations. A combined organi-zational - technical threat is that such accesses are not under strict scrutiny causing too many people including unauthorized ones having access to the ICS domain. Once inside the ICS domain, the ICSs currently offer very limited controls to block any malicious activity.

Although the VPN technology for remote access seems to be secure, a hacker taking control of the system of the operator or engineer at home will be able to access the ICS domain as soon as the VPN connection has been opened legitimately (sometimes even automatically). At that moment, the hacker may launch specific toolkit packages which create an opening and persistent access for further penetra-tion. In this way, a hacker penetrated and manipulated the ICSs of a Harrisburg, Pennsylvania water filtering plant (Esposito 2006).

5.5.3   Dependencies of ICT Systems

Organizations let systems in the ICS domain use systems located in the ICT domain for acquiring critical information to the controlled processes. The reason may be to reduce costs or just for a never ending temporary test as one forgets to configure and install the system in the end in the ICS domain. That works well until the ICT system engineers decide to upgrade and/or restart such a system or the router

providing a cross-boundary service without realizing the potential impact to the
ICS controlled processes. The impact may be high as shown by the simple reboot
of a computer on the business network of the Hatch Nuclear Power Plant near
Baxley, Georgia. It led to a 48-h emergency shutdown of the whole nuclear power
plant in 2008.

A similar type of threat is the shared (*multiplexed*) use by ICT and ICSs of long
distance telecommunication links of limited bandwidth capacity. In case the ICT
side becomes infested with malware, the link may be overwhelmed with communication packets at the ICT side of the communication link. ICS traffic is delayed. The
threat is that this may cause a loss of view to operations or an incorrect situation
view. Delayed state information may cause operators to react out of sync as they
judge the situation based on a state of minutes ago. Packets delays may also cause a
loss of control. Such a condition increased the Big Blackout in the USA 2003.
According to Verton (2003) such as grid operations were hindered by slowness of
control and incorrect situational awareness at the HMI displays of the EMS. This
threat is large for sectors where quick state polling cycles and low latency are
required, for example electricity, refineries, and safety critical processes.

5.5.4 Direct Connection to the Internet

Unexpectedly, given the threats of malware and hacking, hundreds of thousands of
ICSs and sensors are directly connected to the internet. This number is growing
every day. In 2005, a system engineer of a waste water processing system processing the waste water of 1.5 million households, businesses and factories proclaimed
that: "If millions of people make their financial transactions via the internet, one
shall be able to control the waste water processing system in a similar way. When
an alarm situation occurs, the automated system will be blocked and manual procedures will be followed." Since then, many more ICS owners have followed the same
risky path of not taking care of the cyber security of the ICSs. The Industrial Risk
Assessment Map (IRAM) project by the Freie Universität Berlin, Germany used the
Shodan search engine to globally locate ICSs connected to the Internet. Project
SHINE (SHodan INtelligence Extraction) which ran from 2012 till October 2014
did the same and found 2.2 million of internet-connected ICS devices (Radvanosky
and Brodsky 2014). The ICS threat here is that internet-connectivity of ICSs is
regarded to be normal.

5.6 Human Factors

In this section we will discuss various aspects of how human factors create credit-
able threats to ICSs.

5.6.1 User Awareness

The average ICS system or maintenance engineer concentrates on the 24/7 continuous operational state of the monitored and controlled processes. Their cyber security awareness and exposure do not go further than some security controls for the administrative system when filling in time sheets and the security controls securing electronic payments made at home. Many organizations knowingly or unknowingly do not consider their ICSs and network components as assets that potential may fall victim to unauthorized activities in the ICS network. Management, system and maintenance engineers should have a responsibility to think "cyber secure ICSs" alike their way of working in any other ICT domain they use either at work or privately.

5.6.2 Policies and Procedures

Some part of the set of organizations which deploy and use ICS learned that the Stuxnet Trojan (Nicolas Falliere 2011) jumped the 'well-protected' connections between the ICT and ICS domains of the nuclear enrichment factory in Naţanz, Iran via malware on a USB-stick. The stick was brought to the inside by a third party maintenance engineer according to several analysis reports. Since then, many of those organizations developed a doctrine which states "USB sticks shall not be plugged into ICS equipment". Some exemptions are made for the engineering workstation. Unfortunately, these organizations miss the main issue. While the no USB stick doctrine is followed very strictly, one can see process operators charging their MP3 players and smart phones via an USB-cable connected to an ICS component. That the USB-plug and connected personal equipment may carry malware is a largely overlooked threat in both the ICT and ICS environments (Finkle 2013; Kovacs 2015).

5.6.3 Disgruntled Employees

Alike in the ICT-domain, the threat of disgruntled (former) employees exists. As people in the ICS domain are often much longer employed before their contract is or may be discontinued, the threat seems to be higher. A number of cases exist where employees or ex-employees sabotaged or manipulated ICS equipment, see for instance Abrams and Weiss (2008), Potter (1997), King (2014), Wells (2011), Vijayan (2009), and McMillan (2007).

5.7 Operations and maintenance of ICS

This section highlights some ICS threats related to the operations and maintenance of ICS covering both technical and organizational aspects.

5.7.1   Passwords

Security measures in general need to be logical and shall have an as limited impact as possible on the daily operational tasks. Otherwise, humans will seek a work-around which certainly will reduce the overall security posture of the organization. One, much debated issue is the use of passwords, the required password strength (length and entropy), and the password expiration time. In the ICS domain, that debate is even more complex than in the ICT domain.

First, in a considerable number of ICS environments, operations use a single (group) user name and password which has been set during installation or was even left to the factory default and which never has been changed since. In several utility sectors this seems to be common practice in a quarter to one-third of the utilities although their sector-wide cyber security baselines state the requirement that only individual passwords ought to be used. The threat is that neither the security officer, nor law enforcement is able to attribute security incidents to individuals as logs do not show which individual did what (King 2014). Even worse, over time many unauthorized people such as personnel of external parties and those who left the organization may have knowledge of the password. Even when an organization uses individual username-password combinations, the mandatory password change may occur only once in a year. In many cases a change is required on an ad hoc basis after an even longer period than a year. Organizations with ICSs seldom use the password change frequency of 3–6 months which is common use in their own ICT domain and which may be mandated by their own sector-wide good practices for ICSs.

5.7.2   Who Is "Empowered"?

Traditionally, the culture of the process engineering is one of making changes to tune the process to become more efficient and to take corrective action when a process tends to run out of control. In order to be able to do so, they require superpowers in ICSs to make changes 24/7 h a day. The threat is that changes to the ICSs are made without proper change management procedures and consequence analysis (MSB 2014, pp. 38–39). In one case in the Netherlands, 26,000 households were deprived for three days of gas for heating and cooking as the mixing process of high-caloric gas with nitrogen resulted in only nitrogen to be delivered. After a failed experiment with the operational ICSs, it was forgotten to remove the experimental software modifications as proper change management procedures were lacking.

5.7.3   Change Management

A major threat to ICS operations is a lack of change management and up to date ICS configuration documentation and back-ups. Given the often complex ICS and odd hour maintenance needs, current documentation and insight in the last software and configuration changes may help to reduce business process disruption time. In case equipment is destroyed, good configuration documentation and remotely stored back-ups may help to recover the ICS operations as fast as possible (ICT Qatar, p. 9).

Proper change management also requires a separation of the ICS development and testing environment from the operational ICS environment. The threat of unauthorized and inadvertent changes to the operational system is high (ICT Qatar, p. 9).

5.7.4 Patching

Within the ICT domain, it has become common practice to patch those vulnerabilities which have become known as soon as possible. Within the 24/7 ICS environment, the "If it ain't broken, don't fix it" mentality rules. Moreover, ICS manufacturers and system integrators often take a long time to verify whether a patch for an underlying operating system or communications software may not break their ICS application. Then, the system and process engineers need to consider the local risk of applying a validated patch and find the right maintenance moment to apply the patch. Automatic applying of patches is most often infeasible as that may cause the loss of control during a crucial period of the controlled process; only in certain relatively slow processes such as waste water movement that might be an option if it is supported at all in the ICS domain.

Patching in the ICS domain often causes an organizational dilemma of business process continuity versus taking the specific cyber risk (MSB 2014, p. 24). That is, if the underlying operating system and application software are still supported. The risk exists that a Trojan or worm finds a way to penetrate the ICS network and infects the underlying operating system of the HMI or other ICS applications.

Benchmarks in multiple critical infrastructure sectors show that between one-third and a half of utilities currently have a patching policy of 'never applying a patch' or apply a patch 'when the ICS manufacturer or the ICS application manufacturer threatens with no support and no guarantees anymore when a patch is not applied'.

The ICS domain threat is that the organizational window of exposure, which is the time between the application of the patch and the time the vulnerability became known, is far too long given the risk of deliberate disruptions by outsiders (Pauna and Moulinos 2013). An organizational window of exposure of many months is more common than uncommon whereas ICS good practices state a relaxed period of 7 (Waterschappen, p. 93) or 15 days (ICT Qatar, p. 10).

Another surprise, and therefore threat to organizations, is that certain software libraries and modules of a single ICS manufacturer are embedded in a wide set of ICS products put on the market by a diverse set of diverse ICS manufacturers. When a vulnerability becomes known in such a core module, it may take long before patches are distributed by all manufacturers that use the modules. Reselling manufacturers may even not deliver patches to their customers for such vulnerabilities.

The vulnerabilities found in the CoDeSys Control Runtime System are a case in point (Tofino Security 2012).

Patch management in the ICS domain is a topic for which the ISA/IEC standardization organization has developed a good practice document (ISA 2015).

5.7.5   Malware Protection

In the ICT domain it is common to run anti-malware software which often automatically acquires and applies updates found on the internet. Anti-malware solutions for ICS require processor and memory capacity which, due to aging and legacy ICS components in the ICS domain, are hard to apply. When applied, updating of the anti-malware software may take that many processor and memory resources of an ICSs that the monitoring and control of the controlled processes are delayed or even disrupted for a while.

For those reasons some twenty percent of utilities do not apply antimalware solutions in their ICS domain and another ten percent have a window of exposure (Pauna and Moulinos 2013) of several weeks as the malware signatures are only updated ad hoc or after several weeks. On the other hand, sector-wide regulation may state that such updates need to be applied within 24 h after becoming available, e.g. (Waterschappen 2013, p. 67). Benchmarks in various critical infrastructure sectors using ICSs have shown that such gaps between regulation and practice exist. The risk to the business shall not be neglected as malware incidents in ICS domains have happened and have affected large operations. A near miss happened at the grid control center of the Australian power grid operator Integral Energy. They almost lost their HMI due to malware affecting Windows systems in their control center. A loss of power supply due to the inability to control the power grid could have affected 2.1 million households (Farrell 2009).

5.7.6   Hardware Access and Networking

As discussed above, often a friction and lack of understanding exists between the ICT and ICS departments. As their services meet at the level of networking, crucial components to the ICS continuity may be controlled, maintained and upgraded by the ICT department without informing ICS operations as they are just a network user alike the financial department. Loss of view and loss of control of the full ICS environment may be the impact.

ICT maintenance staff may need once in a while physical access to network components in the rooms or buildings where the monitored and controlled physical processes take place. Inadvertently, they manage to unplug cables critical to the ICS domain or inadvertently power off ICS components, a threat to the continuity of ICS operations not to be taken too lightly. Moreover, ICT staff may connect unauthorized equipment to crucial network elements of the ICSs neglecting all cyber security procedures, see for example (WBPF.com 2009). Such incidents even have happened and are likely to happen in future in critical ICS networks of nuclear power plants, why not in your ICS network?

5.8 The ICS Environment

Last but not least, a set of external threats may threaten the ICS monitored and controlled operations with the risk of a major impact to the business, critical infrastructures through dependencies, safety and the environment.

5.8.1 Physical Security

Careful planning of ICS controlled systems may have considered the physical security of the components and restricting physical access to authorized personnel only. At a number of installations, however, less thought is given to the physical security of ICS components, networking equipment and telecommunication lines as no one is interested to damage or manipulate ICSs of a waste water facility, power plant, drinking water pump station, and etcetera.

An example of such lack of attention was, some years ago, an unlocked door of a pumping station adjacent to a biking path somewhere in The Netherlands. Behind the door, a couple of PCs with HMI application software remotely monitored and controlled RTUs at tens of small pumping stations and weirs in a number of polders, each four to five meters below sea level. Theft of the equipment would have caused a very long disruption as there obviously was a lack of asset, backup and configuration management. Moreover, drunken youngsters biking home late night could have stumbled in and manipulated the various water levels changes that could have caused a lot of damage.

5.8.2 Dependencies

Like with all information and communication technologies, emergency generators and batteries may supply power for the continuation of the ICSs and the controlled processes, or may provide a graceful shutting down of the operations. Not well-maintained generators and batteries often fail when their power capacity is really needed for the ICSs and controlled physical processes. The impact of a backup power failure to the primary operation objectives may be high, see for example (Hrenchir 2015).

ICS equipment often is physically able to operate under wide humidity and temperature range conditions. As the old specialized equipment and components are being replaced by not industrially hardened commercial-off-the-shelf ICS components, e.g., networking components, some additional protection measures for the ICS equipment may be required. Moreover, as some ICSs operate in rooms located in remote locations such as tunnels, underground pumping stations, one easily might forget the need for proper lightning protection. Lightning has damaged ICS and networking components, a risk that increases with the move from discrete components to more sensitive microprocessors in for instance RTUs and PLCs.

Much deeper in the ICSs are hidden dependencies due to the use of technical components which can be disturbed or manipulated externally at some distant of the premises. A first example is precise time in ICS networks that is increasingly derived from cheap GPS-based clocks. The threat of external accidental or deliberate manipulation, or temporary loss of GPS signal shall not be neglected as shown by a UK study (Vallance 2012). GPS jamming devices can be bought for less than 20 US dollars. Depending on the range, GPS jamming devices can be pretty small, so small that they can be hidden in plain sight, for instance in a trashed soft drink can.

GPS spoofing devices can be commercially bought as well. With spoofing one can change the location and time on the output side of the GPS receiver affecting controlled processes. The ICSs of various industries are susceptible to GPS manipulation as is explained by (ICS-CERT 2011).

Similarly, relatively cheap wireless communication is brought into the ICS domain to connect sensory equipment with PLCs in order to avoid a Christmas tree of cables. Another reason may be that it is technically infeasible to add more electric circuits than the 24V power supply to continuously rotating equipment, for instance a waste water settling tank, while one wants to add modern sensors. Jamming and manipulation of such wireless communication is cheap and easy. One of the most well-known hacking attacks on ICSs, the one by Vitek Boden affecting Hunter Watertech's waste water system, caused a number of ecological incidents is a case in point (Smith 2001).

And last but not least, ICSs may increasingly depend on and interact with normal ICT services in the ICS domain such as SQL-database services. Sometimes such dependencies are not so obvious, as was demonstrated at a natural gas power plant when the SQL database trial license expired and all PLCs halted (N.N. 2015).

5.8.3   Third Parties on Site

Third parties such as ICS maintenance engineers and system integrators may need access to engineering stations, the ICS hardware and components, network equipment and the monitored and controlled equipment. There is a set of threats connected to their abilities to inadvertently or deliberately disrupt ICS operations. Often their activities are not monitored during their activities. This is a threat cause as set points may be changed and other uncontrolled modifications may occur in the ICS environment. Another threat is that they may bring a USB device or laptop and connect that to the ICS domain causing a malware infection, e.g. (Finkle 2013), or use the laptop to perform network activities that disrupt ICS operations, or even create an uncontrolled and unauthorized external network connection.

5.8.4 Remote Access

Providing authorizations to third parties for using remote access to the ICS domain requires the building of trust. Nevertheless, a threat exists that the third party is sloppy with protecting the information about one's configurations.

That trust in a third party is not always justified was shown in case where a utility had regular breakdowns of their services. After a while a correlation was made with 'maintenance activities' by a third party which were said to be necessary. In the end it became clear that the third party maintenance engineer used the operational ICSs of the utility as a demonstration site on how a control system works; he/she changed set points and valve settings during the demonstrations. Because he/she stupidly forgot to reset the values, the utility services broke down some hours or even a day later.

Larger manufacturers, application providers and ICS maintenance firms may remotely support many ICS installations across multiple nations and states across the globe on a 24/7 basis. They like to have immediate access, meaning that the ICS network needs to have external connectivity where the authentication of the access is provided globally to unknown people at the manufacturer's support centers operating from various nations. For ease of operations, such support centers want to use 'standard' username–password combinations such as support*manuf*–support*xy* where *xy* denotes the ISO-code for a nation or US-state. Once one knows the access to ICSs in, for instance, CA(nada), it is easy to deduce the support password for France, Austria and India. The threat is obvious: when a hacker found his or her way into one ICS-controlled installation, he/she has the keys to ICSs and their controlled physical processes globally. Nevertheless, it is hard to convince the manufacturer or maintenance firm to change the password or even to accept a customer controlled and regularly changing username-password combination. Certain contracts in the utility sector, where the manufacturer both delivered the ICS and guarantees a minimum level of performance during a number of years, state that the customer is not allowed changing the manufacturers' (default) username-password access, otherwise the performance contract will be void.

5.9 Summary and Conclusions

ICSs were traditionally designed around reliability and safety; cyber security was not a design and operational consideration. A lack of understanding of the cyber security threat can be found at all organization levels. Most ICS departments convey their needs to the executive level, in which there is a general lack of understanding. The cultures of the IT/ICT and ICS departments often largely differ. The ICS domain first focuses on the availability, visibility, and operability of the 24/7 ICS-controlled processes, the process efficiency, and safety. ICT departments, on the other hand, focus mainly on ICT controls related to confidentiality and integrity. They then mandate strict application of their ICT controls to the ICS domain when those controls are not optimum, or relevant. ICS operators and engineers, vendors, system integrators, and maintenance personnel are not generally trained in cyber security of ICSs. A number of ICS global hack incidents stem from this ICS threat.

Technological aging of ICS hardware is a significant threat as old technology with limited processing and memory capacities are not able to run secure ICS applications of the current or future age. Threats stem from the need to make old ICS technologies compatible with new technology. ICS components are packaged with factory default passwords. ICSs and their protocols were designed in the period of proprietary products and benign closed environment.

Security policies (e.g., for USB sticks) are not followed well, effectively removing the physical protection of a closed environment. Current desires and requirements for remote access, access by third parties, and freer access between the ICT domain and the ICS domain create new threats to ICSs. Security measures in general need to be logical and shall have an as limited impact as possible on the daily operational tasks. Otherwise, humans will seek a work-around which certainly will reduce the overall security posture of the organization.

Avoidance of some of these threats can be accomplished using some of the following measures:

1. Map the ICS network and understand all connectivity and performance issues. Then reduce the set of external connections to a single logical well-guarded and audited connection, and for larger installations put legacy on a separate firewalled network.
2. Executives should build trust and mutual understanding of all staff in the ICS department with the ICT department staff. You need them!
3. Get leadership support top down, otherwise any attempt to improve ICS security will be a waste of effort. Organizational change may be needed.
4. Perform a threat-risk assessment and start managing threats like user awareness, legacy, third party access, and procurement in a balanced way.

References

Abrams, M., & Weiss, J. (2008). *Malicious control system cyber security attack case study— Maroochy water services Australia.* Washington, DC: NIST. Retrieved November 8, 2015, from http://csrc.nist.gov/groups/SMA/fisma/ics/documents/Maroochy-Water-Services-Case-Study_report.pdf.

Anderson, R., & Moore, T. (2006). The economics of information security. *Science, 314*(5799), 610–613. doi:10.1126/science.1130992.

Averill, B., & Luiijf, E. A. (2010). Canvassing the cyber security landscape: Why Energy companies need to pay attention. *Journal on Energy Security*, May 18. Retrieved November 8, 2015, from http://www.ensec.org/index.php?view=article&id=243%3Acanvassing-the-cyber-security-landscapewhy-energy-companies-need-to-pay-attention.

National Transportation Safety Board. (2010). *Collision of two Washington metropolitan area transit authority metrorail trains near Fort Totten station, Washington, D.C., June 22, 2009.* Washington, DC: NTSB. Retrieved November 8, 2015, from http://www.ntsb.gov/investigations/AccidentReports/Reports/RAR1002.pdf.

BSI. (2014). *Requirements for network-connected industrial components v1.1..* Bad Godesberg, Germany: BSI. Retrieved November 8, 2015, from https://www.allianz-fuer-cybersicherheit. de/ACS/DE/_downloads/techniker/hardware/BSI-CS_067E.pdf.

CIPedia(c). (2015, November 8). *Critical infrastructure.* Retrieved from CIPedia(c): http://www. cipedia.eu.

Computerwoche. (2008, February 2). *Softwarepanne sorgt für Koffer-Chaos in London-Heathrow.* Computerwoche. Retrieved November 8, 2015, from http://www.computerwoche.de/ nachrichten/1856437/.

Dubowski, S. (2004, January 6). *B.C. researchers urge improved industrial IT protection.* BC, Canada. Retrieved November 8, 2015, from http://www.itworldcanada.com/ article/b-c-researchers-urge-improved-industrial-it-protection/11622.

Duggan, D. P. (2005). *Penetration testing of industrial control systems.* Albuquerque, NM: Sandia National Laboratories. Retrieved November 8, 2015, from http://energy.sandia.gov/wp-content/gallery/uploads/sand_2005_2846p.pdf.

Espiner, T. (2010, July 20). *Siemens warns Stuxnet targets of password risk.* CNet. Retrieved November 8, 2015, from http://www.cnet.com/news/siemens-warns-stuxnet-targets-of-password-risk/.

Esposito, R. (2006, October 30). *Hackers penetrate water system computers.* ABC News. Retrieved November 8, 2015, from http://blogs.abcnews.com/theblotter/2006/10/hackers_penetra.html.

EWICS. (2015). *European workshop on industrial computer systems reliability, safety and security.* EWICS.org. Retrieved November 8, 2015, from http://www.ewics.org.

Farrell, N. (2009, October 1). *Linux saves Aussie electrical grid.* The Inquirer. Retrieved November 8, 2015, from http://www.theinquirer.net/inquirer/news/1556944/linux-saves-aussie-electricity.

FBI. (2009, June 30). *Arlington security guard arrested on federal charges for hacking into hospital's computer system.* Dallas. Retrieved November 8, 2015, from http://dallas.fbi.gov/ dojpressrel/pressrel09/dl063009.htm.

Finkle, J. (2013, January 16). *Malicious virus shuttered power plant: DHS.* Reuters. Retrieved November 8, 2015, from http://www.reuters.com/article/2013/01/16/us-cybersecurity-powerplants-idUSBRE90F1F720130116.

Kovacs, E. (2015, December 29). Trains Vulnerable to Hacker Attacks: Researchers, Securityweek. Fromhttp://www.securityweek.com/trains-vulnerable-hacker-attacks-researchers.

Fovino, I. N. (2014). SCADA system cyber security. In K. Markantonakis & K. Mayes (Eds.), *Secure smart embedded devices, platforms and applications* (pp. 451–471). New York, NY: Springer Science+Business Media. doi:10.1007/978-1-4614-7915-4_20.

Frontline. (2003, April 24). *Interview: Joe Weiss.* Retrieved November 8, 2015, from http://www. pbs.org/wgbh/pages/frontline/shows/cyberwar/interviews/weiss.html.

GAO. (2015). *Federal facility security: DHS and GSA should address cyber risk to building and access control systems.* Washington, DC: GAO. Retrieved November 8, 2015, from http:// www.gao.gov/products/GAO-15-6.

Hrenchir, T. (2015, April 27). 3 million gallons of sewage leak into Kansas River after pump station power outage. *The Topeka Capital Journal.* Retrieved November 8, 2015, from http://cjonline.com/ news/2015-04-27/3-million-gallons-sewage-leak-kansas-river-after-pump-station-power-outage.

Huitsing, P., Chandia, R., Papa, M., & Shenoi, S. (2008). Attack taxonomies for the Modbus protocols. *International Journal on Critical Infrastructure Protection, 1,* 37–44.

ICS-CERT. (2011). *Advisory federal aviation administration GPS testing.* Washington, DC: ICS-CERT. Retrieved November 8, 2015, from https://ics-cert.us-cert.gov/advisories/ ICSA-11-025-01.

ICS-CERT. (2015). *The industrial control systems cyber emergency response team (ICS-CERT).* ICS-CERT. Retrieved November 8, 2015, from https://ics-cert.us-cert.gov/.

ICT Qatar. (2014). *National ICS security standard version 3.0..* Doha, Qatar: Ministry of Information and Communications Technology. Retrieved November 8, 2015, from http://www. qcert.org/sites/default/files/public/documents/national_ics_security_standard_v.3_-_final.pdf.

Igure, V. M., Laughter, S. A., & Williams, R. D. (2006). Security issues in SCADA networks. *Computers and Security, 25*(3), 498–506. doi:10.1016/j.cose.2006.03.001.

ISA. (2015). *IEC TR 62443-2-3:2015 patch management in the IACS environment.* Geneva, Switzerland: IEC.

ISO22399. (2007). *ISO/PAS 22399:2007 Societal security—Guideline for incident preparedness and operational continuity management (withdrawn in 2013).* Geneva, Switzerland: ISO.

ISO27000. (2014). *ISO/IEC 27000:2014 Information technology—Security techniques—Information security management systems—Overview and vocabulary.* Geneva, Switzerland: ISO/IEC.

ISO27001. (2013). *ISO/IEC 27001:2013 Information technology—Security techniques—Information security management systems—Requirements.* Geneva, Switzerland: ISO/IEC.

ISO27002. (2013). *ISO/IEC 27002:2013 Information technology—Security techniques—Code of practice for information security controls.* Geneva, Switzerland: ISO/IEC.

Judmayer, A., Krammer, L., & Kastner, W. (2014). On the security of security extensions for IP-based KNX networks. *Proceedings of the 10th IEEE International Workshop on Factory Communication Systems (WFCS 2014).* Busan, Korea: IEEE. Retrieved November 8, 2015, from https://www.sba-research.org/wp-content/uploads/publications/judmayer_KNX_wfcs2014.pdf.

King, R. (2014, October 9). Sabotage investigation highlights poor network monitoring at utilities. *Wall Street Journal.* Retrieved November 8, 2015, from http://blogs.wsj.com/cio/2014/10/09/sabotage-investigation-highlights-poor-network-monitoring-at-utilities/.

Krebs. (2014, February 14). *Target hackers broke in via HVAC company.* KrebsonSecurity. Retrieved November 8, 2015, from http://krebsonsecurity.com/2014/02/target-hackers-broke-in-via-hvac-company/.

Lüders, S. (2005). Control systems under attack? *10th ICALEPCS International Conference on Accelerator & Large Experimental Physics Control Systems* (pp. FR2.4–6O). Geneva: CERN. Retrieved November 8, 2015, from https://accelconf.web.cern.ch/accelconf/ica05/proceedings/pdf/O5_008.pdf.

Luiijf, E. (2013). Why are we so unconsciously insecure? *International Journal of Critical Infrastructure Protection, 6,* 179–181. doi:10.1016/j.ijcip.2013.10.003.

Luiijf, E. (2014). Are we in love with cyber insecurity? *International Journal of Critical Infrastructure Protection, 7*(3), 165–166. doi:10.1016/j.ijcip.2014.07.002.

Luiijf, H., & Lassche, R. (2006). *SCADA (on)veiligheid, een rol voor de overheid? [in Dutch] (SCADA (in)security, a role for the Dutch government?).* Den Haag: TNO/KEMA.

Luiijf, E., & Te Paske, B. J. (2015). *Cyber security of industrial control systems.* Den Haag: TNO. Retrieved November 8, 2015, from http://www.tno.nl/ICS-security.

McMillan, R. (2007, November 29). *Insider charged with hacking California canal system: Ex-supervisor installed unauthorized software on SCADA system, indictment says.* Computerworld. Retrieved November 8, 2015, from http://www.computerworld.com/article/2540235/disaster-recovery/insider-charged-with-hacking-california-canal-system.html.

Moore, T. (2010). The economics of cybersecurity: Principles and policy options. *International Journal of Critical Infrastructure Protection, 3,* 103–117. doi:10.1016/j.ijcip.2010.10.002.

MSB. (2014). *Guide to increased security in industrial information and control systems.* Sweden: Swedish Civil Contingencies Agency (MSB). Retrieved November 8, 2015, from https://www.msb.se/RibData/Filer/pdf/27473.pdf.

N.N. (2015, July 22). *Never trust a subcontractor.* Reddit.com. Retrieved November 8, 2015, from http://www.reddit.com/r/sysadmin/comments/3e3y8t/never_trust_a_subcontractor/.

Nicolas Falliere, L. O. (2011). *W32.Stuxnet Dossier.* Cupertino, CA, USA: Symantec. Retrieved November 8, 2015, from https://www.symantec.com/content/en/us/enterprise/media/security_response/whitepapers/w32_stuxnet_dossier.pdf.

Oosterink, M. (2012). *Security of legacy process control systems: Moving towards secure process control systems (whitepaper).* Den Haag: CPNI.NL. Retrieved November 8, 2015, from http://publications.tno.nl/publication/102819/5psRPC/oosterlink-2012-security.pdf.

Pauna, A., & Moulinos, K. (2013). *Window of exposure... a real problem for SCADA systems?* Heraklion, Greece: ENISA. Retrieved November 8, 2015, from http://www.enisa.europa.eu/

activities/Resilience-and-CIIP/critical-infrastructure-and-services/scada-industrial-control-systems/window-of-exposure-a-real-problem-for-scada-systems.

Potter, W. C. (1997, Augustus 20). *Less well known cases of nuclear terrorism and nuclear diversion in Russia*. NTI. Retrieved November 8, 2015, from http://www.nti.org/analysis/articles/less-well-known-cases-nuclear-terrorism-and-nuclear-diversion-russia/.

Radvanosky, R., & Brodsky, J. (2014, October 1). *Project Shine (SHodan INtelligence Extraction) Findings Report*. USA. Retrieved November 8, 2015, from http://www.slideshare.net/BobRadvanovsky/project-shine-findings-report-dated-1oct2014.

Reaves, B., & Morris, T. (2012). Analysis and mitigation of vulnerabilities in short-range wireless communications for industrial control systems. *International Journal of Critical Infrastructure Protection, 5*(3-4), 154–174. doi:10.1016/j.ijcip.2012.10.001.

Russel, J. (2015). *A brief history of SCADA/EMS*. Scadahistory.com. Retrieved November 8, 2015, from http://scadahistory.com/.

SCADAhacker.com. (2015). *Metasploit modules for SCADA-related vulnerabilities*. Retrieved November 8, 2015, from https://scadahacker.com/resources/msf-scada.html.

Shayto, R., Porter, B., Chandia, R., Papa, M., & Shenoi, S. (2008). Assessing the integrity of field devices in Modbus networks. In M. Papa, & S. Shenoi (Eds.), *Critical infrastructure protection II* (Vol. 290, pp. 115–128). The International Federation for Information Processing. Retrieved November 8, 2015, from http://link.springer.com/chapter/10.1007%2F978-0-387-88523-0_9.

Shodan. (2015). *Shodan*. Retrieved November 8, 2015, from http://www.shodanhq.com/.

Smith, T. (2001, October 31). *Hacker jailed for revenge sewage attacks: Job rejection caused a bit of a stink*. The A Register. Retrieved November 8, 2015, from http://www.theregister.co.uk/2001/10/31/hacker_jailed_for_revenge_sewage/.

Sonnenreich, W., Albanese, J., & Stout, B. (2006). *Return on security investment (ROSI)—A practical approach*. Australian Computer Society Inc. Retrieved November 8, 2015, from https://www.acs.org.au/__data/assets/pdf_file/0003/15393/JRPIT38.1.45.pdf.

Stouffler, K., Pilliteri, V., Lightman, S., Abrams, M., & Hahn, A. (2015). *NIST special publication 800-82 rev 2: Guide to industrial control systems (ICS) security*. Washington, DC: NIST. doi:10.6028/NIST.SP.800-82r2.

Tofino Security. (2012). *White paper v1.1: Analysis of the 3S CoDeSys security vulnerabilities for industrial*. Tofino Security. Retrieved November 8, 2015, from http://www.isssource.com/wp-content/uploads/2012/12/120612Analysis-of-3S-CoDeSys-Security-Vulnerabilities-1.1.pdf.

Vallance, C. (2012, March 8). *Sentinel project research reveals UK GPS jammer use*. BBC. Retrieved November 8, 2015, from http://www.bbc.com/news/technology-17119768.

Verton, D. (2003, August 29). *Blaster worm linked to severity of blackout*. Computerworld. Retrieved November 8, 2015, from http://www.computerworld.com/s/article/84510/Blaster_worm_linked_to_severity_of_blackout.

Vijayan, J. (2009, March 18). *IT contractor indicted for sabotaging offshore rig management system*. Computerworld. Retrieved November 8, 2015, from http://www.computerworld.com/article/2531775/security0/it-contractor-indicted-for-sabotaging-offshore-rig-management-system.html.

Waterschappen, U. V. (2013). *Baseline Informatiebeveiliging Waterschappen [Information security baseline for water boards]*. Den Haag, Netherlands: Unie van Waterschappen. Retrieved November 8, 2015, from http://www.uvw.nl/wp-content/uploads/2013/10/Baseline-Informatiebeveiliging-waterschappen-2013.pdf.

WBPF.com. (2009, Augustus 25). *Employees fired after reporting security breach: Former lake worth utilities employees fear breach could've caused statewide blackout*. West Palm Beach, USA. Retrieved November 8, 2015, from http://www.wpbf.com/Employees-Fired-After-Reporting-Security-Breach/5096936.

Weiss, J. (2009, July 21). *Securing the modern electric grid from physical and cyber attacks*. Statement for the Record, July 21, 2009 Hearing before the Subcommittee on Emerging.

Washington, DC, USA. Retrieved November 8, 2015, from http://chsdemocrats.house.gov/SiteDocuments/20090722115326-92965.pdf.

Wells, L. (2011, January 12). *Fired employee allegedly shuts off Fairfield's gas*. The Carmi Times. Retrieved November 8, 2015, from http://www.carmitimes.com/area_news/x1314139206/Fired-employee-allegedly-shuts-off-Fairfields-gas.

World Economic Forum. (2014). *Risk and responsibility in a hyperconnected world (WEF principles)*. Geneva, Switzerland: WEF. Retrieved November 8, 2015, from http://www3.weforum.org/docs/WEF_IT_PathwaysToGlobalCyberResilience_Report_2012.pdf.

Chapter 6
Attacks on Industrial Control Systems

Nick Evancich and Jason Li

6.1 Introduction

Having discussed a number of broad classes of threats to ICS and SCADA systems, we now explore how such threats enable specific attacks, and the classes and examples of attacks on such systems. The nature and efficacy of these attacks are largely determined by a complex mix of security deficiencies in ICS systems that aggregate architectures and approaches from several epochs of technological history. For example, SCADA systems of the second generation were distributed, but used nonstandard protocols. This enabled centralized supervisory servers and remote PLCs and RTUs. Security was often overlooked in this generation. The third generation of SCADA systems used common network protocols such as TCP/IP. This generation added the concept of Process Control Network (PCN), which allowed SCADA enclaves to connect to the Internet at large. This connection enabled operators to remotely manage the SCADA ecosystem and introduced malware to the enclaves.

The chapter begins by pointing out that security by design was lacking and designers too often relied on hopes that the attacker would lack knowledge about the inner structure and workings of the system (so called security by obscurity). The chapter reviews several examples of known attacks and then introduced elements of common attack approaches, such as buffer overflow, code injection and others. Rootkits are described next. These involve sophisticated attack approaches, commonly believed to require extensive development efforts and resources of a group sponsored by a nation state. Particularly important is the ability of rootkit-based attacks to hide effectively the malicious processes from detection by users or defenders of the ICS.

N. Evancich (✉) • J. Li
Intelligent Automation, Inc., Rockville, MD, USA
e-mail: nevancich@i-a-i.com

© Springer International Publishing Switzerland 2016
E.J.M. Colbert, A. Kott (eds.), *Cyber-security of SCADA and Other Industrial Control Systems*, Advances in Information Security 66,
DOI 10.1007/978-3-319-32125-7_6

To provide a more concrete sample context for discussion of such attacks, the chapter presents a notional system that captures key features on many SCADA systems. Since information about attacks on operational ICS is not easy to come by, vulnerabilities of ICS are often investigated by game-like competitive events. The chapter proceeds to present details of such event. Finally, the chapter discusses Stuxnet—a well-studied and documented rootkit used on a SCADA system—in detail.

6.2   Overview

Most Industry Control Systems (ICS) and Supervisory Control and Data Acquisition (SCADA) systems lack security in their design. In many cases, designers of ICS and SCADA systems believed that an air gap, or not having an Internet connection, was the panacea for security (Lee and Seshia 2011). The Stuxnet malware example detailed later in this chapter highlights the fallacy of this argument.

Particularly, SCADA systems often approached security through obscurity. Commonly, they used proprietary interfaces or interfaces that are not well documented (e.g., company is out of business, interface is not currently in production, device predates wide commercial internet adoption, etc.) or with documentation that is out-of-print. This approach has not worked well for SCADA security. Insiders can attack the system by using institutional knowledge. Attackers have spent time studying SCADA elements by gaining physical access to the elements, thereby deriving intimate knowledge of the physical and cyber features of the SCADA elements.

Some SCADA systems or elements were designed before well-founded cyber security principles were settled upon. SCADA system designers would claim that cyber security is not a concern since SCADA systems are not connected to the Internet. However, over time, SCADA systems began appearing on the Internet, and often with no cyber security. These arguments were rendered moot with the advent of Stuxnet, which is considered the first advanced persistent threat (APT) faced by SCADA systems.

6.2.1   Known Attacks

Due to the general lack of SCADA security, various critical infrastructure incidents have occurred in SCADA controlled systems. "The critical nature of these systems also makes these intriguing targets" (Miller and Rowe 2012). SCADA systems have a large attack surface due to the multiple disciplines and domains that SCADA systems control and operate on. SCADA systems are vulnerable to many classes of exploits, like account compromise, malware, denial of service, and physical effects (such as physically preventing a valve from opening).

The following are a brief enumeration of publicized SCADA system security failings. Though not all of the events were caused by a malicious actor, all were caused by intrinsic security lapses in SCADA systems.

In 1982, the first known attack against a critical infrastructure system occurred in Siberia. A Trojan was used to insert a logic bomb into the SCADA system. The logic bomb resulted in a failure that caused an explosion, which disabled the pipeline. "The pipeline software that was to run the pumps, turbines and valves was programmed to go haywire, to reset pump speeds and valve settings to produce pressures far beyond those acceptable to the pipeline joints and welds. The result was the most monumental non-nuclear explosion and fire ever seen from space." (Reed 2005).

In 1999, an employee was performing maintenance on a SCADA data acquisition server that controlled a gasoline pipeline in Bellingham, WA. The database maintenance resulted in a rupture and leaked gasoline in a creek, which ignited and burned a two-mile section of the creek. This incident resulted in loss of life. The SCADA system had no security features that prevented a maintenance procedure from affecting the operation of the system.

In 2003, the SQLSlammer worm infected a SCADA system that controlled the Davis-Besse nuclear plant in Ohio. The worm shut down the HMI and supervisor SCADA systems that handled the plant's safety systems. The SCADA systems had no protections against this type of attack.

Also in 2003, the Sobig virus attacked SCADA systems in Florida controlling CSX freight trains. The virus disrupted signaling and other systems, completely stopping freight train movement in the south eastern United States.

As mentioned earlier, we discuss the Stuxnet attack (2008/2009) in detail in Sect. 6.3.

The take away from this enumeration is that the interest by malicious actors in SCADA systems has increased. This is evidenced by the increase in attack velocity and sophistication. The increased interest ultimately leads to advanced persistent threats such as STUXNET being deployed against SCADA systems.

6.2.2   General Attack Methods

SCADA systems have a large attack surface due to the involvement of multiple disciplines and domains (cyber, physical, etc.), and because many of the subsystems in the SCADA ecosystem are still based on older cyber technology. For example, one major SCADA remote terminal unit (RTU) is built on top of Windows 95 and these RTUs are still in use in 2015. This makes SCADA systems especially vulnerable and they are increasingly under cyber-attack.

Researchers and SCADA system administrators have discovered the standard set of malicious attacks that are normally used against cyber sub-systems of SCADA systems. The classes of cyber-attacks and their effect on SCADA systems are listed below. These have been detected on production SCADA systems, and each has been used against SCADA systems, which are generally vulnerable to existing cyber-attacks.

Buffer overflow is a class of attack that exploits cyber elements such as an array by moving beyond the declared bounds of the element. This allows an attacker to break out of the normal flow of the program's control and modify the operation of the program. For example, write-what-where condition is an attack that can write any value to any location, which usually results in a buffer overflow. The physical elements of a SCADA system are immune to this type of attack, but the various servers that control the programmable logic controllers (PLCs) and RTUs have been shown to be susceptible to this type of attack. Many older SCADA systems are based on 8-bit or 16-bit systems, and, hence integers can easily overflow. This results in the attacker being able to inject and execute arbitrary code.

Broadly speaking, in a *code injection* attack, the attacker gains access to a critical process on the SCADA system (often via a buffer overflow) and forces the system to execute newly introduced code. This is the classic form of a cyber-attack.

Use-after-free is a vulnerability that does not check if a resource has been freed. The Microsys Promotic SCADA application uses a file after one code path has closed it. This vulnerability allows for the attack to arbitrarily execute code.

Related to code injection, in Dynamic Link Library (DLL) hijacking, the attacker replaces a required DLL with a new DLL that contains malicious code. Since many SCADA systems are based on Windows 95 and Windows 95 does not require signing of DLLs, the DLLs can easily be replaced.

Input validation has been shown to be a significant issue with Industrial Control Systems. Modern programming standards have implemented various input validation or sanitation requirements, but due to the vintage of SCADA systems, not all inputs are validated. This attack is performed by sending input to the system that it cannot reconcile. For example, if the system reads character input and will terminate when a specific sequence is found, the attacker simply does not provide the required sequence and the buffer will likely overflow. This may result in giving the attacker the ability to change the program's control flow or may crash the program. As another example, SQL injection attacks prey upon unsanitized SQL query inputs. These attacks allow the attacker to directly command the SQL database. Modern SCADA systems rely on an SQL database for maintaining the history of the SCADA system and for monitoring purposes. If an attacker drops the database, the SCADA system will essentially be blind.

Since most SCADA systems cover a wide physical land area and may be in remote locations (such as mile 600 of the Trans-Siberian pipeline), it is feasible for attackers to gain physical access to the SCADA subsystems. Physical access allows the attackers nearly unlimited range of attacks on the SCADA system. *Access control* is one of the major security threats to ICS and SCADA systems.

Several SCADA systems in production have well known and hard coded passwords. This provides an attacker with an easy entry point into the SCADA ecosystem. Often the hardcoded passwords are used in other aspects of the system, and other functions or software depend on this hardcoded password.

Hard-coded credentials are a vulnerability that is similar to hard-coded passwords and several production SCADA systems have embedded credentials that are not removable. Several SCADA systems have no way to revoke an invalid or compromised credential. This allows an attacker to gain elevated access to the SCADA system with no recourse for the administrator to mitigate.

In addition, processes should execute at the lowest privilege possible. Many SCADA systems require that the processes run as admin or root, which means that once the process is compromised, the attack has full access to the system.

Modern protocols usually involve *authentication* to determine if the command or client is valid and has the permissions for access. Most SCADA remote elements (RTUs and PLCs) do not authenticate the commands that are issued to them. Therefore, they will execute any command sent to them, whether they are legitimate or not.

Due to the vintage of various production SCADA systems, many SCADA systems have weak implementations of cryptography libraries. This is often due to the remote controllers being 8-bit or 16-bit based. Entropy issues are an example of this. Insufficient entropy is a vulnerability caused by encrypted data being not "random enough," decreasing the value of the cipher. Along with cryptographic issues, the random number generator on many SCADA systems is not a "true" random number generator. Hence this makes the password hashing or the 'salt' vulnerable to brute force attacks.

Inadequate encryption strength is tied to previous attacks based off incorrectly implemented encryption techniques. This attack allows for access to data in the SCADA system that the designers believed was safe. For example, if the system uses a short key, attackers can bypass the encryption and gain access to that data. Mis-encryption of sensitive data is a common vulnerability to SCADA systems; for example, some older SCADA systems will store passwords in clear text.

In *Path traversal*, the attacker moves up or down the file system path to gain access to a directory, usually the configuration of the SCADA controller, which is of interest to the attacker. This attack has been used against Honeywell XLWEB SCADA controllers.

In the fourth generation of SCADA systems, Cross-site scripting (XSS) allows management to be done via *web browsers*. This allows an attacker to inject code into the browsing session. This exploit is present on ClearSCADA systems, which was one of the main vectors that Stuxnet used.

Cross-site request forgery (CSRF) has been found on several SCADA systems, such as Schneider Electric StruxureWare and ClearSCADA. This attack exposes the SCADA server infrastructure to the attacker.

A forced browsing attack relies on standard patterns for various web site frameworks. The attacker "guesses" what a web page that isn't normally publically available would be and gets the system to display that page. This can give the adversary access to sensitive information about the SCADA system.

With *resource exhaustion*, the attacker consumes more resources than the system has available. In SCADA systems, this may be accomplished by sending updates faster than the data acquisition server can process. This attack often does not result in the ability to assume control over the system, but usually degrades the functionality of the overall system. *Resource management* is a type of denial of service attack. The attacker sends commands to limit the resources that various SCADA subsystems require and, hence, causes failures.

6.2.3   Rootkits

The attacks on the SCADA ecosystem have become more and more advanced over time and thus attackers include entities with more sophisticated resources. SCADA systems were found with rootkits and advanced persistent threats. This signals that SCADA systems are targets by nation state level adversaries.

A rootkit is software designed to hide processes from detection, and to provide the injected process with an enhanced level of access to the system. The term "rootkit" is a compound of "root" which is a colloquial term for the highest level of access on a system, and "kit" which is a technical term for a bundle of tools.

A rootkit is usually part of a multistage attack. The minimum is a two-staged attack, including initial exploit vector and payload. The rootkit is installed or delivered to the targeted system via a known exploit. Once the rootkit is installed, it elevates its own access to the highest privileged level. It removes traces of its installation and elevation, hides the detection of its execution, and starts countermeasures to stop circumvention. At this stage of the attack, the rootkit is essentially undetectable. It has the ability to start processes that are virtually undetectable, and can deceive malware detection processes and alter logs.

The next step in the attack is to deploy the rootkit's payload. The payload might be included with the rootkit or delivered to the rootkit. The rootkit has prepared the system for exploitation by the payload via altering the system to create an environment that is ideal for the payload and for stealthy execution. In SCADA systems, the goal of the payload is often to modify the physical effects of the system under SCADA control.

Stuxnet is considered the first rootkit for SCADA (Falliere 2010) and it was the first known APT for a SCADA system. Stuxnet will be used as an exhaustive example later in this chapter. Stuxnet was the rootkit used to alter the programming of Iranian PLCs that were controlling centrifuges. A universal serial bus (USB) drive was the initial propagation vector, Stuxnet was the rootkit, and a worm was the payload from the Stuxnet rootkit. With the advent of Stuxnet, several rootkits were found to exist for various SCADA implementations. The U.S. Air Force Institute of Technology created a rootkit for various SCADA PLCs, which hides in the PLCs' firmware. A common SCADA rootkit is the Rootkit.TmpHider that propagates via the USB storage driver. SCADA devices are often slow to be patched, due to the remote nature of several SCADA ecosystems. For example, the Trans-Siberian Pipeline which extends for over 2800 miles, uses SCADA control and many of the SCADA devices are of 1980s vintage. Assuming a patch exists for a device with respect to an exploit, each SCADA device must be patched by physically visiting the device and removing it from the SCADA system.

6.2.4 Example Notional System

Based on the previously described classes of attacks and a marked increase in attack velocity and sophistication, SCADA security has become a popular topic at several cyber security conferences.

DEF CON, started in 1993, is one of the largest hacker/cyber security conferences. DEF CON 22 has a track of talks specifically about SCADA security. Aaron Bayles, who worked in the oil and gas industry as a SCADA system architect and penetration tester, and performed vulnerability/risk assessment, presented a SCADA presentation as part of the DEF CON 101 series at DEF CON 22. This was the first major discussion at a large forum over SCADA and ICS exploits. Several issues that make SCADA vulnerable were highlighted (Bayles 2015). Some SCADA systems contain legacy equipment that may date back many decades, and which may not be designed to be connected to a network, as evidenced by no command authentication. Size, weight, and power are often constrained, which limits the availability for resources to be expended on security. Further, demands/requirements placed on SCADA systems may not overlap with cyber security requirements.

Figure 6.1 is a notional example of the extent of the geographic span of a SCADA system, as presented in the DEF CON talk (Bayles 2015). A SCADA system like a pipeline can span hundreds of miles, making physical security difficult, if not impossible. Therefore, adversaries may have greater physical access to the SCADA elements than the administrators. These vast geographical distances highlight unique challenges for SCADA administrators. A layered security model is appropriate to enhance the cyber security of these SCADA systems.

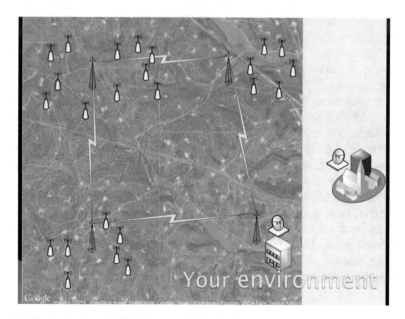

Fig. 6.1 Notional scale of a SCADA network (Bayles 2015)

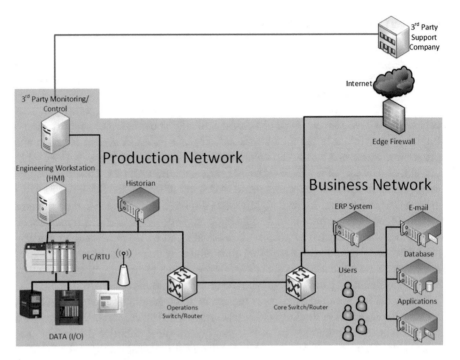

Fig. 6.2 Notional SCADA enterprise (Bayles 2015)

Figure 6.2 shows an example of how many of the SCADA network systems are configured. This network, presented by DEF CON researchers (Bayles 2015) is derived from the published documents of the Hoover dam. The business network side of this example details the various services often present in a notional business network, like enterprise resource planning, email, databases, applications and various users' systems. The production network contains a SCADA system and is connected to the business network via a router. Additionally, the SCADA system's supplier has an external connection into the SCADA system and, hence, to the production network.

Purdue Enterprise Reference Architecture (PERA), shown in Fig. 6.3, recommends a five-layer architecture for ICS and SCADA systems. The goal is to follow well known cyber security principles like isolation, separation, and trust re-establishment. Each layer is isolated by a firewall. This firewall ensures that only the correct, needed, and minimal data is moved between layers. Separation is achieved by not mixing functional elements in a single layer. For example, the operational management layer does not share control elements or functions with the layer below it. Finally, trust is established and re-established when moving from layer to layer via authentication mechanisms.

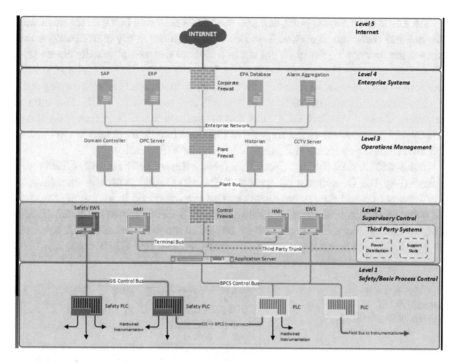

Fig. 6.3 PERA (Bayles 2015)

6.2.5 *Capture the Flag and ICS-CERT*

Many of the vulnerabilities of ICS are best investigated by CTF (Capture the Flag) events since information about attacks on operational ICS is not often easy to come by. Additionally, having ICS as part of CTF events increases the interest level of these systems and may lead to improved security and awareness. In particular, one such CTF event is the S4x15 SCADA CTF, a competition that applied the DEF CON CTF contest idea to SCADA systems. It was held during the 2015 S4 security conference, with the following parameters.

1. 30 teams participated, which made S4x15 the largest SCADA CTF to date
2. 42 flags were available for capture
3. 10 flags were not captured by any team
4. Flags were valued at different points levels (100–1000 points each)
5. Team with the highest score won
6. All flags were taken from SCADA compromises seen in the wild

An example of a 100 point flag was seeding registers with ASCII characters on a Modicon PLC. In this example registers 22 and 23 were overwritten with ASCII values of interest to players in the CTF contest.

An example of a 1000 point flag was the PLC's firmware being overwritten with similar, but malicious firmware. This firmware contained some minor changes that altered the function of the PLC, but not in a manner that was physically observable. Therefore, teams had to reverse engineer the firmware of the PLC and determine what portions of the firmware were malicious, in order to capture this flag and receive points.

The increased exposure of SCADA and ICS exploits by DEF CON talks and the creation of an ICS track at DEF CON and the various ICS CTF games that formed led to public awareness of the fragility of these systems. This in turn led to the creation of several governing and standard boards for ICS security.

Industrial Control System Cyber Emergency Response Team (ICS-CERT) was founded by The Department of Homeland Security (DHS) to provide coordination between public and private organizations that are interested in improving the state of cyber security for industrial control systems. ICS-CERT acts as the clearinghouse for various vulnerabilities related to industrial control and SCADA systems. Figure 6.4 details an example list of vulnerabilities that ICS-CERT produces.

Fig. 6.4 ICS-CERT's reported SCADA vulnerabilities for 2012

Vulnerability Type	
Buffer Overflow	44
Input Validation	13
Resource Exhaustion	8
Authentication	8
Cross-site Scripting	8
Path Traversal	8
Resource Management	8
Access Control	7
Hard-coded Password	7
DLL Hijacking	6
SQL Injection	4
Credentials Management	3
Cryptographic Issues	3
Insufficient Entropy	3
Use After Free	3
Use of Hard-coded Credentials	2
Cross-Site Request Forgery	2
Privilege Management	2
Write-what-where Condition	2
Integer Overflow or Wraparound	2
Inadequate Encryption Strength	2
Missing Encryption of Sensitive Data	1
Code Injection	1
Forced Browsing	1
Miscellaneous	15
Total	171

In addition, ICS-CERT will provide organizations with a Cyber Resilience Review, which evaluates the organization with a rating in ten domains. ICS-CERT is another stepping stone to increasing the awareness of ICS cyber security issues and is a partial response to Stuxnet. The goal of this service is to improve the ICS cyber security across the United States.

6.3 Stuxnet Attack

Stuxnet is widely considered the first SCADA APT and it ushered in an entire field of malware. Stuxnet is a class of cyber physical systems (CPS) malware that was designed to damage a centrifuge being used to enrich uranium. Stuxnet used two different attacks against the centrifuge: overpressure and rotor speed.

The overpressure attack would increase the pressure inside the centrifuge, thereby decreasing the yield of enriched uranium. Technicians would interpret a centrifuge that is chronically in an over pressured state as being at the end of its useful life, and would suggest replacing it.

Altering the rotor speed would cause one of several failures in the centrifuge, since it is designed to spin at one speed for a very long time. Either spinning the rotors above the acceptable limit or varying the speed will greatly impact the useful life of the centrifuge.

6.3.1 Background

It is widely accepted that Stuxnet was released around 2008 or 2009, but it was not detected until at least 2010. The centrifuges were expected to have a 10-year lifespan and a nominal failure rate of 10%. However, at least 2000 centrifuges failed during a period between December 2009 and January 2010. This was a significantly higher failure rate than the expected 10%. Additionally, the Windows systems interfacing with the SCADA systems that control the centrifuges were experiencing an unusual number of the famous Windows "Blue Screens of Death (BSoD)". The operators of the centrifuges contracted VirusBlokAda to help solve their cyber security issues. A security researcher named Sergey Ulasen was assigned to determine why the systems had unusually high rates of BSoDs. He found a unique worm written mostly in C and consisting of about 0.5 MB of compiled code and named it "Stuxnet". 'Stu' derives from a ".stub" file that is used by Stuxnet and 'xnet' comes from MrxNet.sys. His research not only uncovered Stuxnet, but also discovered several zero-day exploits.

The initial exploits found that were related to Stuxnet were MS-10-046, MS-10-061, MS-10-073, and MS-10-092. MS-10-046 was listed as a critical security vulnerability. This exploit allows for remote code execution by using a specially crafted icon. MS-10-061 was listed as a critical security vulnerability that allows for remote code execution using a print spooling service. It allows a specifically formatted print request to execute code contained in the request. MS-10-073 was classified as an important vulnerability. This exploit allows kernel mode drivers to elevate users to a higher privilege level. Finally, MS-10-092 was described as an important security fault. This exploit allows non-validated escalation to privileges of tasks. These four exploits were chained together to deliver and operate the Stuxnet APT.

6.3.2   Deployment and Propagation

Stuxnet can enter a closed network via USB flash memory as shown in Fig. 6.5. In order to accomplish this modality of infection and propagation, Stuxnet must usurp and infect a writable USB device.

Stuxnet starts either via a network or Internet infection and looks for a USB device to jump to. It creates a non-viewable and non-reported window with the handle of AFX64c313. This window's main function is to intercept WM_ DEVICECHANGE, which is a message that is sent by the USB driver to the Windows kernel to notify Windows that a new USB device has been connected and new services may need to be started. Six files are copied:

1. ~WTR4241.tmp
2. ~WTR4132.tmp
3. Copy of Shortcut to.lnk
4. Copy of Copy of Shortcut to.lnk
5. Copy of Copy of Copy of Shortcut to.lnk
6. Copy of Copy of Copy of Copy of Shortcut to.lnk

A ~ before the filename in windows is used to signify that the file is a temporary backup. These backups are often used to recover data when a program such as Word crashes. The four shortcut files are malformed shortcuts to non-existent Control Panel applications.

The multiple copies of the shortcuts target different versions of Windows and are placed in a path that will attempt to run these fictitious Control Panel applications. The shortcuts are executed by "Shell32.LoadCPLModule", which actually executes the .tmp files. This results in a fully infected Windows system.

Stuxnet can spread across the network using two different exploits: windows server service NetPath (**MS-08-067**) and the windows print spooler service (**MS-10-061**).

MS-08-067 was not considered a zero-day exploit. It was widely used by Conficker (an older malware worm) but was often unpatched. Stuxnet uses this exploit to look for C:\ shares and Admin user folder shares on all of the Windows computers on the network. Once it finds either of these shares, Stuxnet copies "DEFRAGxxxx.TMP", the Stuxnet payload and the network propagation code. Stuxnet executes: 'rundll32.exe "DEFRAGxxxx.TMP", DllGetClassObjectEx'.

This command does the following on the targeted system:

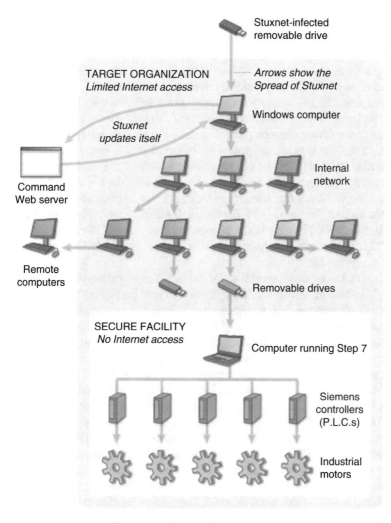

Fig. 6.5 Stuxnet overview (Broad et al. 2011)

1. Rundll32.exe—executes a dll
2. DEFRAGxxxx.TMP—is a dll that Stuxnet uses to execute the exploit associated with MS-10-061
3. DllGetClassObjectEx—gets the handler to the entry point class of the dll

The exploit, MS-10-061, was first discovered along with Stuxnet. The exploit allows for Stuxnet to write files to another Windows computer that does not have a C:\ or admin shared folder. Stuxnet accomplishes this by writing files to a Windows computer that has a shared printer. Two files are copied to the target machine: winsta.exe and sysnullevnt.mof. Winsta.exe executes a "Managed Object File", which is sysnullevnt.mof, and this is the actual payload of Stuxnet.

Additionally, Stuxnet has the ability to create a Remote Procedure Call (RPC) server. RPC allows for functions from one Windows computer to execute on another Windows computer and vice versa. RCP clients and server were often not disabled in the pre-Stuxnet era. Stuxnet can use the mechanism as an additional propagation channel or as an aid for the previously described mechanisms.

Stuxnet has the ability to update itself via two different websites: 'www.mypremierfutbol.com' and 'www.todaysfutbol.com'. The sites were hosted in Denmark and Malaysia. Either site can provide executable or payload updates to Stuxnet. Once updated, Stuxnet will propagate via the mechanisms described previously.

The file, ~WTR4132.TMP, is a user-mode rootkit. This rootkit's main objective is to modify "explorer.exe". Explorer.exe is loaded by the Windows kernel and is required for Windows operation. In order to accomplish this objective, the rootkit will connect to Windows API functions: FindFirstFileW, FindNextFileW, and FindFirstFileExW. These API calls are used to populate the file treeview in "explorer. exe". This rootkit is run only once and its purpose is to infect the system with a kernel-mode rootkit.

Stuxnet's kernel-mode rootkit is "MRxNet". The objective of this kernel-mode rootkit is to hide all the Stuxnet files, in order to load the payloads that will damage the centrifuge and the driver loading mechanism. Since Stuxnet is now in kernel space and running undetected, all it needs to do is present a driver with a valid Microsoft certified driver certificate. Once it completes this step, Stuxnet will have full access to the Windows system. This access will not require any exploits. Stuxnet will now appear to be a valid, approved, and certified kernel-mode application/ driver to the various Windows watchdogs. To accomplish this, the creators of Stuxnet used the private keys of two well-known drivers: one from Realtek and one from JMicron. Both of these companies are physically located in the Hsinchu Science Park in Taiwan and it is widely believed that the private keys were acquired physically. Both of these keys were revoked after Stuxnet was analyzed.

The next step in Stuxnet's attack is to alter the software running on the SCADA elements that directly control the centrifuges. Siemens (the vendor of the SCADA controllers) has SCADA control software, Step 7. Now that Stuxnet is in kernel-mode and has free reign over various Windows systems, it will propagate until it finds itself on a computer that is running Step 7. Once there, Stuxnet will alter a communication library in Step 7, s7othbxdx.dll. This communication library handles communications between the Windows computer running Step 7 and the PLC (SCADA element) controlling the centrifuge. Stuxnet will intercept and alter the communications between these two devices. Additionally, Stuxnet uses a new zero-day exploit, CVE-2010-2772, which is a hard coded password for accessing the PLCs.

Stuxnet will now target two specific PLCs that are attached to the Siemens S7-300 controller system. Once found, the following actions are taken:

1. A rootkit is delivered, which is the first known rootkit on PLCs, which hides the existence of Stuxnet on the PLC

2. Malware is placed into memory block DB890 that monitors system parameters, such as speed
3. The rotational speed is periodically changed from 1410 Hz to a range between 2 Hz and 1064 Hz
4. The changing speed is concealed from the SCADA system at large
5. The vibration is hidden from vibration sensors

At this point, Stuxnet is fully deployed and it will successfully damage the centrifuges slowly and subtly over time, making it difficult for technicians to detect the damage. This will result in an increase in the rate of centrifuge failure and replacement. The increase will be enough to slow the progress of the centrifuge's product, but not high enough to immediately rouse suspicions.

6.3.3 Effects

Stuxnet was specifically enabled by SCADA and ICS vulnerabilities. The Stuxnet APT not only targeted a specific SCADA and ICS system, but Stuxnet would not have been possible without the various cyber security issues associated with both SCADA and ICS based systems.

SCADA enabled Stuxnet by having an intersection between the physical and cyber worlds coupled with exemplifying all of the security faults in both worlds. Stuxnet traded on the specific SCADA requiring an old version of Microsoft Windows, which had well known security faults. Additionally, the ICS element of the targeted system was exploited by Stuxnet to hide the physical effects of the APT.

Once Stuxnet become known, there was a global effort to remove all known copies of Stuxnet in the wild. Several declarations of Stuxnet being eliminated were often followed by a new strain of Stuxnet being discovered within a month of the declaration. The delivery mechanism of Stuxnet has been repurposed as a vector for other non-ICS and non-SCADA payloads. Hence Stuxnet is a popular starting point for malware authors/users. Therefore, it is unlikely that Stuxnet will be completely removed.

The future of ICS and SCADA systems require seismic changes in a post-Stuxnet world. As ICS systems get older and fail, the SCADA elements are also aging out. This results in the components being upgraded to more modern versions that are designed with cyber security in mind. Unfortunately, this velocity is hampered by the cost and complexity of ICSs. Changing out a 30-year SCADA controller on a water control system may have grave unattended consequences that must be understood and mitigated. Additionally, the ICS trade group has a draft version of an updated SCADA protocol. This version addresses many of the cyber security problems present in older SCADA elements' versions.

6.4 Summary and Conclusions

Attackers have been able to execute complicated attacks on ICS and SCADA systems through careful study of the individual elements of the systems. This includes both physical and cyber elements. Over the past 15–20 years, interest by malicious actors in SCADA systems has increased. This is evidenced by the increase in attack velocity and sophistication. Researchers and SCADA system administrators have discovered a wide variety of malicious attack tools, based on reported attacks. Researchers have begun to investigate altering system designs and protocols to manage the cyber security threats for ICS (Lee et al. 2015). Attacks on the SCADA ecosystem have become more and more advanced over time and putative attackers are thought to be using more and more sophisticated resources. Some SCADA systems have been found with rootkits and advanced persistent threats. Stuxnet, from perhaps the most famous SCADA attack, is a class of cyber-physical malware that was designed to damage a centrifuge being used to enrich uranium. The Stuxnet malware was enabled specifically by security faults in both the physical and cyber worlds. The complex delivery mechanism of Stuxnet has been repurposed as a vector for other non-ICS and non-SCADA payloads.

While cyber security problems have continued to emerge in enterprise and personal computing, building security in ICS and SCADA systems needs urgent attention and appropriate controls need to be put into practice before catastrophic and physical damage fundamentally destroy critical national infrastructure. Stuxnet, as sophisticated as it was as the first APT for SCADA and ICS, was only a wake-up call.

References

Bayles, A. (2015). *Protecting SCADA from the ground up*. Las Vegas: DEFCON.

Broad, W., Markoff, J. & Sanger, D. (2011). *Israeli test on worm called crucial in Iran nuclear delay* [Online]. Retrieved June 5, 2015, from http://www.nytimes.com/2011/01/16/world/middleeast/16stuxnet.html?_r=1.

Falliere, N. (2010). *Stuxnet introduces the first known rootkit for industrial control systems* [Online]. Retrieved May 14, 2015, from http://www.symantec.com/connect/blogs/stuxnet-introduces-first-known-rootkit-scada-devices.

Lee, J., Bagheri, B., & Kao, H.-A. (2015). A cyber-physical systems architecture for industry 4.0-based manufacturing systems. *Manufacturing Letters, 3*, 18–23.

Lee, E. A., & Seshia, S. A. (2011). *Introduction to embedded systems—A cyber-physical systems approach*. Berkeley: LeeSeshia.org.

Miller, B., & Rowe, D.C. (2012). Survey of SCADA and critical infrastructure incidents. In: *Proceedings of ACM SIGITE 2012*.

Reed, T. (2005). *At the Abyss: An insider's history of the cold war*. New York: Presidio Press.

Chapter 7
Security Taxonomies of Industrial Control Systems

Angelyn S. Flowers, Sidney C. Smith, and Alessandro Oltramari

7.1 Introduction

With many types of systems, elements, threats, attacks, vulnerabilities, threat actors and so on, it is natural to wonder whether some conceptual order could be imposed on the complex and seemingly chaotic space of ICS security. Taxonomies and ontologies are among means by which humans bring order, meaning and knowledge management to broad domains of things, concepts and principles. For this reason, in this chapter we offer an overview of selected ICS security taxonomies and elements of emerging ontologies. The migration of data processing to open web infrastructures poses a great challenge for ICS in terms of information fusion and knowledge management. In this regard, ICS architectures can benefit from the use of ontologies, namely models of the underlying semantics of data. Ontologies are already used in a variety of applications, from Search Engine Optimization, Knowledge Discovery (e.g. elicitation of patterns of interactions within genomic data), and traditional AI and common-sense reasoning. The use of ontologies to complement ICS security taxonomies is a logical extension. The first section (Sect. 7.2) of this chapter presents key concepts, and their relationships, in a discussion of established taxonomies. Section 7.3 discusses ongoing research related to ICS security taxonomies and extended approaches based on ontologies. Section 7.4 summarizes

A.S. Flowers (✉)
Crime, Justice, and Security Studies, University of the District of Columbia,
Washington, DC, USA
e-mail: aflowers@udc.edu

S.C. Smith
Computational & Informational Sciences Directorate, US Army Research Laboratory,
Adelphi, MD, USA

A. Oltramari
School of Computer Science, Carnegie Mellon University, Pittsburgh, PA, USA

© Springer International Publishing Switzerland 2016
E.J.M. Colbert, A. Kott (eds.), *Cyber-security of SCADA and Other Industrial Control Systems*, Advances in Information Security 66,
DOI 10.1007/978-3-319-32125-7_7

the current status and discusses future trends in regards to ICS security taxonomies. Unless otherwise indicated ICS refers to all control systems, SCADA and DCS; as well as other control system configurations and constituent parts. In those instances where a specific type of control system is the subject, it will be indicated by name.

7.2 Overview

This overview begins with a discussion of the meaning of the term "taxonomy". Since security can be understood from the twin pillars of vulnerability and threat, this section next reviews diverse approaches to an organizing framework for vulnerability. That will be followed by examination of recent developments in the evolution of ICS threats and resulting risk, examining taxonomies that have been developed as a result.

7.2.1 Taxonomy Examples

A taxonomy is a method of classification that enables the grouping of entities into ordered categories. These classifications differ in organizing rationale and purpose. The purpose that a taxonomy is intended to serve plays a significant role in its construction and in its composition. Taxonomy structures vary. They can range from highly structured with multiple levels of delineation to those that are less structured and perhaps not as hierarchal. This can be illustrated by a comparison of two ends of the taxonomy spectrum.

Taxonomy as it is used in the biological sciences represents one end of the spectrum. In biology, taxonomies serve the purpose of defining organisms based on their shared characteristics, organizing them into groups based on those characteristics, giving names to those groups, and organizing the groups into a hierarchy from most to least inclusive. An example is provided in Fig. 7.1.

Fig. 7.1 Biological taxonomy description

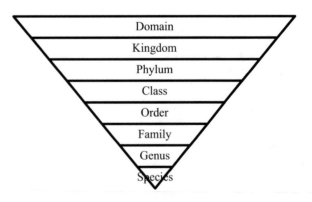

Domain

Kingdom

Phylum

Class

Order

Family

Genus

Species

Fig. 7.2 Bloom's taxonomy, revisited

At the other end of the taxonomy spectrum is Bloom's educational taxonomy (revised, see Fig. 7.2). Instead of enumerating nouns in the taxonomy, Bloom's taxonomy utilizes verbs. The purpose of Bloom's taxonomy is to define the development of critical thinking skills and educational learning objectives as well as assist teachers in developing curriculum content. Rather than ranking the groupings in a rigid hierarchy within the domain, as in biological taxonomic schema, Bloom's taxonomy ranks the domains themselves from higher to lower. Within each domain, instead of seven hierarchically organized levels, there are only two levels. These two levels are not rank-ordered; instead, they are in a logical flow progression.

To compare, biologic taxonomy schema serve the purpose of naming organisms while Bloom's educational taxonomy serves the purpose of describing the actions necessary to achieve a particular goal.

Taxonomies can be viewed as possessing the following characteristics:

- components are grouped into ordered conceptual classifications;
- there is a rationale to the organization; and
- there is a purpose for the taxonomy.

A taxonomy should demonstrate consistency between its organizing rationale and its delineated classification. The delineated classifications should satisfy the taxonomy's purpose. Using the examples above, biology taxonomies have a purpose of naming living organisms. The purpose of Bloom's taxonomy is to provide direction in organizing information to accomplish a teaching/learning activity. A taxonomy is useful when it demonstrates that it is unique, complete, and relational (Smith 2014). Unique means that each component is situated in only one place within the taxonomy. Complete means that the taxonomy either includes everything that it should include, or that it is easily expandable to accommodate the missing aspect. Finally, a taxonomy is relational when similar components are grouped together facilitating the ability to make generalizations.

ICS security taxonomies facilitate risk assessment, as well as enable the development of responses and countermeasures. As noted by Igure and Williams, "several different taxonomies exist because each is mostly applicable only to a particular field of interest" (Igure and Williams 2008, p. 7). For instance, in a survey of computer system security related taxonomies published between 1974 and 2006, Igure and Williams (2008) identified 34 different vulnerability and attack taxonomies created for different purposes. Among them were: Jiwnani and Zelkowwitz's vulnera-

Table 7.1 Vulnerability as
exploitable weaknesses

Domain	Weakness
Configuration	Account management
	Unused services
	Unpatched components
	Perimeter protection
Design/ specification	Cleartext communications
	Poor coding practices
	Network addressing
	Web servers and clients
	Enumeration
Implementation	Poor authentication
	Scripting/interface programming
	Malfunctioning devices
	Poor logging/monitoring

bility taxonomy for auditing software[1]; Welch and Lanthrop's threat taxonomy intended to facilitate the building of a security architecture for wireless networks; and Killourhy et al. whose attack taxonomy organized attacks by the manner in which they present as anomalies in sensor data.

7.2.2 Vulnerability Taxonomies

Vulnerability taxonomies serve a variety of purposes. One purpose for developing vulnerability taxonomies is to aid in the development of automated tools for producing security assessments (Igure and Williams 2008). Other purposes can include risk assessment, identification of needed mitigation strategies or counter-responses. The type of taxonomies required to accomplish these different purposes, will also vary. Since taxonomy development is tied to underlying assumptions or perceptions of vulnerability, understanding ICS security taxonomies begins with understanding vulnerability. In this context, vulnerability, particularly of industrial control systems can be considered as more a concept than a precise description.

Vulnerability has been described as a state which permits an unauthorized user to: read information; modify information; or grant or deny access to a resource (Bishop 1995). Fleury et al. (2008), on the other hand, describe vulnerability as an exploitable weakness. They identify vulnerabilities in the areas of configuration, design/specification, and implementation. A taxonomic schema of this is shown in Table 7.1.

---

[1] This was based on Landwehr's taxonomies on operating system flaws.

Sub-categories could be added to provide a further layer of specificity to the identified weaknesses. However, even without the addition of sub-categories, the weaknesses identified in Table 7.1 would contribute to a purpose of increasing awareness of needed mitigation strategies. While not specifically intended by its authors, Fleury et al's (2008) approach[2] to vulnerability does possess the characteristics of a taxonomy. The identified weaknesses are grouped into ordered conceptual classifications. These classifications serve to provide a definitional and organizational approach to the consideration of ICS vulnerabilities.

As mentioned, the purpose of some vulnerability taxonomies is to facilitate risk assessments. A risk assessment schema has been developed by the National Institute of Standards and Technology (NIST). NIST Special Publication 800-82 r2 (SP 800-82), *Guide to Industrial Control Systems (ICS) Security*, describes ICS vulnerability as a "weakness in an information system, system security procedures, controls, or implementation that could be exploited or triggered by a threat source" (Stouffer et al. 2015, p. C-2). SP 800-82 organizes ICS vulnerabilities into six categories. These categories are: policy and procedure, architecture and design, configuration and maintenance, physical, software development, and communications and network. Four potential threat sources for ICS were also identified: adversarial, accidental, structural, and environmental. NIST SP 800-82 is an overlay for ICS systems, providing supplemental guidance to NIST Special Publication 800-53 r4 (SP 800-53)[3] *Security and Privacy Controls for Federal Information Systems and Organizations* (2013).

NIST SP 800-53 is relied on by the Department of Homeland Security's (DHS) Industrial Control Systems Cyber Emergency Response Team (ICS-CERT). ICS-CERT utilizes the family groupings identified in NIST SP 800-53 to organize and analyze vulnerabilities discovered while conducting onsite assessments of critical infrastructure assets (Department of Homeland Security 2014). The 18 families identified by NIST 800-53, and used by DHS ICS-CERT in their assessments, are shown in Table 7.2.

ICS-CERT's *Industrial Control Systems Assessment 2014 Overview and Analysis* identified weakness across all of the control families in NIST SP 800-53. However, there were six vulnerabilities that were most prevalent, occurring in 28% of all assessments. These are identified in Table 7.3, along with their relevant NIST SP 800-53 family grouping.

Of the six most frequently found vulnerabilities from risk assessments, 50% were in the Access Control family.

---

[2] It was initially developed as a component in a model intended to contribute to development of a larger taxonomy (See, Fleury et al. 2008).

[3] Previously titled *Recommended Security Controls for Federal Information Systems*. Revision 4 represents the most comprehensive re-write of SP 800-53 since 2005. It was developed by an interagency partnership consisting of the Department of Defense the Intelligence Community, and the Committee on National Security that began working in 2009, culminating with the release of revision 4 in 2013 (Joint Task Force Transformation Initiative 2013).

Table 7.2 NIST security control families

Identifier	Family
AC	Access control
AT	Awareness and training
AU	Audit and accountability
CA	Security assessment and authorization
CM	Configuration management
CP	Contingency planning
IA	Identification and authentication
IR	Incident response
MA	Maintenance
MP	Media protection
PE	Physical environment protection
PL	Planning
PS	Personnel security
RA	Risk assessment
SA	System and services acquisition
SC	System and communication protection
SI	System and information integrity
PM	Program management

Table 7.3 ICS-CERT most prevalent vulnerabilities with related Family

Vulnerability	Family	Identifier
Boundary protection	System and communication protection	SC
Information flow enforcement	Access control	AC
Remote access	Access control	AC
Least privilege	Access control	AC
Physical access control	Physical & environmental protection	PE
Security function isolation	System and communications protection	SC

7.2.3 Attack Taxonomies

As the incidence of attacks on all ICS systems continues to rise, taxonomies focused on cyber-attacks have emerged. The 2015 Dell Security Annual Threat Report, when looking at SCADA systems, noted that attacks worldwide increased fourfold in 2014 going from 163,228 in January 2013 to 675,186 in January 2014. This followed an almost twofold increase during the previous time period. The primary method of attack continues to be buffer overflow vulnerabilities accounting for 25 % of attacks, followed by improper input validation at 9 % (Dell 2015).

Since 2000, the number, nature, and purpose of attacks on industrial control systems have escalated. In 2009, Stuxnet surfaced. Stuxnet has been identified as the world's first digital weapon due to its ability to cause actual physical damage. A worm which uses a three-prong attack, it is typically introduced via a USB flashdrive. Stuxnet targets Microsoft windows machines and networks, then targets Seimens PLCs and SCADA systems (Kusher 2013) (see also Sect. 6.3 in Chap. 6). Stuxnet caused substantial damage to the centrifuges of Iran's nuclear reactors before its presence was even recognized. Stuxnet, later, "escaped" from the Iranian facilities and began to propagate in the wild, putting all Siemens control systems at risk. Stuxnet was a "game changer" both in the manner in which it targeted controls systems and in the damage it can cause. Stuxnet later gave rise to related malware such as Flame and Duqu.

Post-Stuxnet, cyber-attacks requiring the resources of a nation-state to implement have proliferated. While Stuxnet was designed to cause actual physical damage, other types of cyber-attacks are geared towards espionage. Two cyber espionage attacks involving control systems were: Dragonfly and NightDragon. Dragonfly, targeted businesses in the U.S., Spain, France, Italy, Germany, Turkey, and Poland; compromising industrial control systems used to control sections of power plants (Brewster 2014). Prior to shifting its focus to energy firms, Dragonfly initially targeted U.S. and Canadian defense and aviation companies (Symantec 2014). Symantec noted that Dragonfly appeared to be a state-sponsored operation, evidencing a high degree of technical capability. Dragonfly used a remote access tool (RAT) type malware to gain access and control of compromised computers. Among the methods used for infection were: spear-phishing (targeting selected executives and senior employees); watering hole attacks; and Trojanized software (malware inserted into the legitimate software bundles made available for download by ICS equipment providers) (Symantec 2014). Dragonfly ultimately compromised more than 1000 energy companies.

NightDragon stole confidential data from global oil, energy, and petro chemical companies including proprietary information about oil and gas field operations, financial transactions, and bidding data using RAT malware (McAfee et al. 2011). The malware was deployed using: SQL injection attacks on extranet web servers; spear-phishing attacks on mobile worker laptops; and though compromised corporate VPN accounts.

In addition to the headline attracting cyber attacks, are the "ordinary" attacks that ICS operators guard against on a daily basis.

A cyber-attack on the control system of an Illinois water utility system burned out a water pump. The hacker may also have stolen passwords and other information needed to gain access to many more water utility systems across the United States. The attack suggested an interest in controlling and sabotaging the ICS. The attack came from the internet address of a computer in Russia (Clayton 2011).

- Cyber-attacks on energy companies and the ICS used to heat and light homes and businesses focused on their IT suppliers, inserting malware into the software sold by third parties to hundreds of energy providers, which was designed to control levels of energy supply. Each time an engineer downloaded an update the infection was interjected as well (Rockall 2014).

- A "brute force" attack, believed to be launched via an internet portal, compromised an ICS network without affecting operations (Peter 2014). By leaving operations unaffected, there can be a delay in awareness that an attack has occurred.
- Technical breaches of both General Electric Co. (GE) and Siemens software systems that provide the user interfaces and controls for the ICS in manufacturing and power plants (Yadron and Mann 2014).

The increase in cyber-attacks on control systems means that emerging efforts in taxonomy development for these systems are oriented towards this new threat vector. The remainder of this section, discusses emerging taxonomy developments utilizing three different approaches. The Attack-Vulnerability-Damage (AVD) Model is presented as a method to facilitate understanding of cyber-attacks. The next taxonomy looks at attacks directed towards ICS in general, while the third taxonomy is focused specifically on SCADA systems

7.2.3.1   Attack-Vulnerability-Damage Model (Fleury et al. 2008)

Fleury et al. (2008) advocated for the development of an attack taxonomy that would provide a comprehensive understanding of cyber-attacks against ICS in the energy critical infrastructure sector. They identified four questions that a taxonomy should address. These questions include analysis of the: different manner in which attacks against control systems can be perpetuated; type of damage that can be caused; challenges involved in defeating the attacks; and finally, requirements for development of adequate defense mechanisms. As the first step towards the development of an attack taxonomy an AVD Model was created. The AVD Model consists of three components:

- Attack,
- Vulnerability, and
- Damage.

An attack is an action originating either within or outside the target. The attack is directed against an exploitable weakness (vulnerability). Finally, the attack causes damage represented by descriptions of both state change and performance degradation, and quantified by the level of impact on the target. An illustration of the model is provided in Table 7.4.

Vulnerability and attacks are typically the subject of separate taxonomies. A taxonomy developed from the AVD Model would not only provide equal footing to both, but would also include consideration of the significance of any potential or actual damage. As indicated in Table 7.4, the second component of the AVD model incorporates the Vulnerability as Exploitable Weakness approach described in Table 7.1. This represents a more expansive approach than is typically utilized. An attack taxonomy based on the AVD Model would view an attack as more than the action precipitating the attack. The components

Table 7.4 Attack vulnerability-damage model (Fleury et al. 2008, p. 78)

Attack		
Origin	*Action*	*Target*
Local	Probe	Network
Remote	Scan	Process
	Flood	System
	Authenticate	Data
	Bypass	User
	Spoof	
	Eavesdrop	
	Misdirect	
	Read/Copy	
	Terminate	
	Execute	
	Modify	
	Delete	
Vulnerability		
Configuration		
Specification		
Implementation		
Damage		
State effect	*Performance effect*	*Severity*
None	None	None
Availability	Timeliness	Low
Integrity	Precision	Medium
Confidentiality	Accuracy	High

of this taxonomy would be conceptualized to cover the span of an ICS attack. It would incorporate into its analysis the vulnerability enabling the attacks as well as the damage resulting from the attack.

7.2.3.2 A Taxonomy of Targeted Attack (Line et al. 2014)

A more narrowly drawn taxonomy developed by Line et al. (2014) looked at the characteristics of the attack itself. The Taxonomy for Targeted Attacks was developed after identifying common characteristics from several well-known attacks on ICS. This taxonomy incorporates four attack elements:

- purpose of the attack;
- initial attack vector;
- lateral movement; and
- location of the command and control server.

Table 7.5 Taxonomy of targeted attacks

Elements	Method	Examples
Purpose of the attack	Exfiltration of sensitive information from target	Industrial espionage
		Intellectual property theft
		Identify theft
	Sabotage	Inference with proper operation of system
Initial attack vector	Automatic	Attacker can compromise a machine without internal assistance (e.g., *drive-by-download* attack)
	Manual	Interaction required from individual within target company (e.g., spearphising)
Lateral movement	Automatic	Attacker establishes presence in victim's network then attempts to compromise additional computers
	Manual	
Location of the command and control (C&C) server	Inside the victim's network	Compromised computer used as C&C to give orders to infected machines
	Outside the victim's network	Connected computers connect to remote servers to receive orders

These elements are described in Table 7.5.

The components of this taxonomy are conceptualized around characteristics of the nature of the attack on ICS. The four attack elements incorporate methodologies by which attacks on ICS are initiated and the desired end-product of the attack. This taxonomy is not limited to the examples provided in Table 7.5. It is expandable to incorporate other examples to the extent they fit within the identified attack elements and methods.

After developing their taxonomy, Line et al. (2014) applied it to four well-known attacks. Among their findings were that:

- The purpose in three of the four attacks was exfiltration and one was sabotage;
- The initial attack was automatic in one case, manual in two cases, with the fourth case using both automatic and manual strategies;
- For the three attacks where lateral movement information was available, two attacks utilized an automatic lateral movement, and one attack used both automatic and manual lateral movements; and
- The C&C location was external in three attacks, and internal in one attack.

Utilization of this taxonomy adds to our understanding of characteristics associated with attack methodologies.

Table 7.6 Taxonomy of cyber attacks on SCADA systems

Hardware	Software	Communications stack
Ex: "doorknob-rattling" attack	• Absence of privilege separation in embedded operating systems	*Network layer*
	• Buffer overflow (most common)	• Diagnostic server attacks through UDP ports
	• SQL injection	• Idle scans
		• Smurf
		• Address resolution protocol (ARP) spoofing/poisoning
		• Chain/loop attack
		Transport layer
		• SYN flood
		Application layer
		• MODBUS
		• DNP3
		Attacks on implementation of protocols
		• TCP/IP
		• OPC

7.2.3.3   Taxonomy of Cyber Attacks on SCADA Systems (Zhu et al 2011)

A broadly inclusive taxonomy of cyber-attacks on SCADA systems was developed by Zhu et al. (2011). In addition to limiting its application to SCADA systems, this taxonomy also differs from the previous taxonomy in the nature of its focus. The Taxonomy of Cyber Attacks on SCADA Systems focuses on the target of the attack, as distinct from the attack itself. The attacks are classified based on whether the target is: hardware, software, or the communications stack. As illustrated in Table 7.6, this taxonomy is a mixture of methods of attack and vulnerabilities.

The methods and vulnerabilities identified in Table 7.6 are only examples rather than an exhaustive listing. Zhu et al. (2011) advocated for a taxonomy connecting computer security, communication network and control engineering. This taxonomy facilitates identification and classification of potential cyber-attacks on SCADA systems.

Table 7.7 Taxonomy foci comparison

Approach	Vulnerability as exploitable weakness	Attack-vulnerability-damage (AVD) model	Taxonomy of targeted attacks	Taxonomy of attacks on SCADA systems
Central focus	Weaknesses which can be exploited for an attack	Characteristics and consequences/damage of an attack	Methodology for, and desired end-product of, an attack	Target of the attack

7.2.4 Comparison of Taxonomy Area of Interest

Taxonomies vary based on their purpose. The taxonomies and taxonomy-like structures presented in this section are consistent with the definition of taxonomy presented in Sect. 7.2.1. For each: their components are grouped into ordered conceptual definitions; there is a rationale to the organization; and there is a purpose for the particular taxonomy. One basis for difference in taxonomies is the area of interest addressed by their development. Those variations have been discussed above. As is illustrated in Table 7.7, the taxonomies and taxonomy-like structures in this section while all addressing ICS attacks, each had a different organizing rationale reflected in the different attack aspects which they addressed.

7.3 Emerging Developments and Research

Examples of ongoing research are described in this section. These examples were selected because they reflect different threads in the continuing diversity of ICS security taxonomy developments. The first example is a proposed taxonomy for system vulnerabilities, followed by a discussion of ontological approaches to SCADA attacks and vulnerabilities. The section concludes with taxonomic development from the ever growing ICS cyber threat sector.

7.3.1 A Proposed Taxonomy for Vulnerabilities

One challenge confronted in the area of ICS security has been increased difficulty in the ability to draw a bright line separating hardware and software when it comes to the operation and hence the vulnerability of these systems to attack (*See generally*, Yadron and Mann 2014). The Proposed Taxonomy for Vulnerabilities recognizes that difficulty and seeks to fill the void by combining a vulnerability taxonomy with a control taxonomy. This is the approach taken by Smith (2014) who combined the NIST 800-53, control taxonomy with Tsipenyuk et al. (2005) "Seven Pernicious Kingdoms"

Table 7.8 Seven pernicious kingdoms

Number	Kingdom	Phyla
1	Input validation and representation	26
2	API abuse	11
3	Security features	9
4	Time and state	7
5	Errors	4
6	Code quality	9
7	Encapsulation	10
*	Environment	9

vulnerability taxonomy. While neither of these taxonomies are specific to ICSs, they are presented to illustrate the effects of merging two taxonomies of different types.

The NIST 800-53 taxonomy (previously discussed in Sect. 7.2.2) was selected because it was considered to be the most focused and relevant of the control taxonomies, while Tsipenyuk et al. (2005) was regarded as the richest and most detailed vulnerability taxonomy. As shown in Table 7.8, the Seven Pernicious Kingdoms taxonomy included 85 phyla which were organized into seven kingdoms, and a bin repository. The phyla represent individual vulnerabilities.

As noted earlier in this chapter, software development was identified as an area of ICS vulnerability by NIST 800-82. However, where previous efforts focused on vulnerabilities in operating systems; Tsipenyuk et al. (2005) expanded to cover application coding errors including web application coding errors. Their taxonomy was designed to be incorporated into a static code analysis tool.

In the proposed new taxonomy the three classes from NIST 800-53—management, technical, and operational[4]—are joined by a fourth class, development, to become four kingdoms. The families from NIST 800-53 (See, Table 3.2, *supra*) and the phyla from the seven kingdoms will become classes. The subject areas from the NIST 800-53 plus the kingdoms from the seven kingdoms become phyla (Smith 2014). Tsipenyuk et al. contains an eighth kingdom called environment, which is a bin for those vulnerabilities that are in the configuration of the system and not in the software development. The proposed taxonomy incorporates elements from the eighth kingdom into one of the other kingdoms where they are already addressed. Table 7.9 describes the organization of the first two levels for the proposed taxonomy for vulnerabilities. It does not include the third level which would consist of the phyla.

This is a vulnerability taxonomy, but reflecting an organizing rationale of broad inclusion, its components are conceptualized to include: management, operational, technical, and development vulnerabilities. The taxonomy's purpose is to provide a framework for accessing current countermeasures, as well as a framework for security assessments and risk scoring.

---

[4] Revision 4 of NIST SP 800-53 has removed the class designations from the security control families. This was because many of the security controls within a family may be linked to various classes. However, this is not meant to preclude the use of the classes where they would be helpful (Joint Task Force Transformation Initiative 2013, p. F-3).

Table 7.9 Kingdoms and classes in a proposed taxonomy for SCADA vulnerabilities

Kingdom	Management	Operational	Technical	Development
Classes	Security assessment & authorization	Awareness & training	Access control	Input validation & representation
	Planning	Configuration management	Audit & accountability	API abuse
	Personnel security	Contingency planning	Identification & authorization	Security features
	Risk assessment	Incident response	System & communication protection	Time & state
	Systems & services acquisition	Maintenance		Errors
	Program management	Media protection		Code quality
		Physical environment protection		Encapsulation
		System & information integrity		

7.3.2 Ontological Approaches to SCADA Vulnerabilities or Attacks

SCADA taxonomies offer important support to monitor and control critical infrastructures and industrial environments. Ontological approaches proceed from the premise that while a hierarchical organization of SCADA attacks and vulnerabilities can improve the situational awareness of ICS operators, it cannot by itself capture the structural dependencies between system components, assets, countermeasures and vulnerabilities/attacks. Capture of these structural dependencies would be greatly facilitated by an expanded SCADA model where vulnerability monitoring, attack mitigation and system recovery can jointly become effective. To accomplish this, an ontological approach would enrich SCADA taxonomies with semantic relationships,[5] thus evolving into ontologies.

Ontologies can be considered as effective knowledge management tools in support of analysis. Just as "data" is the essential bedrock of human decision making, situational awareness can only emerge from "knowledge", namely from a comprehension of the underlying data model. When the semantics of a data model are described using just natural language, an ontology yields a *dictionary* of relevant

---

[5] General ones, like "part-of" and "associated with", or domain-specific, like "exploited-by", "connected-to", "runs-on", "installed-on" (see Choraś 2009 for a list of relevant semantic relationships).

terms or data labels. It is only when semantic primitives are represented using a logical framework (e.g., predicate logics), that *formal ontologies* properly emerge. More importantly, when logical structures are encoded into a machine-readable language,[6] formal ontologies turn into computational artifacts.

In addition to being conceptually richer and formally more expressive, computational ontologies have a major advantage over dictionaries and taxonomies in that they can be used as *software components* in combination with automatic inference engines (Allemang 2011). As a result, computational ontologies are now seen as a fundamental apparatus of knowledge representation and reasoning for information systems.[7] A full-fledged computational ontology of SCADA systems and vulnerabilities could also serve both at runtime as an analysis tool to gain insight during an ICS-related incident, and also postmortem as an instrument for improving forensics and possibly contingency planning. For these reasons, building ontologies of SCADA systems and related data is becoming more and more crucial. These ontologies would provide information about SCADA vulnerabilities; specifically, which architectural components and assets are affected, and how they are affected.

The underpinnings of an example of this type of ontology is illustrated by the European project INSPIRE[8] (Choraś 2009). The overall goal of the project is to use a comprehensive ontology of SCADA as part of a decision aid tool for critical infrastructure protection. The resulting framework is a hybrid architecture merging ontology-based reasoning with Bayesian networks for assessing threat severity (Kozik 2010).[9] It is not possible at present to gauge the level of maturity of the INSPIRE project since the link to the official website is broken. In addition, the two papers mentioned above only sketch the backbone structure of the ontology, skipping any analysis of property constraints and discussion on reasoning algorithms.

An adequate level of detail is achieved in "ScadaOnWeb" (Dreyer 2003), a semantic technology developed in the context of the homonymous European project (see Fig. 7.3). Unfortunately, ScadaOnWeb does not explicitly deal with security aspects. Its descriptive ontology is designed to only capture a general model of representation of SCADA data types, focusing on standard engineering requirements for quantity-measurements (e.g. mass, temperature, etc.). Despite this lack of focus on vulnerabilities and attacks, ScadaOnWeb represents an important framework of reference. The integration between RDF/OWL and MathML markup language[10] can be used as the bedrock for developing an ontology module for ScadaOnWeb centered on vulnerabilities and attacks.[11]

---

[6] Such as RDF and OWL: see http://www.w3.org/standards/techs/owl#w3c_all.

[7] As attested by the FOIS conference series (Formal Ontology in Information Systems): http://www.iaoa.org/fois/.

[8] ftp://ftp.cordis.europa.eu/pub/fp7/ict/docs/security/project-summary-inspire_en.pdf.

[9] Interestingly enough, one of the contributors to this book chapter has recently presented a similar hybrid approach, where the Bayesian statistical computation was performed by ACT-R cognitive architecture (Oltramari 2014).

[10] http://www.w3.org/Math/.

[11] Regarding ontology modularity and implications at the level of semantic interoperability (see Parent 2009).

```
<rdf:RDF
... (Definition of namespaces)>
 <ppqs:PhysicalQuantitySpace rdf:ID="Force">
  <rdf:type rdf:resource="#DerivedPhysicalQuantitySpace"/>
  <rdfs:label xml:lang="en">force</rdfs:label>
  <pqs:hasPhysicalDimension rdf:parseType="Literal">
   <mathml:apply>
    <mathml:times/>
    <ppqs:PhysicalQuantitySpace rdf:about="#Mass"/>>
    <ppqs:PhysicalQuantitySpace rdf:about="#Acceleration"/>
   </mathml:apply>
  </pqs:hasPhysicalDimension>
 </rdfs:Class>
</rdf:RDF>
```

Fig. 7.3 Definition of derived physical property in the ScadaOnWeb ontology (Dreyer 2003)

The work by Sahil Nabil and colleagues: an original—yet very exploratory—methodology to block semantic attacks on SCADA systems, should also be mentioned (Nabil 2012). The main objective of the proposed methodology is the prevention of XML injection attacks by using the information represented in the UDDI registry and an analysis of SOAP messages. However, the paper describing this research includes only a couple of screenshots depicting stages of a Mitnick attack said to be detected through an enhanced semantic-based SCADA architecture. No evaluation was provided and no mention of full-scale experimentation was made in the concluding section of the paper.

7.3.3 Cyber Attacker Taxonomy

Threats to ICS systems have been identified as being among the top ten cyber security threats for the near future (Lyne 2014). Since these attacks typically target operational capabilities within power plants, factories, and refineries, as opposed to credit card information; they are believed to be political rather than financial in motivation (Dell 2015). ICS cyber-attack taxonomies were described in Sect. 7.2.3. This taxonomy adds to those, by the introduction of a taxonomy focused on the attacker. Understanding the characteristics associated with ICS cyber incidents aids risk assessment and subsequent mitigation and response efforts. Attackers are generally grouped into the following categories, which can be considered domains (see Fig. 7.4):

- State-Sponsored;
- Hacker;
- Criminal; and
- Insider.

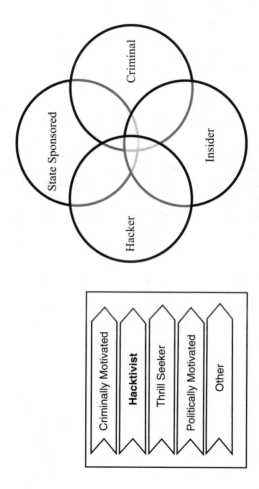

Fig. 7.4 Cyber-attacker taxonomy

A study of a sample of attacks on the energy and utility critical infrastructure sector revealed that the greatest number of cyber-attacks came from hackers at 50 % of the total (Flowers 2015). Another 40 % were state-sponsored with approximately 5 % each attributed to criminals and insiders (id.). Due to the overlap among the categories however, this breakdown is somewhat imprecise.

State-sponsored in this context refers to nation-states. These attacks can be the product of government employees. In May 2014, the United States government charged five Chinese military hackers with cyber espionage against U.S. corporations as well as a labor organization (U.S. v. Wang Dong, Sun Kaillian, Wen Xinyu, Huang Zhenyu, and Gu Chunhui 2014). They are believed to be part of Unit 61398 a division of the Chinese army thought to be responsible for extensive cyber-attacks against western interests. State-sponsored activity can also be the work of "hired-guns" overlapping into the criminal or hacker category. The target is typically the critical infrastructure of another nation-state, including both government and private-sector operations. In the United States, approximately 85 % of the nation's critical infrastructure is owned by the private sector.

The term Hacker broadly encompasses everyone from: the criminally motivated individual; the "hacktivist" with a political agenda such as the group "Anonymous"; thrill seekers and others. The criminally motivated hacker can also be in the employ of a nation-state for a particular attack. For instance, in 2007 during the brief war between the Russian Federation and Estonia, the Russian government is believed to have employed virtually every criminal hacker in Europe. This was done both to conduct their massive distributed denial of service (DDoS) attacks against Estonian government, business, and private websites; but also to prevent those individuals from being available for hire by the Estonian government. It should be noted that a characteristic shared by many taxonomies that focus on the cyber attacker is that at first glance they do not always conform to the taxonomic standard that an item only belongs in one category. The Estonian cyber-attack is a good illustration of that phenomenon. It originated in the state-sponsored domain, but utilized the hacker domain (sub-category criminally motivated) for implementation. This would still be considered as state-sponsored, however, because that domain was the primary instigator.

The goal of criminally inspired cyber-attacks is financial. It can range from the massive theft of identities or credit card information, such as the Target Store credit card breach in December 2013 or the theft of corporate information for profit. Insider attacks generally fall into one of two categories. The first involves a disgruntled current or former employee or contractor who deliberately initiates the attack. The most common type of insider attack however is inadvertent. It involves an attack initiated by an unknowing employee who was the victim of social engineering or spear-phishing. In the instance of an insider attack involving an unknowing employee, the attack could more properly be placed in the category of its originator, either state-sponsored or criminal.

For ICS, the relevant actor in the Cyber Attacker taxonomy is typically state-sponsored.

The purpose of the Cyber Attacker Taxonomy is to provide increased awareness of the categories of attackers in ICS cyber incidents. Unlike other taxonomies which focus on inanimate entities such as hardware or software, or attack vectors or targets; the organizing rationale underlying the Cyber Attacker Taxonomy is how to label and group the behavior and motivations of human actors.

7.3.3.1   Incident-Based Matrix

The Cyber Attacker Taxonomy can stand alone, or be integrated into a larger framework. The Incident-Based Matrix (Flowers 2015) focuses on the incident itself to glean additional information to use in the development of countermeasures. The domains for an Incident-Based Matrix would be:

- Target industry;
- Location;
- Type of Malware;
- Attacker Type (as described above, most ICS cyber attackers will be state-sponsored).

The Incident-Based Matrix would overlap with the Cyber Attacker Taxonomy in the attacker type category. It could also incorporate taxonomies associated with its other domains to produce a four-dimensional analytic matrix. This offers an approach which integrates individual taxonomies into a larger shared framework. The purpose for developing this type of robust incident-based matrix would be to assist in the understanding of characteristics of ICS cyber-attack incidents. This in turn could lead to the development of new risk mitigation and response strategies.

The Cyber Attacker Taxonomy and the Incident-Based Matrix present a new analytic framework for ICS security taxonomies responding to the expanded nature of cyber risks that require new approaches to ICS risk assessment. As distinct from other ICS security taxonomies vulnerability is not the central focus. In the Cyber Attacker Taxonomy, characteristics of the attacker are the central focus. In the Incident-Based Matrix, the central foci are characteristics of the incident.

7.4   Future Developments and Directions

While ICS security taxonomies may share overall goals, such as enhancing risk mitigation, prevention, or response, the structures presented approach ICS security from different vantage points. This is illustrated by Table 7.10 which presents a comparison of the purposes of the ICS security taxonomies and taxonomy-like structures reviewed in this chapter.

Table 7.10 Comparison of ICS security taxonomies and related measures

Name of approach	See section	Author/reference	Purpose
Vulnerability as exploitable weakness	7.2.2	Fleury et al. (2008)	Identify areas of weakness to facilitate mitigation planning
Attack-vulnerability-damage model	7.2.3.1	Fleury et al. (2008)	Serve as a precursor to a full developed taxonomy to provide a comprehensive understanding of cyber-attacks against ICS in the energy critical infrastructure sector
A taxonomy of targeted attacks	7.2.3.2	Line et al. (2014)	Education and for prioritizing preventive measures
Taxonomy of cyber attacks on SCADA systems	7.2.3.3	Zhu et al. (2011)	Identification and classification of potential cyber-attacks on SCADA systems, including cyber physical attacks
A proposed taxonomy for vulnerabilities	7.3.1	Smith (2014)	Provide a framework to assess countermeasures currently available to protect ICS systems
Ontological approaches to SCADA vulnerabilities or attacks	7.3.2	Oltramari (2014)	Use semantic language to capture structural relationships among systems and vulnerabilities for use as an incident analytic tool, forensic analysis, and mitigation planning
Cyber attacker taxonomy	7.3.3	Flowers (2015)	Increase awareness of categories of attackers in ICS cyber incidents, can be used to complement other taxonomies
Incident-based matrix	7.3.3	Flowers (2015)	Provide an integrated approach to viewing cyber incidents

7.5 Summary and Conclusions

In the biological sciences, physical characteristics of the organism are used to determine its placement in the taxonomy. In security, the defining characteristics are not as well defined. Security taxonomies are developed with a specific purpose in mind and characteristics are selected to fit that purpose. As a result, there are many types of ICS security taxonomies, each of which was developed using a different rationale. Vulnerability taxonomies are used to aid in the development of automated tools for producing security assessments, or for aiding in the execution of the security assessment itself. Since the incidence of attacks on ICS systems has recently risen significantly, taxonomies focused on cyber-attacks have flourished. Fleury et al. (2008) combine vulnerability, attack, and damage characteristics to provide a taxonomy that focuses on the severity of the security incident. A more narrowly drawn attack taxonomy developed by Line et al. (2014) focuses on specific attack aspects: purpose, initial attack vector, lateral movement, and location of command and control server for the attack. Broad taxonomies such as that developed by Zhu et al. (2011) center on whether attacks target hardware, software, or the communications stack. A cyber attack taxonomy can also be developed by grouping by the origin of the threat (state-sponsored, hacker, criminal, insider; Flowers 2015). If ICS taxonomies are enriched with semantic relationships, ontologies can be developed to enhance their use for runtime analysis tools to gain insight during incidents, for postmortem forensics, and for contingency planning. All of the cyber security taxonomies discussed in this chapter address cyber threats in ICSs in one way or another—the value of the taxonomy depends entirely on whether the intended rationale and purpose of the taxonomy match those of the user.

References

Allemang, D. H. (2011). *Semantic web for the working ontologist: Effective modeling in RDFS and OWL*. Amsterdam: Elsevier.

Bishop, M. (1995). *CSE-95-10 A taxonomy of unix system and network vulnerabilities*. Davis: Department of Computer Science, University of California at Davis.

Brewster, T. (2014, July 13). *US energy firms report cyber attacks*. Retrieved from Tech Week Europe: http://www.techweekeurope.co.uk/workspace/energy-firms-cyber-incidents-dragonfly-energetic-bear-148457.

Choraś, M.F. (2009). Decision aid tool and ontology-based reasoning for critical infrastructure vulnerabilities and threat analysis. In E.R. Bloomfield (Ed.), CRITIS (Vol. 6027, pp. 98–110). Berlin: Springer-Verlag.

Clayton, M. (2011, November 18). *Cyberattack on Illinois water utility may confirm Stuxnet warnings*. Christian Monitor. http://www.csmonitor.com/USA/2011/1118/Cyberattack-on-Illinois-water-utility-may-confirm-Stuxnet-warnings.

Dell. (2015). *Dell security annual threat report*. Round Rock, TX: Dell Inc.

Department of Homeland Security, Office of Cybersecurity and Communications. (2014). *Industrial control systems assessment FY 2014 overview and analysis*. Washington, DC: Department of Homeland Security.

Dreyer, T. L. (2003). ScadaOnWeb—Web based supervisory control and data acquisition. *The Semantic Web—ISWC 2003* (pp. 788–801). Berlin: Springer.

Fleury, T., Khurana, H., & Welch, V. (2008). Towards a taxonomy of attacks against energy control systems. In M. Pappa, S. Shenoi, & IFIP International Federation for Information Processing (Eds.), *Critical infrastructure protection II* (Vol. 290, pp. 71–85). Boston: Springer.

Flowers, A. (2015, March 31). An organizational typology of cyberattacks: Implications for the energy and utility critical infrastructure sector. In *4th Annual Cyber Security for Energy & Utilities Conference, Abu Dhabi, United Arab Emirates*.

Igure, V., & Williams, R. (2008). Taxonomies of attacks and vulnerabilities in computer systems. *IEEE Communications Surveys & Tutorials, 10*, 6–19.

Joint Task Force Transformation Initiative. (2013). *NIST Special Publication 800-53r4: Security and privacy controls for federal information systems and organizations*. Gaithersburg: U.S. Department of Commerce, National Institute of Standards and Technology.

Kozik, R.C. (2010). Fusion of Bayesian and ontology approach applied to decision support system for critical infrastructures protection. In P. Chatzimisios (Ed.), *MobiLight* (Vol. 45, pp. 451–463). Institute for Computer Sciences, Social Informatics and Telecommunications Engineering.

Kusher, D. (2013, February 26). *The real story of Stuxnet*. IEEE Spectrum. Retrieved from http://spectrum.ieee.org/telecom/security/the-real-story-of-stuxnet/.

Line, M., Zand, A., Stringhini, G., & Kemmerer, R. (2014). Targeted attacks against industrial control systems: Is the power industry prepared? *CCS'14 2014 ACM SIGSAC conference on computer & communications security SEGS, Proceedings of the 2nd workshop on smart energy grid security*. Scottsdale, AZ: Association of Computing Machinery (ACM).

Lyne, J. (2014). *Security threat trends in 2015: Predicting what cybersecurity will look like in 2015 and beyond*. Chicago: Sophos.

McAfee Foundstone Professional Services and McAfee Labs (2011, February 10). *White paper: Global energy cyberattacks: "Night Dragon"*. McAfee. Retrieved from http://www.mcafee.com/us/resources/white-papers/wp-global-energy-cyberattacks-night-dragon.pdf.

Nabil, S.B. (2012). *Security ontology for semantic SCADA* (pp. 179–192). ICWIT.

Oltramari, A.B. (2014). General requirements of a hybrid-modeling framework for cyber security. *Proceedings of the military communications conference (MILCOM), Baltimore*.

Parent, C. (2009). *Modular ontologies: Concepts, theories and techniques for knowledge modularization*. Berlin: Springer.

Peter, T. (2014, May 21). *US utility's control systems hit by advanced cyber attack—DHS*. Reuters. Retrieved from http://rt.com/usa/160328-utility-cyber-attack-hack/.

Rockall, W. (2014, July 24). *Cyber attacks on energy companies: Do we need specific laws to protect us?* Media Network Blog. Retrieved from http://www.theguardian.com/media-network/media-network-blog/2014/jul/24/cyber-attacks-energy-energetic-bear.

Smith, S. (2014). *A proposal for a taxonomy for vulnerabilities in supervisory control and data acquisition (SCADA) systems*. Aberdeen, MD: Army Research Lab Aberdeen Proving Ground.

Stouffer, K., Pillitteri, V., Lightman, S., Abrams, M., & Hahn, A. (2015). *NIST Special Publication 800-82: Guide to industrial control systems (ICS) security, R2*. Gaithersburg: National Institute of Standards and Technology.

Symantec (2014, July 7). Dragonfly: Cyberespionage attacks against energy supplies: Symantec security response. Retrieved from http://www.symantec.com/content/en/us/enterprise/media/security_response/whitepapers/Dragonfly_Threat_Against_Western_Energy_Suppliers.pdf.

Tsipenyuk, K., Chess, B., & McGraw, G. (December, 2005). Seven pernicious kingdoms: A taxonomy of software security errors. *IEEE Security & Privacy*, 81–84.

U.S. District Court Western District of Pennsylvania (2014, May 12). *U.S. v. Wang Dong, Sun Kaillian, Wen Xinyu, Huang Zhenyu, and Gu Chunhui*. Criminal No. 14-118.

Yadron, D., & Mann, T. (2014, October 29). *Computer spies target control systems made by GE, Siemens*. The Wall Street Journal. Retrieved from http://www.wsj.com/articles/computer-spies-target-control-systems-made-by-ge-siemens-1414630558.

Zhu, B., Joseph, A., & Sastry, S. (2011). A taxonomy of cyber attacks on SCADA systems. *Proceedings of the 2011 international conference on internet of things and 4th international conference on cyber, physical, and social computing* (pp. 380–388). Washington, DC: IEEE Computer Society.

Chapter 8
Cyber Risk in Industrial Control Systems

Matthew H. Henry, David R. Zaret, J. Ryan Carr, J. Daniel Gordon, and Ryan M. Layer

8.1 Introduction

To enhance the security of any system, and to defend it effectively, one must under-stand the risk due to the potential for security failures in its computing and communications infrastructure. Practitioners in the cyber security field often identify three modes of failure: (1) breach of confidentiality, which is a failure to protect sensitive system information from unauthorized disclosure, (2) loss of availability, which is a failure to provide reliable access to system data for those users or machines that legitimately require it, and (3) violation of integrity, which is a failure to protect system data from unauthorized manipulation. A useful definition of cyber risk, then, is the potential for any of these failure modes and their corresponding consequences. In the case of industrial control systems (ICS), these consequences can extend into the physical domain.

This chapter focuses on the problems of cyber risk assessment and management, with emphasis on application to ICS analysis. The *cyber risk assessment problem* is to determine the degree to which a specified network-dependent system is at risk due to the potential for computer network attack, where risk is due to the potential for detrimental outcomes and their associated consequences. The *cyber risk management problem* is to determine the relative costs and benefits of implementing candidate risk mitigation policies in terms of resources expended and operational consequences avoided, respectively.

M.H. Henry • D.R. Zaret • J.R. Carr • J.D. Gordon
Johns Hopkins Applied Physics Laboratory, Laurel, MD, USA
e-mail: david.zaret@jhuapl.edu

R.M. Layer
Department of Human Genetics, University of Utah, Salt Lake City, UT, USA

© Springer International Publishing Switzerland 2016
E.J.M. Colbert, A. Kott (eds.), *Cyber-security of SCADA and Other Industrial Control Systems*, Advances in Information Security 66,
DOI 10.1007/978-3-319-32125-7_8

There are important benefits in such quantifications of risks and risk mitigations. They open doors to comprehensive risk management decision-making, potentially highly rigorous and insightful. Employees at multiple levels—from senior leaders to system administrators—will be aware of continually updated risk distribution over the network components, and will use this awareness to prioritize application of resources to most effective remedial actions. Quantification of risks can also contribute to rapid, automated or semi-automated implementation of remediation plans.

This chapter begins with an overview of several common approaches to risk analysis, such as expert elicitation, attack graphs, games and Petri nets. Then, the chapter focuses on one of these approaches in detail, and presents a comprehensive method for applying Petri net risk models to ICS. It includes a detailed example Petri net analysis of a hazardous liquid loading system process, its failure modes and costs associated with the failure modes.

8.2 Approaches to Risk Modeling and Analysis

Multiple schools of thought on how to construct and use models to support risk analysis have emerged over the last several decades. We describe at a high level the usage of several classes of cyber risk analysis methods, and we briefly consider their relative merits and shortcomings. Specifically, we discuss modeling and model-based analysis methodologies intended to better enable an analyst to evaluate measures of cyber-physical risk, where a common application of these measures is informing risk management strategy development.

8.2.1 Expert Elicited Models

Practitioners of this school of thought construct computational models to assess risk based on expert elicited identification and characterization of cyber system attributes such as network data flows amongst users and network resources, the relative importance of network resources and data flows to mission sustainment, and the estimation of the susceptibility of those resources and data flows to different types of compromise. Exemplars of this class of methods include those presented by Kertzner et al. (2006) and Llanso and Klatt (2014). In each of these cases, the computational models in question are used to prioritize investments in security as a means to better assure mission success in the event of cyber attack.

This general approach proceeds as follows. First, the system under review is decomposed into sets of resources (computers, databases, applications, etc.), data flows amongst resources, vulnerabilities of resources and data flows, and consequences of resource or data flow compromise. Second, for each element in each of these sets, the model builder interviews experts and reviews available system documentation to estimate measures of importance for resources and data flows, measures of likelihood of vulnerability exploitation, and measures of consequence due to malicious exploitation of vulnerabilities and subsequently accessible resources and data flows. Finally, these measures are combined in an arithmetic framework, often using spreadsheets and similarly accessible tools, to estimate overall measures of risk.

This general approach possesses tremendous appeal for many applications, including cases involving complicated networks for which little design information is readily available, cases in which intrusive data collection methods are infeasible, and cases in which a relatively quick analysis is needed to inform high-level decisions on short time-lines. The value of the approach lies in its comprehensive, structured methodology for organizing and making good use of existing institutional knowledge, which for legacy operational networks is often feasibly accessible only through expert elicitation. That is, by collecting and organizing existing institutional knowledge of a network, this approach enables an analyst to readily achieve analytic results that will resonate with key decision-makers because the underlying models will have been derived from trusted experts. Moreover, the process of eliciting the information needed to construct the models forces system stakeholders to wrestle with subjective measures of probability, consequences, and vulnerability, and therefore often requires the realization of some degree of consensus amongst experts who may come to the problem from different points of view corresponding to their areas of expertise. As a result, the process of eliciting information from experts and constructing the models can be as valuable as the analysis itself.

One major drawback of this general approach is lack of completeness. In particular, there are two aspects of completeness that often suffer in the application of these approaches, and they are both related to operational use of the network in question. The first of these is due to bias in favor of *normal* operations. That is, resources and data flows and their respective measurements of importance, vulnerability, and consequence are identified and estimated from the perspective of how the system is normally used. More to the point, system elements that are less frequently used tend to be ignored or under-valued. This can happen when their value is dependent on mission conditions. It can also happen when their value to the legitimate system users may be viewed a relatively low, perhaps due to the mundane nature of the resource, but their value to a malicious actor as a means to an end is relatively high. As with any analysis, of course, this bias can be mitigated through meticulous investigation. However, because the expert elicitation and therefore model construction are inherently subjective, this bias cannot be completely overcome in general.

The second drawback is due to the tendency to describe the system in terms of how it *should* be used, with less attention often given to how it *could* be used (or abused) by a malicious actor. This bias is due, in large part, to the propensity for most system experts to be more familiar with how the system is used by legitimate operators than how it could be deliberately mis-used by an actor with malicious intent. As a result, risk can be underestimated. This bias, again, can be mitigated through meticulous system investigation. Cyber red teaming is one useful approach to exposing non-obvious ways in which a system in whole or in part can be abused by deliberate malicious actors.

8.2.2   Attack Graphs

A second school of thought advocates the construction of attack trees or graphs, either by hand or through automated interrogation of a system of interest, to enumerate potential attack sequences. Exemplars are discussed by Ingols et al. (2009) and Byres et al. (2004). In this class of models, cyber attacks are modeled as graphs (trees are a special case) in which nodes correspond to system resources, privileges on hosts or network domains, exploits that abuse network resources by way of vulnerable software or unwitting users, and, sometimes, ostensible attack objectives. In these graph representations of attacks, edges generally correspond to association properties such as local reachability, e.g., "this privilege is reachable by exploiting this other vulnerable application." In some cases, researchers augment attack graphs with edge costs to estimate "shortest path" attack sequences as a means to enumerate highly valuable, from an attack perspective, hosts on a network that could be used to gain an initial foothold, pivot to other targets, and so proceed toward a specified attack goal. Other graph-based models, including our own (Henry et al. 2009, 2010), deliberately choose not to account for attacker goals and instead focus on the degree of intrusion progression and associated consequences that can be achieved by an attacker, given a set of initial conditions. A recent survey (Khaitan and Raheja 2011) reviews recent work in this area. Solutions yield insight into system architectural features, including network partitions, access control policies, and access control enforcement mechanisms.

Deterministic graph-based models, including the attack graphs due to Ingols et al. (2009), avoid dependencies on explicit or surrogate measures of probability, which continue to be difficult to credibly evaluate in practical applications (Holm et al. 2012). Instead, these approaches focus on evaluating ordinal risk measures that account for reachable attack states, regardless of difficulty, given initial conditions on the attacker's access to network resources and host configuration on the network. By developing such measures, these approaches explicitly account for all reachable attack states and thereby permit a more flexible notion of risk that can be resolved as one of several computable measures on the discrete attack space.

This approach has many advantages. Principal among these is a very light data requirement. Specifically, there are no parameters corresponding to the difficulty or probability of attack step success. The estimation of parameters such as these presents a significant data collection and analytic problem in itself. Instead, attack graph model construction requires the ingestion of only easily collected system configuration data. As a result, models in this class do not suffer precision or fidelity shortcomings because they are constructed directly from system data without abstraction or aggregation, though these approximations can be used to improve scalability of computation, interpretability of results, and so forth, as needed. Another advantage of this approach is flexibility in terms of utility for direct risk management assessment and rapid adaptability to consider dramatic changes in network architecture or to account for patches and other security operations for quasi-real time analysis.

Our graph-based approach based on Petri nets (Henry et al. 2009, 2010) is also deterministic in the sense that state transitions, when actuated, occur with certainty and have non-probabilistic outcomes. The only source of randomness stems from the potential for multiple state transitions to be enabled at the same time. However, because outcomes in this model are non-probabilistic, it enjoys the same benefits of not having probabilistic parameters to estimate.

In spite of their advantages, attack graphs do have drawbacks. One of these is that they account only for static defenses. That is, the model is one in which the attack proceeds in the context of obstacles and opportunities that remain unchanged for the duration of the attack. This is a reasonable approach for analyzing many networks, where defenses are effectively passive barriers such as authentication and protocol constraints imposed by firewalls or gateway devices. However, in cases in which an analyst would like to include an assessment of active defenses such as intrusion prevention appliances or network watch floor operations, this approach provides only limited insight.

Another drawback for some models in this class is that vulnerabilities and exploits in the model are assumed to be known in advance of the attack, and there is typically no capacity to model the discovery of new (0-day) vulnerabilities or develop new exploits. As such, these models cannot account for an adaptive attacker or defender. One approach to overcoming this limitation is the estimation of a *time to compromise* measure, as presented by McQueen et al. (2005).

8.2.3   Games

A third school of thought advocates models that explicitly account for the interaction of attackers and defenders in a game theoretic framework. Pioneering work in this area includes the application of stochastic games to attack analysis by Lye and Wing (2002) and the application of differential games to security analysis by Alpcan and Basar (2003, 2004). Henry and Haimes (2009a) applied the principles of stochastic games to network risk analysis and incorporated structured methods for constructing the state space and estimating model parameters. Recent work by Zonouz et al. (2014) has also taken into account the partially observed nature of attacker-defender interactions in cyber space. In these approaches, system state evolves in a space defined by conditions of interest in the network, and state dynamics are driven by actions taken by an attacker and a defensive system. Solutions corresponding to Nash equilibria yield insight into design and operational objectives such as sensor placement, defensive tactics, and recovery procedures.

Models in this class are much more varied, and the approach is much less mature than the expert elicited and graph-based approaches described previously. However, the process for constructing the models shares some similar elements. In particular, the first step in constructing game-theoretic models, as with graph-based and expert elicited models, is to choose and apply a system decomposition strategy that will result in a model structure that is appropriate to shed light on analytic questions of interest. In the case of cyber risk analysis, system decomposition strategies tend to focus on computer resources, access control, and data flow. Game theoretic models then also include attacker and defender "action sets" that permit the acquisition (on the part of the attacker) and denial (on the part of the defender) of access to those resources. The game solution provides insight into how each actor can optimally "play" under different conditions. More importantly, games can inform how the playing field can be better tilted in favor of the defender by adopting architectural changes, new access control policies, and so forth. This is analogous to the so-called *mechanism design* problem in economics.

8.2.4   Petri Nets

In addressing the cyber risk assessment problem, we model the network-dependent system as a Petri net in which the attack state dynamics are coupled to failure modes and effects using an appropriately designed interface (Henry et al. 2009, 2010). Our coupling scheme represents the functionality of network hosts (over which an attacker can gain control via intrusion and privilege escalation) in terms of process interface and control applications. By adopting this scheme, we increase the dimensionality of the attack state space to include the process state space. The result is a compound state space over which coverability (an abstraction of state reachability) can be computed directly to assess risk, which is defined in this case to be the extent to which an attacker might intrude into a protected network, accumulate privileges and access to resources on that network, and then exploit those accesses and privileges to adversely affect an infrastructure system by manipulating its ICS. Each process state has a set of operational consequences associated with it expressed in terms that are meaningful for cost-benefit analysis of risk mitigation alternatives.

In addressing the cyber risk management problem, we conduct informed searches over the coverability set to identify network host vulnerabilities, access control policy failures, and architectural weaknesses that, if mitigated, yield high returns in terms of avoided operational consequences. These returns are compared against the cost of implementing the candidate corrections in the cost-benefit space to identify the efficient courses of action.

Our approach based on Petri nets is derived from the attack graph school of thought. However, due to the noted limitations of static graphs, we have extended this approach by formulating partially observed stochastic games in which actors in the game drive Petri net state changes through selection of offensive and defensive actions. By this extension, we are developing the means to account for active defender strategies, the development of new exploits, and model attacker and defender behaviors in the context of partial observability as a means to evaluate the value of different sources of information from both an attacker's and a defender's perspective. While we expect the approach to provide valuable insight into cyber defense analysis, there are significant research challenges ahead, which we will discuss in Sect. 8.2.5.

Petri nets have been discussed in the literature as a useful formalism for network security evaluation (Dahl 2005; Helmer et al. 2007; McDermott 2000; Zhou et al. 2003). In this section, we present a holistic methodology that constructs and computes properties of Petri net representations of cyber attacks for the assessment of risk due to vulnerability inherent in computer networks. We compute other properties to identify high-value opportunities for risk management.

A Petri net (Reisig 1985; Murata 1989) is a directed bipartite graph, in which the two types of nodes are *places* and *transitions*. Each place is depicted by a circle; each transition is depicted by a bar. A Petri net has *input* arcs that point from places to transitions; and *output* arcs that point from transitions to places. Dots within places denote *tokens*. A *marking* is a mapping $m : P \rightarrow \mathbb{N}$ that specifies the number of tokens assigned to each place, where $P = \{p_1,,,p_2,,,\ldots,,,p_n\}$ is the set of n places and $\mathbb{N}$ is the set of natural numbers. A marking can be viewed as a vector $m(p_1),m(p_2),\ldots,m(p_n)$, where $m(p_i)$ indicates the number of tokens in place p_i.

Formally, a Petri net is defined by a pair P,T, where P is a finite set of places and T is a finite set of transitions. For a place p and transition t, p is an *output place* of t if there is an edge pointing from t to p, and p is an *input place* of t if there is an edge pointing from p to t. We let t° denote the set of output places of t and $^\circ t$ the set of input places. For example, in Fig. 8.1a, $t_1^\circ = \{p_2\}$ and $^\circ t_1 = \{p_1\}$.

Let m be a marking and t a transition. Then t is *enabled* at m if *every input place of t* is marked in m ($m(p) > 0$ for every input place p). If t is enabled, it may *fire*. When t fires, it removes a token from every input place and adds a token to every output place, transforming m into a new marking m'.

We use $m \rightarrow m'$ to denote the fact that m' results from m by the firing of t, and $m \rightarrow m'$ to denote the fact that m' results from m by the firing of some finite sequence of transitions. As an example, Fig. 8.1a shows a Petri net in which the current marking is $m = 1,,1,,0$, and t_1 and t_2 are the enabled transitions. After t_2 fires, the net's marking is transformed from m to $m' = 1,,1,,1$, as shown in Fig. 8.1b. The double arrow between p_2 and t_2 indicates that p_2 is both an input and an output place for t_2. If there had been a single arrow pointing from p_2 to t_2, the marking after t_2 fired would have been $m' = 1,,0,,1$.

A cyber attack is modeled as the successive exploitation of vulnerabilities on hosts to escalate privileges in the network. New privileges are achieved when the attacker uses existing privileges and the accompanying access to hosted applications to exploit vulnerable applications hosted on the same or other networked computers.

Fig. 8.1 Petri net before (a) and after (b) t_2 fires

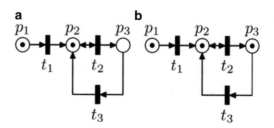

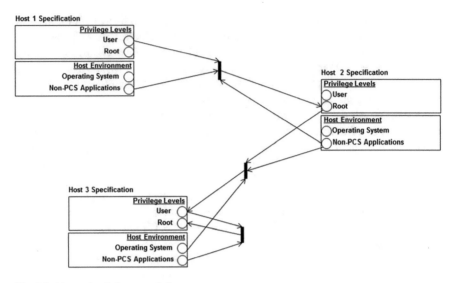

Fig. 8.2 Network privilege escalation

In Petri net terms, each escalation of privilege constitutes a state transition where the new state is indicated by a new marking m' and is reached from the previous state indicated by the marking m in which the pre-conditions of the transition corresponding to the executed exploit are met. This dynamic is illustrated in Fig. 8.2, which presents three exploits. The first escalation yields root access to Host 2, given user access on Host 1, the presence of a vulnerable non-PCS application on Host 2 and a corresponding application running on Host 1. The second escalation yields user access to Host 3. The third escalation yields root access to Host 3. Note that the applications and exploits are illustrated here in abstract terms for the purpose of exposition, whereas in a real attack model, the places would be replaced by specific application names, versions, and patch level; transitions would be replaced by exploits reported in the National Vulnerability Database (NVD) maintained by the U.S. National Institute of Standards and Technology (NIST).[1]

Cyber attacks generally follow a sequence of stages:

1. Improve knowledge of the target network through reconnaissance.
2. Achieve access to one or more hosts on the network through exploitation of a software vulnerability or the deception of a legitimate user.
3. Increase privilege on one or more hosts on the network through exploitation of a software vulnerability or the deception of a legitimate user.
4. Establish sustainable access to one or more hosts on the network by, for example, installing a back door.
5. View, steal, manipulate, or prevent legitimate access to protected information.

---

[1] NVD is a product of the NIST Computer Security Division and is sponsored by the Department of Homeland Security's National Cyber Security Division. NVD is accessible via the web interface at https://nvd.nist.gov/.

Fig. 8.3 Simple attack model

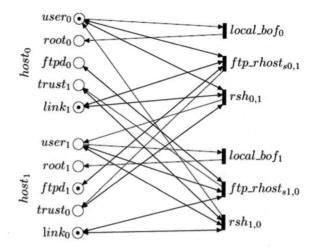

Each stage comprises multiple steps. In the Petri net model, each attack step is represented by a transition: arrows point in from places that represent preconditions, and point out to places that represent post-conditions. This scheme is similar in its basic features to the one proposed by McDermott (2000). A Petri net for a simple network attack scenario is displayed in Fig. 8.3. This example will be used as a reference for the remainder of this section.

The places in the Petri net of Fig. 8.3 represent host attributes in the network being modeled. The attributes and associated places include privilege levels (e.g., $user_0$, $root_0$), services (e.g., $ftpd_1$), trust relationships (e.g., $trust_0$), and connectivity (e.g., $link_0$).

Let P_h be the set of places corresponding to host h. In order to represent the fact that h is characterized by a particular attribute, the corresponding place must be marked by a token. Thus P_h represents the attributes that host h can have; the places in P_h that are marked represent the attributes that h actually does have. For example, the place $ftpd_1 \in P_{h_1}$ is marked by a token, indicating that $host\_1$ is running an ftp server, while the place $ftpd_0 \in P_{h_0}$ is not marked, indicating that $host_0$ is not running an ftp server.

For the purposes of attack analysis, transitions represent attack steps such as buffer overflow exploits for local privilege escalation (e.g., $local\_bof_0$) or remote privilege acquisition (e.g., $ftp\_rhost_{0,1}$). We consider an exploit to be any action an attacker takes, including abuse of legitimate resources such as rsh to achieve additional access. For every exploit e there is a set of preconditions and a set of post-conditions, as described above for transitions. In our example, a precondition for performing a local buffer overflow exploit is that the attacker has user privileges on the target host, and a post-condition is that the attacker has root access on the target host. The use of an exploit by the attacker to escalate privileges is represented by the firing of the corresponding transition.

As mentioned, it is possible for a place to be both an input place and an output place for a given transition. In this case, the place is connected to the transition by a double arrow. For example, the place $user_0$ is both an input and output place for $ftp\_rhost_{s0,1}$. Intuitively, this means that obtaining user privileges on $host_0$ is a precondition for exploiting an ftp vulnerability from $host_0$ to $host_1$, and that the attacker, upon exploiting the vulnerable ftp server, does not lose user privileges on $host_0$. This last point involves the issue of monotonicity, which is discussed shortly.

The initial marking m_0 of the net indicates the conditions that are met at the beginning of the attack. Formally, these are the conditions that have been met before any transitions in T have fired. Intuitively, m_0 corresponds to the initial state of the attack, which was the product of whatever initial exploit gave the attacker initial privileges on the network. In practice, this often corresponds to *user* privileges on a host gained through some phishing attack, web browser exploit, or similar exploitation of a user-induced vulnerability. In the illustrated example, the attacker initially has *user* privileges on $host_0$; $host_1$ is running an ftp server; and $host_0$ and $host_1$ are linked, meaning that they can communicate directly with each other without intermittent obstacles or checks. Accordingly, the places $user_0$, $ftpd_1$, $link_0$, and $link_1$ are marked.

Section 8.3 develops this technique further, including methods for developing coupled models of process control systems and the processes they control. Techniques for assessing and managing risk are also developed in more depth.

8.2.5   Stochastic Cyber Attack Models with Petri Nets

This section introduces at a high level a less mature but potentially much more powerful approach to modeling and analyzing cyber attacks on ICS and other networks. The work that we and other research groups are doing in this area is motivated by three salient properties of cyber attacks on ICS and other networks. The first of these is the recognition that not all aspects of network defense are passive. That is, whereas Petri net analysis examines the potential degree of intrusion based on the passive aspects of network defense technologies and security-minded architectures, today's comprehensive network defense strategies are increasingly taking on a more active posture. A corresponding problem, therefore, is to determine the value of investing in any one or collection of these strategy elements. To address this problem, an attack model must be equipped to represent attack dynamics on an equivalent basis, whether defenses are provided by network defense operators responding to alerts or responsive access controls.

The second salient property of cyber attacks is that attackers and defenders are learning and adaptive agents. A corresponding problem is related to the extent to which attacker and defender learning play a role in attack progression. Specifically, attackers have opportunities to discover new vulnerabilities and develop new exploits. Similarly, defenders have opportunities to observe malicious code segments, for example, and develop detection signatures for them. Both cases motivate a model that is not dependent upon specific vulnerabilities and exploits, but rather

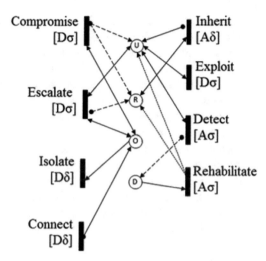

Fig. 8.4 Stochastic game-theoretic attack model for a single host

constructed from attacker and defender sub-models that represent the processes of learning and adaptation.

The approach we have taken to address the role of active defenses and the adaptive nature of attackers and defenders is to augment the Petri net representations of attacks with dynamics corresponding to actions taken by a network defense operators, which necessitates the representation of actions taken by the attacker in response to (or in a proactive attempt to evade) defender actions. Specifically, we have replaced the exploit-specific transitions with transitions that correspond to Attacker and Defender actions as well as other events, such as automated intrusion detection, that take place without conscious decision-making.

The result is the stochastic game-theoretic model overlaid on the Petri net machinery illustrated by Fig. 8.4. For this game-theoretic model, we have focused on simultaneous move games in the sense of Shapley (1953). However, we have also explored the utility of treating them as Stackelberg games, which is the approach taken by Zonouz et al. (2014).

In this model, we have places, as before, that correspond to the attacker having User (U) or Root (R) privileges on the host. We have added places corresponding to whether the host is Online (O) or whether attacker presence is Detected (D). Transitions in this model can be either *deliberate* (D) or *autonomous* (A). Deliberate transitions are driven by an agent decision. Autonomous transitions take place without any need for agent prompting. Likewise, transitions can be either stochastic (σ) or deterministic (δ). Stochastic transitions have probabilistic outcomes. Deterministic transitions have certain outcomes.

We have also added a constraint on some edges indicated by a black circle at one end of the arrow. This signifies that the transition to which the black circle is attached has the potential to fire only if the place to which the arrow is pointing is not marked. This enforces the binary state of each place (places can be unmarked or marked only with a single token). By doing so, we avoid the potentially infinite state spaces possible with the general Petri net formalism.

Some of the specified transitions are abstractions, in some cases, of the exploit-specific transitions of the previous Petri net models. For example, the *Compromise* transition, which is *deliberate* and *stochastic* ($D\sigma$), represents an attacker action intended to gain execution on a target host. This would have been represented by one or specific exploits in the previous model. Similarly, the *Escalate* ($D\sigma$) transition represents an attacker action intended to achieve Root privileges on a host to which the attacker already has User privileges.

Both of these transitions have probabilistic outcomes. In the case of *Compromise*, the outcome may be any one of the following: User privileges, Root privileges, or no privileges (failure). This represents the uncertainty, as discussed above, associated with achieving success in a specified time frame and, given success, the degree of success that is the result of the specific exploit that succeeds, the context in which the vulnerable application or service is running when it is exploited, and so forth. In the case of *Escalate*, the uncertainty in outcome is due only to the probability of achieving success in a specified time interval as discussed. Inherit is autonomous and deterministic.

On the defender side, *Detect* and *Rehabilitate* are *stochastic* transitions corresponding to, respectively, the processes of detecting malicious activity, whether due to automated signature-based detection or human observance of anomalous behavior, and removing attacker privileges and accesses. Detect is *autonomous*, meaning that no agent action, per se, is required for it to fire. Rehabilitate, however, is *deliberate*, meaning that the defender much choose to take this action. Note that the model depicted in Fig. 8.4 indicates that detection is a required precondition for rehabilitation. More recently, we have relaxed this requirement such that no detection is required to take proactive measures. *Isolate* and *Connect* are defender-driven (deliberate) transitions that, respectively, disconnect and connect the host from its network connections.

A comprehensive attack model is constructed by linking multiple host models with each other and with failure modes using the *Compromise* and *Exploit* transitions, respectively, as shown in Fig. 8.5. *Compromise* models the process of gaining privileges on as-yet uncompromised hosts. *Escalate* models the process of using existing privileges to realize some mission-relevant effect on the target network. Both are driven by attacker actions, and both are deliberate, stochastic transitions. In this example model, the process effects, *Transceiver Fouling* and *Spurious Traffic*, are related to a tactical radio mesh network that is under attack.

The third salient property of cyber attacks is that no agent has complete information regarding the true state or state history of the attack when it is in progress. Arguably, no agent ever has complete information regarding state histories, though forensics scientists are becoming more adept at recovering artifacts that yield insight into state histories after the fact. To solve the induced partially observed stochastic game, we have developed a family of algorithms derived from fictitious play (Berger 2007; Brown 1951), and partially observable Monte Carlo planning (Silver and Veness 2010).

There are several active areas of research seeking to address open problems in this domain. We will briefly discuss three: (1) conditions of and for convergence in

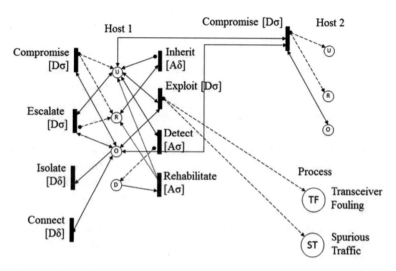

Fig. 8.5 Comprehensive attack model

solvers of the type we are developing, (2) credible methods for estimating model parameters from available data, and (3) methods to efficiently and effectively validate model results.

The convergence characteristics of algorithms designed to solve perfect information stochastic games have been studied extensively. Raghavan and Filar (1991) provide an excellent survey of several algorithms and their convergence properties. However, algorithms to solve partially observed games are relatively immature and, correspondingly, less well understood. Specifically, it isn't clear whether there are well-defined conditions under which convergence is guaranteed, much less what those conditions might be.

One approach we are examining as a means to practically address this problem is to use a scripted strategy for one of the agents, namely, the defender, and play it against a strategy-learning adversary. This effectively transforms the partially observed stochastic game into a partially observed stochastic decision process. While this is also an active area of research, it is more mature and relatively better-understood than its multi-agent counterpart. For example, Lovejoy (1991) presented an excellent survey of methods for solving partially observed Markov decision processes (POMDP). More recent approaches, including the POMCP algorithm (Silver and Veness 2010) we adapted for our work are achieving improved performance.

Another approach we intend to explore is seeding the solvers with heuristics derived from attack and defense experts. The rationale for pursuing this is that, by given the agents a well-informed push in the right direction, we may avoid some of the wilder and woolier regions in solution space, thereby achieving at least near-convergence in practice.

Parameter estimation continues to be a significant problem across the broader cyber modeling community. In particular, the estimation of many of the measures that are common in the community, including *time to compromise*, *level of effort*, and even measures of *consequence* is still heavily dependent on subject matter expert (SME) elicitation. Several researchers have made attempts to use the widely cited National Vulnerabilities Database, specifically its collection of Common Vulnerability Scoring System (CVSS)[2] scores, to estimate parameters such as mean time to compromise (McQueen et al. 2005). Our model, in fact, uses the mean time to compromise measure as a subordinate parameter for estimating Poisson process distributions, which ultimately yield probability measures for state transition in our model. However, recent work by Holm et al. (2012) demonstrated that McQueen's model and several others designed to estimate similar parameters from the same data were in fact poor predictors of actual mean time to compromise. While Holm and colleagues did offer a few broad suggestions, they readily acknowledged the need for much more progress in this area.

We are interested in two specific measures, as indicated previously: time to compromise and time to detect. One of the alternatives to estimation models such as that discussed by McQueen et al. (2005) assessed favorably by Holm et al. (2012) is the size of the vulnerability population on a host. They demonstrated, using exercise data, that the size of the population of vulnerabilities in a particular category is roughly inversely proportional to the time required to compromise the host. On the basis of this insight, we investigated the potential utility of vulnerability population models, with growth due to vulnerability discovery and decay due to vulnerability patching. This remains an open problem.

Lastly, validation remains an open problem for this and many other modeling endeavors. Without a large sample of known intrusions and the conditions under which they took place, the research community is dependent on live exercise data, which are costly to collect, and simulated cyber interactions. However, even costly exercise data are not without their detractors. Chief among these is the observation that cyber attacks are, and will always be, highly tailored to their targets. Therefore, data collected in one instance may provide no useful insight into other situations unless the conditions are strongly correlated.

The situation is not, however, hopeless. Much useful insight can be gained by considering relative analysis. That is, comparing model results for multiple system configurations, attack scenarios, and so forth, to gain insight into the relative costs and benefits of different defensive strategies, system architectures, et cetera. Moreover, varying model parameter values for sensitivity analysis can lend a sense of robustness to these results. Most of the value in models is the extent to which they accurately reflect the structure of the real-life phenomena they purport to represent. On this basis, we assert that our models and others like them, while imperfect, yield much needed insight into problems for which we traditionally rely on intuition and experience for guidance. This is not to discount the value of intuition and experience, but rather to suggest these model-based approaches as a worthy complement to such methods.

---

[2] A specification for CVSS v3.0 can be found here: https://www.first.org/cvss/specification-document.

8.3 Petri Nets for Control Systems

This section further describes the Petri net modeling technique introduced in Sect. 8.2.4. Specifically, we discuss methods for modeling process control systems and coupling those models to models of the processes they control. The result is a straight-forward approach to assessing risk due to cyber manipulation of control systems in terms of the material consequences that can be achieved through abuse of their control authority. These models permit a simple heuristic for identifying opportunities for high-value risk mitigation.

8.3.1 Attack Model

The operational impact of an attack on an ICS-controlled process depends on the extent to which network resources can be accessed and manipulated by the attacker to induce process failure. To examine the interactions between an attacker and the ICS-controlled process, we augment each host specification with properties that correspond to process control functionality, e.g., sensor and actuator I/O, operator interface, and automation functions. An attacker induces physical process failure by corrupting specific applications or data on one or more hosts.

For example, by manipulating an instrument calibration data file, the attacker may affect state estimates to achieve process failure by misleading the legitimate control scheme. Alternatively, the attacker may overwrite the control application to achieve a similar failure mode. Moreover, the attacker may create and send a data stream to the operator interface to give the outward impression that the process is executing normally, thereby delaying operator response.

Specifying host functionality is heavily dependent on the application. For process control networks, we specify host functionality in terms of control authority (subsystems over which the host exerts direct influence or indirect influence through its data and applications), application type (development, process control, state estimation or operator interaction), data in memory and I/O relationships. These properties are modeled as places in our Petri net model as illustrated in the left side of Fig. 8.6 in the box labeled *PCS Functionality*, where PCS refers to Process Control System.

Manipulation of data resident on a host permits an attacker to affect host functionality. We model the interaction between the manipulated functionality and the ICS-controlled infrastructure or process by a set of *PCS Manipulation* places as shown on the right side of Fig. 8.6.

Figure 8.7 illustrates a similar dynamic, but one which requires attacker privileges on multiple hosts.

The set of *PCS Manipulation* places corresponds to global process control failure modes and includes places corresponding to instruction spoofing for specific actuators, operator deception for specific sub-processes, mis-calibration of

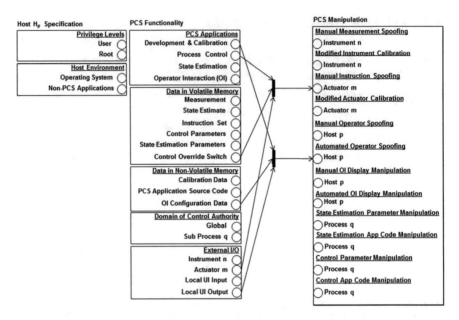

Fig. 8.6 Augmented host specification and coupling to ICS functionality

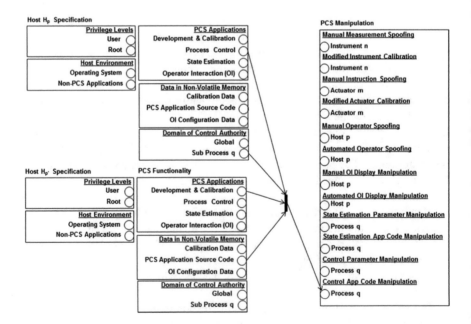

Fig. 8.7 PCS manipulation requiring access to multiple hosts

specific instruments, state estimation parameter modification, control parameter modification and application code modification. Each of these failure modes is a post-condition of one or more transitions that model attacker actions, where the pre-conditions include access to data on different hosts, control authority of the hosts, applications running on the hosts, and some prerequisite level of privilege on the host.

As in the attack model, the transitions that couple process failure modes to the host specification are expressed in terms of pre-conditions that belong to the set of places associated with the augmented host specification; and post-conditions that belong to the set of places associated with process control system manipulation. For example, Fig. 8.6 illustrates two such coupling transitions. The first employs a process control application, control override switch and an I/O relationship with a particular actuator to manually spoof instructions to the actuator. The second coupling transition employs a development application, access to the operator interface (OI) configuration data, and the local user interface (UI) output (typically a graphical representation of system state) to automatically manipulate the OI display.

As with escalation, some types of process control system manipulation may require access to multiple hosts. Note that what is not shown in Fig. 8.6 is the level of privilege required (user or root) to fire the coupling transitions. This has been omitted for the sake of visual clarity. However, these requirements are part of the pre-condition set for each coupling transition.

The set of process failure mode places corresponds to physical process failure states induced by the manipulation of the physical system via malicious actuator control or denial of control authority to legitimate operators. Each failure mode has an assessed consequence, e.g., c^i corresponding to the ith failure mode m^i, where the consequence is measured in terms of the assessed material outcome associated with the failure mode, including the risk of personnel injury, property damage, production loss, etc. Note that the analyst may wish to develop a distribution over possible values for each c^i and compute a variety of metrics (including the expected value or conditional expected value) to achieve a comprehensive risk assessment that takes into account likely and extreme events.[3]

As shown in Fig. 8.8, we couple the process control failure modes to the physical process failure modes through transitions corresponding to actions taken by the attacker after gaining access to network resources. Formally, these transitions are defined by a set of pre-conditions amongst the set of process control failure modes and a set of post-conditions that include all the pre-conditions and a single process failure mode. Intuitively, each of these transitions represents a sequence of actions taken by the attacker (given the ability to induce the prerequisite process control failure modes) to induce component faults at the right time and thereby cause the desired process failure mode.

---

[3] Cf. the techniques for analyzing the risk of extreme events presented in Haimes (2004).

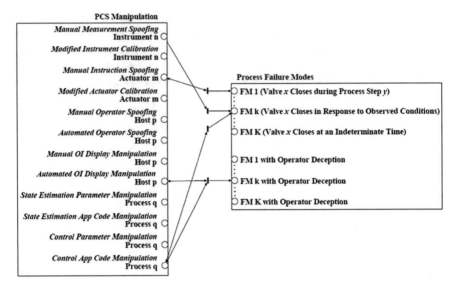

Fig. 8.8 Process manipulation

8.3.2 Computing State Reachability

Given a Petri net representation of an attack, risk can be assessed in terms of the resources to which an attacker can gain access over the course of the attack. As we have discussed, resources are represented as places in the Petri net formalism. Therefore, in order to develop the formal notion of risk, we must solve the following problem: given a Petri net with initial marking m_0, find all the markings (i.e., sets of places that are simultaneously marked) that materialize at some time during the execution of the Petri net. Intuitively, a solution to this problem identifies the resources that an adversary can potentially control, given the initial state m_0.

The problem just described falls in the domain of *reachability analysis*. Let Π be a Petri net with initial marking m_0. The *reachability tree* $RT(\Pi)$ of Π enumerates all markings (states) that can be reached from m_0 by some finite sequence of transition firings. The *reachability problem* for Petri nets is the problem of determining whether a given marking m is reachable from a particular initial state. In other words, it is the problem of determining whether $m \in RS(\Pi)$. It is well known that this problem is computationally intractable in general (Esparza 1998; Murata 1989). However, it turns out that the complete reachability tree is not needed for risk analysis. Instead, we require only the more manageable *coverability graph* (Finkel 1991; Reisig 1985).

The coverability problem for Petri nets is the problem of determining whether a given Petri net marking m is *coverable*; i.e., whether there exists a reachable marking m such that $m(p) \leq m'(p)$ for every place p. The coverability problem still exhibits bad worst-case behavior, but is often manageable for practical applications. In particular, a *coverability graph*, in contrast to the reachability tree, is always finite. The set of all labels of a coverability graph for a Petri net Π is called the *coverability set*, denoted $CS(\Pi)$, a finite abstraction of the reachability set.

The coverability graph does not solve the reachability problem, *per se*. For our purposes, however, a place represents a Boolean condition: we are interested in the question of whether there is some marking in which the place is marked by at least one token. And in order to answer this question, coverability is sufficient. Specifically, the coverability graph yields the set of reachable places as follows: a place p is reachable when there is some node in the coverability graph whose label is an ω-marking m such that $m(p) > 0$. The relationship between state reachability and coverability is discussed in more detail by Henry et al. (2009).

8.3.3 Reachability under Monotonicity

The monotonicity assumption was proposed by Ammann et al. (2002) and adopted, for example by Ammann et al. (2005) and Wang et al. (2006). According to this assumption, an attacker never relinquishes a capability once he has obtained it. This simplifying assumption is not entirely realistic, but does provide the basis for a scalable approach to vulnerability analysis that utilizes attack graphs. The Petri net model, on the other hand, can accommodate non-monotonic behavior if the analyst believes it to be an important aspect of the attacks of interest.

Monotonic behavior, as discussed previously, is encoded by places that are both input and output places for a given transition. Such places are connected to their transitions by bidirectional arrows, and retain their tokens after the transition fires. On the other hand, non-monotonic behavior is characterized by the consumption of resources (without reconstitution) during an attack step. It is therefore represented in a Petri net by a one-directional arrow from pre-conditions to the transition that exhibits non-monotonicity such that the removal of tokens from input places when a transition fires is not paired with the replacement of tokens, as would be the case with double-sided arrows..

For example, as illustrated by Fig. 8.9, the preconditions for an *sshd* buffer overflow attack from $host_0$ to $host_1$ are user privileges on $host_0$ and *sshd* running on $host_1$. There is a bidirectional arc between $user_0$ and $sshd\_bof_{0,1}$, indicating that the attacker maintains user privileges on $host_0$ after performing the exploit. However, there is single arc from $sshd_1$ to $sshd\_bof_{0,1}$, indicating that the *sshd* is disabled as a result of the exploit. This loss of resources is important because without *sshd* running the attacker cannot transfer his root kit from $host_0$ and therefore cannot gain root privileges on $host_1$.

Petri net attack models can be generated in polynomial time from a network specification, without requiring a monotonicity assumption. Analysis of Petri net models using coverability also does not require monotonicity. However, in contrast to the case of automated generation of Petri nets, the monotonicity assumption does

Fig. 8.9 Attacks with
monotonic and non-
monotonic behavior

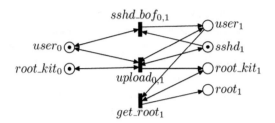

have a substantial impact on the complexity of this sort analysis technique, and it is
only practical to model non-monotonic behaviors in small graphs. Otherwise, we
invoke monotonicity, particularly when our objective is approximate results for
larger networks.

The reachability problem *is* tractable when we proceed under the monotonicity
assumption: an attacker never relinquishes a capability once he has obtained it. The
implication of this assumption for Petri nets is that a place never becomes unmarked,
once it has become marked. For this special case, the full reachability set can be
computed in polynomial time. The set of reachable places is given by the final
marking m_f of the net. In other words, a place p is reachable if and only if
$m_f(p) > 0$.

8.3.4 Measuring Risk

The Petri net model developed in this chapter is non-probabilistic. Thus, the model
does not provide any measure of the relative difficulty for any sequence of attack
states. Consequently, there is no measure of the relative likelihood for any particular
outcome. The model enables us to ascertain only whether any particular outcome is
possible.

Nevertheless, the model does enable us to estimate an upper bound on risk, and
this upper can serve as a useful risk metric. To evaluate this metric, we first compute
the coverability set for the coupled Petri net, which includes places and transitions
corresponding to process failure modes and attacker actions needed to induce the
failure modes, respectively. The risk metric, R, takes the value of the most materi-
ally costly outcome in the coverability set $CS(\Pi)$: $R = \max\{c^i | m^i \in CS(\Pi)\}$.

Note that there is an inherent assumption in this evaluation scheme that the combined consequence due to multiple failure modes is no worse than the worst consequence due to any one of the failure modes. This assumption is based on the
observation that, for most industrial processes, mechanical fail-safe devices are
typically employed for damage control during one catastrophic failure by preventing another catastrophic failure through sub-process isolation. As such, our reasoning covers the equivalent cases of multiple attackers and a single attacker with

multiple targets. However, this assumption can be relaxed without introducing any additional complexity in the analysis. An alternative metric, for example, could be the sum of possible outcomes for any one marking in the coverability set.

8.3.5 Backtracking for Risk Management Planning

In this section, we introduce a heuristic for identifying high-value risk mitigation opportunities via informed search over the coverability set. These opportunities are identified in accordance with their potential for preventing outcomes of estimable severity as given by the failure modes and effects analysis. Once identified, these alternatives are evaluated in a cost-benefit tradeoff analysis to identify a favorable mitigation strategy.

We employ the following procedure to identify and characterize risk management opportunities. First, we search over the set of process failure modes marked in the coverability set in order of decreasing severity. For each process failure mode we identify the *first-order transitions*, where a transition t is a first-order transition for failure mode m if (i) m is an output place of t; and (ii) there exists at least one marking in the coverability set in which t is enabled (all input places of t are marked). Thus, somewhere in the reachable state space, the transition t must be enabled and its firing must result in the marking of the reachable failure mode. For example, Fig. 8.10 illustrates one first-order transition for $FM1$ and two first-order transitions for $FM1A$.

To formally specify the backtracking algorithm, we let T_1 denote the set of first-order transitions. Each subset of first-order transitions $S_1 \subseteq T_1$ is assigned a value V^{S_1}, which is derived from the consequences associated with the failure modes that are reachable uniquely via S_1:

$$V^{S_1} = \sum c^i \mid \left(\forall t \in S_1 \right) m^i \in t^{\circ} \wedge \left(\forall t' \in T_1 \right) \left(t' \notin S_1 \rightarrow m^i \notin t'^{\circ} \right)$$

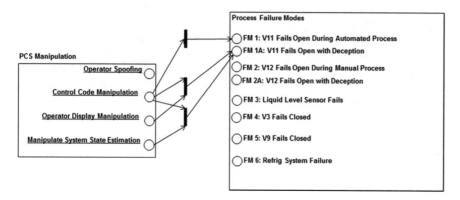

Fig. 8.10 First-order transitions

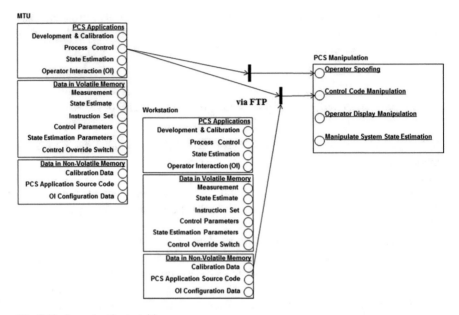

Fig. 8.11 Second-order transitions

Thus, c^i contributes to V^{S_1} if disabling each transition in S_1 would prevent m^i from being reachable, but no proper subset of S_1 has this property. Intuitively, the V^{S_1} are interpreted as the values of the consequences avoided if the given transition or transitions are rendered inactive by implementing a suitable risk management policy.

Next, we identify *second-order transitions*, where t_2 is a second-order transition if (i) at least one output place of t_2 is an input place for some first-order transition; and (ii) there exists at least one marking in the coverability set in which t_2 is enabled. For example, Fig. 8.11 illustrates one second-order transition (via FTP exploitation) for $FM1$.

Let T_2 denote the set of second-order transitions. A set $S_2 \subseteq T_2$ is assigned a value V^{S_2} in the following way. Consider the first-order transitions, each of whose input places is the output place of some transition in S_2. For such a set $S_1 \subseteq T_1$, V^{S_1} contributes to V^{S_2} if disabling each transition in S_2 would disable each transition in S_1, but no subset of S_2 has this property. More precisely,

$$V^{S_2} = \sum_{S \subseteq T_1} \left\{ V^{S_1} \mid CondA \wedge CondB \right\}$$

where

$$CondA : \left(\forall t_1 \in S_1 \right) \left(\exists t_2 \in S_2 \right) \left(\exists p \in \left(t_2^{\circ} \cap {}^{\circ}t_1 \right) \right)$$

and

$$CondB : \left(S_2' \subset S_2 \right) \rightarrow \left(\exists t_1 \in S_1 \right)\left(\forall t_2 \in S_2' \right)\left(t_2^{\circ} \cap {}^{\circ}t_1 \right) = \varnothing$$

The interpretation of value for second-order transitions is similar to that for first-order transitions: the value corresponds to the avoided consequences when the process failure mode is made unreachable through risk management.

It is useful to note that the first-order transitions couple the process failure modes to the global process control failure modes, and second-order transitions couple global process control failure modes to host resources (applications and data) that can potentially be controlled by an attacker with sufficient access to network resources.

The third step in our procedure is to identify third-order and fourth-order transitions that exist in the attack model and assign values to them by extending the technique described above. Finally, we identify high-value risk management opportunities by identifying the host resources or global process control failure modes that serve as pre-conditions for high-value second-, third- and fourth-order transitions. We assume that the first-order transitions, which couple global process control failure modes to process failure modes, are a product of the control system architecture and should be treated separately.

High-value second-, third- and fourth-order transitions are rendered impossible by taking actions such as patching vulnerable applications and encrypting sensitive data. Each of these opportunities is assessed a value equal to the value of the transitions that it renders impossible. Each opportunity is then assigned a cost measure derived from the expense or operating costs likely to be incurred while repairing the vulnerability or making the network resource inaccessible. We then evaluate each opportunity in the cost-value space and eliminate inefficient options, or those which are strictly dominated in a Pareto sense.

From the efficient options, the decision-maker selects an appropriate choice based on his or her posture with respect to the cost-benefit tradeoff. Moreover, to address the uncertainty associated with presumed initial conditions that specify initial attacker access to the network, minimax Pareto frontiers (Henry and Haimes 2009b) can be employed to identify the options that are both efficient in the cost-benefit space and robust with respect to attack scenario.

8.4 An Example Petri Net Analysis of a Control System

In this section we illustrate the risk analysis methodology developed in earlier sections by considering a specific process control network application. Our application builds on the non-automated hazardous liquid loading system analyzed by Balasubramanian et al. (2002). This system is employed to support the liquid ammonia loading operation described below. All system labels (e.g., for valves and pipelines) refer to the system diagram presented by Balasubramanian et al. (2002).

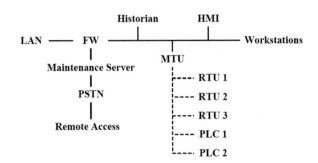

Fig. 8.12 Example ICS

Liquid Ammonia Loading Operation

1. Ammonia carrier (truck) couples to gas pipeline (A–E) at V6 and liquid pipeline (F–H) at V7
2. Compressor primes to operating pressure under isolation by V2 and V3 with bypass through V4
3. Compressor de-isolates and high-pressure gas forces transfer of liquid from truck to tank
4. Compressor shuts down after tank level reaches predetermined threshold

For the purpose of demonstrating our methodology, we contrived an ICS to permit remote operator control and partial automation of the liquid loading process. The process control network comprises a data historian, a human-machine interface (HMI), an engineering workstation, a master terminal unit (MTU), three remote terminal units (RTUs) and two programmable logic controllers (PLCs). The ICS topology is shown in Fig. 8.12.

In our example ICS, RTU 1 controls valves V1, V2, V5 and V13; RTU 2 controls valves V4, V8 and V11; RTU 3 controls valves V9, V12 and V14; PLC 1 controls valves V1 and V10 and the refrigeration system; and PLC 2 controls valves V2, V3 and V4 and the compressor. The MTU communicates with the RTUs and PLCs via a radio serial link (RSL); the maintenance server is accessible via dial-up modems from the public switched telephone network (PSTN); all other communications are conducted over TCP/IP on Ethernet.

Process control applications automate compressor warm-up, tank fill and compressor shutdown (Tasks 3, 4 and 5 described by Balasubramanian et al. (2002). They also permit the remote manual control of valves V1-V3 and V9-V14 in the execution of Tasks 1, 2, 6 and 7 by Balasubramanian et al. (2002). Manipulation of the isolation valves V5-V8 and VN1-VN4 remains manual and local (at the valves). The Petri net formalism is used to model hosts in the process control network (specified by two levels, user and root); several business applications such as an FTP client, the Microsoft Windows suite and web browsers; connectivity to other hosts; and process control data and functionality. This last set of characteristics is divided into several subsets: process state estimation, process control, user interaction, I/O devices, support functions and control authority

Fig. 8.13 Remote
operations Petri net model

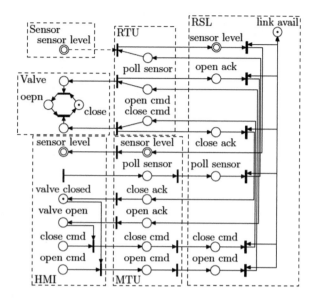

A partial Petri net encoding of these remote operations, specifically the remote operation of a valve, is illustrated by Fig. 8.13. To open the valve, an operator must issue an open command at the HMI, and the valve's state at the HMI must be closed. If these preconditions are met, the HMI relays the command to the MTU via the Ethernet connection, the MTU communicates the command to the appropriate RTU via the RSL, the RTU driver delivers power to actuate the valve, and the open state is then registered at the RTU and relayed back to the HMI through the MTU.

Similarly, Fig. 8.14 illustrates the PN model of automated compressor warm-up and subsequent tank fill. The PLC issues instructions autonomously based on sensor input from the differential pressure measurement across the compressor and the liquid fill level in the tank.

In one modeled configuration, a firewall (FW) is used to control traffic between the process control network, the corporate local area network and the maintenance network. In alternate configurations, the historian and workstations are also isolated by the firewall, i.e., they reside in separate so-called *demilitarized zones* (DMZs).

The coupling of host properties to global process control failures is specified by transitions representing attacker actions that employ controlled resources (preconditions)—such as application source code on the engineering workstation and compiled application code on a PLC—to achieve a process control failure (postconditions) such as control code tampering.

Process failure modes are derived from the process model. Of the large number of possible process failures, Balasubramanian et al. (2002) discuss six in detail by describing the corresponding component failure, the state of the process at the time of failure and the resulting impact. We added two others to model a failure mode coupled with operator deception.

Fig. 8.14 Petri net model
of an automated process

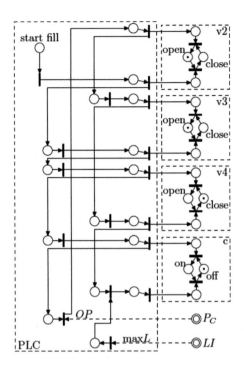

We relate each process failure to a set of ICS attacks, where each ICS attack has the same result as the induced process failure, but is caused by an attack on the ICS computing infrastructure. Moreover, for each process failure, we assign a measure of its severity in terms of expected number of personnel injuries due to inhalation or skin irritation. This measure is a function of the quantity and phase (liquid or gas) of potential ammonia discharge due to the process failure, coupled with the number of personnel likely to be in the vicinity of the discharge and the time required to evacuate those personnel from the affected locations.

For example, one process failure goes as follows: if valve v11 (component) fails open before the execution of Task 4, then a large amount of gaseous ammonia will be discharged into the dilution drum. Due to the location of the dilution drum with respect to the truck operator and plant personnel, we estimate an expectation of three injuries due to inhalation. We relate this process failure and associated consequence to a set of attacks on the ICS system as shown in Fig. 8.15.

In failure mode (FM) 1.1 the attacker gains user privileges on the HMI and issues a command to open the valve v11 before the execution of Task 4, and ammonia will discharge into the dilution drum. A similar, but possibly more devastating attack can occur in FM 1.2 when and attacker gains root privileges on the HMI, opens valve v11 before Task 4, and spoofs a closed state for v11. This attack gives the legitimate HMI operator the impression that the process state is correct for the task at hand and can increase the amount of ammonia discharged. As a result, the expectation of injuries doubles. A third attack (FM 1.3) targets the MTU. This attack has the same effects as the HMI super-user attack.

Fig. 8.15 ICS Attack induces process failures

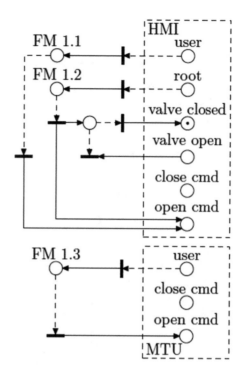

For the purposes of this example, we assessed consequence measures for each of eight process failure modes, each of which is inducible by manipulating the process control system (PCS), based on possible co-location of ammonia system equipment and other plant facilities, including work areas where people may be exposed to ammonia in the event of a leak. The resulting eight failure modes and their corresponding costs are shown in Fig. 8.16 along with the PCS manipulation modes that serve as the pre-conditions for failure.

We computed the coverability set for three cases: (1) a baseline case, (2) a re-architected ICS network, and (3) the re-architected ICS network with additional protocol constraints imposed by the firewall rules and local access control policies. These cases are illustrated below along with the assumed initial conditions, the results of the coverability analysis, and the corresponding risk metric evaluation.

Figure 8.17 illustrates the baseline case. The enterprise network is composed of three segments: (1) the corporate network (Corp Net), (2) the ICS, and (3) the Process Control System (PCS), which is an element of the ICS. Workstations on the Corp Net are Windows XP machines running MS Office and host web browsers. On the ICS network, the Historian is hosted on a Windows XP system and uses the Open Database Connectivity (ODBC) protocol to service database updates and queries; the Engineering Workstation is hosted on a Windows XP system that also hosts a web browser, MS Office products, and an FTP server; and the PCS provides operator control over the process as well as gateway services to the local controllers (RTUs and PLCs) and the Public Switched Telephone Network (PSTN).

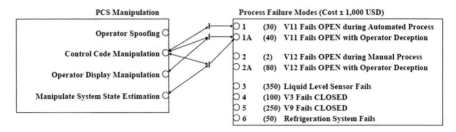

Fig. 8.16 Process failure modes and costs

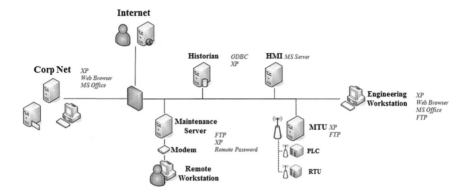

Fig. 8.17 Baseline case: ICS architecture and host attributes

Specifically, the PCS is composed of the HMI, which is hosted on an MS Server system; the Maintenance Server, which is hosted on a Windows XP system, supports data requests via the File Transfer Protocol (FTP), and supports remote log-in via dial-up modem; and the Master Terminal Unit (MTU), which is hosted on an embedded Windows XP system and supports data requests via FTP. These system attributes are indicated by text labels on Fig. 8.17. In the baseline case, we assume the following protocol constraints imposed by the firewall.

- BLOCK inbound connections from Internet to ICS network
- ALLOW outbound from ICS network to Internet
- ALLOW ODBC and FTP from Corp to ICS network

For the initial attack case (and for all other attacks), we assume that, initially, the attacker has root privileges on a host on the Internet and a Remote Workstation with dial-up capability. The results of the coverability analysis are illustrated by Fig. 8.18.

Without conducting any backtracking analysis, we can posit two potential, incrementally more stringent security measures. The first, illustrated in Fig. 8.19, re-architects the ICS network by further partitioning it and imposing more restrictive firewall rules. Specifically, the new rules BLOCK all connections from Internet to and from the PCS, Historian, and Engineering Workstation.

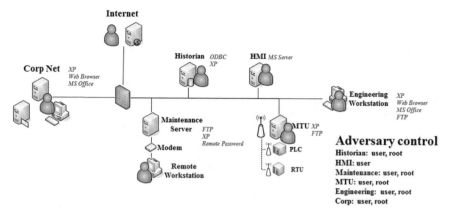

Fig. 8.18 Baseline case: coverability results

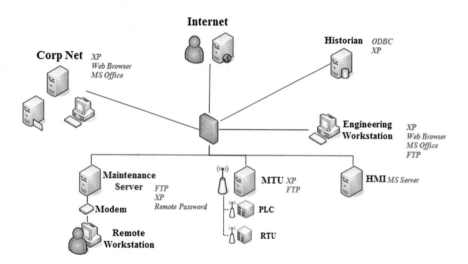

Fig. 8.19 ICS network with new architecture

This approach induces the coverability results illustrated in Fig. 8.20, which are qualitatively similar to the baseline case.

The second security measure, illustrated in Fig. 8.21, adopts the same new architecture but also disallows remote dial-in access to the maintenance server and blocks all FTP traffic between the Engineering Workstation and the Process Control System (PCS) maintenance server and MTU.

The coverability results for this case are illustrated in Fig. 8.22, and they are measurably improved over the baseline case.

The cases and their coverability results are summarized in Fig. 8.23. Here, we have also highlighted the failure modes inducible in each case.

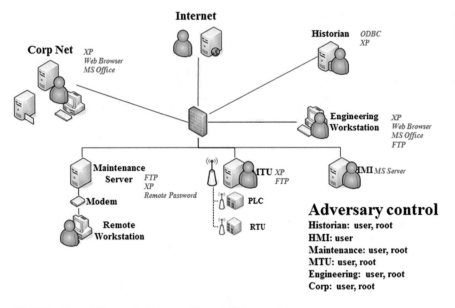

Fig. 8.20 Coverability results for re-architected ICS network

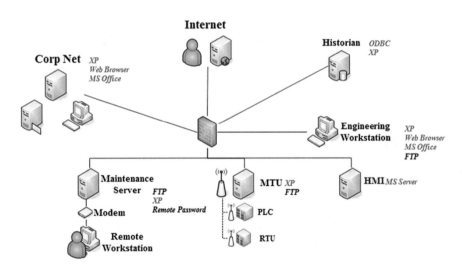

Fig. 8.21 ICS network with new architecture and more restrictive access control

We arrive at a similar conclusion via backtracking analysis. Coverability analysis of the baseline model reveals that the maximum cost induced by a cyber attack on the process control system is due to the induction of Failure Mode 3, the most costly of the identified failure modes. Therefore, the highest value first-order transitions

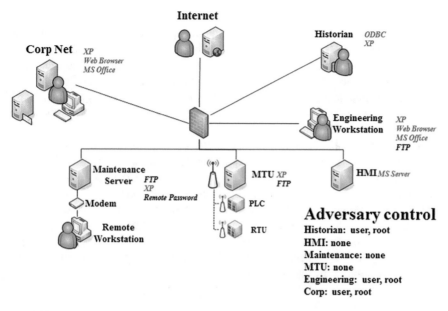

Fig. 8.22 Coverability results for case with new architecture and restrictive access control

Coverability Set (Base Case)

Historian: user, root
HMI: user
Maintenance: user, root
MTU: user, root
Engineering: user, root
Corp: user, root

Coverability Set (with DMZs)

Historian: user, root
HMI: user
Maintenance: user, root
MTU: user, root
Engineering: user, root
Corp: user, root

Inducible Process Failure Modes:

1.   Small qty gaseous ammonia discharge to dilution drum
1A. Large qty gaseous ammonia discharge to dilution drum
2.   Automated fill task disabled
2A. Large qty liquid ammonia discharge to dilution drum
3.   Tank Overfill
4.   High-pressure gaseous ammonia discharge from damaged plumbing
5.   High-pressure liquid ammonia discharge from damaged plumbing
6.   Low-pressure gaseous ammonia discharge from damaged plumbing

Coverability Set (with DMZs and Restrictive Access Control)

Historian: user, root
HMI: none
Maintenance: none
MTU: none
Engineering: user, root
Corp: user, root

Inducible Process Failure Modes:

None

Fig. 8.23 Summary of cases and coverability results

are those that include Failure Mode 3 in their post-condition set. The pre-conditions for these transitions include the control code manipulation failure mode. Thus, the highest-value second-order transitions are those that include the control code manipulation failure mode in their post-condition sets. These transitions include in their pre-condition sets the following places: MTU root access, workstation root access and maintenance server root access. It turns out that exploiting a vulnerability in the FTP client permits all of these transitions and, by disabling the FTP client, the risk measure is reduced to zero.

This security enhancement would generally be accompanied by an operational cost, particularly if FTP is the primary tool used to transport critical information across the network. The decision to be made, then, is if the operational cost of removing the FTP client and introducing the new network partitions is offset by the potential for operational consequences in the event of a computer network attack launched against the process control network. If it is deemed to be a worthwhile change, then the introduction of any new applications to reduce the operational cost of removing the FTP capability should be considered in terms of the cost savings and the risk imposed by the new applications.

8.5   Summary and Conclusions

This chapter discusses five classes of methods for cyber risk assessment and management, with emphasis on application to ICS analysis. The Expert Elicited Model method involves computational models to assess risk based on expert elicited identification and characterization of cyber system attributes such as network data flows and the estimation of the susceptibility of those resources and data flows to different types of compromise. This approach possesses significant appeal for many applications, including cases involving complicated networks for which little design information is readily available and cases in which a relatively quick analysis is needed. One major drawback of this approach is lack of completeness. Second, the Attack Graph method advocates construction of attack trees or graphs, either by hand or through automated interrogation of a system of interest. This approach has many advantages. Principal among these is a very light data requirement. Models in this class do not suffer precision or fidelity shortcomings because they are constructed directly from system data without abstraction or aggregation. Another advantage of this approach is flexibility. Third, game theoretic models explicitly account for the interaction of attackers and defenders in a game theoretic framework. Models in this class are much more varied, and the approach is much less mature than the expert elicited and graph-based approaches described previously. Games can inform how the playing field can be better tilted in favor of the defender by adopting architectural changes and new access control policies. The fourth method is Petri Net models, which are favored by the authors of this chapter. This chapter's Petri net approach is derived from the Attack Graph school of thought. A Petri net is a directed bipartite graph, in which a cyber attack is modeled as the successive exploitation of vulnerabilities on hosts to escalate and then exploit privileges on the network. The final method described involves stochastic games overlaid on Petri nets, creating a much more powerful, and more challenging, approach. In this model, transitions based on attacks corresponding to network defense measures replace exploit-specific transitions. Methods for applying Petri net risk models to ICS are described, including a detailed example Petri net analysis of a hazardous liquid loading system process, identifying eight failure modes and corresponding costs associated with the failure modes.

References

Alpcan, T., & Basar, T. (2003). A game theoretic approach to decision and analysis in network intrusion detection. *IEEE Conference Decision and Control (CDC03)*.

Alpcan, T., & Basar, T. (2004). A game theoretic analysis of intrusion detection in access control systems. *IEEE Conference Decision and Control (CDC04)*.

Ammann, P., Pamula, J., Ritchey, R., & Street, J. (2005). A host-based approach to network attack chaining analysis. *21st Annual Computer Security Applications Conference*, pp. 72–84.

Ammann, P., Wijesekera, D., & Kaushik, S. (2002). Scalable, graph-based network vulnerability analysis. *9th ACM Conference on Computer and Communications Security*, pp. 217–224.

Balasubramanian, N., Chang, C., & Wang, Y. (2002). Petri net models for risk analysis of hazardous liquid loading operations. *Industrial and Engineering Chemistry Research, 41*(19), 4823–4836.

Berger, U. (2007). Brown's original fictitious play. *Journal of Economic Theory, 135*, 572–578.

Brown, G. W. (1951). Iterative solution of games by fictitious play. In T. C. Koopmans (Ed.), *Activity analysis of production and allocation* (pp. 374–376). New York: Wiley.

Byres, E., Franz, M., & Miller, D. (2004). The use of attack trees in assessing vulnerabilities in SCADA systems. *International Infrastructure Survivability Workshop*.

Dahl, O. (2005). *Using coloured Petri nets in penetration testing*. Master's Thesis, Department of Computer Science and Media Technology, Gjovik University College, Gjovik, Norway.

Esparza, J. (1998) Decidability and complexity of Petri net problems—An introduction. In W. Reisig & G. Rozenberg (Eds.), *Lectures on Petri nets I: Basic models; advances in Petri nets* (pp. 374–428). Lecture notes in computer science. Berlin: Springer-Verlag.

Finkel, A. (1991). The minimal coverability graph for Petri nets. *Twelfth international conference on applications and theory of Petri nets*, pp. 210–243.

Haimes, Y. Y. (2004). *Risk modeling, assessment, and management* (2nd ed.). New York: John Wiley & Sons.

Helmer, G., Wong, J., Slagell, M., Honavar, V., Miller, L., Wang, Y., et al. (2007). Software fault tree and coloured Petri net-based specification, design, and implementation of agent-based intrusion detection systems. *International Journal of Information and Computer Security, 1*(1/2), 109–142.

Henry, M., & Haimes, Y. Y. (2009a). A comprehensive network security risk model for process control networks. *Risk Analysis, 29*(2), 223–248.

Henry, M., & Haimes, Y. Y. (2009b). Robust multiobjective dynamic programming: Minimax envelopes for efficient decisionmaking under scenario uncertainty. *Journal of Industrial and Management Optimization, 5*(4), 791–824.

Henry, M., Layer, R., & Zaret, D. (2009). Evaluating the risk of cyber attacks on SCADA systems via Petri net analysis with application to hazardous liquid loading operations. *IEEE International Conference on Technologies for Homeland Security*, pp. 607–614.

Henry, M., Layer, R., & Zaret, D. (2010). Coupled Petri nets for computer network risk analysis. *International Journal of Critical Infrastructure Protection, 3*, 67–75.

Holm, H., Ekstedt, M., & Andersson, D. (2012). Empirical analysis of system-level vulnerability metrics through actual attacks. *IEEE Transactions on Dependable and Secure Computing, 9*(6), 825–837.

Ingols, K., Chu, M., Lippmann, R., Webster, S., & Boyer, S. (2009). Modeling modern network attacks and countermeasures using attack graphs. *Twenty-Fifth Annual Computer Security Applications Conference*, pp. 81–90.

Kertzner, P., Watters, J., & Bodeau, D. (2006). *Process control system security technical risk assessment methodology and technical implementation*. Institute for Information Infrastructure Protection (I3P) Technical Report 06-0707.

Khaitan, S., & Raheja, S. (2011). Finding optimal attack path using attack graphs: A survey. *International Journal of Soft Computing and Engineering, 1*(3), 2231–2307.

Llanso, T., & Klatt, E. (2014). CyMRisk: An Approach for computing mission risk due to cyber attacks. *8th Annual IEEE Systems Conference (SysCon)*, pp. 1–7.

Lovejoy, W. S. (1991). A survey of algorithmic methods for partially observed Markov decision processes. *Annals of Operations Research, 28*(1), 47–65.

Lye, K.W., & Wing, J. (2002). Game strategies in network security. *Foundations of Computer Security Workshop (FLoC'02), 2002 Federated Logic Conference*.

McDermott, J. (2000). Attack net penetration testing. *New Security Paradigms Workshop*, pp. 15-21.

McQueen, M., Boyer, W., Flynn, M., & Beitel, G. (2005). Time-to-compromise model for cyber risk reduction estimation. *1st Quality of Protection Workshop at the University of Trento, Milan. Springer*.

Murata, T. (1989). Petri nets: Properties, analysis and applications. *Proceedings of the IEEE, 77*(4), 541–580.

Raghavan, T. E. S., & Filar, J. A. (1991). Algorithms for stochastic games—A survey. *Journal of Operations Research, 35*(6), 437–472.

Reisig, W. (1985). Petri Nets: An introduction. Springer-Verlag.

Shapley, L. S. (1953). Stochastic games. *Proceedings of the National Academy of Sciences of the United States of America, 39*(10), 1095.

Silver, D., & Veness, J. (2010) Monte-Carlo planning in large POMDPs. *Advances in Neural Information Processing Systems*.

Wang, L., Noel, S., & Jajodia, S. (2006). Minimum-cost network hardening using attack graphs. *Computer Communications, 29*(18), 3812–3824.

Zhou, S., Qin, Z., Zhang, F., Zhang, X., Chen, W., & Liu, J. (2003). Colored Petri-net-based attack modeling. *Ninth International Conference on Rough Sets, Fuzzy Sets, Data Mining and Granular Computing*, pp. 715–718.

Zonouz, S., Khurana, H., Sanders, W., & Yardley, T. (2014). RRE: A game-theoretic intrusion response and recovery engine. *IEEE Transactions on Parallel and Distributed Systems, 25*(2), 395–406.

Chapter 9
Security Metrics in Industrial Control Systems

Zachary A. Collier, Mahesh Panwar, Alexander A. Ganin, Alexander Kott, and Igor Linkov

9.1 Introduction

Risk—the topic of the previous chapter—is the best known and perhaps the best studied example within a much broader class of cyber security metrics. However, risk is not the only possible cyber security metric. Other metrics such as resilience can exist and could be potentially very valuable to defenders of ICS systems.

Often, metrics are defined as measurable properties of a system that quantify the degree to which objectives of the system are achieved. Metrics can provide cyber defenders of an ICS with critical insights regarding the system. Metrics are generally acquired by analyzing relevant attributes of that system.

In terms of cyber security metrics, ICSs tend to have unique features: in many cases, these systems are older technologies that were designed for functionality rather than security. They are also extremely diverse systems that have different requirements and objectives. Therefore, metrics for ICSs must be tailored to a diverse group of systems with many features and perform many different functions.

In this chapter, we first outline the general theory of performance metrics, and highlight examples from the cyber security domain and ICS in particular. We then focus on a particular example of a class of metrics that is different from the one we

Z.A. Collier • M. Panwar • I. Linkov (✉)
US Army Engineer Research & Development Center, Concord, MA, USA
e-mail: Igor.Linkov@usace.army.mil

A.A. Ganin
University of Virginia, Charlottesville, VA, USA

A. Kott
US Army Research Laboratory, Adelphi, MD, USA

© Springer International Publishing Switzerland 2016
E.J.M. Colbert, A. Kott (eds.), *Cyber-security of SCADA and Other Industrial Control Systems*, Advances in Information Security 66,
DOI 10.1007/978-3-319-32125-7_9

have considered in earlier chapters. Instead of risk, here we consider metrics of resilience. Resilience is defined by the National Academy of Sciences (2012) as *"The ability to prepare and plan for, absorb, recover from, or more successfully adapt to actual or potential adverse events"*.

This chapter presents two approaches for the generation of metrics based on the concept of resilience using a matrix-based approach and a network-based approach. Finally, a discussion of the benefits and drawbacks of different methods is presented along with a process and tips intended to aid in devising effective metrics.

9.2 Motivation

Under President George W. Bush, the Department of Energy issued best practices for improved industrial control system (ICS) security (US Department of Energy 2002). Some of these include taking steps such as "disconnect unnecessary connections to the SCADA network", "establish a rigorous, ongoing risk management process" and "clearly identify cyber security requirements." Additionally, Executive Order 13636, signed by President Barack Obama in 2013, brought forth the issue of cyber security and resilience, and proposed the development of a risk-based "Cybersecurity Framework" (EO 13636, 2013). The framework was presented by the National Institute of Standards and Technology (NIST) and offers organizations guidance on implementing cybersecurity measures.

Despite existing guidelines and frameworks, designing and managing for security in cyber-enabled systems remains difficult. This is in large part due to the challenges associated with the *measurement* of security. Pfleeger and Cunningham (2010) outline nine reasons why measuring security is a difficult task as it relates to cybersecurity in general, but all of which also apply to the security of ICS domain (Table 9.1).

Pfleeger and Cunningham (2010) note that one way to overcome these challenges is to thoughtfully develop a clear set of security metrics. Unfortunately, this lack of metrics happens to be one of the greatest barriers to success in implementing ICS security. When ICSs were first implemented, "network security was hardly even a concern" (Igure et al 2006). Although efforts are being made to draft and enact cyber security measures, that gap has yet to be closed, even at a time of greater risk.

9.3 Background on Resilience Metrics

9.3.1 What Makes a Good Metric?

According to the management adage, "what gets measured gets done". As such, well-developed metrics can assist an organization in reaching its strategic goals (Marr 2010). Reichert et al. (2007) define metrics as "measurable properties that quantify the degree to which objectives have been achieved". Metrics provide vital

Table 9.1 Challenges with cybersecurity measurement (adapted from Pfleeger and Cunningham 2010)

Challenge	Description
We can't test all security requirements	It is not possible to know all possible configurations and states of the system, intended uses and unintended misuses from users, etc.
Environment, abstraction, and context affect security	Systems are built to evolve as they process new information, and not all system changes are derived from malicious sources
Measurement and security interact	Knowledge about a system's vulnerabilities and safeguards can affect the types of further security measures implemented, as well as modify the risks that users are willing to take
No system stands alone	Systems are networked to interact with other cyber systems and assets
Security is multidimensional, emergent, and irreducible	Security exists at multiple levels of system abstraction, and the security of the whole system cannot be determined from the security of the sum of its parts
The adversary changes the environment	Developing an accurate threat landscape is difficult due to adaptive adversaries who continually develop novel attacks
Measurement is both an expectation and an organizational objective	Different organizations with different missions and preferences place differing values on the benefits of security
We're overoptimistic	Users tend to underestimate the likelihood that their system could be the target of attack
We perceive gains differently than losses	Biases in interpreting expected gains and losses based on problem framing tend to affect risk tolerance and decision making under uncertainty in predictable but irrational ways

information pertaining to a given system, and are generally acquired by way of analyzing relevant attributes of that system. Some researchers and practitioners make a distinction between a measure and a metric (Black et al. 2008; Linkov et al. 2013a), whereas others may refer to them as performance measures (Neely et al. 1997), key performance indicators (Marr 2010) or strategic measures (Allen and Curtis 2011). For the purposes of this chapter, these are referred to generally as metrics.

When used efficiently, metrics can help to clarify one's understanding of the processes of a particular area of a system, and from there, provide information for external review and assist towards further improvement, among other outputs (Marr 2010). This can be done by establishing benchmarks for a given metric, where thresholds or ranges can be established (Black et al. 2008). Benchmarks, or standards, help form the basis for decision making and taking corrective action (Williamson 2006).

A critical element in eliciting a meaningful metric is to gather the relevant information about one's system and to align that metric with measurable goals and strategic objectives which lie within the scope of a given project or the domain of a particular organizational structure (Beasley et al. 2010; Neely et al. 1997).

Table 9.2 Characteristics of good metrics (adapted from Keeney and Gregory 2005; McKay et al. 2012)

Characteristic	Description
Relevant	Metrics are directly linked to decision making goals and objectives
Unambiguous	Consequences of alternatives can be clearly measured by metrics
Direct	Metrics clearly address and describe consequences of interest
Operational	Data exist and are available for the metric of interest
Understandable	Metrics can be understood and communicated easily
Comprehensive	The set of metrics address a complete suite of goals and consequences

There is also the issue of scale and adaptability. Smaller organization may have metrics dealing with rudimentary security measures, but as they grow larger, these measures may need to be scaled appropriately to deal with the security needed for a larger organization (Black et al. 2008).

There are key elements that contribute to producing a successful metric. Metrics should be actionable: they are not simply about measuring numerous attributes of a project; merely gathering information without a goal in mind will not provide a discernible solution (Marr 2010). Such information in and of itself would not be substantial enough to be considered a metric. Gathering relevant metrics requires delving deeper into the issues faced by a given system and asking pertinent questions which can lead to actionable improvement. These include questions such as "Does it link to strategy? Can it be quantified? Does it drive the right behavior?" (Eckerson 2009). From these, one can obtain metrics which can in turn inform actionable results. Table 9.2 summarizes the desirable characteristics of metrics in general terms and describes how the characteristics apply to all types of systems including ICSs.

Metrics may be described as natural, constructed, or proxy. Natural metrics directly describe an objective in units that are straightforward (e.g., dollars as a metric for "costs associated with ICS downtime"). Constructed metrics may be used when natural metrics do not exist (e.g., scales from 1 to 10 where each number corresponds to a defined level of ICS performance), and usually incorporate expert judgment. Proxy metrics can be used to indirectly measure an objective (e.g., the number of users with certain administrative privileges as a proxy for access) (Keeney and Gregory 2005; McKay et al. 2012).

There are different types of information that metrics gauge and the project team has the responsibility of appropriately selecting and evaluating them. These can be separated into quantitative, semi-quantitative and qualitative approaches. Quantitative metrics have measurable, numerical values attached to them. Semi-quantitative metrics are not strictly quantifiable but can be categorized. Qualitative metrics provide non-numeric information, for example in the form of aesthetics.

9.3.2 Metrics for IT Systems

As described above in Table 9.1, cyber systems provide unique challenges. In particular, the cyber domain extends beyond just the immediate system and requires a holistic viewpoint, with many different technical and human factors to be accounted for (Collier et al. 2014). Threats to the system are also constantly evolving and growing in sophistication, and as a result, there is a high degree of adaptability required in order to remain current. Due to the constantly evolving threat space, there is often little historical data for potential threats (Collier et al. 2014).

With cyber metrics, a significant number of the main issues are tailored towards security and resilience. The Defense Science Board (2013) argues that effective cyber metrics should be broad enough to fit different types of systems, yet also be precise enough to dial down into the specifics of a given system. The following are some examples of cybersecurity metrics currently in use.

The Common Vulnerability Scoring System (CVSS) was introduced to provide various organizations with actionable information in regards to assessing IT vulnerabilities (Mell et al. 2007). CVSS groups their metrics into three categories, namely Base, Temporal, and Environmental metrics. A few of these security metrics include Collateral Damage Potential, Target Distribution, Report Confidence, Exploitability, Access Complexity, Access Vector, Authentication, Integrity Impact, Availability Impact, and Confidentiality Impact (Mell et al. 2007). There are general scoring tips for the way that vulnerabilities are assessed; vulnerabilities are not scored based on interactions with other vulnerabilities, rather, they are scored independently. The main measure of vulnerability is its impact on the key service. Vulnerabilities are scored according to commonly used privileges, which might be a default setting in certain situations. If a vulnerability can be exploited by multiple exploits, it is scored with the exploit that will present the maximum impact (Mell, et al. 2007). CVSS allows vulnerability scores to be standardized, and Base metrics are normalized on a scale of 0 to 10. They can be optionally refined by including values from Temporal and Environmental metrics.

The Center for Internet Security (CIS) has also established metrics for organizations to use (CIS 2010). CIS has divided their metrics into six critical business functions. These are Incident Management, Vulnerability Management, Patch Management, Configuration Management, Change Management and Application Security. It also recognizes hierarchies and interdependencies of metrics, for instance citing management metrics as being of primary importance to an organization, while noting that some of those metrics may depend on the prior implementation of technical metrics (CIS 2010). Some of the metrics include Cost of Incidents and Patch Policy Compliance. Cost of Incidents refers to a number of potential losses, such as customer lists or trade secrets under a "direct loss" and a "cost of restitution", for example in the event that fines are levied due to an incident. This is measured by the summation of the numerical values of all the costs associated with the metric. Examples relating to security include Mean Time to Incident Discovery, Mean Time Between Security Incidents and Mean Time to Incident Recovery (CIS

2010). For an example of measurement, Mean Time to Incident Discovery measures the summation of the time between incidents and discoveries of incidents, divided by total number of incidents recovered during those time frames (CIS 2010).

The Cybersecurity Framework developed by NIST stemming from EO 13636 was released in February 2014 (NIST 2014). The final Cybersecurity Framework consists of a Framework Core, which presents a set of five "concurrent and continuous Functions—Identify, Protect, Detect, Respond, Recover" (NIST 2014). These functions are the "high-level, strategic view of the lifecycle of an organization's management of cybersecurity risk," which feature subsequent categories and subcategories for the functions, relating to outcomes and activities (NIST 2014). For example, the Respond function consists of five categories, among which includes Mitigation. Mitigation is then further subdivided into metrics related to containing and eradicating incidents. The Framework Core is used as a scorecard of progress – the current guidance calls for first developing an organization's Current Profile, which consists of assigned scores based on the organization's performance in each of the categories and subcategories. This Current Profile is then compared to a Target Profile, representing the desired state of the organization in each of the same categories and subcategories. The shortfalls between these profiles can be viewed as gaps in an organization's cyber-risk management capabilities which can inform prioritization of corrective measures (Collier et al. 2014; NIST 2014).

The Software Engineering Institute (SEI) at Carnegie Mellon University developed a framework for assessing operational resilience which features a set of Top Ten Strategic Measures, which aim to be mapped down to the level of specific Process Area measures (Allen and Curtis 2011). Under the heading of High-Value Services and Assets, one of the measures is related to the percentage of high-value services that do not satisfy their assigned resilience requirements (Allen and Curtis 2011). The SEI framework also contains a large amount of resilience measures, spanning 26 different Process Areas. For example, under the Process Area of Environmental Control, there are measures such as Percentage of Facility Assets that have been Inventoried, Elapsed Time Since the Facility Asset Inventory was Reviewed, and Elapsed Time Since Risk Assessment of Facility Assets Performed (Allen and Curtis 2011), where the term "assets" applies to high-value services. These are presented in a table with traceability, assigning an identification number to each metric along with their applicability to goals within the Process Areas.

MITRE proposed a framework entitled Cyber Resiliency Engineering Framework, which, among its goals aims to "motivate and characterize cyber resiliency metrics" (Bodeau and Graubart 2011). The framework contains four Cyber Resiliency Goals: Anticipate, Withstand, Recover, and Evolve. There are a total of eight objectives which are a subset of the goals. For example Anticipate has three objectives: Predict, Prevent, and Prepare (Bodeau and Graubart 2011). This hierarchy can be used to inform and categorize the appropriate resilience metrics. These are meant to be performed simultaneously, and bear a resemblance to the NIST framework mentioned earlier.

9.3.3 Metrics for ICS Networks

The above metrics were developed for "cyber" systems generally speaking, not specifically for ICSs, although they can be tailored with ICSs in mind. ICSs in particular are a unique case; in many situations, these systems have older models, and were designed for functionality rather than security (US Department of Energy 2002). They constitute a diverse group of systems that have different requirements for their various operations (Pollet 2002).

Specifically as it relates to ICSs, time, safety and continuation of services are of great importance, since many systems are in a position where a failure can result in a threat to human lives, environmental safety, or production output (Stouffer et al. 2011). Since these risks are different than those faced by information technology (IT) systems, different priorities are also necessary. Examples of some unique considerations in comparison to cyber security include the longer lifespan of system components, physically difficult to reach components, and continuous availability requirements (Stouffer et al. 2011). Additionally, these systems typically operate in separate fields than cybersecurity, such as in the gas and electric industries, and so metrics must be adapted to fit these different organizational structures (McIntyre et al. 2007). Critical infrastructures are common for ICSs, and as a result "downtime and halting of production are considered unacceptable" (McIntyre et al. 2007).

Stouffer et al. (2011) compare the differences between information technology (IT) system and ICSs, focusing on the safety-critical nature of many ICS networks. For example, "high delay and jitter may be acceptable" as a performance requirement for IT systems, whereas for ICSs, it may not be acceptable (Stouffer et al. 2011). This is due to the fact that there is a time-critical nature to ICSs, whereas for IT systems there is high throughput, allowing for some jitter (Stouffer et al. 2011). Similarly, for IT, "systems are designed for use with typical operating systems" and for ICSs, there are "differing and possibly proprietary operating systems, often without security capabilities built in". There are also availability requirements, in that sometimes an IT strategy may require restarting or rebooting a process, something which, for ICS processes, requires more careful planning as unexpected outages and quickly stopping and starting a system are not acceptable solutions (Stouffer et al. 2011). With these key differences between the two domains, there are varying levels of adaptation needed in order to begin the process of securing ICS networks.

The US National Security Agency (NSA) drafted a framework for ICS networks, focusing on potential impact and loss relating to a network compromise (NSA 2010). They suggested assigning loss metrics incorporating NIST's framework: compromises pertaining to Confidentiality, Integrity and Availability for each network asset (NSA 2010). A Confidentiality compromise is defined as an "unauthorized release or theft of sensitive information" e.g. theft of passwords (NSA 2010). An Integrity compromise is defined as an "unauthorized alteration or manipulation of data", e.g. manipulation of billing data (NSA 2010). An Availability compromise is defined as a "loss of access to the primary mission of a networked asset" e.g. deletion of important data from a database (NSA 2010).

These may also be streamlined into one metric, using the highest value (e.g., of Low, Moderate or High) among the three areas.

The assignment of a threat metrics at each potential attack vector was suggested, but specific examples were not provided. Five threat sources were identified: Insiders, Terrorists or Activists, Hackers or Cyber-Criminals, Nation/State Sponsored Cyber-Warfare and Competitors (NSA 2010). Both loss and threat metrics can be rated on a constructed scale (Low, Moderate or High) and given a numeric rating on a set scale. It was mentioned that the important consideration is to have a scale, and that the number of graduations in the scale is not important, so long as the constructed scale remains consistent (e.g. a potential for loss of life will rank as High) (NSA 2010). Combining results of metrics was also discussed as a possibility. As an example, for a given point in the network, a Loss Metric is assigned a score of High on the constructed scale (3) and a Threat metric at that same network point is rated at Moderate (2). From this, one can arrive at a composite priority value, which is simply the sum of those two scores. Other such points can be evaluated and then prioritized and ranked (NSA 2010). The scoring methodology is a basic example, (and not the only method—weighing metrics was listed as a possibility (NSA 2010)) and more robust methods can be devised.

Boyer and McQueen (2008) devised a set of ideal-based technical metrics for control systems. They examined seven security dimensions and present an ideal, or best case scenario, for each of them. The ideals are Security Group Knowledge, Attack Group Knowledge, Access, Vulnerabilities, Damage Potential, Detection, and Recovery. For the Access dimension, the ideal states that the system is inaccessible to attack groups. The security dimension of Vulnerabilities has an ideal stating that the system has no vulnerabilities (Boyer and McQueen 2008). By the very nature of an ideal, these may be impossible to achieve and maintain in the real world. But from them, metrics were devised that could best represent the realization of these ideals. Under the vulnerability dimension, the metric Vulnerability Exposure is defined as "the sum of known and unpatched vulnerabilities, each multiplied by their exposure time interval." It was suggested that this metric could be broken down into separate metrics for different vulnerability categories, as well as including a prioritization of vulnerabilities, citing CVSS. Under the Access dimension, there is the metric Root Privilege Count, which is the count of all personnel with key privileges, arguing in favor of the principle of least privilege, which states that "every program and every privileged user of the system should operate using the least amount of privilege necessary to complete the job" (Saltzer 1974). This logical ordering of metrics within the scope of ideals can be of value to those wishing to devise their own set of metrics.

The ideal-based metrics (Boyer and McQueen 2008) also acknowledge the physical space of ICS networks. The metric Rogue Change Days, which is the number of changes to the system multiplied by the number of days undetected, includes Programmable Logic Controllers and Human-Machine Interfaces and other ICS related systems. Component Test Count, a metric measuring the number of control system components which have not been tested is a simple measure, but of significance due to numerous components in use in an ICS system.

Table 9.3 Comparison between ICS metrics

	National Security Agency (2010)	Boyer and McQueen (2008)
Focus	Loss and threat focused metrics (p. 10, 15)	Quantitative technical metrics (p. 1), ideal based: attempted to have metrics that could strive toward ideal scenarios within seven security areas
Amount	Three loss metrics (per networked asset), one Threat metric (per potential attack vector)	13 total metrics (suggested total: less than 20)
Applied or theoretical	Suggests deployable metrics	Discusses both deployable and theoretical metrics (p. 10, 11)
Quantitative or qualitative	Semi-qualitative (suggests high, medium, low, with allowance for numeric attachment to these values)	Does not focus on qualitative metrics (p. 1), but on quantitative metrics
Combination of metrics	Presents method to combine results of metric scores for ranking	No combination of metrics
Consequence considerations	Loss metrics are related to confidentiality, integrity, availability	Acknowledges the purpose of security is protection of Confidentiality, Integrity and Availability (p. 4)

Within the ideals, the metric of Attack Surface (defined by Manadhata and Wing (2011) as ICS networks. The metric Rogue Change Days) was determined to not be developed enough for real world use. Boyer and McQueen further argue that "a credible quantitative measure of security risk is not currently feasible" (Boyer and McQueen 2008). But with the inclusion of a theoretical metric, and a framework for security, this demonstrates a forward thinking attitude that can be built upon by those aiming to establish their own security protocols. This represents important future work for the ICS and security communities. Comparisons between the NSA approach and the approach outlined by Boyer and McQueen are presented in Table 9.3.

Complementary research to metrics development in the ICS realm is currently being conducted. One such effort is to develop a standardized taxonomy of cyber attacks on SCADA systems (Zhu et al. 2011). A common language for describing attacks across systems can facilitate the development of further threat and vulnerability metrics for ICSs. In addition, the development of a national testbed for SCADA systems is being developed by the Department of Energy which will enable the modeling and simulation of various threat and vulnerability scenarios, which will allow researchers to develop a better understanding of what metrics may or may not be useful in monitoring and management of these systems (US Department of Energy 2009). Another development related to metrics research is the investigation of tradeoffs between certain critical metrics. One example is between optimizing system performance with system security, where additional security measures may result in reduced performance. Zeng and Chow (2012), developed an algorithmic technique to determine the optimal tradeoff between these two metrics, and the method can be extended to tradeoffs between other metrics as well.

9.4 Approaches for ICS Metrics

While various frameworks and sets of metrics exist, such as the ones mentioned in the previous section, it can be difficult for managers and system operators to decide whether to adopt or modify an existing set, or to create an entirely new set of metrics. Balancing the tradeoffs between generalizable metrics and specific system-level and component-level metrics can be challenging (Defense Science Board 2013). The following approaches provide a structured way to think about developing metrics, allowing users to leverage existing metrics but also identify gaps where new metrics may need to be created. The use of such structured and formalized processes requires the thoughtful analysis of the systems being measured, but also how they relate to the broader organizational context, such as goals, constraints, and decisions (Marr 2010). Moreover, the development of a standardized list of questions or topics helps to simplify the process of designing a metric. The development of metrics should be a smooth process, and such a list can provide insight into the "behavioral implications" of the given metrics (Neely et al. 1997).

9.4.1 Cyber Resilience Matrix Example

The first method is based on the work of Linkov et al. (2013a). Unlike traditional risk-based approaches, this approach takes a resilience-centric theme. Much has been written elsewhere on the relative merits of a resilience-focused approach (see Collier et al. 2014; DiMase et al. 2015; Linkov et al. 2013b, 2014; Roege et al. 2014), but we shall briefly summarize the argument here. Traditional risk assessment based on the triplet formulation proposed by Kaplan and Garrick (1981) becomes difficult to implement in the cybersecurity context due to the inability to frame and evaluate multiple dynamic threat scenarios, quantify vulnerability against adaptive adversaries, and estimate the long-term and widely distributed consequences of a successful attack. Instead of merely hardening the system against potential known threats in a risk-based approach, the system can be managed from the perspective of resilience, which includes the ability of one or more critical system functionalities to quickly "bounce back" to acceptable levels of performance. As a result, a resilient system can withstand and recover from a wide array of known and unknown threats through processes of feedback, adaptation, and learning.

Following this thought process, Linkov et al. (2013a) established a matrix-based method. On one axis, the steps of the event management cycle identified as necessary

Table 9.4 Generic Resilience Matrix

	Plan & prepare	Absorb	Recover	Adapt
Physical				
Information				
Cognitive				
Social				

for resilience by the National Academy of Sciences (2012) are listed, and include Plan/Prepare, Absorb, Recover, and Adapt. Note that the ability to plan/prepare is relevant before an adverse event, and the other capabilities are relevant after disruption. On the other axis are listed the four domains in which complex systems exist as identified by Alberts (2002), and include Physical, Information, Cognitive, and Social domains. The Physical domain refers to the physical resources and capabilities of the system. The Information domain refers to the information and data that characterize the Physical domain. The Cognitive domain describes the use of the other domains for decision making. Finally, the Social domain refers to the organizational structure and communication systems for transmitting information and making decisions (Alberts 2002).

Together, these axes form a set of cells that identify areas where actions can be taken in specific domains to enhance the system's overall ability to plan for, and absorb, recover, and adapt to, various threats or disruptions (Table 9.4). Each cell is designed to answer the question: "How is the system's ability to [plan/prepare for, absorb, recover from, adapt to] a cyber disruption implemented in the [physical, information, cognitive, social] domain?" (Linkov et al. 2013a).

A resulting set of 49 metrics are produced that span the various cells of the matrix, and selected metrics are shown in Table 9.5 (see Linkov et al. 2013a for the complete list). Metrics are drawn from several sources and are meant to be general and not necessarily comprehensive. For example, under Adapt and Information, a metric is stated to be "document time between problem and discovery, discovery and recovery," which has a parallel to the Mean Time to Incident Discovery within SEI's guidance. The metrics under Plan and Information, related to identifying internal and external system dependencies can be compared to the Temporal Metric of Access Complexity from CVSS, which relates to how easily a vulnerability can be exploited. The metric under Prepare and Social presents a simple yet important message that holds true in all of the frameworks: "establish a cyber-aware culture."

The resilience matrix approach described in Linkov et al. (2013a) has several strengths in that the method is relatively simple to use and once metrics have been generated, it can serve as a platform for a multi-criteria decision aid (Collier and Linkov 2014). It has the potential to serve as a scorecard in order to capture qualitative information about a system's resilience, and aid managers and technical experts in identifying gaps in the system's security. However, the resilience matrix does not capture the explicit temporal nature of resilience (i.e., mapping the critical functionality over time) or explicitly model the system itself. In this regard, it can be viewed as a high level management tool that can be used to identify a snapshot where more detailed analyses and modeling could potentially be carried out.

Table 9.5 Selected cybersecurity metrics derived from the resilience matrix (adapted from Linkov et al. 2013a)

	Plan/prepare	Absorb	Recover	Adapt
Physical	Implement controls/sensors for critical assets and services	Use redundant assets to continue service	Investigate and repair malfunctioning controls or sensors	Review asset and service configuration in response to recent event
Information	Prepare plans for storage and containment of classified or sensitive information	Effectively and efficiently transmit relevant data to responsible stakeholders/ decision makers	Review and compare systems before and after the event	Document time between problem and discovery, discovery and recovery
Cognitive	Understand performance trade-offs of organizational goals	Focus effort on identified critical assets and services	Establish decision making protocols or aids to select recovery options	Review management response and decision making processes
Social	Establish a cyber-aware culture	Locate and contact identified experts and responsible personnel	Determine liability for the organization	Evaluate employees response to event in order to determine preparedness and communications effectiveness

9.4.2 Network Simulation Example

The second method is based on modeling of complex cyber and other systems as interconnected networks, where a failure in one sector can cascade to other dependent networks and assets (Vespignani 2010). This is a reasonable assumption for ICS networks; for example, a disruption of the electrical grid can directly impact dependent sectors such as the network controlling ICS devices leading to a cascade of failures as it is believed to have happened during the Italian blackout in 2003 (Buldyrev et al. 2010). Thus the assessment of the security of a single ICS network should be viewed in the context of a larger network of interdependent systems.

Ganin et al. (2015) took this network-oriented view in developing a methodology to quantitatively assess the resilience (and thus security) of networked cyber systems. They built upon the National Academy of Sciences (2012) definition of resilience as a system property that is inherently tied to its ability to plan for, absorb, recover from, and adapt to adverse events. In order to capture the state of the system the authors propose to use the concept of critical functionality defined as a time-specific performance function of the system considered and derived based on the stakeholder's input. For instance in the network of power plants, the critical functionality might represent the total operational capacity. In the network of computers it might represent the fraction of servers and services available. Values of critical functionality are real numbers from 0 to 1. Other key elements to quantify resilience are the networked system's topology and dynamics; the range of possible adverse events (e.g., a certain damage to nodes of the network); and the control time T_C (that is the time range over which the performance of the system is evaluated). Then the dependency of the critical functionality (averaged over all adverse events) over time is built. Ganin et al. (2015) refer to this dependency as the resilience profile. As it is typically computationally prohibitive or not possible at all (in case of continuous variables defining nodes' states) to consider all the ways an adverse event can happen, it is suggested to utilize a simulation based approach with Monte-Carlo sampling.

Given its profile in normalized time (where time T_C is taken to be 1), the resilience of the network can be measured as the area under the curve (yellow region in Fig. 9.1). This allows mapping of the resilience to real values ranging between 0 and 1.

Another important property of the system is obtained by finding the minimum of the average critical functionality. Some researchers refer to this value as robustness M (Cimellaro et al. 2010), while Linkov et al. (2014) note that $1 - M$ corresponds to the measure of risk.

In their paper Ganin et al. (2015) illustrated the approach on a directed acyclic graph. Each level in this graph represents a set of nodes from certain infrastructure system (e.g. electrical grid, computers etc.). Nodes of different levels are connected by directed links representing a dependency of the destination node on the source node. In the simplest case a node in a certain level requires supply (or a dependency link) from a node in each of the upper levels and does not depend on any nodes in the lower levels. Other parameters of the model include node recovery time (T_R)—a measure of how quickly a node can return to an active state after it's been inactivated as a result of an adverse event; redundancy (p_m)—the probability controlling the number of additional potential supply links from upper levels to lower levels; and switching probability (p_s), controlling ease of replacement of a disrupted supply link with a potential supply link. These parameters could be extended to other situations to inform how a system may display resilient behavior, and thus increasing the security of the system as a whole.

The authors found that there is strong synergy between p_m and p_s; increasing both factors together produces a rapid increase in resilience, but increasing only one or

Fig. 9.1 A generalized resilience profile, where a system's resilience is equal to the area below the critical functionality curve (adapted from Ganin et al. 2015)

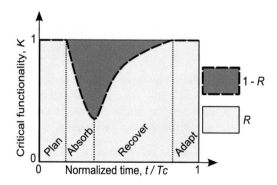

the other variable will cause the resilience metric to plateau. Resilience is strongly affected by the temporal switching time factor, T_R. This temporal factor determines the characteristics of the recovery phase and has a greater impact on the calculated resilience than does the potential increase in redundancy. This is particularly true when the switching probability p_s is low. An important long term challenge is to model adaptation, which, according to the National Academy of Sciences, is part of the response cycle that follows restoration and includes all activities that enable the system to better resist similar adverse events in the future.

Ganin et al. (2015) note that the main advantages of the approach include its applicability to any system that can be represented as a set of networks. Also both the resilience and the robustness of a system are metricized using a real value in range between 0 and 1 (where 1 corresponds to the perfect resilience or robustness) making comparison of resilience of different systems easy. On the other hand mapping the resilience property of a system to a single value necessarily shadows some system's important characteristics (for instance, the rate of recovery). The resilience profile could be used as a more holistic representation of the system's resilience noting that even in that case only the average value of critical functionality (at each time step) is taken into account. To fully describe a system one should consider the distribution of the value of critical functionality (at each time step) for different initial adverse events. Finally, it is not possible to simulate all adverse events from the range used to estimate resilience and the approach is Monte-Carlo based. It means that in order for the results to be reliable the number of simulations is typically required to be very high.

9.5 Tips for Generating Metrics

9.5.1 Generalized Metric Development Process

The following process towards the development of metrics is adapted by McKay et al. (2012).

1. Objective Setting: Articulate clear, specific goals. This should be done in a structured manner. Gregory and Keeney (2002) outline a structured approach to do this.

    (a) Write down all of the concerns that the project team feels is relevant.
    (b) Convert those concerns into succinct verb-object goals (e.g., minimize downtime).
    (c) Next, these should be organized, often hierarchically, separating goals which represent means from those which represent ends.
    (d) Finally, review and clarification should be conducted with the project team. This may be an iterative process.

2. Develop Metrics: Once the objectives are clearly articulated and organized, metrics can be formally developed.

(a) The first step is to select a broad set of metrics, which may be selected from existing lists or guidelines, or created by a project team or subject matter experts for the particular purpose at hand. This step is where the Resilience Matrix could facilitate metric development.
(b) Next, this set of metrics should be evaluated and screened to determine whether it meets the project objectives and the degree to which the metrics meet the desirable qualities of metrics, explained earlier in this chapter. At this stage, remaining metrics can be prioritized.
(c) Finally the remaining metrics should be documented, including assumptions and limitations, and other supporting information.

3. Combination and Comparison: A method should be developed for how the metrics will ultimately be used to support decision making and drive action. Some methods include:

(a) Narrative Description: Techniques where trade-offs may be simple such as listing evidence or best professional judgement.
(b) Arithmetic Combination: Simple mathematical techniques for combining dissimilar metrics such as simple aggregation of metrics with similar units (e.g., cost), converting to similar units (e.g., monetization), or normalizing to a similar scale (e.g., 0 to 1).
(c) Multi-Criteria Decision Analysis: A method for weighting and scoring dissimilar decision criteria based on their relative importance and performance with respect to an objective.
(d) Interdependent Combination: For systems that are complex, usually involving intricate internal relationships, more intensive modeling efforts may be necessary, such as Bayesian networks or other complex systems modeling techniques.

The above-mentioned process, along with a solid metric development process, can greatly aid in devising effective metrics. Often it is necessary to develop a conceptual model of the system in order to identify the functional relationships and critical elements and processes within a system. This can be done using the Network Science approach described above.

9.5.2 Best Practices in Metric Development and Validation

Validation of metrics is an often overlooked aspect of the metric development process. Neely et al. (1997) provide some questions to ask regarding whether the output from the metrics is appropriate, specifically whether the metrics have a specific purpose, are based on an explicit formula and/or data source, and are objective and not based solely on opinion (Neely et al. 1997). Similarly, Eckerson (2009) lays out a series of questions that can serve as a quality check on developed metrics, to ensure that they are of high relevance:

- Does it link to strategy?
- Can it be quantified?
- Does it drive the right behavior?
- Is it understandable?
- Is it actionable?
- Does the data exist?

Regarding the number of metrics necessary, it isn't necessarily the quantity of metrics that constitute a successful implementation, but whether these metrics are collectively comprehensive enough to address everything deemed important (McKay et al. 2012). Neely et al. (1997) provide some questions to ask regarding whether the output from the metrics is appropriate, specifically whether the metrics have a specific purpose, Eckerson (2009) recommends that a set of metrics be *sparse*, since with a limited number of metrics it is easier to analyze how metric-level changes drive the performance in the system, as well as the practical fact that gathering, synthesizing, and presenting multiple data streams often takes quite some time. More granular, process-level metrics may still be required however, and Eckerson (2009) proposes a MAD (monitor, analyze, drill) framework for presenting different levels of resolution to different users of that information.

Another ongoing element of validation is traceability, as evidenced in the framework presented by Neely et al. (1997), which includes a list of information (known as the performance measure record sheet) such as how often data is to be collected, and by whom, as well as important questions such as "who acts on the data?" and "what do they do?". If these questions are considered and answered as the need arises, it is known who is responsible for making the measurement and what actions are to be taken as a result. This can reveal insight into the metric and how they are measured and being utilized, not just for the current project but for future reference. An item on the list asks what the metric "relates to." This can assist in entering the mindset of approaching metrics with an interconnected and goal-oriented viewpoint.

Other validation-related efforts include standardizing methods for ICS metric development and implementation, as well as institutionalizing a clear means to integrate metrics with decision analytic tools to support the risk management process. Finally, given the dynamic nature of cyber threats, periodic review and updating of ICS metrics should be conducted to keep abreast of the latest developments in the field.

9.6 Summary and Conclusions

Despite existing guidelines and frameworks, designing and managing security for cyber-enabled systems remains difficult. This is in large part due to the challenges associated with the *measurement* of security. A critical element in eliciting a meaningful metric is in gathering the relevant information about one's system and aligning that metric with measurable goals and strategic objectives. For ICSs, time, safety and continuation of services factor considerably into overall goals, since many systems are in a position where a failure can result in a threat to human lives, environmental safety, or production output. Often it is necessary to develop a conceptual model of the system or develop a standardized list of questions or topics which helps to identify critical process elements, the functional relationships and critical elements and processes within a system. In this chapter, we discuss in detail two approaches for the generation of broadly applicable security and resilience metrics and their integration to quantify system resilience. The first method is a semi-quantitative approach in which the stages of the event management cycle (plan/prepare, absorb, recover, and adapt) are applied across four relevant domains (physical, information, cognitive, social), forming a matrix of potential security metrics. Second is a quantitative approach based on Network Science, in which features such as network topologies can be modeled to assess the magnitude and responsiveness of the critical functionalities of networked systems. Validation of metrics is an often overlooked aspect of the metric development process; however a series of questions can serve as a quality check on developed metrics.

References

Alberts, D. S. (2002). *Information age transformation, getting to a 21st century military.* Washington, DC: DOD Command and Control Research Program. Retrieved from http://www.dtic.mil/get-tr-doc/pdf?AD=ADA457904.

Allen, J., & Curtis, P. (2011). *Measures for managing operational resilience.* Pittsburgh, PA: Software Engineering Institute, Carnegie Mellon University. Retrieved from http://www.sei.cmu.edu/reports/11tr019.pdf.

Beasley, M. S., Branson, B. C., & Hancock, B. V. (2010). *Building key risk indicators to strengthen enterprise risk management.* Durham, NC: The Committee of Sponsoring Organizations of the Treadway Commission (COSO).

Black, P., Scarfone, K., & Souppaya, M. (2008). Cyber security metrics and measures. In J. G. Voeller (Ed.), *Handbook of science and technology for homeland security* (Vol. 5). Hoboken, NJ: John Wiley and Sons, Inc.

Bodeau, D., & Graubart, R. (2011). *MITRE cyber resiliency engineering framework, MTR110237.* Bedford, MA: MITRE Corporation. Retrieved from http://www.mitre.org/sites/default/files/pdf/11_4436.pdf.

Boyer, W., & McQueen, M. (2008). *Ideal based cyber security technical metrics for control systems.* Retrieved from http://www.if.uidaho.edu/~amm/faculty/Ideal%20Based%20Cyber%20Security%20Technical%20Metrics%20for%20Control%20Systems.pdf.

Buldyrev, S. V., Parshani, R., Paul, G., Stanley, H. E., & Havlin, S. (2010). Catastrophic cascade of failures in interdependent networks. *Nature, 464,* 1025–1028.

Cimellaro, G. P., Reinhorn, A. M., & Bruneau, M. (2010). Framework for analytical quantification of disaster resilience. *Engineering Structures, 32,* 3639–3649.

CIS (The Center for Internet Security). (2010). *The CIS security metrics v1.1.0..* East Greenbush, NY: The Center for Internet Security. Retrieved from https://benchmarks.cisecurity.org/tools2/metrics/CIS_Security_Metrics_v1.1.0.pdf.

Collier, Z.A., & Linkov, I. (2014). *Decision making for resilience within the context of network centric operations.* 19th international command and control research and technology symposium (ICCRTS), June 16–19, Alexandria, VA, USA.

Collier, Z. A., Linkov, I., DiMase, D., Walters, S., Tehranipoor, M., & Lambert, J. H. (2014). Cybersecurity standards: Managing risk and creating resilience. *Computer, 47*(9), 70–76.

Defense Science Board. (2013). *Task force report: Resilient military systems and the advanced cyber threat*. Washington, DC: Office of the Under Secretary of Defense for Acquisition, Technology, and Logistics. Retrieved from http://www.acq.osd.mil/dsb/reports/ResilientMilitarySystems.CyberThreat.pdf.

DiMase, D., Collier, Z. A., Heffner, K., & Linkov, I. (2015). Systems engineering framework for cyber physical security and resilience. *Environment Systems & Decisions, 35*(2), 291–300.

Eckerson, W. W. (2009). *Performance management strategies: How to create and deploy effective metrics. TDWI best practices report*. Renton, WA: The Data Warehousing Institute. Retrieved from https://tdwi.org/research/2009/01/bpr-1q-performance-management-strategies.aspx.

Executive Order No. 13636 (2013). *Improving critical infrastructure cybersecurity*. Retrieved from http://www.gpo.gov/fdsys/pkg/FR-2013-02-19/pdf/2013-03915.pdf.

Ganin, A.A., Massaro, E., Gutfraind, A., Steen, N., Keisler, J.M., Kott, A., et al. (2015). *Resilient complex systems and networks: Concepts, design, and analysis*. Nature scientific reports, submitted.

Gregory, R. S., & Keeney, R. L. (2002). Making smarter environmental management decisions. *Journal of the American Water Resources Association, 38*(6), 1601–1612.

Igure, V., Laughter, S., & Williams, R. (2006). Security issues in SCADA networks. *Computers and Society, 25*(7), 498–506.

Kaplan, S., & Garrick, B. J. (1981). On the quantitative definition of risk. *Risk Analysis, 1*(1), 11–27.

Keeney, R. L., & Gregory, R. S. (2005). Selecting attributes to measure the achievement of objectives. *Operations Research, 53*(1), 1–11.

Linkov, I., Bridges, T., Creutzig, F., Decker, J., Fox-Lent, C., Kröger, W., et al. (2014). Changing the resilience paradigm. *Nature Climate Change, 4*, 407–409.

Linkov, I., Eisenberg, D. A., Bates, M. E., Chang, D., Convertino, M., Allen, J. H., et al. (2013a). Measurable resilience for actionable policy. *Environmental Science & Technology, 47*(18), 10108–10110.

Linkov, I., Eisenberg, D. A., Plourde, K., Seager, T. P., Allen, J., & Kott, A. (2013b). Resilience metrics for cyber systems. *Environment Systems & Decisions, 33*(4), 471–476.

Manadhata, P. K., & Wing, J. M. (2011). An attack surface metric. *IEEE Transactions on Software Engineering, 37*(3), 371–386.

Marr, B. (2010). *How to design key performance indicators*. Milton Keynes, UK: The Advanced Performance Institute. Retrieved from www.ap-institute.com.

McIntyre, A., Becker, B., & Halbgewachs, R. (2007). *Security metrics for process control systems. SAND2007-2070P*. Albuquerque, NM: Sandia National Laboratories, U.S. Department of Energy.

McKay, S. K., Linkov, I., Fischenich, J. C., Miller, S. J., & Valverde, L. J., Jr. (2012). *Ecosystem restoration objectives and metrics, ERDC TN-EMRRP-EBA-12-16*. Vicksburg, MS: U.S. Army Engineer Research and Development Center.

Mell, P., Scarfone, K., & Romanosky, S. (2007). *A complete guide to the common vulnerability scoring system version 2.0*. Morrisville, NC: Forum for Incident Response and Security Teams. Retrieved from https://www.first.org/cvss/cvss-guide.pdf.

National Academy of Sciences (2012). Disaster resilience: a national imperative. National Academic Press, Washington.

National Security Agency (NSA) (2010). *A framework for assessing and improving the security posture of industrial control systems (ICS)*. Retrieved from https://www.nsa.gov/ia/_files/ics/ics_fact_sheet.pdf.

Neely, A., Richards, H., Mills, J., Platts, K., & Bourne, M. (1997). Designing performance measures: A structured approach. *International Journal of Operations & Production Management, 17*(11), 1131–1152.

NIST. (2014). *Framework for improving critical infrastructure cyber security. Version 1.0*. Gaithersburg, MD: National Institute of Standards and Technology. Retrieved from http://www.nist.gov/cyberframework/upload/cybersecurity-framework-021214-final.pdf.

Pfleeger, S. L., & Cunningham, R. K. (2010). Why measuring security is hard. *IEEE Security & Privacy, 8*(4), 46–54.

Pollet, J. (2002). *Developing a solid SCADA strategy.* Sicon/02—Sensors for industry conference, November 19–21, 2002, Houston, Texas, USA.

Reichert, P., Borsuk, M., Hostmann, M., Schweizer, S., Sporri, C., Tockner, K., et al. (2007). Concepts of decision support for river rehabilitation. *Environmental Modeling and Software, 22*, 188–201.

Roege, P. E., Collier, Z. A., Mancillas, J., McDonagh, J. A., & Linkov, I. (2014). Metrics for energy resilience. *Energy Policy, 72*(1), 249–256.

Saltzer, J. H. (1974). Protection and the control of information sharing in Multics. *Communications of the ACM, 17*(7), 388–402.

Stouffer, K., Falco, J., & Scarfone, K. (2011). *Guide to industrial control systems (ICS) security. Special Publication 800-82.* Gaithersburg, MD: National Institute of Standards. Retrieved from http://csrc.nist.gov/publications/nistpubs/800-82/SP800-82-final.pdf.

US Department of Energy. (2002). *21 steps to improve cyber security of SCADA networks.* Washington, DC: US Department of Energy. Retrieved from http://energy.gov/sites/prod/files/oeprod/DocumentsandMedia/21_Steps_-_SCADA.pdf.

US Department of Energy. (2009). *National SCADA test bed: Enhancing control systems security in the energy sector.* Washington, DC: US Department of Energy. Retrieved from http://energy.gov/sites/prod/files/oeprod/DocumentsandMedia/NSTB_Fact_Sheet_FINAL_09-16-09.pdf.

Vespignani, A. (2010). Complex networks: The fragility of interdependency. *Nature, 464*(7291), 984–985.

Williamson, R. M. (2006). *What gets measured gets done: Are you measuring what really matters?* Columbus, NC: Strategic Work Systems, Inc.. Retrieved from www.swspitcrew.com.

Zeng, W., & Chow, M. Y. (2012). Optimal tradeoff between performance and security in networked control systems based on coevolutionary algorithms. *IEEE Transactions on Industrial Electronics, 59*(7), 3016–3025.

Zhu, B., Joseph, A., & Sastry, S. (2011). *A taxonomy of cyber attacks on SCADA systems.* In *Internet of things (iThings/CPSCom), 2011 International conference on cyber, physical and social computing* (pp. 380–388).

Chapter 10
Situational Awareness in Industrial Control Systems

Blaine Hoffman, Norbou Buchler, Bharat Doshi, and Hasan Cam

10.1 Introduction

This chapter discusses Situation Awareness (SA)—science, technology and practice of human perception, comprehension and projection of events and entities in the relevant environment—in our case cyber defense of ICS. The chapter delves into SA's scope, and its roles in the success of the mission carried out by the cyber-physical-human system (CPHS) and processes that an Industrial Control System (ICS) or Supervisory Control and Data Acquisition (SCADA) system supports. Such control systems provide the cyber-physical-human couplings needed to collect information from various sensors and devices and provide a reporting and control interface for effective human-in-the-loop involvement in managing and securing the physical elements of production and critical infrastructure. ICS implementations are involved at various scales necessary for the proper functioning of our society, including water distribution, electrical power, and sewage systems (Smith 2014). Civil society depends upon such systems to be properly operated, and malicious cybersecurity threats to ICS have the potential to cause great harm. The characteristics of ICS environments add additional considerations and challenges for defenders. Cybersecurity operations typically require a human analyst to understand the network environment and the attackers. In defending an ICS environment,

---

B. Hoffman (✉) • N. Buchler
Human Research and Engineering Directorate, US Army Research Laboratory USA
e-mail: blaine.e.hoffman.ctr@mail.mil

H. Cam
Computational and Information Sciences Directorate, US Army Research Laboratory USA

B. Doshi
Senior Research Scientist, US Army USA

© Springer International Publishing Switzerland 2016
E.J.M. Colbert, A. Kott (eds.), *Cyber-security of SCADA and Other Industrial Control Systems*, Advances in Information Security 66,
DOI 10.1007/978-3-319-32125-7_10

however, an analyst must also understand the physical dimension of the ICS environment. This poses serious challenges to maintaining cybersecurity and SA as it spans the human, cyber, and physical dimensions and a myriad of possible interactions and exploits. Maintaining SA is critical to the cybersecurity of an ICS. This chapter addresses the specific challenges posed by the physical, cyber, and human dimensions that must be considered and understood in order for human analysts to best assess and understand the requirements to successfully defend against potential attacks. We demonstrate that these requirements can be defined as focal features for developing and maintaining SA for the cyber analyst in ICS environments.

SA is extremely important to human decision-making in operational contexts; the analyst must know what is happening to increase the speed and effectiveness of decision-making and determine how best to mitigate threats in the future. SA can depend upon the specific context of the mission and the role of the individual within that mission. Sensors and operational data provide the raw material about what is going on. Analytics and human intelligence convert that into an understanding of what is going on, how it impacts the mission, and what actions effectively achieve a desired outcome. Theoretically, Mica Endsley (Endsley 1995) conceptualized SA as a cumulative three level model: Level 1 is the *perception* of the elements of the environment within a volume of time and space, Level 2 is the *comprehension* of their meaning, and Level 3 is the *projection* of their status in the near future. Related to the SA hierarchy is the processing framework of data, information, knowledge, understanding, and wisdom (Ackoff 1989). It is evident that increased processing and analysis is necessary for advancing levels of SA from perception, comprehension, and projection in the Endsley model.

Beyond management and information collection, human cognition and reasoning are required to piece together the overall picture and make sense of what is happening, ascertain potential implications, and reasonably predict what is likely to happen next. For the foreseeable future, artificial intelligence capabilities are still emerging and are unlikely to handle the task of managing safety critical systems without human-in-the-loop oversight. As a result, humans are essential in the development of optimal SA, regardless of the domain, requiring an increasing need for human cognition across the three levels. Perception implies monitoring, recognition, and identification of the current states of critical elements. Comprehension involves understanding the big picture impacts to the mission, interpretation, and evaluation against targets and goals. Projection involves understanding future systems impacts, generating proactive actions, and predicting future states. The development of SA is context dependent and requires adjusting to the cyber-physical domain, mission requirements, and system specifications. In ICS, information spans multiple domains and levels of abstraction, introducing a complexity in analyzing it and comprehending it properly.

10.2   Cyber-Physical Systems are Complex

Human challenges in managing and maintaining SA of cyber-physical systems stems from the multi-layered complexity of the environment. These multiple-layers of abstraction are composed of interfaces, computer systems, networked devices, and sensors. A key challenge facing cyber defenders is the need to maintain and integrate SA across multiple layers. Sensing and understanding one's current physical environment is both direct and immediate; one simply observes, his or her perceptual system attuned to changes as they occur without abstraction. Digital environments are also directly observed by the human, but require human-computer interaction as mediated by the use of a computer to maintain awareness and affect control. Cyber environments introduce an additional layer of networked complexity to the digital interactions, including a network environment monitored and controlled through one or more computer systems. Cyber-physical environments, such as in ICS, are further abstracted by the use of networked sensors; a simplified representation is shown in Fig. 10.1. The physical nature of the environment is recorded and reported by sensors and devices, which in turn are monitored and connected via some kind of network accessed by another network and/or a computer through which the human finally observes information about the environment. In this context, the sensors refer to the devices directly paired with physical elements of the environment, and those related to monitoring the cyber network itself are conceptually rolled into the network item. We refer to this model as the Chain of Situation Awareness, shown in Table 10.1.

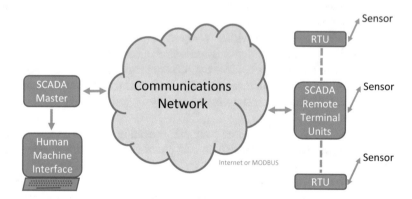

Fig. 10.1 Simplified representation of an ICS/SCADA system

Table 10.1 Examples of the chain of situation awareness

Chain of situation awareness	
Physical	Human—World
Digital	Human—Computer
Cyber network	Human—Computer—Network
Cyber-physical system	Human—Computer—Network—Sensors—World

Increasingly complex environments introduce additional layers of abstraction in maintaining SA. The many layers to a cyber-physical system increase the overall attack surface and highlight additional vulnerabilities or points of failure for exploitation and deception. With so many dependencies, the attack surface is increased, and human understanding of causality is continually challenged. Maintaining good SA requires commanding expertise to assess and integrate across the overall chain rather than a single segment. It also means there is increased potential for mistakes. In a complex cyber-physical system, for instance, an abnormal sensor reading could be due to a faulty sensor, network tampering, or the installation of malware. When the potentially devastating consequences of tampering with, disabling, or destroying ICS services and infrastructures are taken into consideration, not addressing these significant human-in-the-loop challenges is simply not an option. ICS intrusions could mean the loss of power and electrical services (Govindarasu et al. 2012; Mo et al. 2011), damage to the environment (Abrams and Weiss 2008; Weiss 2008), and the destruction of nuclear facilities (Langner 2011; Matrosov et al. 2011). For instance, on August 14th, 2003 an electrical blackout plunged much of the northeastern United States into darkness, affecting over 50 million people and costing over six billion dollars; forensic analysis of the available data suggests that it could have been prevented with adequate SA among the human operators (Marchelli 2011). One attack involved a disgruntled ex-employee of an Australian sewage control company who interfered with the system 46 times before being identified, causing pumps to fail, alarms not to trigger, and sewage to flood the nearby environment (Abrams and Weiss 2008; Weiss 2008).

The interconnected web of computers, workstations, monitors, sensors, valves, switches, and so on expands the attack surface that cyber defenders need to navigate and observe. Independently, individual components of the system may be engineered for specific functions, straightforward with respect to their use and effects on the environment. In the aggregate, however, ICSs are complex and essentially nondeterministic in nature when human variability is introduced through the interactions of attackers, defenders, and users. Variability is compounded by computer operating system use.

Both the human and the networked computer operating systems introduce variability and are essentially uncontrolled control processes. Humans will bring with them assumptions about the system and environment. Assumptions range from naïve to functional as they can serve to simplify and reduce the problem dimensions. Assumptions also often favor convenience over consequence analysis. Ultimately, they lead to incorrect understandings of reality by both defenders and users, including knowledge of the domains involved and likely consequences, and can contribute to human errors, such as misconfigurations that introduce new vulnerabilities into the system. Computers provide a means to alter, update, and break the control logic of the system through a range of interactions, including unintentional errors by users and intentional alterations from attackers.

Constructing SA within ICS requires overcoming deficient assumptions and knowledge gaps to better understand and comprehend the pertinent risks and shortcomings. It is not sufficient to know what function a device serves within the system; knowing how it connects to and exerts control over others is also necessary. Likewise, control and maintenance of the whole environment requires traversing each of the involved layers of abstraction and understanding the relationships that exist among and between the layers. Access and control in one may grant access and control in others, and similarly failure in one may result in failures across the board. There is a cascading nature to failures in a complex system like an ICS (Helbing 2013), making the complexity of understanding consequences non-linear and emphasizing the need for sufficient SA. Human reasoning and cognition are the key to developing optimal SA within ICS environments, enabling the human agents accessing the environment through the multiple levels of abstraction representing it to project appropriate consequences and enact successful action plans.

10.3   SA as a Human-driven Process

SA relies on the use of all of the relevant data in order to know the truth of the world. With the right data, the facts can be perceived such that proper comprehension of the situation is built. Thus, the first level of SA is bolstered by data fusion and analysis. Data fusion has been described and modeled as a framework for the construction of a comprehensive, sensor-based aggregation system to support human analysts (Kessler et al. 1991). The various sensors and field devices involved in ICS present a wealth of information about the environment itself. Depending on the enterprise, the data may also include network relationships and interactions, and the mission may define specific, appropriate contexts. The information can be identified and defined through patterns and relationships, and tools can be used to automate data collection and presentation, directly supporting the perception phase of SA. However, tools and automation lack the cognitive and reasoning capabilities to achieve SA, necessitating human involvement (Biros and Eppich 2001; Blasch et al. 2011).

The idea of cognitive information fusion integrates data fusion further with SA, emphasizing the necessity and strength of the human element in order to perceive the truth of a given situation—the human is at the center of the driving force that enacts changes to the environment and processes information in order to facilitate appropriate data-to-decision paths (Bedny and Meister 1999; Blasch 2008; Blasch et al. 2011; Endsley 1995; Giacobe 2010; Smith and Hancock 1995). What is described, then, is a human-on-the-loop scenario wherein human agents can focus on higher-level analysis of data rather than fine-grained data in large volumes (Albanese et al. 2014). The better the process and information collection, the better the humans involved can identify and react to rapidly evolving security scenarios and events.

Considering what makes a process of establishing SA in the cybersecurity of ICS "better" leads to two pertinent questions. First, how can the challenges of ICS be highlighted and met by defense efforts? Typically, SA is not sufficiently addressed within ICS settings (Govindarasu et al. 2012; Mo et al. 2011). Perhaps this is in part due to the immense amount of relevant information required to maintain SA. ICS command and control monitoring must be integrated with security thresholds in relevant tools, alert configuration, and data fusion processes if SA is to be properly constructed (Skare 2013). The challenges arise not only in the volume of the information but in the aforementioned layers of abstraction and complexity embedded in the association of these layers required for navigating and observing the attack space. Second, how do you evaluate the quality of SA within a defensive effort? Cybersecurity is an adversarial space, involving interactions among and between users, attackers, and defenders. Understanding the human elements will support understanding and evaluating SA development. Answers to both of these question spaces can be found in modeling the process, detailing the information, steps, and individuals involved relevant to data-to-decision paths.

By modeling cyber defense and ICS scenarios, we can establish an understanding of how strategies affect outcomes and how sensor placement and monitoring influences comprehension of evolving situations. For example, consider the speed with which defenders are able to mount a response. Intrusions are more successful the longer it takes to detect and stop them; the quicker an analyst can identify what is happening and consider potential mitigation strategies the quicker appropriate measures can be taken to stop the intrusion. The decision making process benefits from selecting a suitable course of action without taking the time required to exhaustively search for the absolute best solution (Klein 1989; Klein et al. 1986). Humans are ideally suited for this skill, following their hunches when "something just doesn't look right". A macro-level cognitive process that considers heuristics and less reliance on precise observations may benefit a more rapid response.

Such rapid assessment and decision making can be modeled within the concept of an OODA loop (observe, orient, decide, act). John Boyd, a fighter pilot, observed how capitalizing on an efficient and rapid OODA process enabled superior action in dogfighting, reaching conclusions before the enemy could observe and orient themselves (Boyd 1987). The OODA loop represents an understanding of how the humans involved interpret and comprehend a situation, and the decisions that lead to actions rely on that understanding. OODA then can be used for modeling within information fusion, military systems, and semi-automated decision-making processes, for example (Blasch et al. 2011). In military settings, such as Boyd's, the OODA loop is a simple representation of a control process, and extensions of the concept, such as the Cognitive Observe-Orient-Decide-Act (C-OODA) model, enable modeling of user and team analysis in the context of the Data Fusion Information Group (DFIG) Information Fusion model (Blasch et al. 2011). The development of appropriate SA from data fusion techniques and tools can be modeled within the O-O portion of the process for the involved users, and the execution of defense strategies against intrusions is represented within the D-A portion.

The OODA loop is one way to model the human process of establishing SA, focusing on the defenders and their understanding of the environment as time progresses. Another is to directly model the adversary, helping enable defenders to evaluate their own networks relative to the likely reconnaissance and intrusions directed their way. In fact, establishing information about the attacker is one way to create superior SA. However, describing the attacker in detail is difficult, due in no small part to the nature of gathering evidence. Evidence can be scattered across events, and often the human agent has to attempt to properly piece it back together to create the whole picture. Without doing so, some missed data point or log item may lead to the wrong conclusion, i.e. a less ideal perception and comprehension of the situation, which may motivate the wrong action plan. Establishing correct situation perception includes asking and answering several questions about what is happening, how a situation is evolving, and what are the impacts (Albanese et al. 2014). Of particular interest are those that focus on the attacker(s)—what appears to be the strategy of attack? Where is it coming from (perhaps helping to answer who is attacking?)? If available, the information gleaned from these questions can serve to build a foundation for establishing the end goal of the attack and identifying what is actually happening when evidence is pieced together. Of course, this information may not be readily available. No attacker is going to announce him- or herself ahead of time, but there may be patterns or clues that suggest behavior and intent. Regardless, the onus is still on the human agent to piece the information together in order to try to predict attacker behavior, identify strategies, and predict plausible paths from the current situation. In other words, understanding the attacker is a deductive process reliant on analysts' skills that can model potential projections for a given situation (Albanese et al. 2014).

Modeling attackers with respect to ICS environments can explicate the features that make ICS cyber defense more challenging. For example, attackers targeting ICS devices likely possess a level of knowledge relevant and required in order to properly harm and exploit them. Additionally, they may have domain knowledge that includes the physical locations involved, which PCMs and HMI elements are embedded throughout the system, and where weaknesses exist. Attack models may include backdoors present from unpatched systems and misconfigurations or put in place by malicious insiders, enabling an attacker to pivot from some attack vector to the device(s) needed to exploit the ultimate target (Mo et al. 2011). Unlike a more typical intrusion scenario, the motive may not be financial reasons but, instead, a desire to disrupt the infrastructure(s) supported and cause physical damage and societal harm. It is likely there is a clear, directed intent in an intrusion aimed at ICS environments beyond what is normally seen in typical cyber attacks.

The other goal is to evaluate SA development and maintenance. Models can help to suggest how well-equipped defenders are with the information needed to assess a situation, suggesting opportunities to perceive, comprehend, and project scenarios as they evolve. These models and analysis of attacks can be paired with an assessment of ongoing defense efforts in order to reveal the effectiveness of the defense. The idea here is that a successful defense was able to build upon appropriate SA. More importantly, the sooner an intrusion is identified and mitigated, the better off the systems involved are. There are two points to the evaluation, then: (1) was the attack mitigated, and (2) how far did it progress before being stopped?

10.4 Cyber Kill Chain: Adversarial Reasoning

The "cyber kill chain" idea enables the evaluation of incident response and protection efforts—the further along the chain before an intrusion is detected and an action applied, the less successful defense efforts have been. The cyber kill chain model has its roots in military doctrine, evolving from the Air Force's six-stage cycle useful for analyzing mission success, referred to as the kill chain (Hebert 2003). Its original development was motivated by the desire to minimize, or compress, the time required between identifying a target and eliminating it (Hebert 2003; Stotz and Sudit 2007) and has been applied in the evaluation of surveillance, intelligence, and reconnaissance capabilities (Tirpak 2000; U.S. Department of Defense 2007). The use of a phased model like the kill chain enables an understanding of both the attacker/attack type and contextual information with which defenders can more effectively approach a situation or problem. The Air Force has used a Department of Defense kill chain model to evaluate Intelligence, Surveillance, and Reconnaissance capabilities (Tirpak 2000; U.S. Department of Defense 2007), and they have been used to model improvised explosive device (IED) attacks, accounting for everything from attacker funding to delivery and execution (National Research Council 2007). They are effective in emphasizing the data needed in order to make decisions, enabling human agents to draw appropriate conclusions and enact better plans of action. In other words, using and understanding a kill chain model affords superior SA.

Researchers at Lockheed Martin refined and presented a cyber version of the kill chain and this version has become the standard for the cyber realm. An intrusion is rarely ever a singular event, making a phased progression model an appropriate way to investigate them. The chain is an integrated, end-to-end model wherein any successful defense breaks the chain and interrupts the process (Hutchins et al. 2011a, b). By creating a chain for cyber events, one can illustrate the behavior of cyber attackers as well as offer a framework with which organizations can evaluate their defensive efforts. Understanding the phases of the cyber kill chain can clarify where and how the perception and orientation processes of defenders need to be improved in order to support decision-making and action. In part, following along the phases of the chain also invites comparison between the efforts of attackers and defenders, the further along the chain directly relating to the latter having a slower or inadequate OODA process. Within the context of ICS, the chain can help direct attention to difficulties navigating through the layers of abstraction to observe the environment, lack of knowledge or poor assumptions that prevent proper comprehension of evolving scenarios, and an inability fully or adequately piece together evidence and disparate vulnerabilities into an accurate projection of overall risk and consequences.

The chain begins with initial reconnaissance, the stage wherein an opposing force probes a network or system for weaknesses, points of entry, viable targets, etc. It ends with a successful attack action, such as intellectual property or PII being taken, systems disabled, business interrupted or re-directed, etc. (Hutchins et al. 2011a, b). We present a brief summary of the cyber kill chain stages in Table 10.2; more detail can be found in (Hutchins et al. 2011a, b).

Table 10.2 The phases of the cyber kill chain (Hutchins et al. 2011a, b)

Phase	Description	Examples/methods
Reconnaissance	Probing; researching and identifying targets	Exploring websites, mailing lists, social engineering
Delivery/attack	"Weaponization"—crafting the attack using the recon intel; creating the payload that will carry out some exploit on the target(s)	Crafting a Trojan inside a legitimate-looking file
	The actual transmission of the payload to the target environment	USB sticks, email attachments
Exploitation	Executing the code needed to capitalize on a vulnerability, gaining access to a network or system or group of machines	Capitalizes on target vulnerability (zero-day exploit, known software bug)
Installation	Once within the target system, installation enables attackers to deliver the necessary payloads (applications, DLLs, configurations) to elevate their user privileges and persist within the network	Capitalizes on exploit to run code with escalated privileges, delivers malicious code from payload or external source
Command and control	Once sufficient access is achieved, the intruder can establish communication with external servers to carry out additional instructions and escalate attacks	Network connections, modification of target to enable communication and code execution
Action	At this point, the primary goal is achieved, and defense becomes more a matter of recovery than prevention	Data exfiltrated to a remote IP, system or service shut down, physical harm to target device/network/business

These phases in the chain cover the basic steps behind successful attacks, and each of these steps can be modeled and represented in order to dynamically analyze distributed control systems and SA. One means to model that chain is to use a Petri net, a representation of an ICS process and its evolution using a five-tuple (P, T, F, M_o, λ) (Caldero et al. 2011; Zeng et al. 2012). Within Petri net models, the P represents the set of places describing network states and transition conditions, while T is the set of transitions. These places represent attributes of hosts, including privilege levels, services, trust relationships, and connectivity. The characterization of hosts within the modeled system is handled by the use of marking tokens within the corresponding place; thus, an initial marking (M_o) evolves over time as transitions occur. The phases of the kill chain can be directly represented by the transitions, with the environment state depicted by the marking of tokens within places.

Appropriate SA benefits from awareness and identification of vulnerabilities in a system as well as comprehension of how the impact of a potential attack or exploitation will ripple throughout and influence the overall mission. The marking of tokens

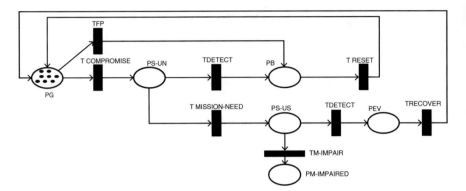

Fig. 10.2 Time Petri Net (TPN) modeling the impact of attacks on assets (Cam et al. 2014)

within places reveals the state of the environment with respect to the conditions of an attack; the connections in the model from a place to a transition and to a place from a transition represent the pre- and post-conditions of attacks (Henry et al. 2009). Using the Petri net visualization, defenders can perceive the status of their assets and project potential future states, interpreted through the token marking and placement/transition relationships. The impact of attacks can be assessed through attack modeling, using places to represent various potential statuses of mission assets during an attack, a technique known as Time Petri Net (TPN) (Cam et al. 2014). Within a TPN model, mission assets are characterized based on whether or not they have been compromised. As shown in Fig. 10.2, all assets begin in the "Good" (uncompromised) set, and as conditions are satisfied to fire transitions they are moved accordingly based on their necessity to the mission, whether a compromise is suspected or confirmed, and whether compromised assets have been repaired and reset to an uncompromised state.

Running a TPN model over attack scenarios against the cyber-physical system enables defenders to explicate the potential transitions and conditions that enable attacks and exploits to escalate across assets and to observe attack progression in real-time. The state changes, as represented by the movement of tokens among places across transitions in the model, visualize the kill chain path, providing feedback on defense capabilities and suggesting areas where additional understanding and comprehension of attack properties and features need to be studied and recognized.

Being aware of the characteristics and indicators that are associated with exploits may increase the chances of detecting them more quickly. By recognizing evidence of an attack and being able to categorize it to the appropriate kill chain phase, an organization is better able to discover and close holes before the actual action intended by the intrusion is completed. In other words, even if resources or expertise is lacking to address all stages with equal vigor, being aware of them and approaching security with them in mind is beneficial to maximizing effective response. Likewise, couching an analysis of a cyber intrusion within the cyber kill chain highlights where the attack was successful and how defensive efforts stack up against it appropriately.

10.5 Stuxnet Through the Cyber Kill Chain: An ICS Example

In 2010, motivated hackers partnered well-designed code with social engineering efforts to capitalize on vulnerabilities within an ICS environment. They established a presence within victim networks and attacked programmable logic controllers (PLCs), causing centrifuges controlled by the ICS devices to spin out of control to the point of self-destruction. This attack became known as Stuxnet, named after the worm and exploits involved, and it serves as a prime example of the challenges faced in securing ICS/SCADA systems in the modern, networked world (Karnouskos 2011; Matrosov et al. 2011).

Discovered in July 2010, Stuxnet was estimated to have infected 100,000 computers, targeting machines residing within ICS for nuclear centrifuges (Chen and Abu-Nimeh 2011; Karnouskos 2011; Langner 2011; Matrosov et al. 2011). Additionally, unlike attacks motivated by espionage or economic gains, Stuxnet was arguably "the first cyber-warfare weapon ever", as it "didn't steal, manipulate, or erase information. Rather, Stuxnet's goal was to physically destroy a military target—not just metaphorically, but literally" (Langner 2011, p. 49). Malware and malicious intrusions via worms were not new to the IT and security industries, yet researchers who have studied Stuxnet since its release agree that it was an unprecedented cyber-attack involving a level of planning and organization not typical of malware distribution. As a result, the understanding and awareness of what was happening as it spread throughout systems was insufficient, enabling Stuxnet to carry out its exploit before being detected and mitigated. We can discuss Stuxnet through the lens of the cyber kill chain to enumerate how the ICS environment increases the complexity of SA.

10.5.1 Phase 1: Recon and Probing—Stuxnet Development

The first phase of any attack is one of scouting and reconnaissance in order to plan an appropriate course of action. Within the cyber realm, this typically means searching for exploitable points within a network or system and designing code to capitalize on it. Research exploring Stuxnet code suggests that it was produced by multiple authors bringing together their collective—and relevant—expertise to different parts of the attack, reflecting a huge investment in time and cost (Chen and Abu-Nimeh 2011; Karnouskos 2011; Matrosov et al. 2011). The eventual victims of it were specific PLCs. To ensure success, Stuxnet's developers would have had to have been familiar with their target PLC's configuration, probably relying on access to similar hardware to test and improve their code (Chen and Abu-Nimeh 2011).

In general, it is difficult to detect an attack before it has been launched. For the defenders of these networks, there may have been no indications that an attack on their PLCs was being designed and constructed. Moreover, the sophistication and planning behind Stuxnet suggest it was highly customized for specific industrial systems. In this case, the attackers had a greater SA through the use of their domain knowledge and expertise. It is difficult to say for certain how the defenders' SA was affected at this phase, but that does not mean no SA can be established.

As outlined, the cyber-physical nature of ICS imposes additional levels of abstraction with respect to observing the relevant world. In order to properly understand what is being observed vs. what is actually happening, the human agents need to understand the components involved in monitoring and representing the environment, including how they might be compromised and how to verify the validity of information. Assumptions must also be challenged, such as the notion of an air gap providing sufficient protection against malicious activity when connections within and across networks exist (Karnouskos 2011; Matrosov et al. 2011). For the defenders, recon and probing should include performing penetration tests on their own networks and running security audits to evaluate best practices and assess defense efforts. By modeling potential attackers and potential avenues of exploitation, defenders can identify gaps in detection and better understand ICS characteristics. Cyber-defense is often reactive, but regular evaluation can at least minimize the chance for error in processing and comprehending a real situation when it arises. Defenders must know what adversaries may be looking for and what relative vulnerabilities exist or might exist. Previous experience, domain knowledge, and regular self-evaluation will enable conjecture of possible exploit paths.

Other evidence may suggest probing by attackers, such as web analytics and traffic to external-facing sites of the company. Stuxnet's designers had knowledge of ICS environments; running an analysis of internal network traffic and searches may also reveal probing actions. Staying on top of information in the early stages of a situation can enable defenders to block or prevent the attack from progressing, even if they don't have knowledge of the ultimate goal.

10.5.2   Phase 2: Stuxnet Delivery

The primary delivery of Stuxnet to the victim networks was via USB drives, likely via social engineering techniques. To avoid suspicion, these USB drives were given a sense of legitimacy with two digitally signed certificates, relying on the reputation of global certificate-granting services for digital entities (Chen and Abu-Nimeh 2011; Matrosov et al. 2011). Two human assumptions were exploited in order for Stuxnet to be successfully delivered: (1) that the PLCs and workstations within the ICS were not directly connected to the Internet and, thus, not vulnerable to outside attack and (2) digital signatures imply benign intent.

Stuxnet is a good example of users and defenders of the ICS holding an improper mental model of security. While unintentional, the fact that employees likely introduced Stuxnet to the victim networks via USB drives shows that the cyber-physical defense of the ICS was insufficient. Stuxnet was not the first attack to make use of auto-run capabilities, yet the Windows-based workstations originally infected had no policies or controls on the connection of these drives. Related to the recommendations of Phase 1, defender (and user) SA would benefit from conducting in-house pen testing and brainstorming about possible attack vectors. Understanding that the PLCs and workstations are potential targets means ensuring that they are locked down as best as possible without preventing regular work. While it is unlikely that a user would be able to identify a forged certificate, preventing the use of USB drives within the ICS network could have stopped Stuxnet from ever gaining access.

When considering how to establish superior SA, defenders should enumerate various intrusion methods and exploit types. Even if the security at the walls is considered top-notch, analysts should understand what to look for within those walls and evaluate what-if scenarios. Doing so will improve detection methods and means. While exploring potential delivery methods, defenders should identify where current defense tools and analysis does and does not manage to prevent and/or detect these intrusions. Answering the question of how and where an attack may originate or gain access as well as what can be and should be observed and recorded will ensure that the defenders won't have to answer those questions after an attack exploits their systems.

Defenders are not the only component of SA here. The USB delivery method likely preyed on unsuspecting users through social engineering, making them available in locations they would find the drives (e.g., conference, parking lot). In this case, educating users about security policies and best practices can help to mitigate the potential for delivery methods to succeed. Training paired with system policy can improve baseline vulnerability of the environment and address assumptions—assumptions from both users on what is actually safe technology use and defenders on what users are actually doing in practice and what they understand regarding security.

10.5.3   Phase 3: Exploiting SCADA Systems

Infection relied on two main stages: (1) access into the SCADA network via a workstation computer and (2) infection of a Siemens PLC in order to execute malicious code. A significant amount of Stuxnet's development focused on the first stage—the creation of a "dropper" that would plant the worm onto a SCADA system from where it would seek out its targets and spread. Stuxnet relied on "an unprecedented four zero-day Windows exploits", reflecting "an unusually high investment" in its success (Chen and Abu-Nimeh 2011, p. 92). These exploits took advantage of vulnerabilities in the workstation operating systems and the ICS network. The worm element of Stuxnet capitalized on vulnerabilities within the Windows-based PCs in the SCADA system to propagate itself across the network, and it attacked specific Siemens control software by taking advantage of hard-coded passwords that couldn't be changed or deleted (Chen and Abu-Nimeh 2011; Matrosov et al. 2011).

ICS environments rely on stability and assurance of device longevity and accessibility. Security often has to take a backseat as a result, and many legacy devices and systems are still involved in ICS operation. Knowledge of ICS vulnerabilities that stem from these legacy devices and unpatched operating systems of the machines involved is necessary to comprehend the baseline situation and scenarios that may arise. When possible, patches or fixes can be pushed to these elements; otherwise, tools should be used as available to protect and observe vulnerable points of access and interaction. While a zero-day exploit itself is likely impossible to see coming, comprehension of how the ICS environment interconnects with itself and other networks within the enterprise should directly pair with setting up and assessing system behavior to increase perception. For example, a typical IDS may not have a signature of the new attack, but a human analyst may be able to understand when new and unusual traffic is observed if relevant sensors and monitors are paired with the cyber and physical elements of the ICS.

10.5.4 Phases 4 and 5: Stuxnet's Foothold and Control

Like any other cyber worm, Stuxnet made use of peer-to-peer communication to search for additional targets and spread itself throughout a network or system once it had access. However, its designers limited its spread, relying on local distribution rather than Internet propagation (Langner 2011). In addition to its specific targeting of Siemens PLCs, minimized activity resulted in Stuxnet managing to go undetected for several months, mitigation not coming until well beyond its installation phase. Local network communication also enabled Stuxnet to keep itself updated automatically if new copies were detected (Karnouskos 2011; Matrosov et al. 2011). Once embedded within victim machines, Stuxnet inserted a malicious.dll file into the target PLCs in place of the original; the malicious code existed alongside legitimate code and only took over control under certain conditions (Karnouskos 2011; Langner 2011; Matrosov et al. 2011).

Defender SA should build upon a solid understanding of the ICS structure in order to combat the installation of a worm like Stuxnet. As with Phase 3, knowledge of the interconnections of systems and devices is necessary to project intrusion paths and determine how attacks might reach potential targets. In order to expand across the network Stuxnet had to modify assets to embed itself. Defenders with knowledge of worm attacks could develop techniques to scan for their effects. For example, a controlled access set of signatures for legitimate applications within the ICS network environment could provide comparisons to detect alterations or malicious usage (Mo et al. 2011). Defense cannot focus only on the entry points from the outside, such as physical control of access to devices or external firewalls. Better SA would be served by maintaining vigilance within the ICS components and traffic flow inside the enterprise's network(s). An observation of packets that are being sent to certain machines over others, especially if associated with certain PLCs, should indicate malicious intent and guide defense actions.

Likewise, updates to PLCs should be closely monitored and recorded. Since the reliability of these devices often motivates holding off on updates and security patches, the defense tools should include logging of any changes to code and settings. For example, file change logs would reveal when a.dll file was changed on the PLCs, enabling a human agent to perceive a change in the environment and decide if action is necessary. Specific machines should be assigned to providing updates to devices, with access and control over these machines closely guarded and secured, increasing accountability while reducing illegitimate update vectors. Without equipping the cyber-physical environment with sensors and control in multiple locations and levels, the human agents are unable to construct and process a complete understanding of the situation. Being mindful of ICS structure and layout can motivate the implementation of additional sensors and tools to report on changes to the environment in order to respond rapidly and accurately.

10.5.5   Phase 6: Stuxnet in Action

The ultimate aim of any cyber attack is to carry out some action. In the case of Stuxnet, even with the use of four zero-day exploits and the directed spread and control of the local peer-network worm, the actual attack had not yet occurred. However, all of the previous phases set the stage for Stuxnet to remain hidden as it commenced its attack on the devices controlled by the Siemens PLCs. The.dll it replaced enabled it to intercept communication between Windows machines and their associated PLCs, blocking commands, warnings, and error messages as well as to falsify information to remain hidden and in control (Karnouskos 2011; Matrosov et al. 2011). All of its actions were done within system memory, providing zero hard disk evidence, and triggered by a complex timer and process conditions so that no external control or signals were required (Karnouskos 2011; Langner 2011). It wasn't until the centrifuges it attacked by periodically modifying the frequency of their rotation had spun themselves apart that Stuxnet's attack was observable.

In the end, Stuxnet was successful. The SA of involved defenders was insufficient to observe and comprehend the worm's propagation throughout the SCADA systems and prevent the installation and execution of malicious code on the PLCs. It was assumed that the reports coming from the monitoring systems were authentic. The trail from initial infection to attack was not detected along the way. As a result, SA was incomplete and based on false data, preventing proper comprehension of the evolving situation until after it occurred. Convenient practice overrode implementing stronger security in the face of potential consequences. If additional security steps and devices were involved in each segment of the environment, could Stuxnet traffic and activity have been detected in the earlier phases? Can steps be taken to reduce the levels of complexity between the human agents and the observable environment, potentially enabling defenders to see harmful centrifuge behavior despite false reports from infected devices?

Research suggests that at this point Stuxnet might have been impossible to stop, having already successfully hidden and embedded itself within its targets. Thus, in this case the kill chain analysis shows that greater effort must be taken to prevent such an attack at an earlier phase, stemming from better SA and security practices and policies. For ICS, this may mean updating design and maintenance structures for devices such as PLCs to allow for more flexibility with respect to patching, updating, and replacing. However, the safety and integrity of the services these devices support may still outweigh the desire to update or replace them, emphasizing that a holistic understanding of the cyber-physical environment is the best bet at maintaining optimal SA. Using knowledge of how the physical and cyber entities of the environment relate to themselves and each other and what features or traits are the most critical to monitor, defenders can place more appropriate sensors, employ more optimal tools, and cast aside incorrect and harmful assumptions in order to observe, comprehend, and project an assessment of current, evolving, and potential situations throughout cybersecurity efforts within the involved networks.

10.6   Guidelines

An essential function of the ICS is to provide details of the physical mission system so that the health of that system can be assessed and appropriate control actions can be chosen and executed as needed. Unfortunately, complex ICS are themselves susceptible to failures and malicious cyber and physical attacks. A failed or compromised ICS cannot be utilized to construct an accurate representation of the mission system or to ensure that chosen controls are faithfully executed by that system. Thus, SA plays an important role in monitoring overall system capabilities and effectiveness and determining appropriate courses of action as part of incident management and mission assurance. Success depends on overall SA, which includes developing an accurate account of the physical system, the involved networks, and all interactions. Developing SA of the ICS and associated cyber, physical, and human systems in isolation is not enough. In this section, we build upon our earlier discussions in the chapter and provide guidelines on maintaining mission-tailored SA and developing effective courses of action.

10.6.1   Expertise of the Operator(s) Responsible for Developing SA

As we discussed earlier, human actors play critical roles in developing the SA of the physical system; each of these roles is cognitively demanding, requiring a deep understanding of the corresponding domain. Traditionally, ICS and their Human Machine Interfaces (HMIs) are manned by control engineers who understand the physical system, sensors, and controls. They can build SA of the physical mission system using the information provided by the ICS, decide on a course of action, and execute the plan. However, they typically do not have domain expertise in cyber systems. For a relatively simple physical system and associated ICS, it is difficult to afford two sets of experts. The following are some recommendations for such systems:

(a) Eliminate or minimize the exposure of the ICS to other networks.
(b) Use standards-based, formally verified software where possible. Given that the ICS in question is relatively simple, formal verification by the vendor is feasible.
(c) Maintain a tight control on access points to the ICS. This includes strong authentication, physical security, and control of removable media.
(d) Train the operator(s) manning HMI in basic cybersecurity, interpretation of the alerts, routine messages, and log files from commercial-grade cyber protection and detection tools; operators must understand the relationships between cyber and physical systems. This is doable for a relatively simple cyber physical system with minimal connectivity.
(e) Where possible, provide independent monitoring of key components of the physical system to identify anomalous behavior. For monitor placement, refer to our discussion of the cyber kill chain. Depending on the system, establishing real-time communication protocols for user feedback and/or complaints may supplement this monitoring.
(f) a-e focus on the physical system; monitoring of cyber elements should be implemented with respect to understanding and evaluating their impact on the mission to support operator SA.

More complex environments involve numerous sensors, PLCs, networked computers, historical and current data, and increasing connectivity to other networks, including the Internet. For such systems, it is important to understand and comprehend the cyber elements and the implications of the integrated state of the environment. At a minimum, our policy recommendation requires some expertise specifically related to sensors and data analytics:

(g) Sensors should be deployed to monitor both the physical and cyber elements.
(h) Data analytics to assist the SA process should work on both the cyber and physical data.
(i) Interfaces should present the state of both the cyber system and that of the physical system, possibly on different screens.
(j) Domain experts should work together to build an overall picture, evaluate courses of actions affecting one or both domains, and supervise the execution of selected actions. Over time, the team should be able to move from data to perception to comprehension to projection more quickly and accurately. Analytics, modeling, and machine learning discussed below will help.
(k) The human team should be able to integrate historical data (including successful attacks) and trends, information from outside sources, and real-time data.
(l) Independent sensors should be used to help the human team resolve inconsistencies and address malicious distortion of sensor data.

10.6.2 Sensors and Data

The complexity of cyber-physical systems requires sensor placement in physical elements, cyber elements, their interfaces, and for human activity. These sensors provide real- or near-real-time data presented to and processed by human operators, supplemented by historical data and external open-source intelligence (e.g., from social media, underground malware market, CERT, and security consortia). The selection of the types and placement of sensors for the best SA is a non-trivial problem and will benefit from detailed modeling. However, the following guidelines will help:

(a) Selection of the type and placement of sensors should aim to detect more impactful anomalies faster and more accurately.
(b) For the most critical physical elements, multiple independent sensors should feed information over independent paths to provide independent corroboration and protection against malicious man-in-the-middle attacks. Decreasing cost and footprints of sensors may enable significant independent corroboration.
(c) Where possible, sensors should be designed to identify failures or attacks not just in their own domain but also across domains and in the interfaces between the two domains. For example, physical domain sensors could help identify attack characteristics observed in cyber spaces.
(d) For critical control actions, it is important to have sensors to justify accurate execution.
(e) Previous successful attacks and exfiltration will inform new sensor placement and types.
(f) Insider threats and supply chain attacks are always challenging to detect. They require careful placement of sensors and alerts that are hard to circumvent unless a majority of the human team is compromised.

10.6.3 System Documentation, Assessment, and "Blue Teaming"

In obtaining meaningful SA, it is important to understand and map both cyber and physical states to outcomes and the impact on mission effectiveness. Forensic analysis is a time-consuming process that can take days, weeks, and potentially months depending on the novelty and complexity of the attack. If done reactively after detecting an abnormal state, the consequences of a malicious attack may be felt well before meaningful SA is developed. We recommend the following proactive measures:

(a) Document the design of the cyber and physical system, stressing the relationships between the two. Use these descriptions to carry out a "blue team" assessment of vulnerability and threats. In addition, use external intelligence to assess risks.
(b) Use the above analysis to inform sensor selection and placement, collection and use of external intelligence, and training.
(c) Design analytics and visualizations to incorporate the results of the above and input from the human team.

10.6.4 *Automation*

While human cognition will remain a significant component of the SA process, the increasing complexity of cyber-physical systems and the large amounts of data pulled from sensors suggest incorporating automation and decision-support techniques whenever possible. Human actors should be able to focus on the strengths of human cognition to establish SA, and automation can support that.

Ontologies and relationships: Experts in cyber and physical systems use different terminologies, ontologies, and visualization to describe their systems, interactions among system elements, and interactions with the rest of the world. Automation requires somewhat formal specifications of ontologies and relationships between them. System descriptions and assessments mentioned above will inform these specifications.

Modeling: Physical systems have been modelled extensively in the past. The models are used to predict performance under various operating environments, failure modes, etc. Cyber systems and their behavior are more difficult to model. However, the relationships between cyber state and physical mission systems, threat and vulnerability analysis, and detailed modeling of the physical system will help build an overall representation to automate many objective relationships and help analytics and visualization.

Human-assisted machine learning: The next stage in automation and management of cognitive overload is to take advantage of artificial intelligence and machine learning to automate some of the cognitive processes in the development of SA. Techniques that use human annotations to assist machine learning may be the most effective in CPHS. We can combine objective models discussed above and human interpretations to build analytics and visualization that provide a better starting point for the SA, leading to faster and more effective courses of action.

Integrated SA: The automation mentioned above, along with the team training mentioned in Sect. 6.3, could enable an integrated SA of the cyber and physical elements. The human team could then work together with a common set of analytics and visualization and rapidly develop courses of actions.

Full automation where desirable and feasible: There are situations where the combined state suggests a likely adverse impact in a time frame too short for developing SA and executing a course of action (COA) based on human cognition. The automation discussed here along with the analysis in Sect. 6.3 could be used to identify such situations and develop COA without human involvement (or human involvement only as a monitor). These actions are then part of the system resilience.

Accounting for the Operationally Relevant Time Frame: Full automation describes a situation in which the Operationally Relevant Time Frame (ORTF) precludes any significant involvement of human cognition in real time. Even when ORTF is long enough to allow significant use of human cognition, it may be limited. The intelligence built should identify bounds on ORTF and assist the human team in arriving at the best COA within the ORTF.

10.6.5 Limiting Human Actions and Physical Parameter Controls

While human actors provide the best cognition and robust decision making, human errors and insider threats are facts of life. These errors and deliberate acts may impact the data itself, analytics, SA, COA, and actual execution of selected controls. Two possible checks and balances can help: Limiting the range of actions allowed by human actors with the provision that actions outside the range require more than one human actors to concur; and limiting the range of key parameters in the physical systems.

While the focus above in this section and in this entire chapter is on SA, it is important to note that the success of a large fraction of malicious attacks (including Stuxnet) has been due to the lack of adequate operational hygiene and discipline. Thus, training in operational discipline and hygiene cannot be overemphasized.

10.7 Summary and Conclusions

In defending an ICS, one must understand all of the various dimensions of its environment. This poses serious challenges to providing security as the ICS spans human, cyber, and physical dimensions, offering a myriad of possible interactions and exploits to adversaries. Beyond management and information collection, efficient human cognition and reasoning are required. The human is the driving force that enacts changes to the environment and processes information to facilitate appropriate data-to-decision paths. Important decisions in ICSs are not made automatically from collected data.

The rapid assessment and decision making needed to achieve SA can be modeled within the concept of an OODA loop (observe, orient, decide, act), which represents an understanding of how the humans involved interpret and comprehend the situation. In addition, the "cyber kill chain" idea, which has its roots in military doctrine, can enable the evaluation of incident response and protection efforts. Stages of the kill chain include reconnaissance, exploitation, installation, command and control, and action. A cyber kill-chain analysis of Stuxnet malware infections suggests that it might have been impossible to stop, since it had already successfully hidden and embedded itself within its targets. This kill chain analysis shows that a greater effort should have be taken to prevent such an attack at an earlier phase, stemming from better SA and security practices and policies. For ICS in general, better updating of design and maintenance structures for devices such as PLCs would allow for more flexibility with respect to patching, updating, and replacing.

Some specific guidelines for achieving SA in ICSs are provided. These include ensuring the expertise of operator(s), effective placement and use of sensors and sensor data, improvement of the quality of system documentation, use of assessments and blue-teaming, and wiser use of automation. SA in ICSs plays an important role in monitoring overall system capabilities and effectiveness and determining appropriate courses of action as part of incident management and mission assurance. This includes developing an accurate account of the dimensions of the physical system and the involved networks, as well as developing an understanding all of the interactions between the various ICS components and dimensions.

References

Abrams, M., & Weiss, J. (2008). *Malicious control system cyber security attack case study—Maroochy water services, Australia*. Retrieved 29 May, 2015, from http://csrc.nist.gov/groups/SMA/fisma/ics/documents/Maroochy-Water-Services-Case-Study_report.pdf.

Ackoff, R. L. (1989). From data to wisdom. *Journal of Applied Systems Analysis, 16*, 3–9.

Albanese, M., Cam, H., & Jajodia, S. (2014). Automated cyber situation awareness tools and models for improving analyst performance. In R. E. Pino, K. Alexander, & S. Michael (Eds.), *Cybersecurity systems for human cognition augmentation* (pp. 47–60). Cham, Switzerland: Springer.

Bedny, G., & Meister, D. (1999). Theory of activity and situation awareness. *International Journal of Cognitive Ergonomics, 3*(1), 63–72.

Biros, D., & Eppich, T. (2001). Human element key to intrusion detection. *Signal, 55*, 31–34.

Blasch, E. (2008). Introduction to level 5 fusion: The role of the user. In M. E. Liggins, D. Hall, & J. Llinas (Eds.), *Handbook of multisensor data fusion* (pp. 503–535). Boca Raton: CRC Press.

Blasch, E.P., Breton, R., & Valin, P. (2011). User information fusion decision making analysis with the C-OODA model. In *Proceedings of the 14th International Conference on Information Fusion* (pp. 2082–2089).

Boyd, J. R. (1987). Organic design for command and control. Part of a set of briefing slides titled. *A Discourse on Winning and Losing*. Retrieved from http://www.danford.net/boyd/index.htm.

Caldero, V., Hadjicostis, C. N., Piccola, A., & Siano, P. (2011). Failure identification in smart grids based on Petri net modeling. *IEEE Transactions on Industrial Electronics, 58*(10), 4613–4623.

Cam, H., Mouallem, P., Mo, Y., Sinopoli, B., & Nkrumah, B. (2014). Modeling impact of attacks, recovery, and attackability conditions for situational awareness. In *2014 IEEE International Multi-Disciplinary Conference on Cognitive Methods in Situation Awareness and Decision Support* (CogSIMA), 3–6 March, 2014, San Antonio, USA.

Chen, T., & Abu-Nimeh, S. (2011). Lessons from Stuxnet. *Computer, 44*(4), 91–93.

Endsley, M. (1995). Towards a theory of situation awareness in dynamic systems. *Human Factors, 37*(1), 32–64.

Giacobe, N.A. (2010). Application of the JDL data fusion process model for cyber security. *SPIE Defense, Security, and Sensing 2010.*

Govindarasu, M., Hann, A., & Sauer, P. (2012). Power Systems Engineering Research Center. *Cyber-Physical Systems Security for Smart Grid.* Iowa State University, 2012. Print.

Hebert, A. (2003). Compressing the kill chain. *Journal of the Air Force Association, 86*(3), 50–54.

Helbing, D. (2013). Globally networked risks and how to respond. *Nature, 497*(7447), 51–69.

Henry, M.H., Layer, R.M., Snow, K.Z., & Zaret, D.R. (2009). Evaluating the risk of cyber attacks on SCADA systems via Petri net analysis with application to hazardous liquid loading operations. *Proceeding of IEEE Conference on Technologies for Homeland Security, HST '09, Boston, MA* (pp. 607–614). Retrieved from http://www.airforce-magazine.com/MagazineArchive/Pages/2000/July%202000/0700find.aspx.

Hutchins, E., Clopperty, M., Amin, R., & Lockheed Martin. (2011). *Intelligence-Driven Computer Network Defense*. [White Paper, PDF]. Retrieved 30 March, 2015, from http://www.lockheed-martin.com/us/what-we-do/information-technology/cyber-security/cyber-kill-chain.html.

Hutchins, E., Clopperty, M., & Amin, R. (2011). Intelligence-drive computer network defense informed by analysis of adversary campaigns and intrusion kill chains. *Proceedings of the 6th International Conference on i-Warfare and Security* (pp. 113–125).

Karnouskos, S. (2011). Stuxnet worm impact on industrial cyber-physical system security. *IECON 2011—37th Annual Conference on IEEE Industrial Electronics Society* (pp. 4490–4494).

Kessler, O., Askin, K., Beck, N., Lynch, J., White, F., Buede, D., & Llinas, I. (1991). Functional description of the data fusion process. Report prepared for the Office of Naval Technology Data Fusion Development Strategy, Naval Air Development Center, Warminster, PA.

Klein, G. A. (1989). Recognition-primed decisions. In W. B. Rouse (Ed.), *Advances in man-machine system research Vol. 5* (pp. 47–92). Greenwich, CT: JAI Press.

Klein, G. A., Calderwood, R., & Clinton-Cirocco, A. (1986). Rapid decision making on the fire ground. In *Proceedings of the Human Factors Society 30th Annual Meeting* (Vol. 1, pp. 576–580).

Langner, R. (2011). Stuxnet: Dissecting a cyberwarfare weapon. *IEEE Security and Privacy Magazine, 9*(3), 49–51.

Marchelli, M. (2011). Situational Awareness (SA) in SCADA EMS/GMS/DMS (Data Visualization and Alarm Processing). Presentation. The Structure Group, 2011.

Matrosov, A., Rodionov, E., Harley, D., & Malcho, J., ESET. (2011). *Stuxnet: Under the Microscope*. [White Paper, PDF]. Retrieved 30 March, 2015, from http://www.eset.com/us/resources/white-papers/Stuxnet_Under_the_Microscope.pdf.

Mo, Y., Hyun-Jin Kim, T., Brancik, K., Dickinson, D., Lee, H., Perrig, A., et al. (2011). Cyber-physical security of a smart grid infrastructure. *Proceedings of the IEEE, 100*(2), 195–208.

National Research Council. (2007). *Countering the threat of improvised explosive devices: Basic research opportunities* (Abbreviated Version). Retrieved from http://books.nap.edu/catalog.php?record_id=11953.

Skare, P. M. (2013, November 26). Method and system for cyber security management of industrial control systems. Siemens Industry, assignee. U.S. Patent No. 8,595,831 B2.

Smith, S. C. (2014). *A survey of research in supervisory control and data acquisition (SCADA)*. Adelphi: Army Research Lab.

Smith, K., & Hancock, P. (1995). Situation awareness is adaptive, externally directed consciousness. *Human Factors: The Journal of the Human Factors and Ergonomics Society, 37*(1), 137–148.

Stotz, A., & Sudit, M. (2007). Information fusion engine for real-time decision-making (INFERD): A perceptual system for cyber attack tracking. *2007 10th International Conference on Information Fusion* (pp. 1–8). IEEE.

Tirpak, J. A. (2000). Find, fix, track, target, engage, assess. *Air Force Magazine, 83*, 24–29.

U.S. Department of Defense. (2007). *Joint Publication 3–60 Joint Targeting*. Retrieved from http://www.dtic.mil/doctrine/new_pubs/jp3_60.pdf.

Weiss, J. (2008). *Assuring industrial control system (ICS) cyber security*. Cupertino: Applied Control Solutions.

Zeng, R., Jiang, Y., Lin, C., & Shen, X. (2012). Dependability analysis of control center networks in smart grid using stochastic Petri nets. *IEEE Transactions on Parallel and Distributed Systems, 23*(9), 1721–1730.

Chapter 11
Intrusion Detection in Industrial Control Systems

Edward J.M. Colbert and Steve Hutchinson

11.1 Introduction

Even if the threats, risk factors and other security metrics—which we discussed in previous chapters—are well understood and effectively mitigated, a determined adversary will have non-negligible probability of successful penetration of the ICS. In this chapter we use the word "intrusion" to refer to a broad range of processes and effects associated with the presence and actions of malicious software in an ICS. Once an intrusion has occurred, the first and necessary step for defeat and remediation of the intrusion is to detect the existence of the intrusion.

We begin this chapter by elaborating on the motivation for intrusion detection and briefly sketch the history—surprisingly long and going back to early 1980s—of intrusion detection technologies and systems (IDS). Much of the chapter's attention is on the difficult question of whether insights and approaches developed for IDSs intended for information and communications technology (ICT) can be adapted for ICSs. To answer this question, the chapter explores the modern intrusion detection techniques in ICT such as host-based techniques and network-based techniques, and the differences and relative advantages of signature-based and non-signature methods. Then, the chapter explores how such techniques may or may not apply in ICS environments. It is useful in such exploration to differentiate between early (let us say before 2010) and recent perspectives on such adaptations.

Finally, we introduce approaches based on an appreciable degree of knowledge about the process controlled by the ICS. These methods focus on monitoring the

E.J.M. Colbert (✉)
US Army Research Laboratory, Adelphi, MD, USA
e-mail: edward.j.colbert2.civ@mail.mil

S. Hutchinson
Adelphi Laboratory Center, US Army Research Laboratory, Adelphi, MD, USA

© Springer International Publishing Switzerland 2016
E.J.M. Colbert, A. Kott (eds.), *Cyber-security of SCADA and Other Industrial Control Systems*, Advances in Information Security 66,
DOI 10.1007/978-3-319-32125-7_11

underlying process in the control system rather than monitoring network traffic. One of the methods presented in the chapter attempts to model process variable excursions beyond their appropriate ranges using machine-learning techniques. The second method requires plant personnel input to define critical process variable limits. Semantic modeling of plant control variables is used in both methods. The chapter concludes with a detailed case study of an IDS in the context of a sample plant and its ICS.

11.2 Background

11.2.1 Motivation for Intrusion Detection Systems (IDSs) in Industrial Control Systems (ICSs)

An ideally secure computer system would not have any vulnerabilities and would not be able to be compromised at all. However, as security experts often half-jokingly say, a computer system with this level of security only exists if it can be completely isolated and never used by anyone. This illustrates a point. Even if all hardware, software, and network threats are mitigated fully, the users of the system are human and can still commit disrupting actions, intentional or not. Insider threat cannot be completely removed from any computer system with human users.

With this said, we adopt the premise that there is always a threat against a real computer system, no matter how well technical and physical vulnerabilities are removed. This is certainly true of computers that are part of Industrial Control Systems (ICSs) that are used to automate and control critical processes used in industrial settings. In fact, ICSs typically have far more technical and physical vulnerabilities than ICT systems, merely because modern ICT equipment is often designed with security in mind.

11.2.2 Early Intrusion Detection Systems

If there is always a vulnerability that can be exploited in a computer system, how does one protect that system? Early ideas (e.g. Anderson 1980) were to monitor accounting records that already existed (for the IBM System Management Facility [SMF] mainframe), and perform analytical tests against those data records for anomalous patterns. This work is often referenced as the first Intrusion Detection System (IDS). The idea is to provide anomalous pattern information as a tool for a human security monitor, with the expectation that most of the patterns flagged will not be malicious behavior. Denning (1987) later elaborated this IDS concept with a more sophisticated model and set of processes (for the same IBM SMF mainframe) developed at SRI International a few years earlier (Denning and Neumann 1985).

It is worth noting that vulnerabilities and threats to these early computer systems were quite different from those of most ICT systems used now. The systems were not openly connected to the large number of malicious actors on today's Internet, since the Internet as we know it did not exist, and global networking of computer systems was rare. The technical competence of a computer user was much higher then. Graphical User Interfaces (GUIs) and computer mice were not a common feature of these systems. Recreational computer user activity (e.g. "surfing" the net) was extremely rare, or non-existent at that time, so that external threats via the network were not a main concern. Aside from that, the types of threats and potential alerts examined then

- Attempted break-in
- Masquerading or successful break-in
- Penetration by legitimate user
- Leakage by legitimate user
- Inference by legitimate user
- Trojan horse
- Virus
- Denial of Service

are very similar to those considered today, even though the threat model used on this early system was much less complex.

11.2.3   Evolution from Early to Modern IDSs

As methods for ICT IDSs developed further, additional techniques were implemented to flag alerts. Most of the threats and alerts pertained to the confidentiality of (assumed) private information existing inside the computer systems or networks. Security is often explained using the CIA "triad": Confidentiality, Integrity, and Availability. When one learns of a security breach in an ICT system, the first thought might be to determine if bank account or credit card information or sensitive emails were stolen. Integrity and Availability are important on an ICT system; however, ICT IDS systems were designed primarily to minimize confidentiality. The intent of most malicious actors breaking into ICT systems is different from that of those breaking into ICS systems. ICS systems control a process and the ICS adversary's intent is to undermine that process, i.e. the availability of the system.

Home personal computers (PCs) in the early 1980s had very little in terms of technical or network security. The best method of protecting PC systems was to provide physical security: lock the room, remove the hard drive, or even install a physical lock on the base system power supply. Some early PC users were able to install password authentication. Even so, the system was still usually extremely easy to break if one had physical access, and PC usage without physical access was very uncommon. Physical security was king. ICSs are similar to these early PCs. It is common for ICSs to use equipment that was manufactured in the 1980s, or even before, and to use physical security as the primary line of defense. Why? The reason is because the older equipment still functions well and the main emphasis in ICSs is Availability.

Since then, home PCs have evolved into much more complex systems with much more storage and computing capacity. Network connectivity in home PCs and mobile devices is now commonplace. As a result, extensive information access is possible, often even from a single break-in. On the other hand, ICS systems have not changed much since the 1980s. Even so, there is now a much more significant interest in connecting them with intranet and Internet, so that operators and managers can access them remotely. Once remote network connectivity is established to these inherently insecurity computer systems, Physical Security is no longer king. Break-ins can and will occur via the global network, leaving ICSs (and their processes) extremely vulnerable.

As mentioned, IDSs for ICT networks have become very popular; especially for identifying the signatures of many pieces of known malicious code (e.g. SNORT rules). Some IDSs utilize model-base anomaly detectors, such as those original proposed by Anderson (1980) and Denning (1987).

An important question is: can we really just transfer the methods developed and implemented for early and current ICT systems to ICSs? Most researchers (e.g., see review by Zhu and Sastry 2010) attest that the answer is no. ICS traffic is much different, ICS component security is much different, and as we have described above, the intent of the intruder is likely much different—to disrupt the availability of the process instead of to compromise the confidentiality of information.

It is important to keep these differences in mind while considering techniques and methods for Intrusion Detection in ICSs.

For the purposes of brevity, we abbreviate the term "Intrusion Detection" as "ID" in the remainder of this chapter.

11.3 Modern Intrusion Detection Techniques

We begin with a brief review on ID and IDSs to provide an overview of their history since the early 1980s, and a crude taxonomy.

11.3.1 Host-Based Intrusion Detection Systems (HIDS)

IDSs described by Anderson and Denning are host-based systems (Host-based Intrusion Detection Systems, or HIDs) for the IBM SMF mainframe systems. System data used in the analysis was internal accounting audit trail data from users of the system. Host-based systems still exist in present day ICT networks, and these systems now process much larger amounts of data. Modern operating system audit trails include both general user accounting information such as login times, system reboot events, hardware access records, and specific security information such as login password failures and firewall denial events. Third-party security software such as anti-virus, personal firewalls and browsers can supplement the operating system information and provide an extensive set of current information for HIDs. This information can also be packaged and distributed to a central processing facility to provide situational awareness of the network nodes.

As mentioned, modern ICS equipment does not normally fall in the same category as computer systems in modern-day ICT networks. ICS equipment is not typically designed with security logging and processing in mind. It does not usually run standard operating systems used in ICT desktops and servers. The device operating software is often vendor specific and primitive. The devices are not refreshed as often as ICT network devices, and may very well be so old that they are no longer supported by the vendor. Upgrades or modifications of the operating software may not be available. Vendors will likely not support any security upgrades to unsupported products. While HIDS systems in general are common for ICT systems, they are not generally used on ICS hardware since it is not typically suitable for logging or monitoring processes.

11.3.2   Network-Based Intrusion Detection Systems (NIDS)

Network-based IDSs are a network device that collects network traffic directly from the network, often from a central point such as a router or switch. Data from multiple network sensors can be aggregated into a central processing engine, or processing may occur on the collection machine itself. For NIDS, useful audit data must be extracted from raw, unformatted network packet data itself rather than from pre-formatted audit log information used by HIDs.

In general, two methods are used for alerting. The network traffic can be scanned for known malicious code with specific bit signatures, which is known as signature-based detection. The network traffic can also be analyzed for unsatisfactory traffic or behavior patterns; either patterns that are anomalous to a previously established traffic or behavior model, or specific traffic patterns that display non-conformity to standards, e.g. violations of specific communication protocols.

11.3.2.1   Signature-Based Intrusion Detection Methods

The most common signature-base security tool used in IDSs is Snort, which was developed by Marty Roesch in 1998 and is currently maintained by Cisco at www. snort.org. Signature-based detection methods are sometimes referred to as misuse-based detection or knowledge-based detection, since knowledge of the software threats under search must have already been gained. Signature-based detection is very commonly used by anti-virus scanners as the *de facto* security measure on ICT systems. The intent of this method is often to determine whether software is safe to import into a system, or whether a system hard drive is safe from malicious code. Likewise, it can often be used as the primary method used in NIDs to determine whether malicious traffic is present on the network. A drawback is that adversaries can easily create dynamically changing code for known malicious software so that the code escapes signature-based detection. Unknown malicious code also escapes detection. Thus, while widely used, signature-based detection methods are not fool-proof. As far as security tools go, though, they are very accurate in providing knowledge of specific detectible intrusions of known malicious code. If one considers an intrusion alarm as a "positive," the rate of false alarms, or false positives, is generally low for signature-based detectors.

11.3.2.2 Non-signature-Based Intrusion Detection Methods

Non-signature-based intrusion methods are more difficult to evaluate for implementation since there are a large number of different methods used, and the rate of false positives is often higher than that of signature-based methods. If false positive rates are too high, it becomes difficult or impossible for a security analyst to monitor the system (see, e.g., Axelsson 2000). Calibration processes for the algorithm can be complex as well, potentially thwarting acceptance and implementation by system owners. When the calibration method includes developing a model for comparison (anomaly-based detection), a significant benefit over signature-based methods can be achieved in that *unknown* malicious events can be detected. Anomaly-based detection is sometimes referred to as behavior-based detection when the baseline reference is behavior based, or model-based detection when the baseline is model-based.

Another non-signature-based detection method relies on searching for non-conformity or deviations from accepted industry guidelines, such as protocol standards. IEEE and IETF network communication protocols are often robust, but improper use of the protocols can produce malicious or covert activity. Vendor products do not typically enforce protocol standards strictly or uniformly, allowing adversaries to create and transmit malicious packets. The ability to detect non-conformities requires intensive deep inspection of network traffic. An accurate reference model of both conforming and non-conforming aspects or patterns of the usage of the protocol is also required. This detection method is known as specification-based detection or stateful protocol analysis.

11.3.2.3 Methods Used in Practice

While the taxonomy of modern intrusion detection techniques just described is rough and simplistic, it does show that IDS methods have expanded to include much more data and analytics since the early 1980s. As noted, the primary market for IDSs has been for ICT systems, either networked desktop or server HIDS running standard computer operating systems, or NIDS connected directly to ICT networks. A more comprehensive review and taxonomy of modern IDS techniques and can be found in Liao et al. (2013). In practice, a commercial HIDS or NIDS will often employ many different intrusion detection and alerting methods, including signature-based, anomaly-based, and specification-based methods. For example, the U.S. Army Research Laboratory has designed a network-based intrusion detection framework, Interrogator, which utilizes an array of different detection methods in its network sensors, and a library of different analytical methods for alerting at its central repository (Long 2004).

11.4 Intrusion Detection in ICSs

In this section, we discuss in detail how the general ID methods for ICT systems have been adapted for ICSs. In the previous sections, we described the original concept and some example development of modern intrusion detection for ICT technologies. Although ICS system components are much different from those of ICT systems, many of the same ideas have been brought forward for ICS IDSs.

11.4.1 Anatomy of An Industrial Control System

Before proceeding to discuss ICS IDS systems, we need to understand how a typical ICS "network" is used.

In Fig. 11.1 we show a rough sketch of a simple ICS (see Chap. 2 for additional information on ICS components). This control system has two Programmable Logic Controllers (PLCs), each of which are connected (upper panel) to a standard ICT device network with a few Workstations. The workstations typically run Microsoft Windows or Linux, as in a standard Enterprise network. In the diagram, this network is annotated as "Primary Bus." The traffic on this network is usually IP packet-based, but parts of it could be hard-wired as a set of serial lines.

Downward from the PLCs are Secondary Buses that control field devices, such as boilers, electronic lighting, and packaging units. While these buses or networks may be IP packet-based, they are usually simple hard-wired cables with specialized voltage or current control needed to run the field devices. In other words, they are not meant to have a standard network communication protocol such as TCP/IP.

Also notice that most of the equipment is NOT computer servers, network switches, or routers, such as you might find in an ICT network. Even the workstations connected to the Primary Bus are doing atypical work. They are not meant to be connected to the Internet to browse the web. They are specifically configured to only perform their function in the ICS. There is often little interest in following security measures such as installing anti-virus or keeping the operating system up to date because, ideally, the systems are not supposed to be accessed from the outside, and are not supposed to access the outside. The field devices and PLCs do not run standard operating systems and most likely will not be modified to do so.

Simple Industrial Control System

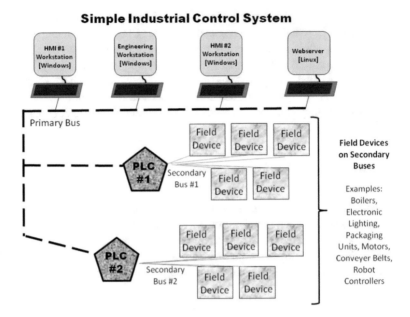

Fig. 11.1 Sample of a simple ICS

11.4.2 Host-Based Intrusion Detection Systems (HIDS) in ICSs

HIDS were developed for standard ICT computer systems, and can certainly be used on normal computer workstations and other similar system on the Primary Bus, or on the corporate network. It would be necessary to ensure that the availability of the workstations would not be affected by the operation of the HIDS or by any central network monitoring system collecting HIDS data over the Primary Bus.

HIDS are rarely if ever able to run on the PLCs or the field devices. First, the device firmware was never intended to run arbitrary software, and second, the devices' processing CPU, memory, and communication links were never designed to accommodate the additional burden. The idea of converting these devices to accommodate a HIDS is tantamount to the idea of replacing and re-testing all of the field hardware devices, which would generate tremendous resistance in an operational environment of an ICS since it implies lack of availability and implies risk of future inoperability.

While future ICS component design may accommodate embedded HIDS-like software or features, these features are not generally used in current ICS devices.

11.4.3   Network-Based Intrusion Detection Systems (NIDS) in ICSs

If we follow the analogous ICT IDS taxonomy, NIDS would be the logical type of IDS to use on ICSs. However, there is the question: What is meant by "network" for an ICS? In our simple ICS network in Fig. 11.1, we have two generally different types of networks (primary and secondary buses). The primary bus is networked (perhaps IP-based), or serial. However, the devices in the secondary buses are arbitrarily diverse. The secondary buses of a complex ICS could use hundreds or thousands of different vendor-proprietary methods of communication.

Network communication protocols in ICSs seldom if ever use any authentication or encryption, which is a critical difference from protocols in ICT networks.

Thus, NIDS methods developed for ICT systems already face a serious challenge if they are to be ported to ICSs. In our simple ICS architecture in Fig. 11.1, the Primary Bus is really the only network that would make sense to apply a NIDS. The Secondary Bus components may not be globally addressable as IP network components are. They may consist of a large number of primitive copper cables, similar to the electrical cords you might find throughout your house. While it is certainly possible that ICT network protocols are used in unique parts of the secondary bus for specific controls, the ICS "network" is uniquely different from an ICT network. Humans may also serve as an essential component in the ICS "network" as they are often a vital component of the underlying ICS process.

We assume throughout the rest of this chapter that the types of IDS systems developed for ICT networks used in ICSs will be NIDS (not HIDS), and those NIDS will be use on the Primary Bus. This ICS IDSs would monitor network traffic between control workstations and ICS hardware devices such as PLCs or RTUs (see Chap. 2). Hereafter the term "ICS network" will imply the Primary Bus network, unless otherwise stated.

11.4.3.1   Signature-Based Intrusion Detection Methods in ICSs

Signature-based ID methods usually aim to find a known bit pattern in network traffic for documented malicious code. Snort "rules" meant for ICT network traffic can easily be ported and used on ICS networks. Since the communication protocols are different on ICS networks, some modification are in order.

Starting approximately 2008, Digital Bond began a DHS-sponsored program called Quickdraw to generate ideas on how to generate security log events for PLCs (see http://www.digitalbond.com/ and http://www.digitalbond.com/tools/quickdraw/). These ideas were developed into rules and pre-processors for Snort signature detection. IDS signatures for ICS protocols BACnet, DNP3, Modbus, Modicon, Niagara Fox, and Siemens S7 became available for anyone wishing to use Snort rules for ICS IDSs.

Digital Bond Snort modifications for IDSs have been used extensively for signature detection. However, signature-based methods have been argued to be far from sufficient in protecting IDS protocol traffic. Due to the inherent lack of authentication and encryption in ICS protocols, unauthorized network access to devices is possible without using known malware. Relatively complex and poorly documented (i.e., unknown) attacks occur on ICSs and these attacks can easily evade signature-based detection methods.

As a result, ICS security researchers often favor a combination of signature-based ID methods and non-signature based ID methods when designing efficient IDSs for ICSs (see, e.g. Verba and Milvich 2008).

11.4.3.2 Non-Signature-Based Intrusion Detection Methods in ICSs

Early Examples (Before 2010)

At this point, we have converged to the ID methods category that seems to be the best fit for ICS networks—non-signature based ID methods on ICS Primary Bus traffic (see Fig. 11.1). Much effort has been devoted to developing efficient non-signature-based ID systems for ICS in the last 10–15 years.

Most of the early works (published before 2010) described or implemented anomaly-based IDSs, with the intention of providing better security protection for inherently highly-vulnerable ICS systems. Physical security methods used previously were no longer sufficient for protecting systems once they are connected to external networks. Some example methods of non-signature based ID methods for ICSs are given below to illustrate progress in solving the issues.

A biologically inspired heuristic model based on ant colony clustering was shown to be feasible for precise clustering and thus accurate, unsupervised anomaly detection (Tsang and Kwong 2005). This model was subjected to some testing with ICT-based IDS attack data, but mostly provided momentum for follow-up studies on anomaly-based IDS methods for ICSs. Normal traffic in ICS networks should consist of only a few regular requests and responses, and the volume should be much lower than that in ICT systems. For example, a PLC likely receives periodic information requests on short regular intervals from the Human Machine Interface (HMI), and other workstations in the ICS produce similarly short periodic network traffic. Occasionally the human running the HMI may make manual requests or changes to field system device variables, but most of the network traffic is very repetitive and easily modeled.

Idaho National Laboratory (INL) funded an ID study that successfully used empirical nonparametric modeling of predetermined network features to compare with current network features, and probabilistically predicted anomalous system activity (Yang et al. 2006). Again, some lab testing was performed against this model-based anomaly ID method, but a full implementation and verification was not performed. The Yang et al. study showed that network anomaly detection had merit for ICSs.

A more complete set of model-based anomaly algorithms was tested at Sandia National Laboratories by Cheung et al. (2007). A Modbus protocol-level model, a model of expected communication patterns, and a learning-based model for system changes were used in the test. Curiously, Snort was utilized to flag the complement of the models, contrary to the normal expectation that Snort is used for signature-detection. All of these alerting methods, together with the Digital Bond Snort rules, were used on the EMERALD ID and correlation framework in the testbed experiments. This work demonstrated that a multi-algorithmic ID implementation not only seems mathematically promising, but functions very well in an real (testbed) environment. Verba and Milvich (2008) provided some further guidance based on their experience with ICS IDS systems at Idaho National Labs. They also describe a multi-algorithmic ID method in which intelligent packet inspection, tailored traffic flow analysis, and unique packet tampering detection are used to provide the much higher level of granularity needed for ICS IDSs. Their conclusion is that multiple methods should be used simultaneously to provide accurate alerting, including signature-based methods.

A solid implementation of an ICS IDS was eventually built and evaluated by Oman and Phillips (2008). This method was based on having all of the ICS device functionality and their configurations documented precisely so that failed logins, configuration changes, and non-compliant network traffic would provide accurate alerts. Testbed experiments showed that the method works well. In practice, however, obtaining and maintaining 100 % accurate device information may be difficult to implement.

These methods and other early (pre-2010) research on ID for ICSs revealed the following key ideas:

- Methods used for ICT networks do not simply apply to ICS networks in the same manner
- Signature-based methods are useful, but cannot be trusted by themselves
- A large number of non-signature-based methods are feasible, although since an operational system is being examined, their unsuitably high rate of false alarm is of concern for implementation
- Using multiple methods simultaneously is beneficial, especially when using both signature-based and non-signature-based methods simultaneously
- Performing real verification testing is very challenging since operational ICSs are not available for experimentation

Recent Examples (2010 or After)

While our cutoff date of 2010 for "recent" methods is somewhat arbitrary, it reasonably marks the time when ICS ID techniques began to diverge from their ICT Enterprise "parents" and develop unique and useful methodologies customized for ICSs. The idea of using multiple methods simultaneously continued, eventually even including unique multi-method prototyping for some less common communication protocols such as IEC 60870-5-104 (Yang et al. 2013). This author utilizes signature-based and model-based techniques together. Full implementation and testing of the ICS ID techniques has not been easy to come by, most likely because few people had testbeds to perform such tests, and operational systems were not available for experimental testing.

A neural network approach for ID was proposed and tested by Gao et al. (2010) at the Mississippi State University. Promising results were shown for most attacks, although the false alarm rate was still high enough to be worrisome. Reply attacks were not well detected, with a quoted testbed accuracy of only 12%.

Automatic machine learning gave rise to the concept of state analysis, starting with a description of a signature-based and state-analysis system using a special rule language for MODBUS and DNP3 (Fovino et al. 2010), designed to express critical states in the system. At this point, the focus of IDSs started to change from "detecting intruders, or events signifying intruders," which would seem to be of concern for ICT systems, to "detecting changes to the underlying process, affecting process availability." This was a significant step forward as this is in fact one of the main difference between ICT and ICS system security. Fovino's embryonic work was more fully developed by Carcano et al. (2011), who tested a prototype system with a more elaborate Critical State Analysis engine and a State Proximity indicator. A multidimensional metric provided the parametric measure of the distance between a given state and any of the defined critical states. As Carcano et al. mention, the processes and critical states in an ICS system are generally well-known and limited in complexity, which is not normally the case for ICT systems. Goldenberg and Wool (2013) use a somewhat similar approach, modeling the current and critical states with Deterministic Finite Automation (DFA) techniques. These authors find that a multiple-DFA method would be superior to the single-DFA method they describe, but leave verification for future work.

A key observation for these "recent" ICS ID techniques is that they are attempting to measure the actual process values as much as possible from the network traffic, and determine anomalous behavior as disturbances in the process.

An n-gram anomaly detection technique described in Tylman (2013) shows that ICT IDS tools can still be used reliably. They developed a Snort pre-processor to detect anomalous communication between devices using the MODBUS RTU protocol. While this technique only applies to a unique scenario (MODBUS communication, which we already widely confront in ICS security), it does demonstrate that implementation does not necessarily mean building new tools from scratch.

Oman and Phillips (2008) described a full implantation of an ID system based on automated gathering, logging, and comparison of RTU device settings. Device settings are stored in XML format and comparisons are made with on-line monitor data. This is one of the most empirical based methods that has been described, and again, applies to a unique scenario (specific RTU devices). One could utilize this method with any ICS hardware configuration, provided one could exactly account for all device configurations and all possible anomalous states for those configurations.

The following research ideas have been established from these "recent" ID methods for ICSs:

- Again, using multiple methods simultaneously is beneficial, especially when using both signature-based and non-signature-based methods simultaneously

- Being able to model the state of the system (or underlying process) is very important, especially since availability of that process is of upmost importance
- Being able to model critical states and proximity to those critical states with various mathematical techniques seems to be a very promising way forward
- While ideas and prototypes are useful, there is not sufficient real testing and verification of many of the published methods
- Detailed and complete accounting of all specific hardware configurations in one's unique ICS provides useful and perhaps vital knowledge for ID

11.5 Process-Oriented Intrusion Detection

11.5.1 Overview

The design intent of an ICS is intended to (1) establish appropriate process values to produce desired output and (2) to allow operators to observe aspects of the plant to assure proper operation and safety and quality conditions. The sole purpose and only capability of ICS network traffic control messages is to support the synchronization of the PLC registers and to provide a local, HMI-side copy of these registers, to effect control of the plant processes. ICT network traffic has a much wider variety of uses, but is not generally used for process control. While both ICS and ICT computers have registers, only an ICS network can change and read register values. Register values directly affect process parameters and hence, the process. Since ICS security is ultimately for safeguarding the process variables and not the network traffic itself, process-oriented designs for monitoring and ID became of interest.

In this section, we discuss two current ID methods that focus on monitoring the underlying process in the control system rather than monitoring network traffic. The first method (Hadžiosmanović et al. 2014) attempts to model process variable excursions beyond their appropriate ranges using machine-learning techniques. The second method, which is based on ongoing ICS research at the Army Research Laboratory, requires plant personnel input to define critical process variable limits. Semantic modeling of plant control variables is used in both methods.

Semantic Security Monitoring (SSM) uses analysis of control-bus traffic messages to construct a 3rd copy of the plant-PLC registers for a new purpose: to detect events that suggest that plant operations may be out of specification, out of compliance, or out of a desired safety range. These events form the basis for a cyber-security monitoring capability. The change in emphasis is necessary; ICS networks are intended to control plant processes to produce quality output. Input sensors are queried at rates and with precision sufficient to accomplish control to maintain quality output. These rates, precision, and monitored parameters may not be appropriate or sufficient for security and safety monitoring operations.

11.5.1.1 Semantic Security Modeling from Network Traffic Data

Hadžiosmanović et al. (2014) describe a novel network monitoring approach that utilizes process semantics by (1) extracting the value of process variables from network traffic, (2) characterizing types of variables based on the behavior of time series, and (3) modeling and monitoring the regularity of variable values over time.

Their prototype system measures MODBUS traffic using scripts written in the policy language of the Bro Intrusion Detection Platform (www.bro.org) and custom C++ code. Data characterization is achieved by using heuristic algorithms to compare project file information with the network traffic information. Their results show good matches (>90 % matched) for constant process variables, but poor matches (20-70 % matched) for attribute and continuous variables. This information is used to create a "shadow" memory map of the ICS process variables.

During a training period, deviations are measured, and a rolling forecasting procedure is used to cross validate the model. A control-limits model and/or an autoregression model are then used to model all of the process variables, providing the basis for alerting.

Approximately 98 % of the process control variables used in real-world plans are reliably monitored by this process (Hadžiosmanović et al. 2014). The remaining 2 % of the variables remain challenging to model with this approach.

11.5.1.2 ARL Collaborative Modeling using SME Input, Network Traffic Data, and Process Monitoring Data

The novel approach by Hadziosmanovic et al. demonstrates that process variables can successfully be modeled for ID. However, as they mention, additional work is needed if all of the process variables are to be monitored reliably. Our ICS ID research at the Army Research Laboratory (ARL) is based on the assumption that all of the process variables do not need to monitored for alerting. Rather, there are critical process variables that need to be monitored for alerting, but abnormal values of the remaining variables are not significant enough to harm underlying plant process. We argue that identifying the critical values and determining the allowed ranges of those critical values is extremely difficult if only network traffic data is used. We use a collaborative modeling approach which uses plant operator or plant Subject Matter Expert (SME) input and out-of-band (OOB) sensor data in addition to data from network packets.

In Table 11.1, we describe general differences between the ARL Collaborative method and SSM model of Hadziosmanovic et al.

Our model recognizes that, just as in ICT ID, reference information from plant sensors, configurations, semantics, and policies (acceptable security/safety value ranges) must be captured, maintained, shared, and made available to the security/safety monitoring analysts in timely, orderly, and priority-relevant means to enhance decision-making. However, it also recognizes that ICS process sampling methods and process control methods (e.g. MODBUS) were never intended to feed security/safety analyses. Thus, as stated earlier, many process parameters seen in network

Table 11.1 General differences between the Hadziosmanovic et al. SSM model and the ARL collaborative model

Step	SSM method (Hadziosmanovic et al.)	Collaborative method (ARL)
Identify variables	• Extract values of process variables from network traffic	• Utilize critical process variable information specifically identified and described by plant process engineer (SMEs)
		• Assemble and update security and safety-relevant models based on SME input
Characterize process	• Characterize types of variables based upon observed behavior of time series (Train Model)	• Identify units, possible ranges, typical ranges, change characteristics, required sampling rates, and extreme-value conditions based on SME input
		• Refine model characterization using network traffic data
Model and alert	• Model the regularity of variable values over time using machine learning approaches to signal anomalous behavior, or significant drift/divergence of the process	• Refine model using network traffic data and OOB data
		• Alert based on excursions of critical process variables beyond SME-provided input

traffic may not be relevant, or may not be sampled at sufficient rate or fidelity. Moreover, there may be other process variables that are indeed critical, but they are not represented in network traffic, i.e. they are out of band. In this case, independent sensing of these parameters would be needed to create sufficient uplift in timeliness, accuracy, and relevance to the security/safety monitoring mission. In the ARL model, the SME defines the critical security model variables based on his knowledge and analysis of the plant processes, and the IDS security engineer implements the appropriate security model.

We refer to this model as "collaborative" since the security engineer utilizes human input from the plant operator/SME for constructing the IDS security model.

11.5.2 ARL Collaborative Intrusion Detection: A Case Study of a Sample Plant

In this section, we describe a case study implementation of the ARL Collaborative ID model. We also illustrate specific operational scenarios in which the collaborative model offers significant advantages over other methods. We end with a description of an effective alerting infrastructure which employs three ID methods, the first of which is the collaborative method outlined here.

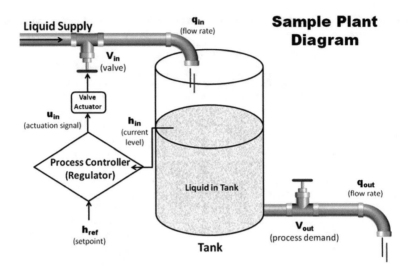

Fig. 11.2 Diagram of a sample plant

11.5.2.1 Background: Description of a Plant

Physical Plant Model

We show a plant diagram of our sample case study plant in Fig. 11.2. The plant uses a process controller (regulator) to maintain liquid level in a tank to the level value prescribed by a set point parameter entered from the HMI.

Output flow, represented by q_{out}, reflects typical outflow to the process. A regulator monitors the current liquid level h_{in} in the tank, and adjusts the actuation signal u_{in} to an inflow supply valve V_{in} to maintain the level at the set point value h_{ref}. The regulator design is intended to maintain the liquid level during anticipated process loading.

Much of the process control for this sample plant is performed by the process controller, or regulator. According to Astrom (2002) more than 95 % of regulators in control loops are of the PID (Proportional-Integral-Differential) or PI (Proportional-Integral) type. In PID type regulator, a sensor measures the process variable and the regulator compares that value with the set point value to provide the current error as a function of time [*error(t)*]. A proportional term provides a contribution to change the output (actuation) directly, according to the magnitude and direction of the error. An integral term accumulates a weighted sum of all past error values and is usually needed to allow for convergence of the process value to the setpoint value. A derivative term can improve stability and reduce oscillatory behavior by responding more to increased changes in the error value. The actuator output u_{in} is a weighted average of these three terms:

$$\text{Actuator Output } \mathbf{u}_{in} = W_{proportional} * error(t)$$
$$+ W_{integral} * \int error(t)\,dt$$
$$+ W_{derivative} * \frac{d[error(t)]}{dt}$$

Most plants encounter unanticipated load changes called disturbances that often present as step changes in the output load. Implementation of this load in the actual plant process can reveal previously unknown issues which can have an impact on plant monitoring data.

Implementation: Electronic Plant Model

For this case study, we implement the plant model (Fig. 11.2) by replacing the fluid mechanic components by electronic counterparts. A diagram illustrating our electronic implementation for the sample plant is shown in Fig. 11.3.

In the electronic implementation, electric current flow represents the liquid supply flow $\mathbf{q}_{in}$ to the tank. The reservoir or tank is equivalent to a capacitor. Valves $\mathbf{V}_{in}$ and $\mathbf{V}_{out}$ (or $\mathbf{a}_{out}$) control flow rates are modeled using a potentiometer and/or a bipolar-junction transistor operating in its linear range.

In our electronic implementation, the regulator is replaced by an Arduino computer programmed to function as a PID process controller. Digital signals are converted to

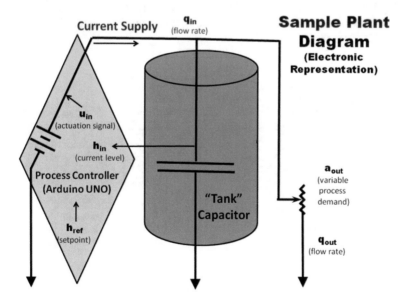

Fig. 11.3 Electronic representation of sample plant

continuous current flow by integrating the digital signal into a resistor-capacitor circuit. The time-based behavior of the physical plant can then be matched in the electrical model system. Thus, an electronic PID controller will appropriately regulate the electronic circuits in the electronic plant model.

Plant Control Network

The network diagram of the plant control network in Fig. 11.4 shows a PLC (PID controller), an HMI, a network traffic monitor (ICS Security monitor), and a high-speed sensor (Independent LEVEL sensor) that monitors the tank level.

Human Machine Interface (HMI)

In this implementation, MODBUS TCP messages are sent from the HMI to the PLC over the control network at regular polling-rate intervals of approximately one second. The HMI also affords monitoring of PLC variables representing the state of the plant process. There are roughly 10 different MODBUS commands which are limited to reading one or more register values, and setting one or more register values. Some commands pertain to 'coils' which are a binary type of register, which can take values of ON or OFF. Some PLC registers are used as inputs into its control algorithms. For example, sensor values obtained from interrogation by the PLC may be made available via MODBUS queries using a specific register. The HMI can also be used to write specific control parameters to the PLC, using MODBUS commands over the network.

The function of the HMI is to periodically query the PLC to obtain and often display important PLC control register values that are indicative of important process variables. The HMI output is then monitored regularly (usually visually) by a human plant operator.

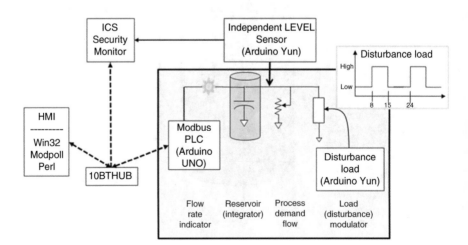

Fig. 11.4 Network diagram of electronic implementation of sample plant

PLC/Regulator (PID Controller)

The Arduino UNO PID controller regulates incoming supply flow q_{in}. (The Ardino UNO is labeled "Modbus PLC (Arduino UNO)" in Fig. 11.4). The controller supports MODBUS TCP communications over a wired Ethernet network. Register and coil number assignments are made arbitrarily by plant engineers, which we will see is an important observation in Section 11.5.2.2.1.

The Arduino PLC implementation diagram for our plant process is shown in Fig. 11.5. We show the use of one coil register (C[1]) as an on/off or RUN/STOP switch which must be set by the HMI controller interface.

During operation, a level sensor (10-bit analog input A/D converter) provides current level values h_{in} to the controller which update register R[2]. The desired set point value h_{ref} is stored in R[1] using a MODBUS write operation from the HMI. The PID algorithm evaluates the error (difference between set point and current level) and provides a copy of this value to update R[9] as the current error value. The PID algorithm calculates a new output actuation signal value u_{in}, and sends the actuation signal to an output actuator (using a pulse-width modulated signal) and provides the corresponding numeric output value to R[3].

In this manner, MODBUS read-register commands can obtain values from all PID parameters including set point, current level, current error, current output, as well as other parameters exposed to the MODBUS registers.

Network Traffic Monitor

To implement network monitoring for intrusion detection, a network traffic sensor is added to the plant control network to enable passive monitoring of all MODBUS TCP traffic. This sensor is labeled "ICS Security monitor" in Fig. 11.4.

Fig. 11.5 Arduino Uno PLC implementation diagram

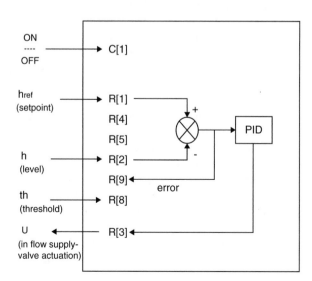

Independent High-Speed Sensor

We also add a high-frequency sensor to the plant which also monitors critical process parameters. This sensor is labeled "Independent LEVEL sensor" in Fig. 11.4.

This high-speed sensor serves two purposes. First, it helps the SME to better characterize some typical behaviors that are not critical, but may appear as such when sampled at the lower rates used by the control system. Second, the sensor provides an independent (out of band) physical measurement that can validate data from the network traffic monitor.

For our specific plant model we use an inexpensive analog sensor to sample the specific critical process parameter 'liquid tank level.' The high speed sensors provides 1500 integer samples during a 1-s interval. This sampling rate and interval were determined experimentally to best illustrate typical oscillatory behavior in response to set point and step disturbances; this practice is also typically performed by SMEs during process control implementations and recipe change testing.

11.5.2.2   Configuration of Plan Security Monitoring Model

In this section we describe how our security model is configured using the collaborative method. We demonstrate that even if the variables captured from 1-s network polling of the PLC are used to populate a decision model, more information is needed to accurately define the security model. One still requires (1) an SME control engineer to verify the typical and over/under limit range bands thus describing the semantics of the observed value time-series, and (2) the SME to categorize these excursion events to allow un-ambiguous labeling of them to use in the semantic message for each corresponding alert.

Although there are many other process variables that could be monitored, we selected the "tank" level as our sole critical process variable. In our collaborative method, this critical process variable will receive priority in monitoring, and a common understanding of typical and alarm values will be determined. Semantics and notification actions to be implemented are achieved by collaborative discussions between plant personnel and the security monitoring analysts. We discuss these aspects in the subsections below.

Inference of Critical Values from Network Traffic Data

A first step in defining the security model is to examine the network MODBUS traffic itself. In our case study implementation, an ICS network traffic security monitor collects MODBUS TCP traffic between the HMI and the Arduino PLC. We use this passive monitoring data to attempt to construct a valid parallel model of the critical plant operating parameters. In the lower right section of Fig. 11.6, we show actual configuration and register content logs from the running plant. The traffic monitor is able to receive and parse all MODBUS traffic, and provide register-labels for each of the values received, but the underlying configuration is not clear.

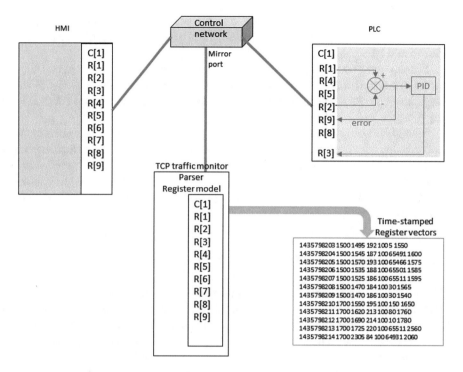

Fig. 11.6 Observed plant parameters from ICS security monitor

Without knowledge of the plant or the monitored process, it is difficult to infer (1) which process variable is represented by each register, and (2) the semantic of each register. Is the register an input, or an output, or a set-point value, or unused, or even more importantly, not used today for this recipe and batch but may be used in a different recipe or batch run?

While machine learning can certainly be applied to this type of model, it will only identify the degree of 'normality' of current observations compared to past observations. A machine learning approach really does not allow inference of the purpose, configuration, or semantic of these parameters. These details and even more useful information concerning the criticality and acceptable value-ranges of the important (critical) values must be obtained from the plant operator/SME.

Determination of Critical Values from SME Input and Network Traffic Data

A next step in defining the security model is to consult with plant personnel on the exact usage of PLC registers and other plan process configuration details that can be monitored. In our case study plant, after consultation with the plant operator/SME, we are able to better understand plant operating processes.

First, we find that the R[2] register values report our critical value of the tank level. Further information is provided in the form of upper- and lower-alarm bands that should be monitored for the R[2] register.

Second, our plant operator/SME also advises that the system is frequently subjected to a disturbance (unpredicted change in load) which presents as a significant step-change to the process. Tank levels may traverse the specified alarm bands during this time and this should not be considered a course for alarm.

Finally, disturbances and set-point changes perturb the controller in similar manners causing a damped oscillatory deviation in the tank level having a frequency of about 5Hz. Since the MODBUS HMI polls every 1000 ms, various peak values from such oscillations may be represented in the logs and model. This information can be used to verify and validate SME input for the allowed ranges of the tank level.

Model Refinement and Verification using Network Traffic Data

Time-stamped log records from the traffic monitor provide input to our semantic security model. In Fig. 11.7, we show the R[2] tank level in column 3 of the log records. With further knowledge from the plant operator/SME, we identify the high-speed sensor tank level measurements as column 7 in f the log records(see Fig. 11.7).

Typically, plant personnel can specify more precise conditions needed to justify issuance of a semantic security monitoring alert by providing an additional qualifier describing the extent or severity of the alarm condition. In the case of our case study, we may be informed that during disturbances, the tank level will often travel outside of the alarm bands, significantly so, but, will not maintain these extreme values for 'longer than 1 s' (as the control algorithm applies output actuation to bring this controlled parameter back into desired range).

Plant personnel provide the information that the level set-point h_{ref} is indicated by the value in R[1]. Referring to the above annotated model, the set-point appears as column 2 in the register vector log. We notice it starts at 1500 and after 8 s, changes to 1700. The process engineer recalls that for this recipe, the batch starts at 1500 and then does an automatic set-point change to 1700 at 8-s. Thus, the alarm bands need to be adjusted in the detection model to reflect this planned event.

As an example of a semantic security monitoring language, we provide a sample implementation of a windowed alarm band integrator to calculate a moving area-under-curve value to use to identify routine excursions as distinct from more severe alarms where the tank level maintains an alarm value for a longer time period and thus justifying alarming and notification.

Now equipped with a level monitoring capability with independent sensor input, we focus on analyses which can determine the magnitude and severity of alarm events. The observation of one alarm is not usually sufficient justification for declaration of a significant event. In process control it is often the case that an alarm condition must persist for a minimum time duration after which it becomes a concern. Many power-conversion processes specify a maximum duration for delivery

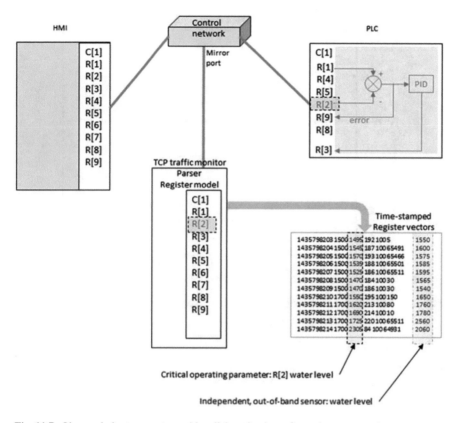

Fig. 11.7 Observed plant parameters with collaborative input from plant personnel

of power at some value above its nominal rating. For example, an aircraft turbine engine might be rated at 90 % power continuous duty, but 5-min at 100 % and 1-min at 120 % power. Our analytic alerting method needs to allow expression of these various alarm bands and provide means to calculate accumulated values over various time-durations.

To illustrate this capability, we implemented a windowed, area-under-curve (AUC) function and applied it to the tank level log data (see Fig. 11.8). The function accumulates net area above the alarm-high level as well as net area below the alarm-low level using trapezoidal integration.

We are then informed by the plant personnel that if the AUC stays above 1000 (unit-secs) for longer than 20 s, then it is an alarm condition that requires notifications. Above, we implement an AUC integrator with sample length of 30, calculated each new sample-time (1000 ms) using alarm bands of 1800 and 1300. Negative excursions are accumulated along with positive excursions providing a cumulative value shown above. Thus, although AUC for the level parameter exceeds the alarm level, it does not persist longer than 6 s in the sample above and no notifications are needed.

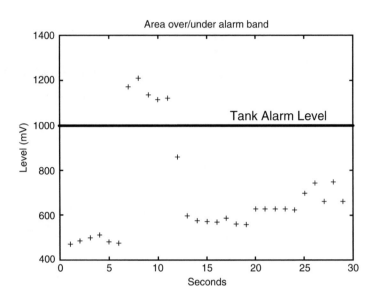

Fig. 11.8 ICS security monitor data showing tank level excursions above tank alarm level

The tank level alarm process described here is somewhat complex, but it represents exactly what the plant operator/SME desire. We argue that our collaborative security model is more effective than one based solely on network packet analysis.

Model Refinement and Verification using Out-of-Band Data (High speed sensor)

Process variables may not be sampled at a sufficient rate or precision to inform security/safety decisions. Our case study plan can clearly show this distinction. It is customary in process control to provide parameter information only as frequently as is needed to control the plant. It is however quite common for many process variables to exhibit wild or oscillatory excursions at much faster rates. This can occur in response to disturbances (changing load conditions) or set-point changes (changing value requirements). In a properly designed plant control environment, such excursions would be anticipated and means provided to diminish these behaviors before any damage is caused. Unfortunately, since the control design can often prevent adverse effects by dampening such excursions, a cyber monitoring system may only receive sampled parameter values which could include some of these extreme parameter values that are clearly out of range. This we anticipate will be the source of most false alarms, or false-positive alerts.

If the (few) monitored parameters are described as critical variables by the SME, then it may be justifiable to augment normal network monitoring of ICS sensors with additional, high-speed out-of-band sensors. Gathering independent measurements of

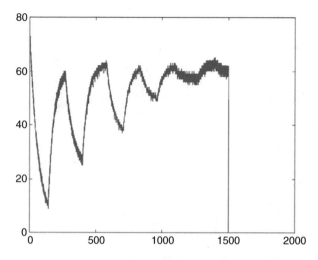

Fig. 11.9 One-second (1500 samples) duration high-speed sensor sampling of tank level during system disturbance. Within 1500 samples (1 sample of the Independent LEVEL sensor), significant deviations are observed

such critical parameters will supply significant uplift to data and decision quality. In our case study implementation, an independent level sensor that polls the tank level at high speeds, in synchronization with the ICS Security monitor.

To more fully understand the excursions in the tank-level values in response to step change disturbances, we obtain a trace from a high-speed sensor. In Fig. 11.9, we show 1500 samples for a 1-s interval triggered by the increased step load disturbance. This oscillatory behavior occurs in response to each load change. Analysis of these samples using a DFT (discrete Fourier transform) confirm the principal component of 5-Hz along with low frequency and DC components. Monitoring of the 1-s MODBUS samples of the tank level with the ICS Security monitor will not represent this signal consistently.

Knowledge of this oscillatory behavior allows us to better interpret the meaning of the tank level when sampled at 1-s intervals. Frequent excursions above and below the alarm bands can be observed for the critical variable of the tank level. It is obvious that one-second network sampling is not adequate to alert reliably on the behavior. Actual value ranges and durations should again be determined in consultation with plant personnel to provide realistic ranges compatible with the analysis, decision, and alert notification time-frames.

11.5.2.3 Intrusion Detection Alerting

We define 'alerting' as automatic information generation to be sent to a human analyst for further consideration. We define an alarm as a determination of a possible compromise or other insecure situation as determined by the human analyst, based on alerting information that was provided by the intrusion detection system.

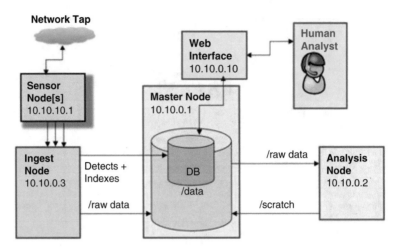

Fig. 11.10 Sample generic intrusion detection architecture

Our collaborative intrusion detection model is implemented at ARL in a live testbed. We report on general findings from our testbed experiments. In Fig. 11.10, we show the implemented IDS architecture in our testbed. A network tap (e.g. SPAN port on a switch) provides network capture data to one or more sensor nodes. Some of the data are pre-processed on the sensor nodes into 'detects' (detect/alert information) and index data. The Ingest node then forwards that data to a master node, which stores raw data and provides indexed information for analyst web tools. More complicated analytics are executed by the Analysis Node, which again places results back on the Master Node for the web interface to display. The Web Interface contains an HTTP web server with web analytics and web links for execution of additional analysis tools. The Human Analyst then examines alerting information that resides in the system using various analytical tools.

In our testbed implementation, IDS alerting by the Sensor Node is generated in one of three methods:

1. Critical Process Values: This is the collaborative method just described. Critical Process variables are those that define whether the control system is successfully operational or not. Sensor nodes are modified specifically to monitor the value of all critical process variables that have been defined collaboratively between the ARL security engineer and the site operations SME. Nominal values, and upper and lower limits for critical values are programmed into the sensor node. The example of a critical value for our case study is the tank level. Danger can incur if the tank overflows.

2. Network Packet Reporting Values: Anomalies identified by deep inspection of the network packets captured by the network traffic monitor are reported by the sensor node. These network values are not necessarily critical process variables, but if they are not within reasonable range, they may indicate a minor issue or

warn of a future significant network intrusion. Collaborative discussions between the ARL security engineer and the plant operator/SME will determine nominal values and ranges, and the ARL security engineer will use network captures to refine the model.

3. <u>Network Traffic Pattern Anomalies</u>: Traffic on a control system network is very minimal and is usually very periodic. Methods similar to the non-signature based ICS anomaly detection discussed earlier in this chapter are used to provide alerting. As we note, we do not regard this alerting information as something the analyst should use exclusively to report an alarm condition. These alerts are expected to have a high enough false-alarm rate that more information should be used to draw a conclusion about reporting an alarm. Metrics and limits to those metrics will need to be defined. These metrics will be specific to the site and will define when anomalous network traffic is indicated. This calibration process should be done carefully to ensure that false alarm (alert) information is not passed up to the Interrogator Analyst. Network traffic pattern anomaly alerts are not necessarily critical in that they do not indicate that the system is not functional. However, they may indicate that an intrusion is in progress, and that the critical process variables are threatened. Providing this alert information to the analyst can help avoid a critical process failure.

11.6   Summary and Conclusions

One of the central themes of IDS research and development for ICSs is whether one can easily transfer intrusion detection methods developed and implemented for early and current ICT systems. ICSs are not merely a collection of networked computer servers, network switches, and routers, such as you might find in an ICT network. ICSs often simultaneously employ many different intrusion detection and alerting methods, including signature-based, anomaly-based, and specification-based methods.

An ICS can be described in terms of a Primary Bus and Secondary Bus architecture, where the Secondary Bus connects field devices to PLCs and other ICS hardware. The Primary Bus is often connected via standard network communication protocols and perhaps even to a corporate network or the Internet, but the Secondary Bus may not have network-addressable components. We assume ICS IDSs will only connect to the Primary Bus.

Digital Bond's Quickdraw adaptation for signature-based methods using Snort was used on ICSs beginning approximately 2008. ICS (and ICT) security researchers however often favor a combination of signature-based ID methods and non-signature based ID methods. Starting approximately 2010, ICS ID techniques began to diverge from their ICT Enterprise "parents" and developed unique and useful methodologies that focused more on characterizing the actual ICS process values, even to the point of creating and monitoring a distinct copy of the ICS plant PLC registers. These register states can be configured automatically via network polling, or with collaborative assistance from plant personnel.

As we demonstrate in our sample plant case study, all of the PLC registers do not need to be monitored for alerting. If PLC register values obtained from polling the network are used to populate a decision model, more information is needed to accurately define a sensible security model. In some cases, higher time precision is also needed to accurately determine the alarming method. Network polling of register values and other network traffic can be used for identifying anomalous behavior once the plant variables are defined. Anomaly detection in ICSs is more effective than for ICT networks due to the small volume and high regularity of ICS network traffic. ARL testbed research on intrusion detection methods for ICSs proposes a three-method approach: collaborate monitoring of specific critical plant process variables, a process-oriented anomaly-based technique based on network polling, and non-signature base anomaly detection technique for network traffic patterns. Alerts from all three methods are sent to a human analyst who investigates further and decides if plant operational personnel should be notified.

References

Anderson, J. P. (1980). *Computer security threat monitoring and surveillance*. Fort Washington, PA: James P. Anderson.

Astrom, K. (2002). Chapter 6. PID control. In *Control System Design Lecture Notes for ME 155A*. UCSB, CA.

Axelsson, S. (2000). The base-rate fallacy and the difficult of intrusion detection. *ACM Transactions on Information and System Security (TISSEC), 3*(3), 186–205.

Carcano, A., Coletta, A., Guglielmi, M., Masera, M., Fovino, I., & Trombetta, A. (2011). A multi-dimensional critical state analysis for detecting intrusions in SCADA systems. *IEEE Transactions on Industrial Informatics, 7*(2), 179–186.

Cheung, S., Dutertre, B., Fong, M., Lindqvist, U., Skinner, K., & Valdes, A. (2007, January). Using model-based intrusion detection for SCADA networks. In *Proceedings of the SCADA Security Scientific Symposium* (Vol. 46, pp. 1–12).

Denning, D. E. (1987). An intrusion-detection model. *IEEE Transactions on Software Engineering, 2*, 222–232.

Denning, D. E., & Neumann, P. G. (1985). Requirements and model for IDES — A real-time intrusion detection expert system. *Document A005, SRI International, 333*.

Fovino, I., Carcano, A., Murel, T., Trombetta, A., & Masera, M. (2010). Modbus/DNP3 state-based intrusion detection system. In *2010 24th IEEE International Conference on Advanced Information Networking and Applications*.

Gao, W., Morris, T., Reaves, B., & Richey, D. (2010). On SCADA control system command and response injection and intrusion detection. In *2010 ECrime Researchers Summit*.

Goldenberg, N., & Wool, A. (2013). Accurate modeling of Modbus/TCP for intrusion detection in SCADA systems. *International Journal of Critical Infrastructure Protection, 6*(2), 63–75.

Hadžiosmanović, D., Sommer, R., Zambon, E., & Hartel, P. (2014). Through the eye of the PLC. In *Proceedings of the 30th Annual Computer Security Applications Conference on— ACSAC '14*.

Liao, H. J., Lin, C. H. R., Lin, Y. C., & Tung, K. Y. (2013). Intrusion detection system: A comprehensive review. *Journal of Network and Computer Applications, 36*(1), 16–24.

Long, K.S. (2004). Catching the cyber spy: ARL's interrogator, *Army Research Lab Technical Report*, (DTIC ACC. NO. ADA432198).

Oman, P., & Phillips, M. (2008). Intrusion detection and event monitoring in SCADA networks. In *IFIP International Federation for Information Processing Critical Infrastructure Protection* (pp. 161–173).

Tsang, C., & Kwong, S. (2005). Multi-agent intrusion detection system in industrial network using ant colony clustering approach and unsupervised feature extraction. In *2005 IEEE International Conference on Industrial Technology.*

Tylman, W. (2013). SCADA intrusion detection based on modelling of allowed communication patterns. In *Advances in Intelligent Systems and Computing New Results in Dependability and Computer Systems* (pp. 489–500).

Verba, J., & Milvich, M. (2008). Idaho national laboratory supervisory control and data acquisition intrusion detection system (SCADA IDS). In *2008 IEEE Conference on Technologies for Homeland Security.*

Yang, Y., Littler, T., Wang, H., Mclaughlin, K., & Sezer, S. (2013). Rule-based intrusion detection system for SCADA networks. In *2nd IET Renewable Power Generation Conference (RPG 2013).*

Yang, D., Usynin, A., & Hines, J. W. (2006, November). Anomaly-based intrusion detection for SCADA systems. In *5th International Topical Meeting on Nuclear Plant Instrumentation, Control and Human Machine Interface Technologies (npic&hmit 05)* (pp. 12–16).

Zhu, B., & Sastry, S. (2010, April). SCADA-specific intrusion detection/prevention systems: A survey and taxonomy. In *Proceedings of the 1st Workshop on Secure Control Systems (SCS).*

Chapter 12
Cyber Physical Intrusion Detection

Carlos Aguayo Gonzalez and Jeffrey Reed

12.1   Introduction

In this chapter, we continue to explore the topic introduced in the previous chapter, but with a special focus on use of physical measurements for intrusion detection. Approaches for protecting the field zone elements (i.e., the devices and networks in charge of control and automation such as programmable logic controllers) from cyber attack are traditionally limited to physical security. Field zone elements are those devices in the Secondary Bus of the Sample ICS shown in Fig. 11.1. Network security (e.g. intrusion prevention and intrusion detection) for the filed zone is often limited to the conduits, and end-point protection to a limited extent.

At the same time, field zone operational environment also impacts the attacker's ability to achieve their malicious objectives without being detected or triggering safety events. In a way, the field zone is the most difficult to attack, since attackers need to have intimate knowledge of the process and systems in order to achieve the malicious objectives without being discovered, and without triggering any of the safety and security mechanisms.

Therefore, monitoring the physical environment in the field zone can get very valuable information, not only about the physical process (control), but also about the execution status of controllers and digital devices. Since field controllers ultimately determine the physical process, it is possible to obtain an indirect assessment of the integrity of the field devices my monitoring the process itself. This concept can be extended to the monitoring of the physical processes happening inside the controllers themselves, and in this way assess directly the execution status of the controllers.

C.A. Gonzalez (✉) • J. Reed
PFP Cybersecurity, Vienna, VA, USA
e-mail: caguayog@pfpcyber.com

© Springer International Publishing Switzerland 2016   239
E.J.M. Colbert, A. Kott (eds.), *Cyber-security of SCADA and Other Industrial Control Systems*, Advances in Information Security 66,
DOI 10.1007/978-3-319-32125-7_12

In this chapter, we focus specifically on approaches that rely on monitoring physical measurements of the process and the controllers and use physical measurements to detect malicious intrusions in critical systems. An IDS based on such an approach characterizes the normal behavior of the physical measurements and detects anomalies from that baseline. The approach involves three main elements common to all pattern recognition systems: sensing, feature extraction, and classification.

The chapter concludes with the case study of an implemented IDS system for a commonly used programmable logic controller. The IDS determines the baseline. Then, we introduce a malicious modification, similar in structure and operation to Stuxnet, into the PLC logic, and show how the IDS uses the baseline to detect the intrusion.

12.2   Leveraging Physical Monitoring in ICS Cybersecurity

The use of physical process data is a key element in approaches to detecting computer attacks on CPS (Mo and Sinopoli 2009) in general, and ICS in particular. This general concept takes a number of variations, e.g., the use of historical data from physical systems, contextual data from multiple and diverse sensors, and human behaviors to enable anomaly detection and obtain a higher-level collective vision of the network for better event correlation and decision analysis (Chow 2011).

The same concept is presented in (Cárdenas 2011), in which the authors incorporate knowledge of the physical system under control to detect computer attacks that change the behavior of the targeted control system. There, when using knowledge of the physical system, a key idea is to focus on the final objective of the attack, and not on the particular mechanisms of how vulnerabilities are exploited, and how the attack is hidden. Moreover, they analyze the security and safety of the defended systems by exploring the effects of stealthy attacks, and by ensuring that automatic attack-response mechanisms will not drive the system to an unsafe state.

Monitoring the physical environment in CPS can provide very valuable information, not only about the physical process (control), but also about the execution status of controllers and digital devices. Since field controllers ultimately determine the physical process, it is possible to obtain an indirect assessment of the integrity of the field devices by monitoring the process itself. This concept, however, can be further extended to the monitoring of the physical processes occurring inside the controllers themselves, and in this way assessing directly the execution status of the controllers. This approach relies on monitoring the physical environment in the immediate vicinity of the controllers to capture what is known as side channel information. The side channel information can be used for integrity assessment and for intrusion detection. We provide a detailed description of that approach in the next section, but first we introduce the concept of side channels attacks.

Side-channel attacks refer to a variety of techniques in which adversary gains useful confidential information about a system by collecting physical evidence about the system's operation—e.g. its power consumption or electromagnetic leaks—and then uses this information leak to defeat the system's security mechanisms. The term "side-channel" refers to the fact that the adversary exploits the sources and channels of information that the designers of the system did not intend to provide to anyone. In the open literature, such side-channel attacks were first introduced in 1996 (Kocher 1996).

The non-invasive nature of side-channel attacks allows them to defeat a device during its normal operation without causing a physical impact. Side-channel attacks have been successfully used to extract cryptographic key material of symmetric and public key encryption algorithms, such as Data Encryption Standard (DES) and Advanced Encryption Standard (AES), running on microprocessors, DSPs, FPGAs, ASICs and high performance CPUs. For example, the execution status information carried by the processor's dynamic power consumption has been exploited in power analysis side-channel attacks to obtain secret cryptographic keys from smart cards (Popp et al. 2007). Other side-channel attacks have been implemented by observing changes in time delay (Kocher 1996), electromagnetic radiation (Gandolfi 2001), or even fault behavior (Biham and Shamir 1997).

Side-channel attacks based on power analysis have been attempted using a number of techniques that vary in terms of resources required, number of observations, and success rate. For example, Simple Power Analysis (SPA) involves directly interpreting power consumption measurements collected during cryptographic operations and can yield algorithm as well as key information (Mangard 2003). Differential power analysis on the other hand, requires more involved statistical analysis of the power measurements, often by correlating the data being manipulated with the side channel information, to exploit specific biases in power consumption during cryptographic operation and to obtain key values (Kocher 1999). In general, all power analysis side-channel attacks rely on having knowledge of the encryption algorithm being employed, the input to the cryptographic device, a model of the device's power consumption, and power measurements from several encryption operations. Attackers use all this information to identify the cryptographic key value that is more likely to generate the observed power consumption give the specific model used.

12.3 Example—SCADA Cybersecurity Monitoring Using Power Fingerprinting

The physical environment in CPS provides very valuable information about the physical process, which in turn can be used to detect cyber attacks on ICS. As shown by side-channel attacks, the physical processes happening inside the controllers themselves produce physical side channels in the immediate vicinity of the controller. These side channels, similar to those exploited in cryptographic attacks, can also be used for integrity assessment and intrusion detection. Integrity assessment based on monitoring the physical side channels is particularly well suited for field devices since it adds no overhead on the target platforms and can be applied to legacy and resource-constrained systems that are often found in the field zone.

Here we consider a particular example of such integrity assessment approach called Power Fingerprinting (PFP) that uses physical measurements from a side channel (e.g. power consumption) to detect malicious intrusions in systems (Reed and Gonzalez 2012). PFP is able to monitor directly the execution of systems with constrained resources and does not require the loading of any software artifacts on the target platform. PFP can perform intrusion detection directly in ICS, even in the systems controlling critical processes. PFP provides an extra layer of protection and is complementary to traditional IDS approaches. Unlike the power analysis side-channel attacks, however, PFP does not attempt to reverse-engineer the executed code, or steal secret keys, but only to characterize the normal behavior of the side-channels and detect anomalies deviating from that baseline.

12.3.1 Monitoring Physical Side-Channels to Detect Malicious Intrusions and Unauthorized Execution

PFP performs fine-grained anomaly detection on the processor's side channels, such as power consumption or electromagnetic emissions, to determine whether it has deviated from expected operation. A PFP monitor, shown in Fig. 12.1, uses a physical sensor to capture side-channels which contain patterns or "fingerprints" that emerge as a direct consequence of state transitions during execution. In PFP, power traces are processed using signal detection and classification techniques on an external device. The observed traces are compared against trusted references to assess whether the execution has deviated from its expected behavior, e.g. when an attack has managed to install malicious software.

Because in PFP the monitoring is performed by an external device, the memory and processing overhead on the target is greatly reduced or eliminated. Also, PFP monitors can be built using Commercial off-the-shelf (COTS) components.

12.3.2 Integrity Assessment and Intrusion Detection

The concept behind PFP integrity assessment and monitoring includes three main elements common to all pattern recognition systems: sensing, feature extraction, and classification. Sensing involves measuring, directly or indirectly, the instantaneous current drain. This measurement can be accomplished using a variety of approaches, including current or electromagnetic probes.

During runtime assessment, PFP compares the captured traces against a baseline references and looks for deviations beyond what is considered normal for that target execution. The baseline references uniquely identify the execution of a given software routine. They are extracted in a controlled environment before the system is deployed. The stored references are used by the PFP monitor to detect unauthorized execution deviations at run-time.

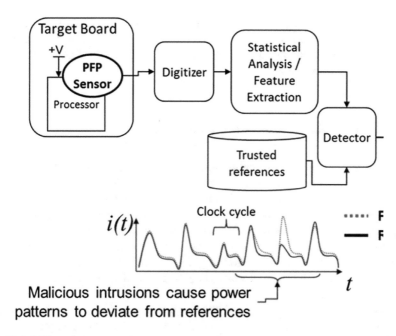

Fig. 12.1 PFP monitor

The level of expected deviation during normal operation is identified during the characterization process and determines a threshold between normal and anomalous execution. When the observed traces cannot be matched with any of the baseline references, within a reasonable tolerance, it is determined that an intrusion has occurred.

12.3.3 Characterization

PFP is based on detecting anomalies and deviations from baseline references. These references describe the expected power consumption and how much variation is considered normal. PFP references can be extracted using several different approaches. One of the most straightforward methods includes developing a "gold sample" of the target platform. In this scenario, PFP baselines are determined by executing the gold sample in a controlled environment while observing its power consumption. This process is close to automated software testing, thus PFP can leverage existing tools to facilitate the baseline extraction process. While references are unique to a specific target system, the process to extract them is general and can be applied across platforms and applications.

Ideally, a reference is extracted from every execution path in the target. ICS and embedded systems with their relatively limited complexity present excellent opportunities for complete characterization as their process execution is limited in functionality (as compared to an enterprise server, for example). In cases when extracting a reference for every execution path is not feasible due to complexity, characterization is focused on critical modules of the system (e.g. Kernel, Boot loader, cypher, etc.) with synchronization support. This way, PFP can monitor the integrity of the target modules every time they are executed.

12.3.4   PFP Advantages and Limitations

PFP enables the continuous, real-time, direct monitoring of elements of ICS systems for which alternative solution for detecting malicious intrusions may not be readily available. PFP is able to detect intrusions even at a minor disruption in execution, even if the malicious intrusion remains dormant or mimics legitimate network traffic. This detection capability allows rapid response to neutralize the threat. PFP does not violate the principle of non-interference in terms of safety and security in critical ICS, allowing the monitoring of sensitive components. PFP can detect zero-day threats and adversarial attacks largely independent of platform, failure scenarios, or attack techniques.

However, PFP provides only a limited support for forensic analysis and attack attribution. PFP can help identifying the modules that have been tampered during attack, but not the type or modifications or the attacker's intentions. PFP should only be applied in a defense in depth approach, as part of a comprehensive security solution.

12.4   Case Study: Siemens S7-1200 Monitoring

Here we describe a case study in which we implement a reference system in a target Siemens PLC and extract its PFP baseline references. We introduce a malicious modification, similar in structure and operation to Stuxnet, into the PLC logic and use thee references to detect the intrusion.

12.4.1   The System

The target platform for this experiment is the Siemens SIMATIC S7-1200 micro PLC. The proof-of-concept PFP monitor for this experiment is implemented using off-the-shelf equipment. The target PLC is first instrumented with a commercial near-field sensor for electromagnetic compatibility testing to capture the side-channel signal. The near-field probe is a commercial probe from Beehive Electronics and has good spatial resolution, reducing the interference from other subsystems in the board. The increased spatial resolution also reduces the sensitivity, which is compensated by a wide-band low-noise amplifier (LNA) with 30dB of gain. This setup is shown in Fig. 12.2.

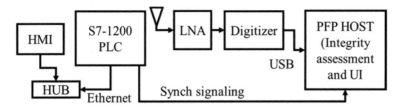

Fig. 12.2 PFP monitor measurement setup

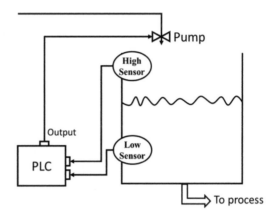

Fig. 12.3 Tank level control application for case study

    The signal captured by the sensor is then digitized using a commercial real-time oscilloscope from Tektronix. The oscilloscope is configured to a sampling rate of 2.5 GSPS and a total of 100K samples are collected in every trace. A physical trigger signal is provided by using one of the available IO pins in the PLC. This signal is used for synchronization purposes, to indicate to the oscilloscope when to start capturing power traces. Once captured, the signals are transferred using USB and processed at the PFP host using custom software tools and scripts.

    The application logic for this experiment is a simple tank-level control application, shown in Fig. 12.3. In the control system, the target S7-1200 PLC controls the level of a tank using two sensors to determine when to turn on and off a pump.

    The sensors are configured to provide a logic 1 when the tank's liquid level is at or above the sensor's level (when they are wet) and a logic 0 when the liquid level is below the sensor.

    The PLC turns the pump on when the tank level drops below the Low sensor (L) and turn the pump off when the level reaches the High sensor (H). When the level is in between both sensors (L=1, H=0) there is no change in the pump state. The last combination of input values (L=0, H=1) is treated as a faulty condition.

    The target logic is implemented in the S7-1200 PLC as a SCL program in block OB1. The pseudocode of the application logic is shown in Fig. 12.4.

Fig. 12.4 Pseudocode of
application logic

```
// PFP Trigger

if L = 0 && H = 0 then

    pump = On
    alarm = Off
else if L = 1 && H = 1 then
    pump = Off
    alarm = Off
else if L = 0 && H = 1 then
    alarm = ON !!!

    pump = Off

    update alarm counter

else

    no change in outputs

end

// Reset PFP Trigger
```

The target logic operation has 4 execution paths, mapping the truth table. The selection of what execution path is taken is determined by the combination of input values at the beginning of the logic cycle.

In order to facilitate the synchronization for this experiment, the application logic includes a physical trigger, which is an electric signal sent to the digitizer using the PLC Output port to indicate when the logic cycle is starting. It is important to note that there are other ways to perform this synchronization without the need for a physical signal.

In order to test the ability of PFP to detect intrusions, we modify the original application logic to mimic a malicious attack. The tamper introduced closely resembles the tampering that Stuxnet introduced in the Siemens S7-315 PLCs. The tamper emulates Stuxnet's hooking of DP_RECV to collect information from normal operation for approximately 13 days.

The attack, depicted in Fig. 12.5, consists of moving the original DP_RECV routine to a different logic block and replacing it with an infected block, which monitors inputs and forwards requests to the original DP_RECV routine.

For this experiment, we introduce a tampering into our target system, similar in structure and operation to Stuxnet's RECV hook, with the goal to modify normal logic operation, i.e. turn pump on regardless of sensor input and disable alarm system

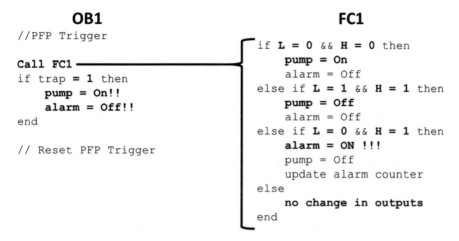

Fig. 12.5 Pseudocode of tampered application (OB1 and FC1)

As shown in Fig. 12.5, the tampered version moves the original logic block and calls it. After the original logic is executed, the tampered block post-processes the results to change the logic behavior. The most important element of the tamper, however, is the fact that behavioral modifications only take place in specific conditions. Similar to Stuxnet, this tamper has the ability to go into a dormant state, in which the tamper simply listens to the trigger condition and original behavior is not affected.

In this case, the trigger condition is another digital input pin, which controls the sabotage routine. This selection of trigger mechanisms is arbitrary and selecting a different trigger mechanism would have no impact on PFP.

12.4.2 Baseline Reference Extraction

In order to perform the run-time assessment of the target PLC, it is necessary to extract the baseline references from all execution paths during the characterization process. Training traces are captured using a controlled environment in which we provide input vectors to exhaustively exercise all different paths.

Once training traces are captured for each execution path, we process each one using a spectral periodogram (spectrogram) to extract the frequency components of each training trace at different time segments. The spectrogram is the magnitude squared of the Discrete-Time Short-Time Fourier Transform (STFT), $X(\tau,\omega)$, as described below:

$$\text{spectrogram}\{x(t)\}(\tau,\omega) = |X(\tau,\omega)|^2$$

Where

$$X(m,\omega) = \sum_{n=-\infty}^{\infty} x[n] w[n-m] e^{-jwn}$$

Where, $x[n]$ is the captured PFP trace and $w[n]$ is a Gaussian window. The PFP references are constructed by averaging the spectrograms of the training traces for each execution path. So, for Path 0, the PFP reference is represented by S_0, for Path 1, the PFP reference is represented by S_1, and so on.

Once the references for each execution path are calculated, the PFP monitor uses them for determining at run-time what path has executed or whether an anomaly has been detected. In order to match the captured run-time test trace to a specific path reference, $r[n]$, we calculate its spectrogram and obtain the difference against each baseline reference over selected time segments and frequency bands.

We select the reference with the smallest difference as the likely origin of the captured test trace. If the difference is within the range of what is considered normal, the PFP monitor classifies the trace as that specific path. If the test traces, however, cannot be matched with any reference within the predefined tolerance, then the PFP monitor determines that an anomaly has occurred and alerts the system operator.

12.4.3 Detection Performance

The ability of PFP to detect malicious intrusions was tested by capturing a set of test traces from each execution path in the original logic, and in the tampered version with the malware in dormant state. This is, with the trigger condition not present and with the tampered version displaying the same observable behavior as the original logic.

The plot in Fig. 12.6 shows the sample distributions (histogram) of the differences against the same path reference of the test traces from the original execution and the traces from the tampered execution in the dormant state. The distribution on the left corresponds to the original logic. The closer to 0 the difference, the most similar it is to the reference. The distribution on the left corresponds to the execution using the same input values for that specific path of the tampered version with the malware dormant. We can see a clear separation between the distributions.

The clear separation indicated the ability of PFP to detect malicious intrusions. Similar results were obtained for the different execution paths. The boxplot diagram in Fig. 12.7 shows an aggregate view of each execution path.

We can see that the separation between the original and tampered distributions is maintained for all execution paths. This result illustrates the ability of PFP to detect malicious intrusion in industrial control systems by monitoring directly the execution of PLCs.

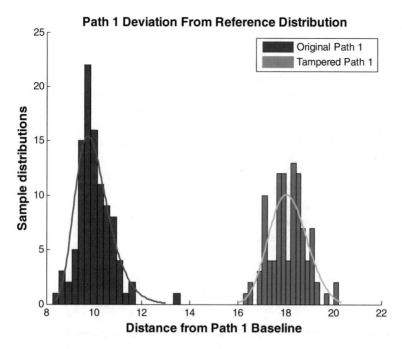

Fig. 12.6 PFP distance from Path 1 baseline sample distribution

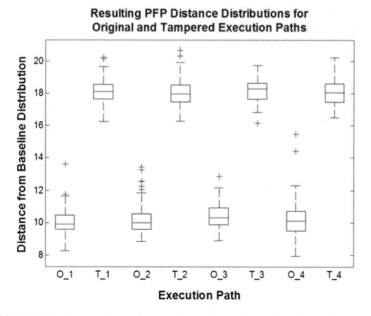

Fig. 12.7 PFP Intrusion detection performance for all execution paths in the original logic

12.5 Future Developments

In terms of technology development, big data analytics and machine learning can be expected to play a significant role in protecting future ICSs (see Chap. 16). In applying big data and machine learning technologies into ICS cybersecurity, it is expected to be leveraged by utilizing a multitude of physical and logical sensors into the analysis, providing a broad picture of the whole logical system and physical process. The objective will be to provide stakeholders with the ability to detect and mitigate malicious threats in real-time, independent of the physical process, communication technology, system architecture, or implementation platforms, including legacy devices. To this end, anomaly detection of the physical process using methods such as PFP, as well as on the behavior of the logical devices, including direct execution assessment, will play a key role in providing system administrators with the tools needed to detect malicious actors..

12.6 Summary and Conclusions

Monitoring the physical environment of ICS components provides very valuable information, not only about the underlying physical process of the system, but also about the execution status of controllers and digital devices. Offensive side-channel approaches (attacks) on ICS components can be executed by collecting physical evidence about the component operation, e.g., power consumption or electromagnetic leaks. The collected information may then be used to defeat system security mechanisms. Side-channel attacks based on power analysis have been attempted using a number of techniques that vary in terms of resources required, number of observations, and success rate. Defensive side-channel approaches can be used as a form of intrusion detection.

Power Fingerprinting (PFP) uses physical measurements from a side channel (e.g. power consumption) to detect malicious intrusions in systems by performing fine-grained anomaly detection on the processor's side channels, such as power consumption or electromagnetic emissions, to determine whether it has deviated from expected operation. The concept behind PFP integrity assessment and monitoring includes three main elements common to all pattern recognition systems: sensing, feature extraction, and classification. Sensing involves measuring, directly or indirectly, the instantaneous current drain. PFP is based on detecting anomalies and deviations from baseline references and is well suited for the repetitive and regular nature of typical operational ICSs. PFP baseline references can be extracted using several different approaches. One of the most straightforward methods includes developing a "gold sample" of the target platform. An example of PFP baselining and anomalous signal detection for a Siemens PLC is given in the chapter, demonstrating that PFP methods are able to detect intrusions even at a minor disruption in execution. A drawback of PFP is that it provides only a limited support for forensic analysis and attack attribution, suggesting that it should be applied in a defense in depth approach, as part of a comprehensive security solution.

References

Biham, E., & Shamir, A. (1997). Differential fault analysis of secret key cryptosystems. In N. Koblitz (Ed.), *Advances in cryptology—CRYPTO'97* (pp. 513–525). New York: Springer.

Cárdenas, A. A. (2011). Attacks against process control systems: Risk assessment, detection, and response. In *Proceedings of the 6th ACM Symposium on Information, Computer and Communications Security* (pp. 355–366). ACM.

Chow, R. U. (2011). Enhancing cyber-physical security through data patterns. In *Proceedings of the Workshop on Foundations of Dependable and Secure Cyber-Physical Systems (FDSCPS)* (p. 25).

Gandolfi, K. M. (2001). Electromagnetic analysis: Concrete results. In *Cryptographic Hardware and Embedded Systems—CHES 2001* (pp. 251–261). Springer Berlin Heidelberg.

Kocher, P. C. (1996). Timing attacks on implementations of Diffie-Hellman, RSA, DSS, and other systems. In N. Koblitz (Ed.), *Advances in Cryptology—CRYPTO'96* (pp. 104–113).

Kocher, P. J. (1999). Differential power analysis. In M. Wiener (Ed.), *Advances in cryptology—CRYPTO'99* (pp. 388–397). New York: Springer.

Mangard, S. (2003). A simple power-analysis (SPA) attack on implementations of the AES key expansion. In *Information Security and Cryptology—ICISC 2002* (pp. 343–358). Springer Berlin Heidelberg.

Mo, Y., & Sinopoli, B. (2009). Secure control against replay attacks. Communication, control, and computing. In *47th Annual Allerton Conference on Allerton 2009* (pp. 911–918). IEEE.

Popp, T., Mangard, S., & Oswald, E. (2007). Power analysis attacks and countermeasures. *IEEE Design & Test of Computers, 24*(6), 535–543.

Reed, J. H., & Aguayo Gonzalez, C. R. (2012). Enhancing Smart Grid cyber security using power fingerprinting: Integrity assessment and intrusion detection. In *Future of Instrumentation International Workshop (FIIW), 2012*. IEEE.

Chapter 13
Experimental Methods for Control System Security Research

Vincent Urias and Brian Van Leeuwen

13.1 Introduction

The need for experimental approaches is particularly acute with respect to ICS cyber security. The ability to assess cyber posture, effectiveness, and impact for predictive analysis is predicated on the assumption that operators, users, and others have prior and complete understanding of the effects and impacts caused by cyber adversaries. Obviously, this is often not the case. When compared to the physical world, cyber is quite different, in that it does not follow physical scientific laws; rather, cyber is unbounded because it is a human-made science. As a result, understanding and quantifying effects are still an immature science. Many systems do not lend themselves to closed form mathematical solutions. Thus experimentation becomes a key method of performing analysis of these systems. In order to develop a foundation for identifying and bounding the issues, one approach to this problem is empirically through experimentation, much like physical sciences such as chemistry and physics.

Many of the challenges in cybersecurity relate to the inability to predict the outcome of an effect, be it the placement of a network element, where to place network sensors, or applications to prevent threat. The non-determinism of cyber systems requires cross-validation and aggregation of several weak indicators to verify and provide confidence in the measures. However, there are several challenges that must be overcome:

V. Urias • B. Van Leeuwen (✉)
Sandia National Laboratories, Albuquerque, NM, USA
e-mail: bpvanle@sandia.gov

© Springer International Publishing Switzerland 2016   253
E.J.M. Colbert, A. Kott (eds.), *Cyber-security of SCADA and Other Industrial Control Systems*, Advances in Information Security 66,
DOI 10.1007/978-3-319-32125-7_13

- Understanding what is measurable,
- Describing the trade space between sensor placement and usefulness measuring effects,
- Understanding where to place sensors,
- Defining what locations and equipment can produce valuable data, and
- Analyzing sampling characteristics, including sampling rate (likely varies by data source) needed to capture data-rich transients.

There exist numerous methods of conducting cyber experimentation, ranging from creating highly constructive mathematical models of observed phenomena to creating large, special purpose hardware representations of the systems. Each of these approaches provides data and analytic capacity to derive knowledge from, but each has drawbacks and limitations.

Before looking at how to construct a cyber experiment, it is important to understand what question we are trying to answer. Like in every other Modeling and Simulation effort, the cyber experiment is not meant to drive all classes of questions that may be asked during a cyber-experiment.

13.2 Overview of the Approaches

13.2.1 Live, Virtual, Constructive

The concept of Live, Virtual, and Constructive (LVC) is a familiar idea in much of the Department of Defense (DoD). In the DoD community, LVC approaches are used to exercise and understand complex systems and processes. The LVC approach is often applied during exercises, where use of a fully "live" system is unfeasible for any number of reasons. These same approaches are valuable in Computer Network Operations (CNO) modeling and simulation efforts—where a fully live implementation of the system of interest is unfeasible (Parker et al. 2009).

Throughout this chapter the terms *simulated* nodes, *emulated* nodes, and *physical (i.e., real)* nodes are used. Here, simulated refers to the nodes represented through simulation tools; in our case Riverbed/OPNET Modeler. *Simulated* nodes generally use unique and abstracted implementations of the protocols and software running on virtualized hardware. *Emulated* nodes use real software, for instance an actual Windows OS, but run on emulated or virtualized machines. *Physical* nodes are the real software running on real hardware. In some cases, we also use *surrogate* applications that represent the functionality of the software, but not the exact software used in the target system under study.

To illustrate the concepts of LVC we describe two example tool development activities that provide capability for overall power system analysis including ICS (McDonald et al. 2008). These are the Real Time Digital Simulator (RTDS) and Critical Infrastructure Protection and Resiliency Simulator (CIPR/sim).

13.2.1.1 Real Time Digital Simulator (RTDS)

The Real Time Digital Simulator or RTDS provides power systems simulation technology for fast, reliable, accurate, and cost effective study of power systems with complex High Voltage Alternating Current (HVAC) and High Voltage Direct Current (HVDC) networks. RTDS employs efficient algorithms that support analysis of electromagnetic transients in power systems in real time. The tool's capability enables realistic representations occurring in a real system since the simulator functions as a real-time tool. Real-time simulation is significant for because it enables experiments with actual physical devices in the loop and thus can be connected directly to power system control and protection equipment. For example, it can be used to test HVDC (High Voltage Direct Current) controllers or protective relays. This capability enables more thorough testing of systems than other test methods because the analyst is able to subject the system or subsystem under study to conditions that are not obtainable any other way. More specifically, it allows for testing of devices that could not be tested on an operational system. These types of experiments are useful to assess system impacts of some ICS security studies (Idaho National Laboratory 2015a, b; RTDS Technologies Inc 2015).

13.2.1.2 Critical Infrastructure Protection and Resiliency Simulator (CIPR/sim)

Scientists and engineers at Idaho National Laboratory have developed an advanced simulation technology called CIPR/sim which allows emergency planners to visualize the real-time cascading effects of multiple infrastructure failures before an actual emergency occurs. This development activity was in collaboration with the United States Department of Defense for the objective of enabling responders to be better prepared, more responsive and accurate when analyzing critical incident data. CIPR/sim is designed to help first responders plan and prepare their response to the cascading effects that natural disasters or terrorist attacks have on infrastructure resources such as the electric power grid and telecommunication networks. The tool provides analysis capability to predict the effects of the event on the critical infrastructure. CIPR/sim is the first critical infrastructure simulation tool to be designed with a common operating framework that adheres to national Institute of Electrical and Electronics Engineers (IEEE) 1516 standards. Importing real-time data from numerous existing analysis modules supports setting analysis parameters. The specific modules include Real Time Digital Simulator (RTDS) for electric grid analysis, QualNet for telecommunications analysis, and PC Tide for wind speed and flood surge analysis (Idaho National Laboratory 2015a, b).

13.2.2 The Need for Cyber Analysis

SCADA systems were not built with the security mindset. They were built to aid in monitoring and controlling the system. Current SCADA systems are often accessed remotely by variety of different users including the utility workers, multiple third-party vendors, among others. One of the primary reasons for this level of access is to reduce costs. To create an entirely isolated SCADA network that was not connected in some fashion in a geographically disperse location would require lots of single-purpose infrastructure (networking, tools, equipment) to access and maintain these systems. These Internet-connected devices control and monitor critical processes and are at risk of disruption by cyber initiated attacks. SCADA systems usually lack inherent security, making them appealing targets for cyber-attacks. SCADA systems also have inherently insecure systems, running un-patched, unsupported, unencrypted communications within their networks.

13.2.2.1 Threat Analysis

Threats to SCADA systems and ICS have been on the rise. Cyber weapons such as Stuxnet reveal an already volatile and under-secured environment. Another challenge is the lack of tools that are intended to help a system owner/operator better understand how their security posture can be used to create exploits. These exploits for ICS infrastructures then can be released for profit. Cyber security challenges are complicated by the highly complex, interconnected networks of ICS that use generationally different physical equipment and applications rather than traditional commodity enterprise applications and infrastructure.

SCADA systems have evolved to include standard PCs, operating systems, and networking. SCADA system networks are interconnected with the critical infrastructure organization's other networks, including those that are connected to the Internet. Connectivity of an organization's various information systems is vitally important to the organization's effective and efficient operation. SCADA systems' diverse and geographically distributed locations require remote access capabilities; for that, the Internet may be used to provide connectivity. Connectivity can introduce additional paths for cyber-attacks.

Cyber security threats to SCADA systems can be grouped as follows:

Malware—SCADA systems are comprised of operating systems and software applications that are vulnerable to viruses, worms, Trojans and spyware. Extensive SCADA system connectivity provides increasing opportunities to become infected with malware.

Hacker—An individual or groups that intend to cause disruption may access SCADA networks and collect data and interrupt data flows within the physical system under control. The physical disruption might be a power outage or water delivery system interruption.

Insider—A person who has permission to access the network and can disrupt a company's physical or information systems. An insider may increase access to physical assets and disrupt operations via the SCADA system.

SCADA systems carry high value information, so often they are targets for cyber attacks. The latest and most advanced security methods are used to protect SCADA systems from such attacks. Important to securing these systems are analysis methods and tools that measure the effectiveness of selected security approaches to an information system's security, reliability, and resilience against cyber-attack.

13.2.2.2 LVC Supports Cyber Fidelity Requirements

Network modeling, simulation, and analysis offers researchers and IT professionals the opportunity to better understand the complex network-based systems that are deployed, being deployed, and under design. To date, much of this introspection has been centered on our ability to understand connectivity, protocols, and quality of service. The same tools that give us insight into the functioning of protocols and topologies are useful when applied to security, reliability, and survivability questions.

Many of today's network-critical analyses involve the use of custom-made test-beds from real hardware components. These test-beds are typically expensive and time-consuming to construct and deploy, nevertheless they are required for critical missions. In some cases, a number of simulation runs are performed before the real network is built. However, the ability to rapidly test prototype network devices is still a major challenge. In many cases, the simulation program code needs to be developed to simulate the devices in question. These codes, sometimes buggy, typically do not depict an accurate enough picture of the system, and feedback from simulations is used to rework the simulation code. This process is time consuming and inefficient to the extent that deployed network setups are not well tested.

The most common security analysis technique used by SCADA system specialists evaluates the hardware prior to installation in the SCADA system. Lab-scale testing environment requires that the specialists purchase physical equipment, and then they build and configure the system. The SCADA system is instrumented using network diagnostic equipment. It is connected to computer networks that generate appropriate traffic. This approach is problematic for three reasons:

- The equipment can be very expensive to acquire, configure, instrument, and maintain,
- Full system-level effects cannot be evaluated without duplicating the full operational environment, and
- Once the system becomes operational, cyber security testing is difficult to perform; it introduces an unacceptable risk to disruption of the critical systems under control.

Numerous simulation tools for studying network performance issues exist. Today's simulation tools have extensive capabilities and high accuracy. Simulation is used extensively by SCADA operators and planners. The simulation tools have probing capabilities making it possible to correlate events and generate system-level information. Simulation tools have been used primarily to analyze data capacity performance and help information system (IS) users accomplish expansion studies. Few simulation tools currently have the necessary network device fidelity to enable specialists to evaluate various security implementations effectively and analyze threats and vulnerabilities at scale. While most simulation tools accurately represent the data link and network transport layers; they do not sufficiently model the application layer and programs.

13.2.2.3 Advanced Modeling Support for SCADA and ICS Applications

Supervisory control and data acquisition (SCADA) systems and industrial control systems (ICS) are vulnerable to the same classes of threats as other networked computer systems, tools and techniques for security testing and performance analysis need to be developed. In practice, security testing is difficult to perform on operational ICS; it introduces an unacceptable risk of disruption to the critical systems (e.g., power grids) that they control. The hardware used in ICS often is expensive; this makes full-scale mockup systems for live experiments impractical. A more flexible approach to these problems is through use of test beds that provide the proper mix of real, emulated, and simulated elements to model large, complex systems, such as critical infrastructures. This chapter describes a testbed and methodology that enables security and performance analysis of ICS.

13.2.3 Modeling Methodology Applied to Industrial Control and SCADA Systems

One cyber-physical security analysis approach includes experimentation on realistic testbeds. Techniques and expertise are used to identify system-level vulnerabilities, consequences of vulnerability exploitation, and how to eliminate the vulnerability. If multiple vulnerabilities are exploited simultaneously, system-level consequences are more difficult to determine. Testing on operational systems or on testbeds is effective in determining system-level impacts. In some cases, testing on operational systems is not possible because of the risk to the operational system and its mission. It may be cost prohibitive to build an experimental system identical to the operational system. Software models of the devices and system may not be available; if available, they lack features for cyber security analysis. An effective alternative is to use a hybrid testbed to create a cyber-physical security experimentation platform.

The methodology described in this chapter is intended to effectively instantiate—via hybrid testbeds—networked information systems that perform cyber analysis and cyber training with high-levels of fidelity and realism. The capability provides an understanding of and planning for cyber operations, evaluation of the effectiveness of deployed defense strategies, and technologies, and effectiveness against expected cyber-attack approaches. Cyber analysis development asks these questions:

- Can data obtained from real-life cyber incidents be leveraged in the cyber analysis capability and platform to create more-realistic and real-time training scenarios?

- How capable is the platform in configuration and deployment of new cyber experiments? How quickly can experiments be designed and implemented (i.e., machine speed vs. human speed)?
- How accurate is the capability and platform in representing and evaluating cyber security technologies?
- What is the process for effectively training and equipping cyber analysts with new approaches, tactics, techniques, and solutions?
- Does the capability include methods for scoring and measuring effectiveness of the approaches, tactics, techniques, and solutions under evaluation?
- What is the scalability of the system-under-study through deployments on the platform? Can the capability and platform replicate systems at desired scales?
- Can multiple information system applications be deployed and have faithful interoperability with other systems and applications? Will the capability and platform accurately represent the operation of mission critical applications and the impacts to it from the approaches, tactics, techniques, and solutions under evaluation?
- Can technology and device specific cyber training and testing be performed? Consider IPv6 and wireless communications? Are mobile communications faithfully represented in the capability and platform?
- In cyber training scenarios, can the defender's actions be observed, assessed, and replayed?
- Will the cyber analysis capability and platform enable analysts and commanders in understand and quantifying the effects of their decisions in executing a plan?

To overcome the challenges with security analysis using either an exclusive hardware SCADA testbed or a simulation of a SCADA system, a hybrid testbed methodology can be used to perform cyber-physical security analysis as well. The methodology enables models to be built of both the SCADA system and the physical system. The SCADA system model may include its connectivity to the various business networks and to the Internet. The physical system model is selected from various solvers for the physical system under study. In a hybrid experiment, the SCADA system events and the physical system events are joined in lock-step to create realistic operation. Fig. 13.1 illustrates the hybrid testbed methodology and how the testbed has variable realism vs. cost and setup time.

Note, although the focus of this paper is on SCADA, there has been application to many other Critical Infrastructure areas, including Oil and Gas, Natural Gas Pipelines, among others.

The testbed methodology is based on modeling, simulating, emulating, instrumenting, and analyzing large-scale networks of engineered and human-coupled subsystems that have significant dependencies on cyberspace capability. The testbeds provide the following:

- Large-scale, vastly heterogeneous networked systems,
- Integrated systems that can be configured and used for controlled experimentation and interactive exploration of system behavior,
- Components that may be real, emulated, or simulated,

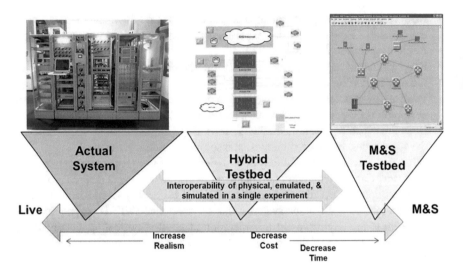

Fig. 13.1 Hybrid tested employs physical, emulated, and simulated models

- Network(s) creation, management, and instrumentation,
- Large high-performance computing (HPC) platform management and monitoring,
- Data extraction and warehousing, and
- Analysis and result visualization.

An example of a hybrid testbed capability is the Emulytics™ program developed by Sandia National Laboratories; it is a cyber security analysis capability using physical hardware, emulated machines, and simulation (Armstrong and Rinaldi 2010). Key aspects of the hybrid approach to cyber security analysis have been published (Parker et al. 2009; Van Leeuwen et al. 2009; Van Leeuwen et al. 2010). Typical capabilities for a hybrid testbed include:

- Mechanisms to rapidly specify and deploy complex networked information systems of routers, switches, hosts, services, and applications,
- Extensive protocol support for network devices, such as switches and routers, and
- Instantiation of ten thousand hosts, such as servers or workstations, in high-fidelity. Currently supporting Windows and Linux operating systems; can be extended to support a greater variety of systems and devices including, for example, VoIP phones and printers,
- Instrumentation at the host and network layers to capture, in high-fidelity, data describing system operation,
- Creation of complex scenarios (e.g., of deployments, intrusion attempts, user impact, etc.) that can be scripted for execution within the experimental platform,

- Incorporation of application-layer overlay systems such as those used for Supervisory Control and Data Acquisition (SCADA) (Urias et al. 2012),
- Representation of mobile communications and their interoperability with fixed-networked systems, and
- Representation of the latest and upcoming security approaches, e.g., Moving Target Defenses (MTD).

A hybrid testbed solution may include procurement of operational system devices and configurations (router, switches, firewalls, security appliances, etc.) and deployment of networked endpoints (e.g., Windows, Linux hosts or servers, embedded controllers, SCADA devices) that represent an operational system. The hybrid testbed includes instrumentation, data collection, and backend analysis capability to digest the unstructured data produced by network devices, applications, hosts, and network defense tools that enable key aspects for analysis under various scenarios and system states. Cyber red teams and blue teams can apply their techniques and develop tools, tactics, and procedures as well.

13.2.3.1 Obtaining Modeled System Specification

Obtaining accurate system specifications for a particular system is another challenge in creation of an emulated system model. Security practitioners may start by examining the original system design and specification documents, if available. Because the system may have been modified for a number of reasons, this may result in a poor system description:

- Original specifications were modified during original deployment because of errors,
- Device configurations were not completely specified and modified overtime,
- Original device firmware and software were upgraded,
- Original system topology was modified for system growth, and
- Device selection changes resulted from vendor performance improvements.

To obtain an up-to-date and accurate view of the information system, a system discovery and mapping capability must be employed. System analysts use it to diagram, inventory, audit, and analyze the system under study.

The discovery and mapping capability accounts for both application and service representation, and network configuration. The capability incorporates custom software that interoperates with various network and information system device management capabilities, device monitoring capabilities such as Windows Management Instrumentation (WMI), and protocol standards such as Simple Network Management Protocol (SNMP) and Dynamic Name Services (DNS). System discovery in critical infrastructure systems may pose significant challenges because of diverse devices not usually found in traditional corporate IT systems. System devices may include embedded devices that do not respond to traditional discovery techniques; discovery may be limited to network protocol scanning mechanisms.

Capability tools use both commercial and open source solutions to fuse data for active device discovery and mapping techniques; also included are protocol based host discovery techniques to discern and create maps of information systems of interest. Passive traffic analysis techniques can identify additional mechanisms to enhance discovery and mapping capabilities.

13.3 Modeling Industrial Control and SCADA Systems Using Hybrid Testbed

To demonstrate the cyber analysis methodology application to SCADA systems, a model of a SCADA system can be created that includes modeled Intelligent Electronic Devices (IEDs). These devices provide a direct interface to control and monitor equipment and sensors. An IED, e.g., a protective relay, may communicate directly to the SCADA Server. Or a local Remote Terminal Unit (RTU) may poll the IED to collect the data and pass it to the SCADA Server.

The modeled SCADA system also includes a Human-Machine Interface (HMI), SCADA server, and other components to manage the overall system. The SCADA system management devices usually are located in a control center. The typical communication between the control center and the remotely located devices is via a wide area network (WAN). The SCADA control center includes a LAN that provides network connectivity to the various devices in the control center. Additional connections link the control center network to the business network. In most configurations, connections between the control center network and business corporate network are protected by a network firewall. The business corporate network usually has connectivity to the Internet. An example topology showing the connectivity between the SCADA system with the corporate network and Internet is shown in Fig. 13.2. Also shown are locations where an attack may take place and the types of attack that can occur at those locations.

Modeling protocols that enable communication in the control system network are integral to cyber analysis. The testbed supports four protocols: ModbusTCP, Distributed Network Protocol (DNP3), International Electrotechnical Commission (IEC) 60870, and IEC 61850 (GOOSE messaging). As new standards of communication for SCADA protocols appear, modular methodology can include new protocols.

IEDs may be polled directly and controlled by the SCADA server or remote terminal units (RTUs). In some cases, there are local configurations and functionality that allow the IED to act independently of the SCADA control center. IED control by the SCADA server requires that ModbusTCP, DNP3, and IEC 60870 packets be transported over the networks that provide connectivity. Network connectivity is what makes the SCADA control so vulnerable to the same classes of attacks as a corporate business network.

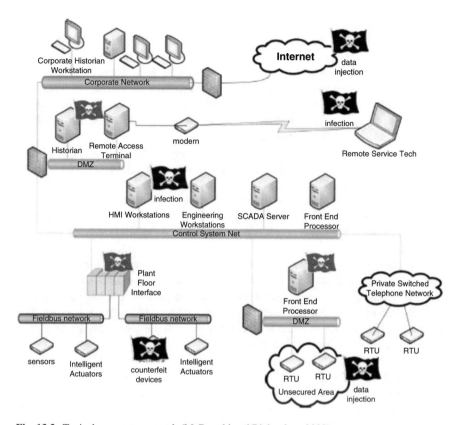

Fig. 13.2 Typical corporate network (McDonald and Richardson 2009)

13.3.1 Simulated and Emulated Devices Used in the Hybrid Testbed Experiment

Use of a hybrid testbed enables the creation of a SCADA system with simulated, emulated, and real devices in a single experiment. Each specific experimental domain has advantages and disadvantages. System components represented in each domain must be carefully selected to maximize the advantages and minimize the disadvantages.

13.3.1.1 Device Model: Simulated

Network simulation tools, such as OPNET Modeler and NS2, are designed in part to allow analysts, engineers, and researchers to gain insight into how network protocols perform under various traffic loads and device configurations. Analysts can implement and deploy these protocols on simulated device networks, trace messages that the devices send between one another, and collect statistics on traffic results, including packet delays.

A recently identified cyber security analysis tool is network modeling and simulation (M&S). A key advancement has been a capability to interface real network devices with simulated ones, then pass network traffic between them. Interfacing real network traffic with simulated traffic is available with OPNET's or NS3's system-in-the-loop (SITL) capability.

The limitations of using M&S for cyber security analysis must be recognized. When using network M&S in a hybrid testbed to perform cyber security analysis, the modeled network components represent behavior of real network devices in their configurations and capability to transport network traffic. This is accomplished via different implementations of the network protocols. Device operating system (OS) and application vulnerabilities are not modeled with network M&S tools.

The network device model can represent a real device in its configuration of security features such as filter rules and access control lists (ACLs). Most devices provide a variety of configuration options that users can set, based on their own security versus convenience tradeoffs. If configurations in a real device permit or deny an attack, the expectation is that a model with the same configuration will permit or deny the same attack vector.

A key part of the hybrid testbed is its ability to interface real SCADA devices and subsystems to simulated SCADA devices and subsystems. The experiment could be a real workstation connecting to a logically distant IED over an extensive simulated network or various traffic sources and sinks communicating over a network comprised of real and simulated parts. The combination of real and simulated devices into a single experiment requires the SITL interfaces to translate data packets or datagrams between real and simulated domains. Translation functions are required for cases where a datagram is created in one domain, either simulated or real, and interpreted in another domain.

In cases where the simulated network is transporting the data from one real device to another, the translations are limited to the header portion of the data packets. The payload of the data packets can remain as a block of bits. Since the simulation may include filter rules in modeled routers and switches, and ACLs in modeled firewalls, data packet headers are read, interpreted, and acted upon in the same manner as a real device with the same configuration.

In the case of ModbusTCP, DNP3, and IEC 60870, if an IED exists outside of the network simulator and the SCADA controller also exists outside of the simulator, then it is not necessary to parse the application-level fields of the data packet. It is necessary only to parse Ethernet and IP fields of the packet. In contrast, if either the IED's or SCADA controller is modeled in the network simulator, then complete parsing of the entire ModbusTCP, DNP3, or IEC 60870 packet is required.

13.3.1.2 Device Model: Emulated

To represent authentic network services, virtual machines (VMs) are used as surrogate systems to function as hosts and servers supporting various applications. In the example SCADA system under test, physical hardware solutions are used to provide DNS and proxy services. It is possible to virtualize a significant portion of the experiment with modern hardware; enabling numerous services and devices to be consolidated into a single, portable computing system. This provides a cost effective alternative approach to the use of proprietary hardware solutions.

Virtualization can represent network devices, such as routers, firewalls, and Layer-3 switches. They can be hosted on the same commodity hardware as the emulated endpoints running Windows or Linux OSes. Example network device operating systems used in experiments include the open-source Vyatta router and numerous proprietary operating systems, such as the Arista vEOS.

13.3.1.3 Device Model: Physical

Physical devices are included in hybrid cyber experiments. These devices are connected to the experiment in the same way that devices are connected to an operational system. They create, consume, and pass traffic as they do in an operational system.

Incorporation of physical devices forces the simulated portion of the experiment to run at a real-time simulation rate. This requires the simulation capability to be throttled to real-time. It is not a problem in most cases if the simulator hardware can simulate faster than real time. For a simulator that runs slower than real time, throttling cannot be used.

Analysts are able to create experiments with varying levels of fidelity by combining virtualized and simulated devices through SITL. The approach provides varying levels of fidelity. Real hardware can be incorporated into critical components or in areas of interest. Virtualization and simulation can be used in other areas of the system. When an entire hardware system does not have to be duplicated, cost savings are realized without a loss of critical experimental fidelity. In Fig. 13.3 a hybrid-experiment topology is illustrated.

13.3.2 Industrial Control and SCADA Systems Security Assessment Demonstration Experiment and Setup

A primary objective of the demonstration experiments is to explore what classes of cyber threats and effects can be modeled using the test methodology. Testing incorporates system modeling using simulation, physical hardware, and extensive virtualization. A modeling capability proves effective when incorporating necessary levels of realism for analysis. System-level modeling includes distributed, replicated subsystems to create experiments of increased scale, while maintaining

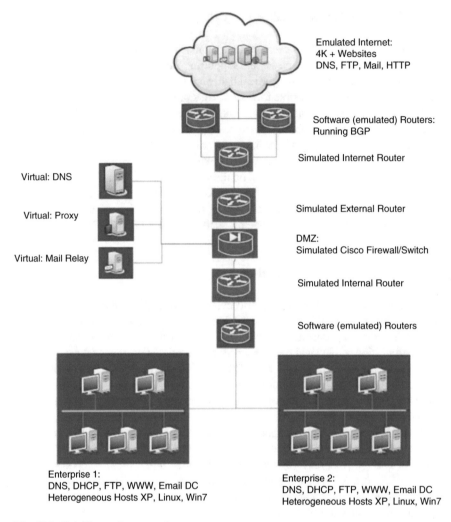

Emulated Internet:
4K + Websites
DNS, FTP, Mail, HTTP

Software (emulated) Routers:
Running BGP

Simulated Internet Router

Virtual: DNS

Simulated External Router

Virtual: Proxy

DMZ:
Simulated Cisco Firewall/Switch

Virtual: Mail Relay

Simulated Internal Router

Software (emulated) Routers

Enterprise 1:
DNS, DHCP, FTP, WWW, Email DC
Heterogeneous Hosts XP, Linux, Win7

Enterprise 2:
DNS, DHCP, FTP, WWW, Email DC
Heterogeneous Hosts XP, Linux, Win7

Fig. 13.3 Hybrid experiment topology

high-levels of realism. A modeling capability includes instantiation of real applications and services running on virtualized hardware to produce realistic system transactions and network traffic. An experiment includes instrumentation and data analytics. A system-level model incorporates many servers and workstations hosting actual applications and network services. Connectivity is provided by various types of network devices that include LANs and WANs.

Another objective is to verify and validate the experimental testbed. A testbed must provide a complex, faithful network representing the real world. Red teams and blue teams will have enough realism and complexity to navigate through a system that is similar to the real world. Experimental components provide diverse traffic sources, destinations, and data traffic. All services, applications, and protocols must minimize potential experimental artifacts. Then a true evaluation of a threat can be examined with confidence in results produced by the testbed environment.

The demonstration information system created in the testbed includes a global Internet-like network. There are multiple cities having cyber cafes, an enterprise system with a DMZ between it and the Internet, and a SCADA system managed by the enterprise system. Details of each sub-system are described below.

13.3.2.1 Global Internet-like System

The demonstration information system represents global connectivity. The global Internet-like network includes Internet service provider (ISP) router representations in cities located around the world as shown in Fig. 13.4. The ISP routers are configured as autonomous systems and peers using Border Gateway Protocol (BGP). Each ISP router is connected to a distribution-like network. This network is comprised of routers using Open Shortest Path First (OSPF) connecting to business network models or cyber café representations. In the demonstration example scenario, multiple cyber café locations have hosts that cyber red teams can use for their reconnaissance and exploit launch points.

13.3.2.2 Enterprise Networked Information Systems

The enterprise network representation is located in Washington D.C. It is connected to the Washington D.C. ISP router via an intermediate router as shown in Fig. 13.5. Connectivity between the enterprise network and Internet-like network is through a

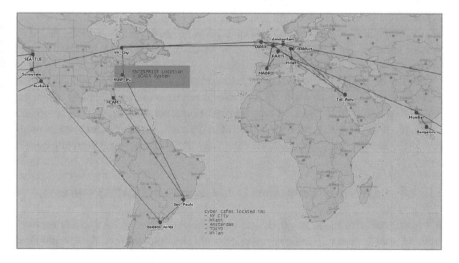

Fig. 13.4 Global internet and cyber cafés

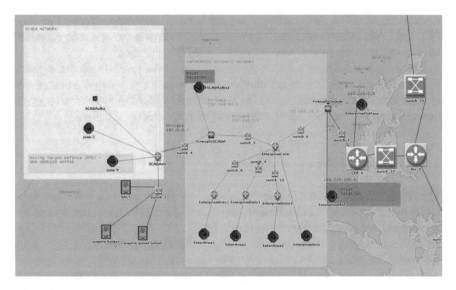

Fig. 13.5 Enterprise networked information system

firewall. It includes a demilitarized zone (DMZ) containing security services and other network gateway functions, such as mail servers, dynamic name service (DNS), and proxies. Several enterprise areas are included, each having approximately 100 end points representing workstations, servers, printers, etc. In the testbed, these end points are Windows or Linux hosts, each configured with unique IP addresses and hosting specific applications. End points respond to network reconnaissance and mapping tools such as Nmap. Responses from the modeled system are similar to responses expected from a live operational system.

In the demonstration scenario, the enterprise network is connected to a SCADA system. The SCADA system, for example, could be an industrial assembly system or a power distribution system. The enterprise network connects to the SCADA system network via a firewall. It includes an enterprise/SCADA interface subnet providing access between the two networks.

For the demonstration scenario, the enterprise DMZ includes several hosts with vulnerable operating systems (OS) available to red teams in their training exercises. Vulnerable hosts are included to provide pivot points for red teams. Pivot points are necessary, since a training exercise is limited in duration. For a red team to make progress in the allotted time, pivot points are used to make progress towards an objective.

13.3.2.3 Supervisory Control and Data Acquisition (SCADA) System

Many critical infrastructure systems rely on complex information systems for control and management. Electrical power critical infrastructure includes the physical systems comprised of power generation, transmission and distribution capabilities.

Control of the physical systems is accomplished via SCADA systems. Today's SCADA systems employ many of the same information system devices as traditional business or enterprise information systems. SCADA system networks and enterprise information system networks are connected to external networks that include the Internet. In the example system, the SCADA network is connected to the enterprise network through a firewall; it includes a SCADA enterprise system interface as shown in Figs. 13.5 and 13.6.

In Fig. 13.3, the devices and subnets in the yellow colored area form the SCADA system. The SCADA system is segmented into three areas—a SCADA business area and two SCADA zones. The business area includes servers that support operations within the SCADA system area, and systems such as power trading tools and broader system management tools. The two zones in the SCADA system segment include a group of remote terminal units (RTUs) that interface with physical equipment and report their state. Also in the zones are front-end processors (FEPs) that communicate with the RTUs and other SCADA resources as shown in Fig. 13.6. Note the various other SCADA system computing platforms represented in each area, such as two human machine interface (HMI) clients and servers, and a historian.

An additional feature employed in the SCADA region, area-9 subnet, is a moving target defense (MTD) system being developed at Sandia. The MTD system is based on a software defined networking (SDN) approach that uses an IP address randomization approach (Chavez et al. 2015). Further details of the MTD approach will be published in an upcoming research paper. The MTD approach is included in

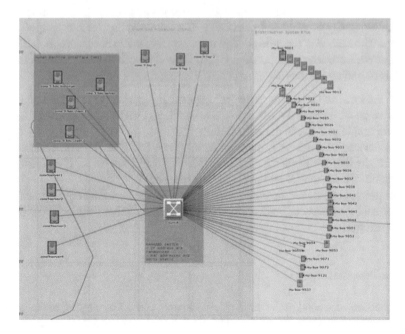

Fig. 13.6 Supervisory control and data acquisition (SCADA) network topology

a single SCADA area where the objective is to observe what a red team is able to discover and exploit in their training exercise. During a training exercise, data is collected from the areas with the MTD approach and without it. The results are used to evaluate the efficacy of the MTD approach.

To communicate with SCADA system nodes, a pivot point must be established within the neighboring enterprise system. More specifically, unauthorized attempts to gain access to SCADA subnets can be launched from a node in the SCADA/enterprise subnet connected to the firewall separating the SCADA system from the enterprise system. A SCADA/enterprise subnet is shown in Fig. 13.5. As with the DMZ located at the enterprise/Internet connection, the SCADA enterprise subnet has several vulnerable hosts that can used as pivot points for a red team activity. In the demonstration experiment, control system devices such as RTUs are modeled and simulated using the testbed (McDonald and Richardson 2009). The devices all produced and responded to authentic SCADA protocols including ModbusTCP, DNP3, and IEC 60870.

13.3.2.4 Models, Simulations, and Emulations Used in Demonstration Experiment

System models deployed in the testbed provide the necessary infrastructure to host experimental environments. As mentioned, these environments may consist of any number of subsystems meant to emulate common computer and communication networks. The underlying components of these systems are the primitives required to build out virtualizations to promote realism and fidelity. The primitives are steeped primarily in emulated machinery, from networking devices to application servers. The testbed is versatile enough to incorporate hardware-in-the-loop (HITL), as required. Between emulation and HITL, the end state is to provide environments to address such questions as:

- Do the local and wide-area networks respond appropriately? Do routes and paths converge as expected? Are quality-of-service (QoS) parameters and metrics comparable to those in the real world?
- Do devices perform as expected? Are servers, SCADA devices, and security stack devices well integrated? Do the devices offer the same, if not extended, capabilities to monitor and perform introspection?
- Do users, such as red or blue teams, feel comfortable in the environment? Do workstations, servers, and applications accurately reflect the settings they're accustomed to?

Device Representations

Emulated devices used in the testbed experiments consist of varying technologies, often packaged as virtual machines. The emulation platform itself allows the instantiation of virtual machines by 'snapshot' (wherein the same virtual machine image may be used for high density experiments), or by 'write-back' as required (where changes made in the virtual machine are written back to the virtual disk image). Those virtual machines running in snapshot still may be uniquely configured using virtual disk image file insertion, SNMP, DHCP and device-specific in-band configuration methods. In virtual machines, Windows and Linux operating systems often are used to represent workstations and servers, as well as endpoint devices in SCADA networks. To represent network infrastructure, virtual routers, Layer-2 and Layer-3 switches are instantiated within the experiments. The latter devices provide a means to apply QoS and promote network realism; they can be used to monitor and assess experiments from a networking perspective.

Application and Traffic Representations

To establish a realistic and high-fidelity model, applications and traffic generation can be added to the primitives of the deployed topology. Through software stubs and scripting, configurations injected at run-time into the virtual machines install, configure, and start applications to provide the look and feel of an enterprise network within the model.

A minimum enterprise network often includes a domain controller and e-mail server. The model is expanded by an array of server-based services, e.g., instant messenger, collaborative wiki, cyber defense tools, and general web servers. To facilitate training environments, exploitable targets are added to the topology to hunt, providing pivot points as well as remediation for multi-day events. These images typically are unpatched versions of Windows server and desktop. They also include some variations of Linux, with known vulnerabilities that are identified easily with tools such as Metasploit.

When the right objects are present in the network, some degree of realism is created, but hardly shows the fidelity required by the demands of most SCADA use-cases. Traffic generation on the wire between endpoints is added to address the gap in fidelity, simply from the emulation environment. A small cross-platform binary is used to generate HTTP(S), SMTP/TLS, and SSH traffic over both IPv4 and IPv6 links.

13.3.3 Industrial Control and SCADA Systems Security Assessment Demonstration Experiment—Security Mechanisms Use Case

The demonstration experiment is based on a variety of concepts of operations. The focus mostly is on applying red team methods on the experimental system to evaluate if the testbed environment can respond faithfully to the red team methods. The red team's objective is to identify security flaws so system security can be increased to prevent unauthorized access to the system. Red team attempts at emulating unauthorized accesses primarily focus in two areas: attempts originating in the control system network and attempts originating from the business environment. Each of these vantage points has vulnerabilities that produce different system-level effects. Vulnerability assessments require different red team methods and hacker tools.

Review of contemporary literature shows very limited information on this topic. Identified references primarily focus on representing denial-of-service cyber-attacks (Nicol and Okhravi 2009). Although this is a very real contemporary attack, many systems may be susceptible to a variety of other exploits that need study as well.

13.3.3.1   Analysis of Cyber-Attacks Targeting the Business Network

The corporate network is a more open and accessible network compared to the control system network. The corporate network has access to Internet resources; hence it is susceptible to a variety of open and known vulnerabilities. Its security posture, however, has a direct impact on overall security, since the network can be connected directly to the SCADA network. This provides a vantage point to infiltrate or exfiltrate data, conduct reconnaissance activities, and capture usernames and passwords amid a variety of different hacker techniques.

To assess the security posture of the network, a variety of experimental red team scenarios can be conducted against the experimental corporate network. The red team can assess system security to resist more against the following:

Reconnaissance—The red team assesses the business network external facing security by examining what data can be collected from this point (e.g. enumerating the DMZ). In the experiment, common tools such as Nmap to conduct the reconnaissance are leveraged. A variety of different types of scans (e.g., x-mas) are used; they return the expected information. This demonstrates that there are no corruptions or artifacts introduced by the hybrid experimentation environment.

Resistance to common hacker tools—The red team examines the experimental system's response to common hacker tools such as Metasploit. Metasploit is used to assess the system's security of business network services (e.g., mail, http, proxy). In the experiment most hacker attempts are filtered and blocked by the simulated firewall; again demonstrating faithful function of the network. Next, a Snort intrusion protection system (IPS) is added to perform signature-based alerting on the inbound traffic. Snort performs as expected by alerting on several hacker attempts launched against the web server.

To examine the testbed's response to known hacker exploits on specific services, a vulnerable service on a DMZ entity is loaded, then its port is exposed to the outside world. In the experiment, this models a zero-day vulnerability in a critical service that was included in the demonstration experiment. This demonstrates that malicious traffic is generated from a physical machine in the testbed. It moved across virtual and simulated routers and switches and passed a physical IPS with a payload that compromised the machine. After adding a Snort rule for that payload, the experiment is repeated. This time the IPS detects the malicious payload as it entered the network. This demonstrates that actual tools and techniques used on the testbed result in the same system response as if they were executed on an operational system with the same security posture.

In order to increase the complexity of the network, a VPN tunnel, which originates outside the external facing firewall and terminates inside the DMZ, is deployed. The VPN is modeled in the simulation part of the testbed. It includes all aspects of a VPN, except the actual encryption of the payload. Using the testbed, assessing the VPN protocol transactions is a valid experiment. Because encryption is not used in the experiment, attempts to assess the encrypted payload are not valid studies on the testbed.

In another experiment, one user is assumed to be compromised. The system's ability to resist and/or alert on malicious activity from that user's machine is assessed. The compromised user either can be inside the business network or accessing the internal applications and services through a VPN from a remote machine. In the testbed, it is demonstrated that system reconnaissance can be performed. As expected, since the IPS is externally facing, it does not alert while several experiments on the testbed were executed. Using common hacker tools, experiments are performed to determine the system's ability to detect malicious activity under different security postures. Included in the experiment are hosts with different operating systems and configurations. Hosts and configurations are subjected to compromise; difficulties are identified in finding the vulnerability using open source tools found in Metasploit. Other open-source tools are used to assess the ability of the system to resist and detect data exfiltration. Attempts are performed to exfiltrate a variety of files from some of the compromised machines, including SAM files, PDFs, and Word documents, to an external server. The testbed system responds as an operational system under these studies.

The testbed is used to assess the system impacts of a number of Business Logic Attacks (BLA) under various system configurations and assumptions. On the testbed, it is assumed that users in the corporate network are infected by a malicious PDF download that included a Trojan onto their machine. Security is assessed by assuming users click on malicious links of a site that has an XSS vulnerability and by examining the impacts while increasing number of users are infected.

13.3.3.2 Analysis of Cyber-Attacks Against the Control System Network

The control system often is overlooked as a target for attack by security personnel. The reasoning is that applications and machines found within these networks are limited and access to other networks is restricted. These networks should be monitored closely. The security posture of these networks should be thoroughly assessed.

The following tests are conducted from a number of vantage points on the control system network. The experiment assumption is that a control system network has been compromised. The testbed is used to assess the capability of the control system network to resist and/or detect malicious behavior. In the experiment, attempts try to faithfully create, modify, and change the state of SCADA specific protocols (both DNP3 and ModbusTCP) using common open-source techniques.

To show how well the testbed represents the various protocol layers, including the lower layers, a generic man-in-the-middle (MITM) attack is created. Scenarios are created in which network devices in the control system are represented as simulated devices and the communication link is intentionally compromised by an emulated computer used by a hacker. The compromised link can be manipulated in the experimental system as if it were in a live system. This demonstrates the testbed's ability to reproduce data traffic on the network lower layers as well as to have the simulated, emulated, and physical domains interoperate. SCADA system networks must be thoroughly assessed to be immune to MITM attacks.

A basic SCADA network topology is used to assess security and performance. Although the field device network is segregated by a firewall, it still is networked to the control systems environment. The HMI reports status derived from FEP polling and sends commands to field devices. With this experimental configuration knowledge, it is possible to leverage several open source tools to perform a MITM attack on the communications between the SCADA applications and any field device. In this experiment, an ARPSpoof technique can advertise a spoofed ARP "is-at" message on the unencrypted link. By testing again, this time with an improved security posture, it shows that the vulnerability is eliminated. Using the testbed methodology it can demonstrate the MITM exploit on emulated devices, physical devices, and even on simulated devices. All these system-level demonstrations respond similarly to the MITM exploit. Verification is established that each device advertising the ARP "is-at" command results in the same SEP ARP tables (the tables included logs of the MITM box as the MAC address) and that Layer-2 traffic is sent to that device.

After the MITM is conducted on the unsecured link, it demonstrates that the link is fully compromised. Since encryption, such as provided by a VPN or SSL, is not used, it is possible to modify anything in that link, including dropping packets or just forwarding them without modification. On the unsecured link, the testbed is used to evaluate a denial-of-service experiment. This experiment demonstrates that it is possible to deny service to a field device and to disrupt heartbeat messages back from a field device. During the experiment, traffic also is forwarded as if in normal operation, showing that operations proceed normally. With presence on the link, all packet traffic is captured, parsed, and assessed with Wireshark and tcpdump. This test demonstrates the feasibility to passively monitor the state of the control system, passively enumerate the devices that communicate back to the SCADA applications and learn what their normal operating conditions are for future action. Following demonstrations on the unsecured link, a simulated VPN is used to show that these vulnerabilities no longer can be executed. This is comparable to what might be seen on an operational system.

Additional experiments evaluate the effects of disrupting ModbusTCP and DNP3 communication with field devices or SCADA applications to assess system-level impacts. It is possible to modify traffic in stream and produce false results to the SCADA applications. Insights into system-level impacts are provided as the number of, and location of, devices are modified. Using open-source tools, an attacker modifies packets to cause disruptive effects; this highlights the importance of securing the links. Results are verified by using a combination of physical system and information system analysis tools to verify that network disruptions lead to the expected physical effects. Evaluating the impacts of an unsecure control network results in the HMI reporting inaccurate states of the physical system. The demonstrations show the importance of effective network security on networked control systems.

The testbed provides security researchers with an environment where they can assess a variety of security postures and their resilience to cyber-attacks. These include assessing SCADA applications and conducting experiments to better understand system effects if networks are insecure and compromised.

13.3.4 Data Collection and Analytics in Hybrid Testbed Experiments

At the crux of any experiment is the ability to extract information about the experiment itself, more specifically, extracting experiment information that is meaningful, concise and actionable for the questions the experiment is designed and is expected to answer. Types and quantity of data pulled from the experiment must be based on the goals of the experiment. Experiment data outputs often have not matched with the user requirements, resulting in lost time and efforts for both sides. In training environments, the chasm can be exacerbating when experiment outputs are required for feedback to the trainees and for further development of pertinent training environments.

An emulation environment supporting the actual experiment must be instrumented and be flexible enough to employ devices that are highly configurable for instrumentation for data collection. Data extraction and collection must pay attention to formatting to ease the parsing and ingestion requirements for analytic applications. Virtual network devices deployed in the environment provide the ability for network monitoring applications to poll SNMP data (e.g., performance metrics, routes, CAM-table entries). Virtual machine instantiations include agents to query and push host data to collection servers with in-band and out-of-band. The emulation platform itself includes capabilities to:

1. Perform introspection on virtual machines from the hypervisor,
2. Capture point-and-click type operations from user VNC sessions, and
3. Collect summary network traffic and full-packet capture on the physical host machine virtual switches.

Network monitoring applications are tooled to ingest active and passive network data to generate general and customized reports. This data may be fed to analytic engines that receive VM host data via VM agents, hypervisor-based introspection, and in-experiment virtual machine services (e.g., firewalls, IPS, etc.). A fusion of the many data sources collectively forms a rich, complex view into the system throughout the course of the experiment. The output may be coarse in nature for high-level discourse or provide fine-granularity for detailed analysis.

13.4 Summary and Conclusions

Analysis testbeds provide important and capable cyber security analysis and experiment methodology to help perform analysis of communication networks and networked information systems. Live, Virtual, and Constructive (LVC) "hybrid" testbed approaches for ICSs are used to exercise and understand complex systems and processes where use of a fully operational system is unfeasible. Hybrid testing with simulated, emulated and physical components can provide the following :

- Evaluation of security architectures of systems,
- An immersive environment for red teams to assess different security models and their security risks,
- Use of a blue team training tool for operators to learn to configure components of the system,
- A red team environment that provides targets for training and evaluation of other systems,
- Cyber range environments for emulation of blue and red team activities,
- An effects-based modeling environment to test computer network defense strategies under a variety of conditions,
- A cloud computing testbed to learn and ask questions about open-source cloud solutions and applications, and
- Data collection techniques to provide rich views and analysis of experiment outcomes
- Improved cyber training environments

Two example tool development activities are described as examples of the utility of hybrid testbeds. These tools provide specific functions of offering fast, reliable, and cost effective studies of power systems in configurations that would otherwise be prohibitive, and predictive visualization analysis of real-time cascading effects of multiple infrastructure failures. When used on hybrid testbeds, these and other tools optimize training of ICS personnel by allowing emulated system configurations that would not be possible on the operational system, often in better than real-time.

Hybrid testbed capabilities, such as the Emulytics™ program developed by Sandia National Laboratories, offer a variety of levels of system fidelity that can be tailored to the specific test or development use case. ICS system events and the physical system events can be joined in lock-step to better emulate realistic operation. To assess the security posture of the operational ICS, a variety of experimental red team scenarios can be conducted against the experimental system. Various security models can be evaluated by changing the security configuration of the experimental system and re-testing. Validation and verification of systems can also be investigated on hybrid experimental ICS testbeds if a sufficient degree of granularity is substantiated in the testbed. LVC hybrid ICS testbeds offer an extensive array of system- and component-level experiments and investigations that would otherwise be impossible, due to the high-availability requirements of operational ICSs.

References

Armstrong, R., & Rinaldi, S. (2010). Emulytics: Concepts for cyber emulation, modeling, and simulation. In *Sandia National Laboratories Report—SAND2010-1639C*.

Chavez, A., Hamlet, J., Lee, E., Martin, M., & Stout, W. (2015). Network randomization and dynamic defense for critical infrastructure systems. In *Sandia National Laboratories Report— SAND2015-3324 (April 2015)*.

Idaho National Laboratory. (2015). *Real time digital simulator.* Retrieved from http://inl.gov/nationalsecurity/factsheets/docs/rtds.pdf.

Idaho National Laboratory. (2015). *INL Research Programs in National and Homeland Security.* Retrieved from https://www.inl.gov/research-programs/.

McDonald, M., & Richardson, B. (2009). Position paper: Modeling and simulation for process control system cyber security research, development and applications. In *Center for Information Management, Integration and Connectivity—Position Papers, 2009.*

McDonald, M., Conrad, G., Service, T., & Cassidy, R. (2008). Cyber effects analysis using VCSE: Promoting control system reliability. In *Sandia National Laboratories Report—SAND Report.*

Nicol, D., & Okhravi, H. (2009). Application of trusted network technology to industrial control networks. *International Journal of Critical Infrastructure Protection, 2*(3), 84–94.

Parker, E., Miner, N., Van Leeuwen, B., & Rigdon, J. (2009). Testing unmanned autonomous system communications in a Live/Virtual/Constructive environment. *International Test and Evaluation Association Journal (ITEA), 2009*(30), 513–522.

RTDS Technologies Inc. (2015). *RTDS simulator description.* Retrieved from http://www.rtds.com.

Urias, V., Van Leeuwen, B., & Richardson, B. (2012). Supervisory command and data acquisition (SCADA) system cyber security analysis using a live, virtual, and constructive (LVC) testbed. In *IEEE Military Communications Conference—MILCOM 2012* (pp. 1–8).

Van Leeuwen, B., Urias, V., Eldridge, J., Villamarin, C., & Olsberg, R. (2010). Performing cyber security analysis using a live, virtual, and constructive (LVC) testbed. In *IEEE Military Communications Conference, 2010—MILCOM 2010* (pp. 1806–1811), 31 October 2010–3 November 2010.

Van Leeuwen, B., Burton, D., Onunkwo, U., & McDonald, M. (2009). Simulated, emulated, and physical investigative analysis (SEPIA) of networked systems. In *2009 IEEE MILCOM Conference*, October 2009.

Chapter 14
Governance and Assessment Strategies for Industrial Control Systems

Daryl Haegley

14.1 Introduction

In spite of decision support technologies, such as experimentation and simulation discussed in the previous chapter, it remains challenging for ICS stakeholders (leaders, managers, operators, etc.) to make informed decisions regarding formulating guidance, assigning responsibilities, balancing security and efficiency, allocating funding, determining return on investment, and measuring performance. Formulating and establishing an overarching plan that supports and guides such decisions is often called governance. This is the subject of the present chapter.

While definitions of governance vary, some of such definitions are better suited to ICS. This chapter will discuss them in detail, but generally governance refers to processes of interaction and decision-making among the actors who are collectively solve the problem such as ensuring and maintaining security of an ICS. Governance includes actions and processes that engender and support stable practices and organizations. In the context of ICS, such processes ensure that benefits of ICS are delivered in a well controlled and are aligned with long-term goals and success of the enterprise.

Governance processes are reflected in, and guided by appropriate documents. The totality of such governance documents can be classified into four types: policies, standards, guidelines and procedures. Policies are the highest level of written governing documents that outline which standards, guidelines and procedures the organization is to follow. Standards offer a frame of reference for compliance and performance. Guidelines are typically not a mandatory governing document, but

D. Haegley (✉)
Department of Defense of the United States
e-mail: dhaegley@gmail.com

© Springer International Publishing Switzerland 2016   279
E.J.M. Colbert, A. Kott (eds.), *Cyber-security of SCADA and Other Industrial Control Systems*, Advances in Information Security 66,
DOI 10.1007/978-3-319-32125-7_14

rather are designed to be dynamic and flexible, updated to reflect relevant processes and adapt best practices and changes to the organizational situation. Finally, procedures represent a step-by-step process to achieve a specified result.

There are multiple benefits to establishing governance processes and the corresponding documents. They specify which organizational components are responsible for procurement, sustainment, and technical refresh of an ICS. They stipulate authorization roles, risk management process and performance accountability. They also standardize process and metrics for conducting security assessments.

This chapter begins with an illustrative story, inspired by real-life experiences of the author, that help the reader to appreciate some of the practical reasons for good governance of ICS. Then the chapter describes the definitions, purposes and sources of governance. Because governance is particularly important for the purposes of ICS security assessments, the chapter continues by focusing on frameworks and methodologies that govern ICS assessments.

14.2   Overview

14.2.1   A Motivating Story

On a not particularly noteworthy day, my boss approached and directed, "investigate why those information technology (IT) folks wont' approve thousands of smart meters recently purchased by the facility engineers to run on the network" (Smart meters are electronic devices that records energy consumption and enable two-way communication between the meter and a central system [Wikipedia]). At the time it did not seem there should be any issues—aren't all networked devices the same? Is the value of the investment to secure the smart meters greater than the risk not to secure them? What technical issues could the IT folks possibly have?

If there was an obvious concern regarding the smart meters, why didn't the facility engineers coordinate with the IT team in deciding which smart meters to purchase? There are a couple reasons why. First, the facility engineers have been managing their networks for decades. Typically they were not interconnected to an enterprise network or the Internet. There were several decentralized or independent facility–related networked systems that were managed by manually observing analog gauges. Some were electronically connected and centrally managed within the building containing the ICS.

Many of these ICSs did not connect to the Internet, although some did. There are instances where a vendor may have established a connection to verify ICS performance and warranty conditions or to install upgrades or patches. But even under these circumstances, the IT department was not informed or integrated into network purchasing decisions. Since it was not part of the email network, why would it be considered IT? The IT SMEs were not consulted for most all ICS network decisions, hardware, software, governance, security procedures, training, etc.

The facility or civil works budget for their network and any corresponding security controls would stand independently and compete among all other resource requests. If ICS networks were considered part of the IT department's purview, then the IT budget, which is often under budgeted according to the IT SMEs, would have even more competing hardware and software security requirements. Now, as the ICS networks are being exploited due to a lack of integrated security, there is an increased need for the IT and engineering communities and departments to collaborate and cooperate in performance, risk, security, resourcing and procurement discussions and decisions. Those conversations and partnering are critical to justify an ICS for authorization to operate or establish proof of net-worthiness on the corporate network or via the Internet.

If worrying about a smart meter being exploited was not on the organization's radar, then chances are that other exploitable devices connected to controls system are not either. For example, in December 2011, the Chamber of Commerce discovered that one of their digital thermostats was configured to communicate back to a location in China. [http://abcnews.go.com/International/chinese-hack-us-chamber-commerce-authorities/story?id=15207642] While technically intriguing, it brings to bear a fundamental question: who in your organization would be responsible for monitoring and cybersecuring controls systems networks and devices? Subsequent questions follow: Would the IT folks know the thermostat is able to connect to the Internet? Would the facility engineers know? Would the IT folks be trained in control systems? How about the facility engineers, would they recognize a fault from a cyber source? What are the governing documents that outline how this should be handled? How have those governing documents demonstrated reasonable measures to ensure the organization's intellectual capital (and the shareholders) were adequately protected?

Although hope and luck can be integral for short-term success, long-term success requires a more structured approach. That begs the question: Where to start? In increasingly connected environments, it can be extremely challenging for executives, leaders, managers, operators to make informed decisions regarding formulating guidance, assigning responsibilities, balancing security and efficiency, allocating funding, determining return on investment, and measuring performance.

Overwhelmingly significant emphasis on interconnectedness and associated security concerns has been evident in the IT community over the past decade; the same concern has recently gathered momentum regarding ICS. Despite the prolific, continuous threats and concerns emanating from every direction, the interconnected benefits and efficiencies gained continue to inspire thoughts of opportunities and growth. A daunting task, specific exploitation risk to ICS was extremely difficult to calculate and seemed impossibly rare to occur on "my network," hopefully exploitation would occur on "someone else's network." Therefore many refrained from implementing security in ICS environments.

But exactly where to start? Westby (2003) offers that in increasingly connected environments, it can be extremely challenging for stakeholders (leaders, managers, operators etc.) to make informed decisions regarding formulating guidance, assigning responsibilities, balancing security and efficiency, allocating funding, determining return on investment, and measuring performance. What should be included in formulating an overarching plan for those interconnected or isolated environments? Many refer to establishing such a plan as "governance."

14.2.2 Some Definitions

Enter "governance." In the Wikipedia entry of governance, subject matter expert Hufty (2011) provides specific definitions that can be aligned to ICS: "processes of interaction and decision-making among the actors involved in a collective problem that lead to the creation, reinforcement, or reproduction of social norms and institutions," and "…governance is a theoretical concept referring to the actions and processes by which stable practices and organizations arise and persist. These actions and processes may operate in formal and informal organizations of any size; and they may function for any purpose."

In the context of IT and ICS, Howe (2009) describes governance referring to "the structure, oversight and management processes which ensure the delivery of the expected benefits of IT in a controlled way to help enhance the long term sustainable success of the enterprise." Those processes yield a simple governance construct that can be applied within organizations. The construct may be divided into the following four subcomponents: policies, standards, guidelines and procedures. This construct is especially useful for those in large or geographically separated organizations:.

Policies are regarded as the highest level of written governing document, outlining which standards, guidelines and procedures to follow. Effective polices must be realistic, identify achievable goals, and focus on elements. Alternately, they may comprise a number of related standards, guidelines and procedures. Policies should receive input from all aspects of the organization with the key stakeholders having the most influence. They can broadly or specifically reflect leadership direction, goals, objectives or mission, leaving execution details to the referenced documents. With few exceptions, these overarching documents routinely apply to all employees and supporting contractors; non-adherence consequences should be clearly articulated to include specified disciplinary action.

Standards offer a frame of reference for compliance and performance. They can span an entire range of options, from minimal to maximum, as well as local, national and international. Often aligned to a statutory law or consequence, the organization determines the most appropriate that apply. Additionally, within an organization there may be different requirements or tolerances and different standards or exceptions that should be detailed, approval and documented. For example, the same NIST ICS security control standard could be applied for two systems but there would be fewer security controls necessary for a building escalator compared to the critical infrastructure supporting a data center. Standards are adapted or internally developed to satisfy compliance or respond to industry competition/rivalry, then organizational leadership would select which to "mandate."

Guidelines are routinely developed by those while trying to meet the requirements outlined by the standards within a specific environment or context. Typically not a mandatory governing document, guidelines are designed to be dynamic and flexible, updated to reflect relevant processes and adapt best practices and changes to the organizational situation. As an example relating to baselining the configuration of an ICS, one may generate an organizational specific guide or adapt what's outlined in the NIST Special Publications. The two NIST special publications offer guidance for controls that can apply to ICS: NIST SP 800–53 "Recommended Security Controls for Federal Information Systems and Organizations," and even more specifically, NIST SP 800–82 "Guide to Industrial Control Systems (ICS) Security."

Examining excerpts from each publication in Tables 14.1 and 14.2, the Configuration Management (CM) family provides the following guidance that IT or ICS managers can employ:

As shown, there are multiple options for the ICS owner/operator/manager to choose. Tailoring the guidance to a specific ICS environment is encouraged. The most important aspect is to document the guidance and obtain leadership approval.

Table 14.1 Excerpt from NIST SP 800–53 CM-2 baseline configuration

	NIST SP 800–53 CM-2 baseline configuration (p. F-64)
Control	The organization develops, documents, and maintains under configuration control, a current baseline configuration of the information system
Supplemental guidance	This control establishes baseline configurations for information systems and system components including communications and connectivity-related aspects of systems. Baseline configurations are documented, formally reviewed and agreed-upon sets of specifications for information systems or configuration items within those systems. Baseline configurations serve as a basis for future builds, releases, and/or changes to information systems. Baseline configurations include information about information system components (e.g., standard software packages installed on workstations, notebook computers, servers, network components, or mobile devices; current version numbers and patch information on operating systems and applications; and configuration settings/parameters), network topology, and the logical placement of those components within the system architecture. Maintaining baseline configurations requires creating new baselines as organizational information systems change over time. Baseline configurations of information systems reflect the current enterprise architecture
Related controls	CM-3, CM-6, CM-8, CM-9, SA-10, PM-5, PM-7
Control enhancements	(2) *Baseline configuration|automation support for accuracy/currency*
	The organization employs automated mechanisms to maintain an up-to-date, complete, accurate, and readily available baseline configuration of the information system
Supplemental guidance	Automated mechanisms that help organizations maintain consistent baseline configurations for information systems include, for example, hardware and software inventory tools, configuration management tools, and network management tools. Such tools can be deployed and/or allocated as common controls, at the information system level, or at the operating system or component level (e.g., on workstations, servers, notebook computers, network components, or mobile devices). Tools can be used, for example, to track version numbers on operating system applications, types of software installed, and current patch levels. This control enhancement can be satisfied by the implementation of CM-8 (2) for organizations that choose to combine information system component inventory and baseline configuration activities
Related controls	CM-7, RA-5

Table 14.2 Excerpt from NIST SP 800–53 CM-2 Baseline Configuration

	NIST SP 800–82 CM-2 Baseline Configuration (p. G-27)
Control enhancements	(1) *Baseline configuration|reviews and updates*
	The organization reviews and updates the baseline configuration of the information system:
	(a) [Assignment: organization-defined frequency];
	(b) When required due to [Assignment organization-defined circumstances]; and
	(c) As an integral part of information system component installations and upgrades
Related control	CM-5
Control enhancements	(2) *Baseline configuration|automation support for accuracy/currency*
	The organization employs automated mechanisms to maintain an up-to-date, complete, accurate, and readily available baseline configuration of the information system
Supplemental guidance	Automated mechanisms that help organizations maintain consistent baseline configurations for information systems include, for example, hardware and software inventory tools, configuration management tools, and network management tools. Such tools can be deployed and/or allocated as common controls, at the information system level, or at the operating system or component level (e.g., on workstations, servers, notebook computers, network components, or mobile devices). Tools can be used, for example, to track version numbers on operating system applications, types of software installed, and current patch levels. This control enhancement can be satisfied by the implementation of CM-8 (2) for organizations that choose to combine information system component inventory and baseline configuration activities
Related control	CM-7, RA-5

Procedures represent a step-by-step process to complete a specified result. Each step should be clearly articulated, simple to follow even when the subject matter expert is not available. A simple example procedure is "press red button when centrifuge is exceeding operating tolerance of 5000 to 7500 RPM." In the configuration example above, procedures would be the "how" outlined for each tool, control and device in the proper order of sequence and or precedence.

In an example guidance, a policy may require all networks to be secured. The referenced standards would list which security controls could apply to the different types of networks (e-mail, cell phone, control systems, wired and wireless, etc.). Guidance documents could identify applicable processes, best practices and lessons learned when applying the security controls to each network type. Procedures could outline the individual steps required in each particular process to implement individual security controls.

- Policy: Secure control system network
- Standard: Routinely change administrator level passwords
- Guidance: Change passwords every 90 days consisting of a minimum of 16 characters, upper/lower case, including special characters

- Procedure: Send email reminder on 15th of each month to change passwords; verify status of changes by logging in to terminal named "Skyrunner," folder located x://ICS polices/monthly reminders; document compliance; lockout/disconnect those non-compliant

If there is no procedure for verifying changing passwords, or if that procedure is not followed properly, then the best practice guidance is not implemented, standards are not followed, and the network may not be secure.

14.2.3 Purpose of Governance

Setting the tone from the top is a critical enabler for the success of ICS security. One must publish policies that promote compliance and performance, incorporate relevant standards, and generate guidelines to facilitate consistent application of procedures. It is critically important to outline the specific expectation as well as the consequences of not adhering to policy. If it cannot be clearly demonstrated that the appropriate standards are in compliance, the ICS may be deemed exploitable and lose its accreditation or permission to operate on the corporate network.

A common concern with ICS stakeholders is the resourcing decisions to secure IT-related or automated assets in another part of the organization. As reflected by Allen (2005), "Governing for enterprise security means viewing adequate security as a non-negotiable requirement of being in business. To achieve a sustainable capability, organizations must make the protection and security of digital assets the responsibility of leaders at a governance level, not of other organizational roles that lack the authority, accountability, and resources to act and enforce compliance."

Tangible benefits to establishing governing documents include:

- Specify organizational resource responsibility for procurement, sustainment, and technical refresh
- Stipulate authorization roles, risk management process and performance accountability
- Provide compliance evidence to regulators, shareholders, insurers, etc.
- Enable continuity of operations despite unpredictable environments and skilled personnel turnover
- Justify certificate of net-worthiness/authority to operate
- Standardize process and metrics for conducting security assessments

14.2.4 Groups Issuing ICS Governance

Various global entities have written many relevant standard documents for assisting with risk management and cybersecurity within ICS environments. Fabro (2012, p. 125) relays a simple, overarching purpose, "Understanding these standards will allow asset owners to create and manage a program to mitigate cyber security risks in their control systems environments. When an asset owner is without formal direction to adhere to a certain security standard or practice, these standards allow for great flexibility to accommodate for the unique challenges presented by control system environments."

Below is a list of the organizations routinely developing authoritative and internationally recognized standards and specific ICS guidance (not all inclusive, see Table 14.3 for more details):

- IEC—International Electrotechnical Commission
- IET—Institution of Engineering and Technology
- ISA—International Standards of Automation
- ISO—International Organization for Standardization
- NIST—National Institute of Standards and Technology
- NRC—Nuclear Regulatory Commission
- U.S. DoD—Department of Defense

14.2.5   ICS Assessments

Unless specifically dictated, the standards listed above can be used as prescribed or modified to apply to unique ICS environments. While no ICS configuration may be exactly the same, the standards can be applied consistently across an enterprise of multiple assets, systems and or networks. Even if the ICS configuration fully complies with all the regulations, standards, guidelines, etc., disruption, exploitation and manipulation may occur. Targeted by undeniably persistent and complex vectors of cyber threats, ICS owners and operators must endeavor to remain proactively vigilant in their security perspective. Therefore, it is critically important to conduct routine evaluations to ascertain operational and security performance.

The assessment process is essential. Among all the governing documents within an organization, assessments are the most powerful for enabling resource decisions, revealing vulnerabilities, and making security modifications. Assessments are applied at the design, construction and completion phases. They establish the baseline and consider modifications when they occur. When regular assessments are completed the organization understands the precise ICS hardware and software configuration. When all is operating well, assessments verify system communications are all according to expectations and plans. On the other hand, assessments can reveal existence of unexpected communications illuminating the extent of malware or exploitation, and/or the lack of updates, patches, and adherence to best security practices.

Despite assessment benefits, due to a general lack of oversight from an IT security context, many ICS assessments were never conducted and, consequently, security was not integrated into the design. When assessments do occur, the following are common negative findings:

- Existence of undocumented network connections (wired and wireless)
- Presence of known or unknown connection to Internet or vendor (for maintenance/warranty)

Table 14.3 List of many standards and guidance documents applicable to ICS (not all inclusive)

Source	Title	Description
IET *Institution of Engineering and Technology*	Code of practice for cyber security in the built environment	Describes cyber security options to consider throughout a building's lifecycle and offers community best practices when integrating building related systems with enterprise cyber environment
ISA 99/IEC 62443 *International Society of Automation/International Electrotechnical Commission*	Industrial automation and control systems (IACS) security	Procedures for implementing electronically secure IACS and security practices and assessing electronic security performance
ISO/IEC 15408 *International Organization for Standardization/International Electrotechnical Commission*	Common criteria for information technology security evaluation; usually referred as simply "Common Criteria"	Established to facilitate a unified set of pre-existing standards enabling mutually agreed evaluation reference for vendors, testing laboratories and government customers combined by Canada, France, Germany, the Netherlands, the UK, and the U.S. governmental organizations
ISO/IEC 27001:2015	Information technology — Information security management systems — Requirements	Specifies requirements for establishing, implementing, maintaining and continually improving an organization's information security management system; requirements for assessment and treatment of information security risks tailored to the needs of the organization
ISO/IEC 27002:2013	Information technology — Security Techniques — Code of practice for information security controls	Designed for selecting controls within the process of implementing an Information Security Management System (ISMS) based on ISO/IEC 27001 or as guidance for implementing commonly accepted information security controls; facilitates consideration of specific information security risk environment(s)
ISO/IEC 27003:2010	Information technology — Security techniques — Information security management system implementation guidance	Describes the process of ISMS specification and design from inception to the production of implementation plans
ISO/IEC 27004:2009	Information technology — Security techniques — Information security management — Measurement	Provides guidance on development and use of measures and measurement in order to assess effectiveness of an implemented information security management system (ISMS) and controls or groups of controls, as specified in ISO/IEC 27001
ISO/IEC 27005:2011	Information technology — Security techniques — Information security risk management	Relevant to managers and staff concerned with information security risk management within an organization and, where appropriate, external parties supporting such activities

(continued)

Table 14.3 (continued)

ISO 31000:2009 *International Organization for Standardization*	Risk management—Principles and guidelines	Establishes a number of principles to enable effective risk management; can be applied to an entire organization, its sub-components, at any time, as well as to specific functions, projects and activities
ISO 50001:2011	Energy management	Outlines how organizations can apply energy management techniques resulting in improved quality and environmental management
NIST SP 39 *National Institute of Science and Technology (NIST)*	Managing information security risk	Organization, Mission, and Information System View; provides guidance for an integrated, organization-wide program for managing information security risk to organizational operations (i.e., mission, functions, image, and reputation), organizational assets, individuals, other organizations, and the Nation resulting from the operation and use of federal information systems
NIST SP 800–53 revision 4	Recommended security controls for federal information systems and organizations	Provides a set of procedures for conducting assessments of security controls and privacy controls employed within federal information systems and organizations
NIST SP 800–82 revision 2	Guide to industrial control systems (ICS) security	Provides an overview of the differences between ICS and transitional IT, typical ICS topologies, threats, vulnerabilities, and mitigation controls
NIST SP 160 DRAFT	Systems security engineering: An integrated approach to building trustworthy resilient systems	Provides recommend steps to help develop a more defensible and survivable IT infrastructure—including the component products, systems, and services that compose the infrastructure
NRC 5.71 *Nuclear Regulatory Commission*	Cyber security programs for nuclear facilities	Regulatory guide that identifies cyber-security program implementation procedures for U.S. nuclear facilities
U.S DoDI 8500.01 *United Stated Department of Defense Instruction*	Cybersecurity	Implements a multi-tiered cybersecurity risk management process
U.S. DoDI 8510.01	Risk management framework (RMF) for DoD information technology (IT)	Establishes using an integrated enterprise-wide decision structure for cybersecurity risk management

- Incorrect configurations (modified from initial installation or adapted to customer environment)
- Incomplete patches and upgrades (HW/SW)
- Non-secure configuration
- Owners/operators not familiar with configuration, appropriate cyber/security practices

14.3   Examples of ICS Assessment Processes

One significant concern is that with many ICSs, taking the system off-line for software upgrades or patches may have operational impacts. For example, if the HVAC system were to come offline, the server room temperature may increase to the point where computers overheat and shut down. In another example, applying a patch to a critical life-support medical device during an operation may cause it to fail. If clear governance exists, all system operators and network administrators would cooperate on specific procedures, would routinely review the systems and devices using network communications, and would work together on implementing upgrades and patches. This would reduce the risk of avoiding lapse in normal operations or initiating catastrophic results.

There exist several documented processes to complete ICS security assessments. They can be performed independently or in concert with the IT assessments. The following list is not comprehensive but reveals varying approaches with underlying common themes. Inclusion does not represent or imply endorsement of any commercial product or government process. A brief overview is provided with the recommendation to further investigate these and others to determine the most relevant, repeatable assessment process for your organization.

1. NIST Cyber security framework
2. Department of Energy (DoE) & DHS Cyber Capability Maturity Model (C2M2)
3. Robust ICS Planning & Evaluation (RIPE) Framework
4. DHS ICS Cyber Emergency Response Team (CERT) Cyber Security Evaluation Tool (CSET)

In the next four subsections, we describe aspects of these assessment processes in more detail.

14.3.1   NIST Cybersecurity Framework

The NIST Cybersecurity Framework (NCF) is a "risk-based" methodology for managing cybersecurity risk, consisting of: Framework Core, Framework Implementation Tiers, and Framework Profiles (http://www.nist.gov/cyberframework/). Each Framework component emphasizes interactions among business drivers and cybersecurity activities.

The NCF systematic process can be used to establish a new cybersecurity program or advance an existing one. Working through each step, the organization can evaluate current capabilities and gaps to attain desired performance. Essentially the NCF (2014, p. 15) can provide "a roadmap to improvement" and ability to "prioritize expenditures to maximize the impact of the investment."

The Framework Core in the NCF (2014, p. 6) is designed to enable "communication of cybersecurity activities and outcomes across the organization from the executive level to the implementation/operations level." In Fig. 14.1, there are five functions on the left side: Identify, Protect, Detect, Respond, and Recover; and four elements across the top: Functions, Categories, Subcategories, and Informative References. The Core (p. 6) is not a simple task-list, it "provides a set of activities to achieve specific cybersecurity outcomes, and references examples of guidance to achieve those outcomes. It presents key cybersecurity outcomes identified by industry as helpful in managing cybersecurity risk."

The NCF (2014, p. 7) describes Framework Implementation Tiers ("Tiers") to facilitate self-evaluation of cybersecurity risk and associated processes. Tiers describe the degree to which an organization's cybersecurity risk management practices exhibit the characteristics defined in the Framework (e.g., risk and threat aware, repeatable, and adaptive). The Tiers characterize an organization's practices over a range, from Partial (Tier 1) to Adaptive (Tier 4)." When selecting the appropriate Tier, "an organization should consider its current risk management practices, threat environment, legal and regulatory requirements, business/mission objectives, and organizational constraints."

Further, the NCF (2014, p. 7) specifies the next level, Framework Profile. *"Framework Profile ("Profile") represents the outcomes based on business needs that an organization has selected from the Framework Categories and Subcategories. The Profile can be characterized as the alignment of standards, guidelines, and practices to the Framework Core in a particular implementation scenario. Profiles can be used to identify opportunities for improving cybersecurity posture by comparing a "Current" Profile (the "as is" state) with a "Target" Profile (the "to be" state). To develop a Profile, an organization can review all of the Categories and Subcategories and, based on business drivers and a risk assessment, determine which are most important; they can add Categories and Subcategories as needed to address the organization's risks. The Current Profile can then be used to support prioritization and measurement of progress toward the Target Profile, while factoring in other business needs including cost-effectiveness and innovation. Profiles can be used to conduct self-assessments and communicate within an organization or between organizations."*

Figure 14.2 provides the next stage in establishing a relevant framenwork template, an organization may include additional "Category" and "Category Unique Identier" to optimally align with the functions.

As the example depicts, it may appear the "intended outcomes" listed in the Functions, Categories, and Subcategories are similar for IT and ICS. However, the operational environments and considerations for IT and ICS differ. The NCF (2014,

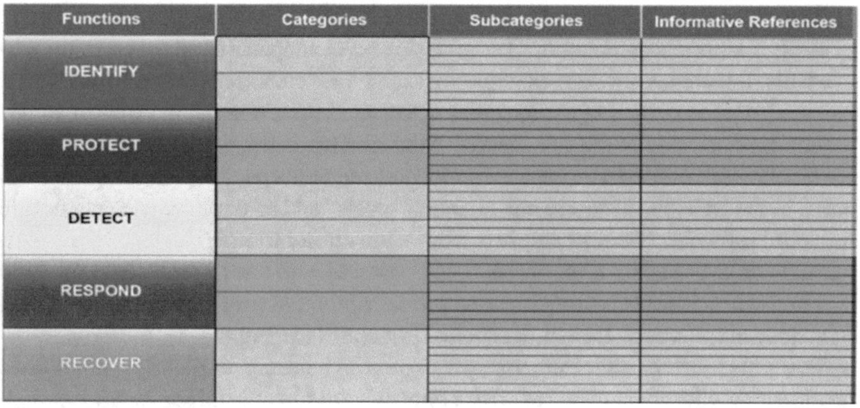

Fig. 14.1 NCF core elements

Function Unique Identifier	Function	Category Unique Identifier	Category
ID	Identify	ID.AM	Asset Management
		ID.BE	Business Environment
		ID.GV	Governance
		ID.RA	Risk Assessment
		ID.RM	Risk Management Strategy
PR	Protect	PR.AC	Access Control
		PR.AT	Awareness and Training
		PR.DS	Data Security
		PR.IP	Information Protection Processes and Procedures
		PR.MA	Maintenance
		PR.PT	Protective Technology
DE	Detect	DE.AE	Anomalies and Events
		DE.CM	Security Continuous Monitoring
		DE.DP	Detection Processes
RS	Respond	RS.RP	Response Planning
		RS.CO	Communications
		RS.AN	Analysis
		RS.MI	Mitigation
		RS.IM	Improvements
RC	Recover	RC.RP	Recovery Planning
		RC.IM	Improvements
		RC.CO	Communications

Fig. 14.2 Example of NCF functions, category unique identifier and category

p. 20) surmises "ICS have a direct effect on the physical world, including potential risks to the health and safety of individuals, and impact on the environment. Additionally, ICS have unique performance and reliability requirements compared with IT, and the goals of safety and efficiency must be considered when implementing cybersecurity measures."

The NCF prescribes separate representative "Profiles" and a separate characterize of an organization's practices or "Tiers." Below is an adoption of all the concepts into one table. It includes only one example for each Function, Category and Subcategory, and integrates the Tier evaluation under a "current" Profile measured against attaining the task outlined in the subcategory column. This is not precisely prescribed by the Framework but offers a means to view all the concepts integrated together. As noted in the NCF, the Tiers are not "maturity levels" and an organization may decide not to invest in resources to progress from a lower Tier to a higher one. Leadership may decide to assume a level of risk commensurate with one or more Tiers.

The NCF provides a template along five functional areas common to IT and ICS: Identify, Protect, Detect, Respond, Recover (see Fig. 14.3). It aligns informative references overarching view of current cybersecurity practice, but it does not identify which specific security controls should be in place to protect ICS networks. It certainly emphasizes collaboration and cooperation among and across all lines of business/operations within an organization to determine the appropriate categories for evaluation. On its own, however, generating a "current state profile" and "to-be state profile" it will not serve as a justification for authorization to operate on the corporate network or proof of net-worthiness. It will undoubtedly serve as another management resource investment decision aid and/ or capability oversight tool.

Profile:			Attain by June 20XX	Current	
Function	Category	Subcategory	Implementation Tiers		Informative References
IDENTIFY (ID)	**Asset Management (ID.AM):** The data, personnel, devices, systems, and facilities that enable the organization to achieve business purposes are identified and managed consistent with their relative importance to business objectives and the organization's risk strategy.	ID.AM-1: Physical devices and systems within the organization are inventoried	Tier 1: Partial		· CCS CSC 1 · COBIT 5 BAI09.01, BAI09.02 · ISA 62443-2-1:2009 4.2.3.4 · ISA 62443-3-3:2013 SR 7.8 · ISO/IEC 27001:2013 A.8.1.1, A.8.1.2 · NIST SP 800-53 Rev. 4 CM-8
PROTECT (PR)	**Protective Technology (PR.PT):** Technical security solutions are managed to ensure the security and resilience of systems and assets, consistent with related policies, procedures, and agreements.	PR.AT-1: All users are informed and trained	Tier 4: Adaptive		· CCS CSC 9 · COBIT 5 APO07.03, BAI05.07 · ISA 62443-2-1:2009 4.3.2.4.2 · ISO/IEC 27001:2013 A.7.2.2 · NIST SP 800-53 Rev. 4 AT-2, PM-13
DETECT (DE)	**Anomalies and Events (DE.AE):** Anomalous activity is detected in a timely manner and the potential impact of events is understood.	DE.AE-1: A baseline of network operations and expected data flows for users and systems is established and managed	Tier 3: Repeatable		· COBIT 5 DSS03.01 · ISA 62443-2-1:2009 4.4.3.3 · NIST SP 800-53 Rev. 4 AC-4, CA-3, CM-2, SI-4
RESPOND (RS)	**Improvements (RS.IM):** Organizational response activities are improved by incorporating lessons learned from current and previous detection/response activities.	RS.RP-1: Response plan is executed during or after an event	Tier 2: Risk Informed		· COBIT 5 BAI01.10 · CCS CSC 18 · ISA 62443-2-1:2009 4.3.4.5.1 · ISO/IEC 27001:2013 A.16.1.5 · NIST SP 800-53 Rev. 4 CP-2, CP-10, IR-4, IR-8
RECOVER (RC)	**Recovery Planning (RC.RP):** Recovery processes and procedures are executed and maintained to ensure timely restoration of systems or assets affected by cybersecurity events.	RC.RP-1: Recovery plan is executed during or after an event	Tier 2: Risk Informed		· CCS CSC 8 · COBIT 5 DSS02.05, DSS03.04 · ISO/IEC 27001:2013 A.16.1.5 · NIST SP 800-53 Rev. 4 CP-10, IR-4, IR-8

Fig. 14.3 Integration of all NCF concepts into single table

14.3.2 Department of Energy (DoE) and DHS Cyber Capability Maturity Model (C2M2)

The C2M2 evaluation can enable organizations to assess and bolster their cybersecurity program, prioritize cybersecurity actions and investments, and maintain the desired level of security throughout the IT systems life cycle (http://energy.gov/oe/services/cybersecurity/cybersecurity-capability-maturity-model-c2m2-program/cybersecurity). Stemming from a diverse set of cybersecurity standards, frameworks, programs, and initiatives, it outlines implementable steps applicable to almost any organization (see Fig. 14.4).

The DoE (2014, p. 1) claims the resulting scores from the C2MC model can reflect the "implementation and management of cybersecurity practices" integrating traditional information technology systems and ICSs, as well as the overall security culture of the organization:

- Strengthen organizations' cybersecurity capabilities
- Enable organizations to effectively and consistently evaluate and benchmark cybersecurity capabilities

	Inputs ➡	Activities ➡	Outputs
Perform Evaluation ⬇	1. ES-C2M2 Self-Evaluation 2. Policies and procedures 3. Understanding of cybersecurity program	1. Conduct ES-C2M2 Self-Evaluation Workshop with appropriate attendees	ES-C2M2 Self-Evaluation Report
Analyze Identified Gaps ⬇	1. ES-C2M2 Self-Evaluation Report 2. Organizational objectives 3. Impact to critical infrastructure	1. Analyze gaps in organization's context 2. Evaluate potential consequences from gaps 3. Determine which gaps need attention	List of gaps and potential consequences
Prioritize and Plan ⬇	1. List of gaps and potential consequences 2. Organizational constraints	1. Identify actions to address gaps 2. Cost-benefit analysis (CBA) on actions 3. Prioritize actions (CBA and consequences) 4. Plan to implement prioritize actions	Prioritized implementation plan
Implement Plans	1. Prioritized implementation plan	1. Track progress to plan 2. Reevaluate periodically or in response to major change	Project tracking data

Fig. 14.4 Table illustrating how the C2M2 can contribute to an overall prioritized implementation plan (2014, p. 19)

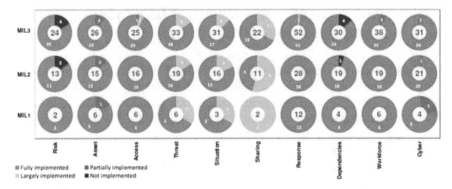

Fig. 14.5 Sample summary scores after completing the C2M2 questions (2014, p. 15)

- Share knowledge, best practices, and relevant references across organizations as a means to improve cybersecurity capabilities
- Enable organizations to prioritize actions and investments to improve cybersecurity

Within the C2M2, there exist ten domains comprised of cybersecurity practices, corresponding objectives, and practices identified by Maturity Indicator Levels (MIL). See Fig. 14.5 for a sample score result. The C2M2 Self Evaluation Toolkit (excel spreadsheet) contains over 600 questions which are graded at a four-point scale using: Fully Implemented (FI), Largely Implemented (LI), Partially Implemented (PI), and Not Implemented (NI).

The process is fairly simple to repeat as "plans are implemented, business objectives change, and the risk environment evolves" (DOE (2014, p.15). The DoE defines two energy sector specific models: Electricity Subsector C2M2 (ES-C2M2) and Oil and Natural Gas Subsector C2M2 (ONG-C2M2).

While the C2MC provides an overarching view of current cybersecurity practice, it does not identify which specific security controls should be in place to protect ICS networks. It does reiterate the need for collaboration and cooperation among and across all aspects of business/operations within an organization to determine the appropriate practices, objectives and corresponding MILs. As a stand-alone product however, it will not serve as a justification for authorization to operate on the corporate network or proof of net-worthiness. It does serve as a resource investment and capability oversight tool.

14.3.3 Robust ICS Planning & Evaluation (RIPE) Framework

Mr. Ralph Langner, founder and director of Langner Communications GmbH, the cyber-security consulting firm focused on ICS security, has developed the Robust ICS Planning & Evaluation (RIPE) Framework (http://www.langner.com/en/solutions/).

The specific details are proprietary information, but some insightful information is publically available from a whitepaper accessible on the company's website (see Tables 14.4 and 14.5). Langer (2013, p. 1) explains that RIPE consists of evaluating "eight different domains, establishing benchmarks and scorecards enabling measurable cyber security capability and identifying weak spots. Such a framework-based approach to ICS security provides economies of scale that can result in significantly improved efficiency compared to risk management exercises that approach every single plant as a completely unique universe."

Unlike the other assessment processes described in this chapter, RIPE requires that an organization purchase RIPE materials to ascertain its cyber security effectiveness

Table 14.4 Captures the whitepaper attributes used to measure cybersecurity capability and indicates these can be routinely "blurred" (2013, p. 4)

Attribute	System properties (Think: Sensors)	Procedural guidance (Think: Actuators)
Verifiability	Documentation on system properties is verifiable by walk-down inspection or experiment	Conformity to procedural guidance documents is verifiable by audit
	Blur example: System documentation claims that a component (such as a PLC, or software application) is "secure" without detailing why and how	Loss example: Security policies that contain language such as "as soon as possible" or "as appropriate", resulting in unpredictable execution that cannot be audited
Completeness	System architecture models are complete, verified by walk-down inspection or experiment	Written procedural execution items (policies, SOPs, guidelines) are provided for all procedures that otherwise leave room for variation that could affect the cyber security posture
	Blur example: Systems used on the plant floor (including mobile devices), or software applications running on computers, are not listed in the system inventory	Loss example: Security policies are produced and enforced for employees, but not for contractors
Accuracy/compliance	Walk-down inspection or experiment verify that documentation of system properties is accurate	Audits verify that procedure execution is compliant with written policy
	Blur example: A system is configured differently than documented, for example in respect to network connectivity, software version, security patch level etc.	Loss example: Mobile devices are configured or used in a manner that violates policy; backups are not performed according to policy; network segregation (firewall rules) is not configured according to policy

Table 14.5 Reveals an example of how the performance characteristics would be measured (2013, p. 7)

RIPE system	Inventory quality
SI quality	Completeness and accuracy of the system inventory
	Computation: SI Accuracy * SI Completeness/100
SI completeness	Percentage of components listed in the system inventory based on total number of components as identified by walk-down inspection
SI accuracy	Percentage of components listed accurately in the system inventory as identified by walk-down inspection
RIPE system	Procurement quality
SP quality	Completeness of system procurement guideline application and compliance of acquired systems
	Computation: SP Completeness * SP Compliance/100
SP completeness	Percentage of system acquisitions during last audit interval for which system procurement guidelines have been applied
SP compliance	Percentage of system acquisitions during last audit interval for which systems proved to be compliant with system procurement guidelines
RIPE training	Program quality
TP quality	Completeness of training program and compliance with training obligations and offerings Computation: TP Completeness * TP Compliance/100
TP completeness	Percentage of user roles relevant for industrial control systems and process IT, including contractors, for which a formal training program beyond awareness is established
TP compliance	Percentage of users, including contractors, eligible or obligated for training actually finishing respective training sessions during the last audit interval

(see http://www.langner.com). One option is to purchase licensed guidelines and templates for an organization and to simply self-populate those guidelines and documents. A much more robust on-site process is also offered, consisting of an audit lasting 30 days, resulting in a RIPE Framework implementation certification.

The RIPE (2013, p. 5–6) focuses on "eight domains of the plant ecosystem" and measures the effectiveness of each as a percentage of the optimal performance:

- System Population Characteristics
- Network Architecture
- Component Interaction
- Workforce Roles and Responsibilities
- Workforce Skills and Competence Development
- Procedural Guidance
- Deliberate Design and configuration Change
- System Acquisition

Once each of the eight domains is scored, the results can be plotted in a spider web diagram as in Fig. 14.6, which is a fictitious comparison of the Atlanta and Birmingham plants, clearly revealing differences in performance.

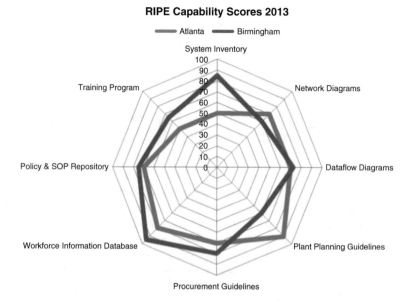

Fig. 14.6   RIPE comparison of the Atlanta and Birmingham plants (2013, p. 7)

As with most assessment processes based on metrics or measures of effectiveness, the results can be used by leadership to make logical, non-subjective risked-based investment decisions. Per the whitepaper (2013, p. 10), "Based on the RIPE Framework documentation, it is also feasible to determine which security controls yield the best mitigation for the cost—if implemented properly (as specified in miti- gation advice). Mitigation advice will usually involve multiple security domains."

However, a common problem seen in many organizations is a lack of insight to the actual problems and relevant mitigating solutions. Moreover, even after a solution is purchased, it is critical to ensure the controls are implemented prop- erly. For example, everyone has a lock on their front door to keep out intruders but sometimes the lock is not engaged. Within the context of cybersecurity, Mr. Langer (2013, p. 9) notes "It is discouraging to see how many asset owners (from management down to control system engineers) are satisfied with the idea to "have addressed the problem" of ICS insecurity by having invested in firewalls, anti-virus solutions, security patching regimes etc. without ever bothering to check their effectiveness."

The RIPE Framework can provide an overarching view of current cybersecu- rity practices, risk management tolerance and measures of effectiveness of eight domains common to plant operations. Once a product license is procured, inde- pendently or with the RIPE team, a holistic view based on performance metrics can be implemented to protect ICS networks. It reinforces the need for an under- standing across all aspects of business/operations within an organization. It may provide relevant artifacts to help justify authorization to operate on the corporate network or proof of net-worthiness. However, the specifics are not detailed in the whitepaper. Similarly to the other methodologies, it can serve as a resource investment and capability oversight tool.

14.3.4 DHS ICS Cyber Emergency Response Team (CERT) Cyber Security Evaluation Tool (CSET)

The Department of Homeland Security (DHS) National Cyber Security Division (NCSD) developed CSET for control systems asset owners (https://ics-cert.us-cert. gov/Assessments). Their primary objective was to assist organizations identified as parts of nation's critical infrastructure and reduce their cyber risk. However, since its initial release in August of 2009, it has become a useful tool suitable for almost all systems that control a physical process, from expansive power utilities, sewage treatment plants, to manufacturing plants, logistical or medical facilities as well as individual buildings. The most recent CSET version as of this chapter's printing is 7.0, released in August, 2015.

CSET (2015, p. 15) can be basically described as "CSET implements a simple, transparent process that can be used effectively by all sectors to perform an evaluation of any network." One can order a free CD or download the file directly from the DHS ICS CERT website. The software tool includes a step-by-step guide to assist user's enter their organizational-specific control system information (hardware, software, administrative policies, etc.) into predefined parameters based on relevant security standards and regulations (see Figs. 14.7 and 14.8):

Fig. 14.7 CSET Step 1—select relevant assessment mode (2015, p. 44)

Fig. 14.8   From selected standards stem appropriate questions in CSET (2015, p.47)

- NIST Cybersecurity Framework
- NIST SPs: 800–39; 800–53 Rev 4; 800–82 Rev 2
- NISTR 7628
- NERC CIP
- ISA 99/IEC 62443
- ISO/IEC 15408; 27001–27005
- ISO 31000 and ISO 50001
- NRC 5.71
- U.S. DoDI 8500.01 and 8510.01
- Others

As with the other assessment methodologies listed in this chapter, CSET should be completed by a cross-functional team consisting of subject matter experts spanning administrative, business, information technology, maintenance, operational and security functional areas. There are hundreds of questions to be answered and while the software is simple to install and use, the breadth and depth of answers required to effectively respond to the questions necessitates knowledgeable and proficient personnel. Those personnel will be routinely located in various parts of the organization. Answering the series of diverse and technical questions is a forcing function to bring them together, potentially enabling unprecedented collaboration among entities that seldom otherwise communicate, if at all.

CSET assessments (see Fig. 14.9) cannot be successfully completed by any one individual as no single person maintains sufficient enterprise knowledge to provide effectual responses to all of the questions. To be truly effective and efficient, completing a CSET (2015, p. 20) assessment requires a cross-functional team consisting of representatives from the following areas:

Fig. 14.9 CSET depiction of general security assessment level (SAL) (2015, p. 70)

- ICSs (knowledge of ICS architecture and operations),
- System Configuration (knowledge of systems management),
- System Operations (knowledge of system operation),
- Information Technology (IT) Network/Topology (knowledge of IT infrastructure),
- IT Security/Control System Security (knowledge of policies, procedures, and technical implementation),
- Risk Management (knowledge of the organization's risk management processes and procedures),
- Business (knowledge of budgetary issues and insurance postures), and
- Management (a senior executive sponsor/decision maker).

Conveniently, CSET can generate the System Security Plan and the Artifacts; adding the Security Assessment Report (SAR), CONOPS, and Incident Response Plan provides an organization with the basic analysis to understand the risks, impacts, and recovery/mitigation options. CSET includes an extensive complement of templates (see Fig. 14.10) to facilitate network, systems and device inventories and diagrams. Since proprietary design and potential vulnerability information will be revealed after completing the assessment, the corresponding reports must be handled appropriately.

CSET is a compliance verification tool rather than a risk or vulnerability assessment tool. Once the assessment is completed, CSET (2015, p. 14) "pulls its recommendations from a database of the best available cybersecurity standards, guidelines, and practices." The resulting reports (see Fig. 14.11) outline specific mitigation actions to obtain full compliance with the selected policies, standards and corresponding security controls and thereby improving the ICS's cybersecurity capability.

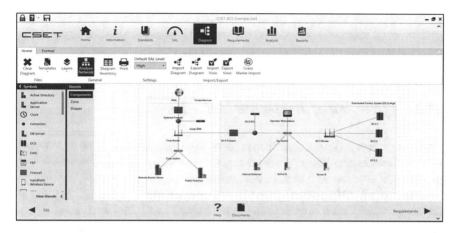

Fig. 14.10 CSET offers many templates to create inventory and network diagrams (2015, p. 111)

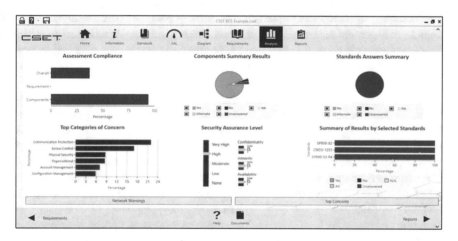

Fig. 14.11 Sample final CSET report summary (2015, p. 153)

CSET should be combined with other tools to fully evaluate the security posture. For example, one may use network scanning, penetration testing, and other tests on nonproduction systems that will not adversely impact mission, operations, health or safety.

CSET is a stand-alone software application that enables organizational self-assessment using national and internationally recognized standards. It can integrate ICS community cybersecurity best practices into the organizational corporate risk management strategy. Since its inception, many have posted video tutorials on-line, demonstrating its wide user community. Within CSET is a comprehensive and expansive reference library. If preferred, DHS ICS CERT has an on-site service that can assist with the assessment process. A benefit of CSET is that a system security plan can be exported as an artifact toward justification for authorization to operate on the corporate network, or proof of net-worthiness. While a CSET "all green" cybersecurity standards compliance evaluation is impressive, as for other assessments, it does not equate to an impenetrable or un-exploitable network.

14.3.5 Overview of Assessment Methodologies

Each assessment approach described is based upon extensive subject matter experience and community best practices. None offer shortcuts or exclusions from their process; the process must be followed in order to obtain an accurate, accountable inventory of all ICS systems, networks and devices. They all recommend that all stakeholders within an organization—especially IT and ICS—work together and systematically conduct self-assessments on the networked assets in order to capture dependencies and interdependencies. The results can inform leadership to help with resource decisions and management task prioritization. It's important to understand not every asset will require robust security controls. Despite many executives stating "securing all these is an impossible task," there are many methodologies available to achieve the security level relevant for a given organization.. When the appropriate people come together and are required to discuss issues related to protecting their assets, they are often able to recognize areas of weakness and the required improvements for their organization.

Improvements are needed in <u>automated</u> identification of assets on an ICS network, its topology, connectedness, adherence to rules/polices/patches, visualization, evaluation of instantaneous performance (and trend analysis) and exploitability based on continuous alerts, intelligence community inputs, 100 % verification of vendor patch authenticity, identification of potential consequences of applying new patch in real-time operational environment versus first applying to test bed. A cyber range or test laboratory can be used for replicating all vendors, all protocols, all levels of updates and patches, as well as automating responses to alerts such as updating and patching. Predictive maintenance and mitigation options incorporating associated expenses would also be very useful. There are tremendous business opportunities in this space. Beyond hardware or software advancements, additional labor and training may need to be considered to complete the job well.

Each methodology can be a catalyst change. Many hesitate to take the first step because security, especially ICS cybersecurity, is unfamiliar territory. It is overwhelming to be faced with reading through the totality of hundreds of security questions to answer in the standards documents. However, if one takes on the challenge one step at a time and embraces the opportunity to safeguard the organization, catastrophes can be avoided. There are a vast number of free resources. One will need to dedicate resources, time and effort, internally and perhaps engage external expertise. It is imperative that the technical specialists representing IT and ICS collaborate instead of compete. Assessments offer a measurable, repeatable, non-subjective process to make informed security related decisions.

It is prudent to invest in community best practices and conduct regular assessments. Security evaluations and investments are reported directly to the CEO. If a breach occurs and the media questions company officers or shareholders, one may confirm that an assessment was performed. Quarterly reports include those investment decisions in cybersecurity solutions as a differentiator. As it is commonly said but rarely implemented: Security should be "baked in" from the beginning and not "bolted on" after all the equipment is installed. If you are in the planning and or design phase, then security capability requirements can be applied now.

If the smart meters mentioned in the very beginning of this chapter are already installed but it is not known if they were securely installed, the organization could use the methods from this chapter to create a relevant governance structure and assess current security procedures via structured and repeatable processes. In the process you one may discover that the ICS networks are unknowingly connected to other networks within the organization, presenting significant risks to critical ICS processes. In the Code of Practice for the Cyber Security in the Built Environment, Boyes (2014, p.57) explains "This cascade from the strategy through policy to process and individual procedures is most important as it provides an audible trail that links specific actions and activities to the overall vision of how the cyber-security risks will be managed and mitigated."

14.4 Summary and Conclusions

ICS networks are being exploited due to a lack of integrated security. This motivates a much stronger need for interdepartmental collaboration and cooperation in an organization. Cooperative discussions can optimize system performance and security while minimizing cost and risk. Contributors must manage procurement practices and weigh consequences of other relevant corporate decisions. Although cooperative motivation can be integral for short-term success, long-term success requires a more structured approach.

Security governance is critically important for outlining both the specific expectation of ICS operations, as well as the consequences for not adhering to specified policies. Once asset owners understand the security standards for their organization, they are able to create and manage a program to mitigate cyber security risks. In addition, it is critically important to conduct routine evaluations (assessments) to ascertain operational and security performance. Assessments are applied at the design, construction and completion phases. Among all the governing documents within an organization, assessments are the most powerful for enabling resource decisions, revealing vulnerabilities, and making security modifications.

Four sample methods of ICS security assessments are discussed in detail in this chapter: The NIST Cyber Security Framework (CSF), DoE/DHS Cyber Capability Maturity Model (C2M2), the proprietary Robust ICS Planning and Evaluation (RIPE) framework, and the DHS ICS CERT Cyber Security Evaluation Tool (CSET). Each of these approaches is based upon extensive subject matter experience and community best practices, and each can be used as a starting point for establishing security practices in an organization. A large amount of informational and tutorial documents are available for using these methods.

Although engaging governance and security assessments requires significant investment by the organization, the benefits can far outweigh the costs. Security evaluations and investments are shared directly with organization executives, who are consequently become integrated in the process. Due diligence or corporate responsibility is usually evident if a breach occurs. Documentation of security processes and well-kept security logs can be instrumental for forensics, and for overall process improvement in an organization.

References

Allen, J. (2005). *Governing for enterprise security (CMU/SEI-2005-TN-023)*. Pittsburgh, PA: Software Engineering Institute, Carnegie Mellon University.

Boyes, H. (2014). *Code of practice for cyber security in built environment* (p. 57). London: The Institution of Engineering and Technology.

Department of Energy. (2014). *Cybersecurity Capability Maturity Model (C2M2) Facilitator Guide* (pp. 1, 15, 19). Retrieved from http://energy.gov/sites/prod/files/2014/02/f7/C2M2-FacilitatorGuide-v1-1-Feb2014.pdf.

Department of Homeland Security Industrial Control System Cyber Emergency Response Team. (2015), *Cyber Security Evaluation Tool (CSET), Users Guide* (pp. 14, 15, 20, 44, 47, 70, 111, 173). Retrieved from https://ics-cert.us-cert.gov/Assessments.

Fabro, M. (2012). *Study on cyber security and threat evaluation in SCADA systems* (p. 125). Ontario: Defense Research and Development Canada Centre for Security Science.

Howe, D. (2009), *Information technology governance*. The Free On-line Dictionary of Computing from Dictionary.com website. Retrieved from http://dictionary.reference.com/browse/information_technology_governance.

Hufty, M. (2011). Investigating policy processes: The governance analytical framework (GAF). In U. Wiesmann, H. Hurni, et al. (Eds.), *Research for sustainable development: Foundations, experiences, and perspectives* (pp. 403–424). Bern: Geographica Bernensia. Retrieved from https://en.wikipedia.org/wiki/Governance.

Joint Task Force Transformation Initiative Interagency Working Group. (2013). *Security and privacy controls for federal information systems and organizations*. Gaithersburg, MD: National Institute of Science and Technology, Special Publication 800–53 revision 4, p. F-64. Retrieved from http://nvlpubs.nist.gov/nistpubs/SpecialPublications/NIST.SP.800-53Ar4.pdf.

Langer, R. (2013), *Robust ICS Planning & Evaluation (RIPE) Framework* (pp. 1, 9). Retrieved from http://www.langner.com/en/solutions/.

National Institute of Science and Technology. (2014), *Cybersecurity framework* (pp. 6, 7, 15, 20). Retrieved from http://www.nist.gov/cyberframework/.

Stouffer, K., Pillitteri, V., Abrams, M., & Hahn, A. (2015). *Guide to Industrial Control Systems (ICS) Security*. Gaithersburg, MD: National Institute of Science and Technology, Special Publication 800–82 revision 2, pp. 2–117, G-27. Retrieved from http://nvlpubs.nist.gov/nistpubs/SpecialPublications/NIST.SP.800-82r2.pdf.

Westby, J.R. (2003). *Information security governance: Toward a framework for action business software alliance*. Retrieved from http://www.bsa.org/country/Research%20and%20Statistics/~/media/BD05BC8FF0F04CBD9D76460B4BED0E67.ashx.

Chapter 15
Responding to Attacks on Industrial Control Systems and SCADA Systems

Frank Honkus III

15.1 Introduction

This chapter discusses potential active and military response to an attack on ICS performed by a nation state, something that rarely if ever enters the purview of a typical ICS stakeholder. However, because ICS attacks are so likely to be perpetuated by a nation state, and because any response to an ICS attack may touch on issues related to a hostile nation state, we feel that this book benefits from exploring this unusual topic.

Evidence exists that nation-state actors have realized the utility of holding industrial control systems (ICS) at risk; they have also demonstrated intent to gain and retain access to ICS networks, and a willingness to use such an access when deemed necessary. In addition to a wealth of intellectual property, ICS can be held at risk for coercion during peace time, or for destruction during times of conflict. This chapter begins with an overview of the notion of Jus ad bellum, or "right to war"—a concept that identifies criteria nation-states use in order to justify engaging in military actions. Then, the chapter discusses considerations and governing factors in use of force in response to cyber attacks, and proceeds to outline a method—the Schmitt Analytical Framework—for determining whether an attack on ICS constitutes the use of force, which constitutes a major factor in determining appropriate response.

The remainder of the chapter is focused on applying the framework to three case studies. The first case, made public in 2013, concerns the alleged Chinese government sponsored cyber exploitation campaign targeting US oil and natural gas companies for ICS information, a ICS vendor, and other control system related targets. The second is discusses Iranian state sponsored cyber actors allegedly conducting several attacks against critical infrastructure as detailed in the Operation Cleaver

F. Honkus III (✉)
Energy Sector Cyber Intelligence Unit, US Department of Energy, Washington, DC, USA
e-mail: Fjhonkus@gmail.com

© Springer International Publishing Switzerland 2016
E.J.M. Colbert, A. Kott (eds.), *Cyber-security of SCADA and Other Industrial Control Systems*, Advances in Information Security 66,
DOI 10.1007/978-3-319-32125-7_15

report. The third case explores the Havex malware, first reported in June 2014, which was presumably developed and distributed by a nation-state actor.

In each case, the Schmitt Analytical Framework is used as a test to measure an actor's cyber behavior and determine if it could be a use of force. The concept of Jus ad bellum, use of force, and the Schmitt Analytical Framework help shape the conversation on security approaches that can provide recommendations for mitigation and resiliency, as well as tools a nation state can use to respond to an attack on an ICS.

15.2   Cyber Warfare

Nation state and non-nation state malicious actors can target, access, and potentially impact ICS networks. Non-state actors are dealt with through local, state, and national laws, while Nation state cyber operations are covered by international law. The Tallinn Manual, which is an academic study and non-binding, describes how international law applies to cyber conflicts and cyber warfare.

It has been established that Stuxnet was created by a nation state actor, but the actor who damaged a German steel mill is 2014 is unknown. Nation state and non-nation state malicious actors can target, access, and potentially impact ICS networks. Non-state actors are dealt with through local, state, and national laws, while nation state cyber operations are covered by international law.

In 1999, a legal framework was created by Professor Michael Schmitt to stymie war between nation-states. This was prior to the concept of cybersecurity or the potential use of offensive cyber operations. More recently in 2013, a basis for the use of cyber warfare, specifically computer network attack (CNA), was developed by NATO Cooperative on Cyber Defense Centre of Excellence in the Tallinn Manual in order to fill the gap of applicable international law with regards to the use of cyber in warfare. The Tallinn Manual, which is an academic study and non-binding, describes how international law applies to cyber conflicts and cyber warfare.

The legal basis for understanding and responding to cyber attacks is not well defined, but a few efforts have been made. In this chapter, we describe some of these efforts and show example use of these methods to analyze specific cyber attacks.

15.2.1   Jus ad bellum ("Right to War")

The intent of Jus ad bellum—the "right to war"—is to determine if a nation state's actions can be construed as a use of force, providing a justification for war. Jus ad bellum criteria include "legitimate or competent authority, just cause, last resort, reasonable hope of success, announcement of intentions, the right intention, proportionality, and just conduct" (Childress 1978). Fulfilling some or all of these criteria provide a justification for the use of force. The concept of Jus ad bellum predates cyber warfare by centuries, but it now applies to cyber warfare. Cyberspace has now become an operational domain for nation-state warfare.

Cyberspace provides a malicious actor a better ability to maneuver and position in their adversary's terrain prior to a military engagement. It complements each of the other warfare domains (land, air, sea and space). Cyber warfare can be used independently or as a force multiplier with the other warfare domains (Department of Defense 2013). ICSs, and the critical infrastructure that it supports, are an ideal target to hold at risk in order to coerce or intimidate. As cyberspace has now matured as a cyber warfare domain, a need has arisen to determine how previously established international law impacts it.

The United Nations Charter, article 2(4) states: "All members shall refrain in their international relations from the threat or use of force against the territorial integrity or political independence of any state, or in any other manner inconsistent with the Purposes of the United Nations" (United Nations 1945). However, cybersecurity as an institution, and cyber as a use of force, has only matured over the past few decades. In July 2012, at the request of the NATO Cooperative on Cyber Defense Centre of Excellence, analysis was conducted on the application of international law to cyber warfare, generating the Tallinn Manual (Schmitt 2013).

15.2.2 Use of Force

According to the International Court of Justice, Articles 2(4) and 51 of the United Nations Charter apply concerning a use of force, regardless of the technology, tactics, techniques, and procedures employed. The International Court of Justice judgment was made concerning nuclear weapons, but is to be considered all-encompassing, and according to the Tallinn Manual (Schmitt 2013), includes cyber warfare. The Tallinn Manual argues that with regards to *Jus ad bellum*, "a cyber-operation that constitutes a threat or use of force against the territorial integrity or political independence of any state, or that is in any other manner inconsistent with the purpose of the United Nations, is unlawful" (Schmitt 2013). The Tallinn Manual also defines the use of cyber force as being proportional to a non-cyber operation "rising to the level of a use of force." A proportional non-cyber operational use of force would equate to an armed physical attack. Accordingly, a cyber-operation designed to sway a political campaign, undermine confidence in a nation state's economy, or otherwise sow disharmony would not be considered a use of force. However, for example, the targeting of the ICSs that supports critical infrastructure such as manufacturing, water purification or reclamation systems, or electric power substations with the intent to cause a negative physical effect would be considered a use of force.

Critical infrastructure, whether civilian or military, has often been a target in past military engagements. For example, during World War II, the United States Air Force targeted German and Japanese cities in order to interrupt production and manufacturing. The concept was that "industrial economies were delicate webs of interdependent factories, power plants, and transportation links" (Searle 2002). Identification and targeting of critical nodes in these webs would enable the Allies to undermine and potentially halt civilian and military production. A similar tactic was used during the Vietnam War, in which 94 industrial, transportation, and infrastructure targets were identified for concentrated bombing in North Vietnam. Targets in the list covered numerous sectors of critical infrastructure (Kamps 2001) including communications, manufacturing, and transportation

Targeting of the underpinning of critical infrastructure, specifically ICSs, would enable a malicious actor to potentially cause a significant impact while remaining anonymous. Nation states have already begun to engage in malicious activity necessary to gain access to, and hold at risk, ICS networks (Mandiant 2013). Classification and identification of these actors would be necessary to determine if the attack is a nation-state attack. In addition, factors characterizing the attack would need to be identified and analyzed to determine if an actor's activity constitutes a cyber-use of force.

15.2.3 Schmitt Analytical Framework

In this section, we describe in detail a method for determining whether use of force has been applied in cyberspace. The Schmitt Analytical Framework was developed by Michael Schmitt (Schmitt 1999) to address the need for how cyber warfare would fit into an international legal framework. Schimitt's analysis was prescient; he created the framework in 1999, and accurately described the global communities' reliance on computers and their networks, and the vulnerabilities inherent in them. He explained how the civilian world relies on global use of computer systems and the Internet. Schmitt further demonstrated the military's reliance on computers and network systems, identifying in 1999 that the United States Department of Defense (DOD) relied on roughly two million computers and 10,000 networks. As of 2010, it was reported (Connelly 2010) that the US DoD needed to defend seven million computers, 15,000 networks, and 1.1 billion DoD Internet users.

Schmitt recognized that computer systems could be held at risk through acts of sabotage that could interfere in a nation's defenses and/or disrupt critical infrastructure and human and natural resources. Identified attack techniques included viruses with the intent of denying or damaging target networks, logic bombs that could lay in wait until a certain time, date, or action caused them to activate, or denial of service campaigns that could flood a target system or network with useless data, causing a shut down. Schmitt's 1999 framework came 10 or 11 years prior to the identification of Stuxnet, and roughly 14 years before malicious actors damaged a blast furnace at a steel mill in Germany.

Even if cyber warfare is used as a standalone cyber operation (e.g. Stuxnet), it would be a use of force. Drawing on the language of the United Nations Charter, Article 2(4), specifically the term, "other manner," Schmitt argues that this term would be interpreted as any use of force, regardless of the method, that is not covered explicitly by the Charter. Essentially, if a CNA operation constitutes force, it will be deemed wrongful unless based on the United Nations Charter (Schmitt 1999).

Schmitt further explores the established international law concerning the use of force and the distinction of "armed force" or an "armed attack." Designation of armed force relies on an instrument based approach for determining Jus ad Bellum. Namely, the instrument used in the attack must be of kinetic nature in order to be classified as an armed attack and consequently a use of force. This instrument-based approach was used when drafting the United Nations Charter. Schmitt argues (Schmitt 1999) that in the context of cyber warfare a consequence-based approach for establishing Jus ad Bellum would better serve to determine use of force. In this way, the consequences of the attack are considered rather than just the instrument used.

Schmitt identified seven determinative factors to consider in order to determine whether an action is a use of force in cyber warfare.

Severity: This would include cyber operations that are intended to cause physical harm or destruction.

Immediacy: Essentially, how fast a cyber-effect's impact occurs. The lower the immediacy, the more time nation states have to resolve their grievances peacefully. The faster the effect manifests, the less time diplomacy has to play a role.

Directness: The connection between the cyber operation's intent and the consequences of the operation.

Invasiveness: The perceived intrusion of the cyber operation against a nation state's sovereignty and/or borders.

Measurability: The more a nation can identify and quantify the consequences of a cyber-operation, the more likely it will be construed as a use of force.

Presumptive Legitimacy: Activities deemed legitimate in the international law, such as psychological operations and economic espionage, apply in the cyber domain as well.

Responsibility: Attributing the cyber operation to the nation state who conducted it will more likely lead to the interpretation of a use of force.

15.2.4 Mitigation and Response

Depending on the nature of the production targeted or impacted, mitigation and response should be applied as warranted. Although ICSs supports critical infrastructure, some infrastructure is less critical than others. For example, it would not be cost effective to devote significant resources protecting a web enabled programmable logic controller for a public drinking fountain that utilized HTTP. The PLC for this fountain only monitors use and can control the valve to turn the water on and off. If the fountain's PLC were hacked, it would be a slight inconvenience for anyone who uses it. A simple and very cost effective solution would be to move communications to port 443 and utilize SSL encryption in order decrease the likelihood of compromise.

However, for ICSs that controls critical infrastructure involving human safety and/or survival, it may be necessary to afford greater protections. Examples of critical infrastructure that warrant greater protections include water and waste water reclamation, oil and natural gas production, refinement, and transmission, and electric power generation and transmission. For the water example, the release of raw sewage into a river that is also used for drinking water downstream can introduce a significant health risk. Oil and natural gas lines run through residential, commercial, and industrial zones. An oil spill can create a hazardous environmental situation as well as the threat of combustion. Manipulation of natural gas compressors could potentially have explosive results. Finally, degradation of electric power generation or transmission can cause localized or regional blackouts. What the ICS network controls should always be taken into account in order to afford the best protections comparable to the risk and impact. Indeed, a similar scale can be used by nation states in order to gauge the appropriate response in the event of compromise or attack against ICS causing impacts in critical infrastructure.

Nation states have a number of tools at the international level that they can use to dissuade or punish a malicious nation state actor. Nation states can use diplomatic tools including the use of national law enforcement, the declaration of "persona non grata", and the concept of a demarche. National law enforcement such as the Federal Bureau of Investigations (FBI) can issue indictments against suspected parties operating on behalf a nation state. Such indictments can be coupled with the concept of persona non grata. Persona non grata is a diplomatic term which means "an unwelcome person." For example, this term might be applied by nation states to remove or revoke travel to individuals who may have been accused or identified to be operating for a foreign government. A demarche is used as a form of protest from one government to another when the first government feels there has been a transgression. Most commonly, they are used during territorial disputes. Nation states can also use sanctions or force themselves. Economic sanctions are traditionally used to punish a nation state perceived negative behavior. For example, economic sanctions are currently enforced against Iran for their Uranium enrichment program. A nation state can also opt to use armed force themselves in retaliation for a perceived attack or in self-defense. The degrading or destruction of ICSs in order to destroy critical infrastructure could push a nation state to respond with a use of armed force, whether with a similar cyber reprisal or physical attack. However, the use of force should be limited in scope to reciprocate appropriately to any perceived attack.

15.3   Case Study Analyses for Use of Force

The seven factors of the Schmitt analytical framework enable an individual to subjectively categorize the individual characteristics of a cyber-attack. By drawing all the factors together, a representation of whether the actions of a nation state engaged in cyber warfare can be construed as a use of force. These seven factors will be applied to two nation state actors identified by security companies—China and Iran. In addition, the Schmitt analysis will be applied to the Havax malware attack. The attack has not been attributed, but it is thought that the Havex attack was executed by a nation state (Symantec 2014). Each of these actors have targeted critical infrastructure, and the Havex malware was designed to targeted ICS networks. The factors will be weighted and combined, and an interpretation of use of force will be determined. Finally, recommendations will be made on mitigation and/or resiliency of ICS networks and tools nation states can use to respond.

15.3.1 China Case Study

According to the FBI and several information security companies, China has engaged in an espionage cyber campaign targeting the United States as well as several other countries. In March 2015, the former Director of National Intelligence and former Director of the National Security Agency (NSA) Vice Admiral (VADM) Mike McConnell stated the Chinese government hacked into the computer networks of the U.S. Congress, Department of Defense, State Department, and major American corporations. The intent of the Chinese campaign is to identify and exfiltrate intellectual property. VADM McConnell stated (Pagliery 2015) that during the final years of President George W. Bush's Presidency, the Chinese government employed roughly 100,000 hackers. A few days following VADM McConnell's comments, it was reported that the Chinese military acknowledged that they had specialized military and intelligence units dedicated to cyber warfare. The admission (Harris 2015) is attributed to a publication produced by the Chinese People's Liberation Army, entitled "The Science of Military Strategy."

As described by VADM McConnell, 100,000 Chinese hackers is far too many to account for here. However, in February 2013, the information security company Mandiant (Mandiant 2013) released a report of their findings specifically identifying APT1 as Unit 61398 of the Third Department of the Chinese People's Liberation Army (PLA). According to Mandiant's analysis, Unit 61398 has conducted economic espionage since at least 2006, compromising nearly 141 targets across multiple industries.

One of the contributions of the Mandiant report was to provide roughly 3000 indicators of compromise that could be used to identify Unit 61398. Mandiant further reviewed media reports of activity, and tied together at least three groups that had been reported in the news or by other information security companies as being Unit 61398. Comment Crew, Comment Group, and possibly a group identified as Shady Rat, all seemed to share similar tactics, techniques, procedures, and infrastructure to carry out their campaigns. There are several cases where Unit 61398 were identified concerning the targeting of ICSs.

Between May and June 2012, media outlets (Clayton 2012) reported that the Department of Homeland Security (DHS) was notifying oil and natural gas owners and operators of a spear-phishing campaign that began in late 2011. DHS released several confidential alerts to the oil and natural gas sector, and identified the intrusions as related to a single campaign. According to DHS (Ryan 2012), the malicious actors who sent the spear-phishing emails appeared to be target a small select group of individuals at U.S. gas companies. DHS released restricted accessed indicators of compromise to compromised oil and natural gas companies and information security companies that specialized in ICSs. Two of these companies, Critical Intelligence and Red Tiger Security, determined that the same intrusion set that under took the campaign against the oil and natural gas sector also conducted a hack against information security company RSA. In March 2012, GEN Keith Alexander, Director of NSA and chief of US Cyber Command at the time, had briefed a Senate committee that China was behind the RSA hack.

While undertaking the oil and natural gas campaign, Unit 61398 also targeted other ICS specific companies. One example is a spear-phishing email that targeted an employee (Wightman 2012) of the ICS security company Digital Bond and was posted to the company's blog in June 2012. The spear-phishing email was carefully crafted with ICS security language in order to entice its target to click the link and ensure compromise. However, the ruse was quickly discovered and the intended target was not exploited. The Mandiant report drew upon the supplied indicators of compromise to identify Unit 61398 as the malicious actor who targeted the employee of Digital Bond.

A second example of Chinese targeting of companies working with ICS occurred against the company Telvent. Telvent produces software and provides services for remote administration and monitoring of ICS. According to researcher and analyst Brian Krebs (Krebs 2012), Telvent was notified of a breach in September 2012. Telvent released a report to its customers outlining the compromise, what was impacted, and included a list of indicators of compromise. The attackers had installed malware and exfiltrated information related to one of its primary products, OASyS SCADA. The OASyS product is used to by energy companies to network their older IT systems with smart grid technology. The indicator list was used by Dell SecureWorks to link the malware names back to the Chinese hacking team Comment Group. As previously discussed, the Mandiant report associated the Comment Crew with Unit 61398.

The Christian Science Monitor (CSM) (Clayton 2013) connected Unit 61398 to the oil and natural gas campaign through the use of the Mandiant report. In February 2013, CSM referenced a restricted DHS report and a source familiar with the investigation and reported that nearly two dozen U.S. natural gas pipeline operators had been targeting and stated that the information exfiltrated from compromised victims could be used to sabotage U.S. pipelines. According to the DHS report CSM cited, the exfiltrated information included "usernames, passwords, personnel lists, system manuals, and pipeline control system access credentials." The DHS report also stated "The data exfiltrated could provide an adversary with the capability to access US [oil and natural gas industrial-control systems], including performing unauthorized operations" and that the attackers used customized malware to search the pipeline companies networks for files with the letters "SCAD," which can be construed as shorthand for the term supervisory control and data acquisition (SCADA).[1] According to CSM, the SCADA files stolen contained information necessary to "locate and operate compressors, valves, switches, pressure settings, and other pipeline operations" (Clayton 2013). One of the more telling files taken during the exfiltration is a list of dialup modem access numbers for remote terminal units used

[1] SCADA is a subset of ICS.

to monitor and control pipeline networks remotely. The CSM reported that the list of indicators of compromise that was provided in the Mandiant report matched with the list of indicators of compromise that had been distributed by DHS in 2012, identifying Unit 61398 as being behind the campaign.

The FBI has also identified Unit 61398 as a threat, issuing criminal charges against five members of the unit. Among other charges in the indictment, counts 10 through 23 are "Transmitting a program, information, code, or command with the intent to cause damage to protected computers" (FBI 2014).

It is clearly evident that Chinese actors, specifically Unit 61398, are engaged in cyber operations. The application of the Schmitt analysis will help to determine if it is a use of force.

Severity: Unit 61398's targets were broadly spread across many sectors of critical infrastructure and the private and sector, the campaign against U.S. oil and natural gas companies, ICS vendors, and ICS software manufactures, demonstrate that ICSs was key. Of specific interest is the exfiltration of the RTU dialup information, and the potential those dialup numbers provide for access and control of these systems. Although there is great potential to cause physical destruction and death, there is no reporting of physical damage to the pipelines at this time, attributed to Chinese actors or otherwise.

Immediacy: The campaign targeting the oil and natural gas sector, ICS software manufacturer, and ICS security company occurred over the course of many months, from roughly December 2011 to September 2012. Although the actual compromises and exfiltration may take no more than the speed of light, the drawn out aspect of the campaign provided several opportunities to engage in diplomacy. The FBI indictment could be construed as an act of diplomacy in the intervening years since the information was taken, drawing from the diplomatic concept of *persona non grata*.

Directness: It is unclear if the collected ICSs information was intended to be used for cyber warfare or economic espionage. The gathered information can be labeled as dual use, serving either an economic or military objective. As there is no reporting of an attack or damage at this time, it can be argued that the information gathered could support future operations while also serving an economic benefit.

Invasiveness: During the oil and natural gas campaign, Unit 61398 used the Internet to target, compromise, and access systems that reside in the United States. Some of the information exfiltrated, for example the RTU dialup numbers, could be used for future military operations against U.S. privately held infrastructure. It is clear that there is a capability to inhibit a state's sovereignty and that the actors crossed the US border, underscored by the indictment against the five members of the unit.

Measurability: The consequences of the campaign against the oil and natural gas sector, ICS software manufacturer, and the ICS security company could be quantifiable, regardless of economic or military intent. Concerning military intent, the exfiltration of sensitive documents on the logical and physical layout of an oil or natural gas pipeline, in conjunction with access information such as the RTU dialup numbers, would enable a malicious actor to cause measurable destruction allowing for the calculation of cost in critical infrastructure, human, and natural resources lost or damaged.

Presumptive Legitimacy: Economic espionage is currently tolerated under international law, however, actors caught in the actor are punished to the full extent of a nation state's laws. It has long been understood that nation state actors spy on one another. However, targeting and exfiltrating information from ICS specific vendors and companies could be interpreted as part of a larger campaign to preposition and hold critical infrastructure at risk during a time of war.

Responsibility: Based off the gathered reporting, and the extensive analysis of the Mandiant report, as well as underscored by the FBI indictments and the Chinese acknowledgement of cyber warfare military and intelligence units, it is all but certain that Unit 61398 operates on behalf of the Third Department of the Chinese People's Liberation Army.

Taking all of the factors into account, most states would not consider China's Unit 61398 actions as a use of force. There is direct attribution, and the campaigns targeting ICSs and the information exfiltrated is startling. There is also the ability to quantify the consequences of a potential attack, and the assets compromised were in the United States. However, there has been no attack. This campaign, although arguably a first step in order to identify vulnerabilities or critical weak points in ICS networks, would appear to be economic espionage or an intelligence campaign. There is no reporting of physical destruction to U.S. oil and gas pipelines since the campaign was first report to present. Additionally, the immediacy of the campaign provided several months from the beginning of the campaign to the end to attempt to resolve the issue. Again, the FBI indictment may have been a gesture of *persona non grata* or could have been interpreted as a subtle démarche in order to diplomatically put the Chinese on notice.

The security professional's response to the Chinese campaign would include best practices such as employee training in how to identify spear-fishing emails, scheduled password resets, stronger email filtering, and network monitoring to include white listing. Control system environments are generally a "quieter" then a typical IT network. The machines involved typically poll and produce in a repetitive way. That is not to say ICS networks are static, but they do have an operational rhythm that can be identified over time. This monotony is useful in white listing, enabling a security professional to identify typical daily, weekly, or monthly activity, and identify rules when anything out of the ordinary arises. A passive intrusion detection system can be used on an ICS network and rules can be built that would send alerts any time there is any deviation from what would be considered normal traffic. Since the infrastructure that could be impacted could cause significant negative impact of denied or degraded, it would also be recommended to develop a resiliency plan in the event that aggressive action were taken against the control systems. However, resiliency can be an expensive proposition, especially if the deployment is over several hundred miles. Moving processes into a local mode with an operator on hand would be difficult, and would best be used only during hostile activity.

Specific to the Chinese intrusions, nation states have some tools that could be considered an equal response. In this case, national law enforcement (the FBI) issuing arrest warrants for the accused perpetrators. Additionally, it would be implied that the accused would be considered "persona non grata" in the United States. A diplomatic demarche could also be used to raise the awareness of the actions to the Chinese government. Finally, economic sanctions could be used to dissuade the Chinese from further targeting of ICS networks, but the costs for both sides would be extraordinarily high.

15.3.2   Iran Case Study

In December 2014, the information security company Cylance released a report named "Operation Cleaver." Operation Cleaver lays out Cylance's argument (Cylance 2014) that Iranian state sponsored cyber actors have conducted several attacks against critical infrastructure. These attacks included targets in the financial services, energy and utilities, oil and natural gas, and chemical sectors. Cylance states that in 2009 and 2010, Iranian cyber actors would have been considered lower tier, using publically available zero days, SQL injection, and social engineering tactics in an attempt to compromise targets. Within the span of roughly four years, Iranian actors had refined their tactics, techniques, and procedures, and created internally developed, customized tools, stating that Iran is of the same caliber as China. Cylance points to several examples of Iranian cyber attacks. The distributed denial of service (DDOS) campaign against the financial services sector in the United States, nicknamed Operation Ababil, the compromise of U.S. military targets including the Navy Marine Corp Intranet (NMCI), and the attacks against Saudi Aramco and RasGas utilizing the Shamoon malware. Similar to the Mandiant report on Chinese cyber actors, Cylance collected and provided a list of indicators of compromise in order to identify adversarial activity and attribute it to Iran. Cylance points out that Persian hacker names were used throughout the campaigns, domains were registered in Iran, infrastructure used during the attacks was hosted by an Iranian service provider, source netblocks and autonomous system numbers were register to Iran, and specific infrastructure was registered to an Iranian company. Finally, Cylance speculates that part of the campaign that Iranian cyber actors have waged may be to damage ICSs in order to cause impacts to critical infrastructure. Although there were impacts against the financial services industry and the NMCI networks, the following will focus on the targeting and destructive attacks against Saudi Aramco and RasGas.

In August 2012, two oil and natural gas companies were targeted with a malware that overwrote the master boot records of systems, causing the systems to become inaccessible upon restart. According to reporting, the first target was the Saudi Arabian company Saudi Aramco. Saudi Aramco extracts and transports petroleum products, supplying the world with a tenth of its oil. On August 15 at 11:08 am., the malware identified as Shamoon (Symantec 2013) was activated, overwriting the master boot records of 30,000 Armaco computers, destroying the machines and the information on them (Arthor 2012). The attack destroyed three fourths of the systems on the network, however, Saudi Aramco claims they were able to clean and reconstitute their network in a matter of weeks. At the time, the company also stated that their petroleum exploration and production systems had not been affected because they run on an isolated network. However, by December 2012, Saudi Aramco and the Saudi government stated that the attackers' intent was to interrupt production and distribution of oil and gas, with Aramco's vice president stating, "The main target in this attack was to stop the flow of oil and gas to local and international market and thank God they were not able to achieve their goal" (Leyden 2012).

Two weeks after the Aramco incident, on August 27, the network of the Qatari liquefied natural gas company RasGas was impacted by a d by a ent, on August 27, the network of the Qatari liquefied natural gas company Ra virus similar to Shamoon had been used to destroy the corporate network of RasGas. According to RasGas, the attack did not impact production. As the attack against RasGas was almost immediately after the attack against Saudi Aramco, it was speculated (Mills 2012) that the malware used was Shamoon. Similar to the pronouncement after the NMCI compromise, U.S. officials claimed (Mount 2012) that Iranian cyber actors were responsible. The Cylance report provides indicators of compromise tying Saudi Aramco and RasGas to Iranian cyber actors, stating that the intent of the malicious actors is to gain initial access in order to later carry out sabotage through cyber means.

Based off of a large body of reporting and the indicators of compromise provided in the Cylance report, it can be determined that Iran has a state sponsored cyber program. Just like the Mandiant report, the indicators of compromise are crucial in order to attain attribution. Reuters was able to attain a FBI confidential "Flash" report, which is supplied to private businesses and provides indicators of compromise in order to identify and stop attacks. Indicators of compromise in the FBI report matched those provided by Cylance, however, the FBI would only claim (Finkle 2014) that they were associated with Iranian hackers. The campaigns and reporting, taken as a whole, will help to determine if the activity would be construed as a use of force.

Severity: The Shamoon malware was designed to, and did destroy, at least 30,000 computers at Saudi Aramco. According to reporting, the hard drives of the affected systems needed to be replaced, and all of the data that had been on that system was destroyed. It is believed that RasGas' systems were also affected.

Immediacy: According to the Cylance report, Iran has been conducting cyber operations since at least 2009. They have consistently developed and refined their capabilities, at least until the date of publication of Operation Cleaver. The Iranians began to attack the critical infrastructure of their neighbors and of the United States as the economic sanctions against them tightened. There was ample time to engage in diplomacy, which Iran and the U.S. have done. Since at least 2013, the United States and Iran have been engaged in discussions pertaining to the Iranian nuclear program. Talks continue at the time of writing, demonstrating that Iran may have used a diplomatic approach allowing both sides an opportunity to discuss all issues and grievances.

Directness: There is a connection between Iran's cyber activity and their intent. The economic sanctions have caused the Iranian economy to deteriorate. In 2010, Stuxnet disrupted Iran's nuclear enrichment program. Iran was becoming isolated, and there would most certainly be an intent to lash out and cause consequences.

Invasiveness: It can be argued that Iran did cross international boarders in order to install the Shamoon malware on Saudi Aramco and RasGas. Striking at Saudi Arabian and Qatari oil and natural gas, both countries' main exports and source of income, could be considered as an attack against the sovereignty of the state.

Measurability: The destruction of computers through the use of Shamoon are measureable and quantifiable.

Presumptive Legitimacy: The destruction of computers at Saudi Aramco and RasGas would be outside of the concept of Presumptive Legitimacy.

Responsibility: There is sufficient evidence that Iran engages in state sponsored cyber operations, based upon the remarks and reports of U.S. officials and information security companies.

Taking all factors into account, most nation states would consider Iran's cyber operations to be a use of force. What stands out in stark contrast is the use of the Shamoon malware against Saudi Aramco and RasGas. The malware was designed to destroy, and it executed that function with startling efficiency. The use of Shamoon is easily measurable, was activated in a sovereign state, with the intent to degrade or destroy the compromised network. It should be noted that no similar attack as Shamoon has been associated with Iranian cyber actors since Saudi Aramco and RagGas. From the perspective of immediacy, It can be argued that due to the drawn out timeframe of events over the course of many years, coupled with the purposeful posting of specific targets and dates during the DDOS campaign, Iran was attempting to demonstrate their cyber capacities in order to have a stronger negotiating position during the ongoing nuclear discussions and deal with the U.S. It could also be reasoned that the use of cyber capabilities was, or is, part of the discussion, whether regarding Iran or concerning Stuxnet.

Security professionals could take similar steps to mitigate the Iranian activity similar to previous recommendations made for the Chinese case study. In this case, network monitoring seems to come to the fore front. A baselined network, although expensive, would have enabled administrators to identify the Shamoon malware prior to launch. Baselining of a network is attempting to identify what would be considered "normal" applications, processes, and network communications. A successful baseline can then be compare to the current state of the network to identify any changes. However, initial baselining can be time consuming and costly if it was not done at the time of implementation and build out. Additionally, baselining after a network has been operating for months or years might be all but impossible as numerous changes, patches, and configurations have been made since its inception. Employee training can still be provided concerning the identification of spear-phishing emails and best practices and diligence can be applied to web facing nodes and/applications including adhering to a patching schedule, deletion of accounts of former employees, password refreshes, and network monitoring. Finally, having a warm site as backup that is segregated from the normal corporate network would be ideal. It would appear that a warm site was maintained for Aramco, or at least a weekly backup of information, as they were able to reconstitute their network in a matter of weeks. Unfortunately the same cannot be said for RasGas, who appeared to suffer greater harm and had much more difficulty coming back online.

From a nation state perspective, the Iranian activity would constitute the use of higher caliber tools. For example, a demarche after the destruction of the corporate network would be too little too late, as the network and the information contained upon it was already destroyed. However, sanctions could be a useful tool. It could be considered an "eye for an eye" in so much as the cost of the destruction of the networks of Saudi Aramco and Rasgas is quantifiable and an economic sanction could be pressed upon Iran in a manner so that they suffer economically to the same degree. Although Iran's actions can be interpreted as a use of force, it would be suggested that a similar attack not be carried out against Iranian infrastructure. It can be argued that Iran was lashing out after they suffered some loss due to Stuxnet, and that their attacks against Saudi Aramco and RasGas may have satisfied a need to retaliate. Ultimately, the attacks enabled Iran to demonstrate their cyber capabilities, which could provide all nation states an opportunity to reevaluate future offensive operations that target Iran.

15.3.3   Havex Case Study

The Havex malware was first reported in June 2014. There is no attribution for this malware at this time, however it is argued that this malware was developed and distributed by a nation state. Therefore, the Havex malware warrants an exploration of its tactics, techniques, and procedures. The scope of the Schmitt analytical framework will be reduced, in this case the framework will be applied to the malware only versus the previous case studies analyzing nation state activity as a whole. The Schmitt analysis has been conducted (Foltz 2012) before to malware, specifically Stuxnet, by Andrew C. Foltz in his article "Stuxnet, Schmitt Analysis, and the Cyber 'Use of Force' Debate." The dynamic developed by Mr. Foltz will be used for Havex.

On June 23, 2014, security companies (F-Secure 2014) began to report on malware identified as Havex, which was targeting ICS networks and users. Targeted companies included major electricity generation firms, oil and natural gas pipeline operators, and energy industry equipment manufactures. The malware was attributed to the advanced persistent threat (APT) group Dragonfly, also known as Energetic Bear. Infection occurred in a multi-pronged approach, the first prong was to send spear-phishing emails to employees of specific companies. The second prong was to compromise legitimate vendor websites likely to be accessed by individuals working in the energy sector, which would redirect them to websites that hosted the exploit kit. The third and final prong was compromising legitimate software bundles of ICSs equipment manufacturers with a Trojan so unsuspecting operators would download and install the compromised software. Essentially, actors of the Dragonfly APT replaced legitimate software installers, such as firmware updates and/or patches, with Havex corrupted installers. The actors compromised (ICS-CERT 2014) the websites of three European ICSs manufactures, two of them suppliers of remote management software for ICSs and a third who deals in high-precision cameras. According to Symantec, the Dragonfly/Energetic Bear APT group "bears the hallmarks of a state-sponsored operation, displaying a high degree of technical capability. The group is well resourced, with a range of malware tool" (Symantec 2014). Symantec also stated that the group's primary motive is cyber espionage, however sabotage is, "a definite secondary capability."

Once Havex is on a computer, it gathers system information, files, and programs installed. It will extract a computers Outlook address book and VPN connections, then writes this information to a temporary file in an encrypted format that is sent to a remote command and control (C&C) server controlled by Dragonfly actors. At the completion of the system enumeration, the C&C server can send the Havex implant an additional "ICS/SCADA sniffing" payload (Wilhoit 2014), which enumerates infected networks looking for object linking and embedding (OLE) for process control (OPC) servers.[2] If an OPC server is discovered, it will be used to gather details of the connected devices and send them back to the C&C server for analysis. Information gathered from the OPC server includes a temporary file in an encrypted server name, Program ID, OPC version, vendor information, running state, group count, and server bandwidth" (ICS-CERT 2014). US ICS-CERT determined that the Havex payload caused multiple common OPC platforms to intermittently crash. The crashing of the OPC server could cause a denial of service to applications that rely on OPC communications.

At this time, there is no reporting of Havex having caused damage or destruction. It can be argued that the Dragonfly APT group is attempted to identify ICSs in order to pre-position before an attack. As Symantec pointed out, it is highly likely that Dragonfly is a nation state sponsored organization, and would have a vested interest in gaining and retaining a foothold in perceived adversary ICS networks during peace time in order to disrupt or destroy them during war. The Schmitt analytical framework will help to define if this malware and its application could be defined as a use of force.

Severity: According to reporting, Havex appears to be an instrument of espionage. Still, it should be taken into account that Havex is specifically tailored to compromise ICS networks, and once inside, enumerate and exfiltrated as much information as possible. This is underscored by the sniffing module designed to search superficially for OPC servers. It is *highly* unlikely that any other network would have an OPC server if it was not used for ICSs. It is additionally striking that the actors compromised vendor websites, including their malware in to the legitimate updates and patches, and then reposted them for download. It seems highly likely that only a nation state actor would have the time and resources to exploit such a supply chain vulnerability.[3] Additionally, failure of the ICSs of the targeted

---

[2] OLE for process control is a standard way for Windows applications to interact with process control hardware.

[3] Barring poor security practices on the webservers and websites of the targeted companies.

companies, including those that support the electric power and oil and natural gas sectors, would have significant impacts affecting not just those sectors but all of those interdependent on them.

Immediacy: Havex was identified in June 2014. The Dragonfly/Energetic Bear APT group has been operating for far longer. It has been almost a year since Havex was identified, and since there is no reporting to suggest Havex has been used to disable or destroy an ICS network, there would still be a diplomatic option in order to avoid violence.

Directness: Symantec states that the intent of the Dragonfly APT group is primarily espionage, with the possibility of a "definite" secondary objective of sabotage. Havex has not disabled or destroyed an ICS network, but it has the potential to do so.

Invasiveness: Havex was found across multiple countries and compromised physical machines in those countries. The methods of website redirects may, but supply chain compromise of updates would, also take advantage of computers in the countries affected. However, as Havex appears to have only gather information from compromised networks, it would not be recognized as a use of force.

Measurability: The cost and consequences for the Havex compromises would be easy to identify and quantify as there is information on targeted sectors of critical infrastructure, and specific business that support those sectors. The Dragonfly APT group used Havex to compromise included major electricity generation firms, oil and natural gas pipeline operators, and energy industry equipment manufactures. Loss of electricity generation and/or oil and natural gas pipelines would be significant.

Presumptive Legitimacy: Although there is the potential for sabotage with Havex, only espionage has been reported. The enumeration of systems and ICS networks, and the exfiltration of data from those networks, would not be construed as a use of force.

Responsibility: There is no attribution of the Dragonfly/Energetic Bear APT group to a nation state at this time. However, it is likely that the Dragonfly group is sponsored by a nation state based off of reporting.

Taking all factors into account, most nation states would not consider the Havex malware to be a use of force. Although it is tailored to target and compromise ICS networks, specifically seeking OPC servers, it has not be liable for disabling or destroying any ICS networks at this time. Only system and network enumeration and data exfiltration have occurred. The creators of Havex, Dragonfly, are believed to be state sponsored cyber actors, however, there is no direct attribution to a nation state at this time. Havex was identified in June 2014, and did not cause any destructive harm, so it stands to reason that the malware is part of an espionage campaign in order to gather information from ICS networks. That being said, Havex also would have the dual use function of enabling a Dragonfly operator to hold the compromised ICSs at risk, potentially disabling or destroying it at some future date.

Mitigation for a security profession for the Havex malware scales up in difficulty with each prong of the attack. First, stronger email filtering and training to identify spear-phishing emails would be useful for the first prong. It would be necessary to maintain patch management on all Internet enabled systems and applications in order to counter the second prong. However, a zero day exploit against a web browser plug in such as flash is comment and could be hosted on the redirected site. Unfortunately, the third prong would be the most difficult to mitigate, as a vendor's patch server would be trusted. It would be necessary to use the known indicators of compromise and engage in network monitoring in order to determine if a network was infected. Since the Havex campaign affected numerous companies who support various members of critical infrastructure, it would be difficult to develop a resiliency plan in the event of attack. Each stakeholder would need to assess their own unique production to include its criticality and the cost or loss before developing a plan. Again, resiliency can be expensive to implement and should be reserved only for the worst case scenario.

It can be inferred that a nation state response would be minimal as there is no attribution as to who developed and deployed the Havex malware. However, if the malicious party were identified, it would most likely lead to the use of a demarche as it appears that the malware is only being used for espionage purposes at this time.

15.4 Summary and Conclusions

The legal basis for understanding and responding to international cyber attacks is not fully specified, but some progress has been made. In 1999, an effort known as the Schmitt Analytical Framework was created, prior to the concept of cybersecurity or the potential use of offensive cyber operations by nation states. Cyber warfare is used independently or as a force multiplier with other warfare domains such as land, air, sea, and space. ICSs and the critical infrastructure they support, are an ideal target to hold at risk in order to coerce or intimidate, and they have recently been targets of nation-state cyber warfare.

Jus ad bellum (the "right to war") for kinetic warfare has been used for centuries and we must now define and understand its use for cyber warfare. In July 2012, at the request of the NATO Cooperative on Cyber Defense Centre of Excellence, analysis was conducted on the application of international law to cyber warfare. The resulting analysis was published in the Tallinn Manual, which determines that a cyber operation that is a threat or is a use of force is unlawful by international legal standards. The target and effect of "cyber force" is proportional to an armed, physical attack.

The Schmitt Analytical Framework addresses the current need for how cyber warfare fits into an international legal framework and it is the focus of this chapter. Schmitt identified seven determinative factors to consider in order to analyze whether an action is a use of force in cyber warfare. These seven factors are applied to three cases studies of international cyber attacks, and results are presented.

Legal definitions of cyber warfare and international norms for cyber behavior will continue to develop and converge as more nation-state engagements are studied by legal and military scholars.

References

Arthor, C. (2012, August 16). *Saudi Aramco hit by computer virus.* Retrieved July 11, 2015.

Charter of the United Nations, Article 2(4). (1945, June 26). Retrieved July 11, 2015.

Childress, JF. (1978). *Just war theories.* Retrieved October 19, 2015.

Clayton, M. (2012, May 10). *Exclusive: Potential China link to cyberattacks on gas pipeline companies.* Retrieved July 11, 2015.

Clayton, M. (2013, February 27). *Exclusive: Cyberattack leaves natural gas pipelines vulnerable to sabotage.* Retrieved July 11, 2015.

Connelly, J. (2010, April 11). *Cyber attacks: The next big security threat?* Retrieved July 11, 2015.

Cylance. (2014, December 3). *Operation cleaver.* Retrieved July 11, 2015.

Department of Defense. (2013, February 5). *Joint publication 3–12 (R) cyberspace operations.* Retrieved July 11, 2015.

F-Secure. (2014, June 23). *Havex hunts For ICS/SCADA systems—F-Secure Weblog : News from the lab.* Retrieved July 11, 2015.

FBI. (2014, May 19). *U.S. charges five Chinese military hackers with cyber espionage against U.S. corporations and a labor organization for commercial advantage.* Retrieved July 11, 2015.

Finkle, J. (2014, December 13). *Exclusive: Iran hackers may target U.S. energy, defense firms, FBI warns.* Retrieved July 11, 2015.

Foltz, A. (2012). *Stuxnet, Schmitt analysis, and the cyber "Use-of-Force" debate. JFQ, (67* 4th Quarter). Doi:40–48

Harris, S. (2015, March 18). *China reveals its cyberwar secrets.* Retrieved July 11, 2015.

ICS-CERT. (2014, July 1). *Alert* (ICS-ALERT-14-176-02A). Retrieved July 11, 2015.

Kamps, C. (2001). The JCS 94-target list: A Vietnam myth that still distorts thought. *Aerospace Power Journal, 15*(1), 67–80.

Krebs, B. (2012, September 26). *Krebs on security.* Retrieved July 11, 2015.

Leyden, J. (2012, December 10). *Saudi Aramco: Foreign hackers tried to cork our gas output.* Retrieved July 11, 2015.

Mandiant. (2013, February 18). *APT1: Exposing one of China's cyber espionage units.* Retrieved July 11, 2015.

Mills, E. (2012, August 30). *Virus knocks out computers at Qatari gas firm RasGas—CNET.* Retrieved July 11, 2015.

Mount, M. (2012, October 16). *U.S. Officials believe Iran behind recent cyber attacks—CNN.com.* Retrieved July 11, 2015.

Pagliery, J. (2015, March 16). Ex-NSA director: China has hacked 'every major corporation' in U.S. Retrieved July 11, 2015.

Ryan, J. (2012, May 8). *DHS: Hackers mounting organized cyber attack on U.S. gas pipelines.* Retrieved July 11, 2015.

Schmitt, M. (2013). *Tallinn manual on the international law applicable to cyber warfare: Prepared by the international group of experts at the invitation of the NATO Cooperative Cyber Defence Centre of Excellence* (pp. 42–45). Cambridge: Cambridge University Press.

Schmitt, M. (1999). Computer network attack and the use of force in international law: Thoughts on a normative framework. *Columbia Journal of Transnational Law, 37*, 885–937.

Searle, T. (2002). The firebombing of Tokyo in March 1945. *The Journal of Military History, 66*(1), 103–133.

Symantec. (2013, August 16). *The Shamoon attacks.* Retrieved July 11, 2015.

Symantec. (2014, June 30). *Emerging threat: Dragonfly/energetic bear—APT group.* Retrieved July 11, 2015.

Wightman, R. (2012, June 7). *Spear phishing attempt.* Retrieved July 11, 2015.

Wilhoit, K. (2014, July 17). *Havex, it's down with OPC.* Threat Research|FireEye Inc. Retrieved July 11, 2015.

Chapter 16
In Conclusion: The Future Internet of Things and Security of Its Control Systems

Misty Blowers, Jose Iribarne, Edward J.M. Colbert, and Alexander Kott

16.1 Introduction

We chose to conclude this book with a look into the future of ICS cyber security. As best as we can see, much of this future unfolds in the context of the Internet of Things. In fact, we envision that all industrial and infrastructure environments, and cyber-physical systems in general, will take the form reminiscent of what today is referred to as the Internet of Things.

Internet of Things is envisioned as multitude of heterogeneous devices densely interconnected and communicating with the objective of accomplishing a diverse range of objectives, often collaboratively. One can argue that in the relatively near future, the IoT construct will subsume industrial plants, infrastructures, housing and other systems that today are controlled by ICS and SCADA systems.

The advent of IoT will be accompanied by a number of developments: miniaturization of devices and sensors, increasing mobility of devices, wearable devices, ubiquitous robotics and growing automation of all functions of IoT. Many of these devices will be smart sensor that contains a microprocessor that conditions the signals before

M. Blowers (✉)
USAF Research Laboratory, Rome, NY, USA
e-mail: mkb333@gmail.com

J. Iribarne
Westrock, Norcross, GA, USA

A. Kott • E.J.M. Colbert
US Army Research Laboratory, Adelphi, MD, USA

© Springer International Publishing Switzerland 2016   323
E.J.M. Colbert, A. Kott (eds.), *Cyber-security of SCADA and Other Industrial Control Systems*, Advances in Information Security 66,
DOI 10.1007/978-3-319-32125-7_16

transmission to the control network. Some of the devices are likely to be nano-robots with overall size of the order of a few micrometers or less in all spatial directions and constituted by nanoscopic components.

IoT will be associated with great increase in automation. In addition to supporting highly autonomous devices, IoT itself will be self-organizing, self-configuring, and self-healing. The increase in automation may cause an increase in system vulnerability. With automation comes the necessity of reducing the need for manual intervention. Automated security monitoring will be essential as control systems grow large enough to exceed the capacity for humans to identify and process security logs and other security information.

Other game-changing development may include radically new computing and networking paradigms. Emerging computing paradigms—nanocomputing, quantum computing, biologically or genome-based computing—might develop soon enough to make most current cybersecurity technologies obsolete, thus drastically changing the market. Quantum computing and networking are already fueling lively debate. Biologically inspired computation and communication paradigms will attract growing interest, especially as they offer promises for autonomous adaptation to previously unknown threats and even self-healing.

In the IoT environments, cybersecurity will derive largely from system agility, moving-target defenses, cyber-maneuvering, and other autonomous or semi-autonomous behaviors. Cyber security of IoT may also benefit from new design methods for mixed-trusted systems; and from big data analytics—predictive and autonomous.

16.2   Overview of Change in Control Systems

16.2.1   Industrial Revolution: Earliest Times to the Present

The first industrial revolution began in Britain in the late 18th century, with the mechanization of the textile industry. Tasks previously done by hand in hundreds of weavers' cottages were brought together in a single cotton mill, giving birth to the factory. The second industrial revolution came in the early 20th century, when Henry Ford improved the moving assembly line and ushered in the age of mass production (The Economist 2012). There is a debate regarding electrification and electronics, including automation, being a possible third industrial revolution leading into a fourth. It is clear that a major change is now underway; manufacturing is becoming digital. The modern world is seeing the convergence of the global industrial systems with large-volume data capture and analysis, all enabled by ever increasing computing power. The distributed growth of networked systems, internet connectivity, low-cost wireless technology, advanced sensors, and satellite systems are shaping a new world where the reliance of man on machine is dominant.

Industry or manufacturing (we will use these terms interchangeably) is largely the process of conversion of raw materials into products. Manufacturing is increasingly dependent on sophisticated equipment and automation to meet simultaneous demands for safety, quality, efficiency and productivity. However, different generations of equipment and automation co-exist as older plants and mills, or different production areas therein, and continue to operate along their more efficient and newer brethren. Increasingly, the distinction between equipment and automation is becoming blurred as new process equipment has embedded sensing, control and communication devices.

According to the US President's Council of Advisors on Science and Technology, advanced manufacturing is "a family of activities that (a) depend on the use and coordination of information, automation, computation, software, sensing, and networking, and/or (b) make use of cutting edge materials and emerging capabilities enabled by the physical and biological sciences, for example nanotechnology, chemistry, and biology. It involves both new ways to manufacture existing products, and the manufacture of new products emerging from new advanced technologies." (Holdren et al. 2012) Additional studies have shown, however, that there is a growing gap between research and development activities and the deployment of technological innovations. There is a recognized need to accelerate the technology life-cycles in the U.S., and growing numbers of entrepreneurial programs are enabling this to happen. The acceleration of the technology life-cycle increases the importance of gaining market share in the commercialization phase so that manufacturers can seize the opportunities associated with the scale-up phase.

These changes will come with a cost, however. The faster we push these technologies into the manufacturing environment, the higher the risk and potential for failure. Economic gain will be realized with evolutions of core products, but the biggest gains will come from the disruptive technologies that can revolutionize current methods or products.

16.2.2 Sustainability of an Industrial Enterprise

In the manufacturing context, sustainability is essential to the long-term survival of an enterprise constrained by economic, environmental and social factors. Those are primary considerations for investments in new technology.

16.2.2.1 Economic Factors

The economic constraints of a modern company include the escalation and volatility of material and energy costs, customer and market pressures to accelerate new product introductions and the continual push for greater productivity and cost reduction. Companies also face the escalation of capital expenditures, as modern equipment is increasingly more costly to purchase and install. Companies also face the inevitable obsolescence of equipment that is still productive but contains parts that are no longer manufactured. This is especially true of ICS, where the trend towards the use of "commercial off-the shelf" computer hardware has reduced initial costs, but also shortened the life expectancy of the computers as their operating systems become unsupported every few years.

16.2.2.2 Environmental Factors

The environmental pressures on manufacturing include increasingly tighter regulations for emissions to the air and water, and waste generation, as well as concerns over global climate change. In response, many companies have adopted targets to reduce their carbon footprint, *i.e.* the direct and indirect emissions of carbon dioxide associated with their operations. The environmental constraints are most acute in industrial operations dealing with dangerous substances and hazardous processes, especially in the chemical and nuclear industry. Major accidents with multiple fatalities continue to occur worldwide in the process industries, causing distress to those affected and massive costs to companies. Accidents at Flixborough, U.K., Seveso, Italy, Bhopal India, and Pasadena, Texas, in the 1970s and 1980s led to tighter regulation of the process industries and raised awareness of the key risk control systems needed to prevent such accidents (Kletz 2009). In the United States, companies need to comply with both the OSHA Process Safety Management and EPA's Risk Management Program. Those rules require a process hazard analysis to be conducted and risks to be reduced to an "as low as reasonable practical" level. Similar regulations exist in other countries and in most cases require inherently safe (Moore 2006) or instrumented safety systems, including a hierarchy of controls and redundancy. The current rules for such systems generally do not allow for Internet and wireless technology, seriously limiting the adoption of IoT technology.

16.2.2.3 Social Factors

A major social constraint on manufacturing, at least in developed countries, is the aging of the technical workforce. Employers find that replacing qualified workers and engineers is increasingly difficult as they retire. In the U.S., the median age of the manufacturing workforce spiked to 46.1 years in 2013, up from 40.5 years in 2000. For high-skilled manufacturing workers, the average age is 57 (Higgins 2015). Cavallaro (2015) cites a study by Deloitte and The Manufacturing Institute that illustrates just how dire the situation has become: six out of ten manufacturing positions remain unfulfilled because of the talent shortage, and the projected shortfall may rise to two million workers in the next decade. And yet, 52 % of American teenagers have no interest in a manufacturing career.

16.2.2.4 The Future

The most likely method for industrial sustainability will be increasing the degree of automation of the manufacturing processes. For example it is possible to reduce the required personnel in assembly lines by up to 90 % through the use of robotics (Forrest 2015). The remaining workforce will need to be highly skilled and better trained to compensate for the smaller number of employees (Young 2015). Outsourcing is another possible solution. Outsourcing allows in-house personnel to focus on day to day priorities, while the less critical work is performed by contractors. Due to the spread of the Industrial Internet of Things with its non-proprietary character, the major suppliers of automation are taking a defensive position by offering service agreements that typically include condition-based monitoring, remote troubleshooting, spare parts and technical labor.

As Industrial enterprises include more and more automation, for example in the forms of robotic hardware and smart machines, the number of vulnerable paths through which the adversary may exploit system processes increases dramatically. This happens almost unnoticeably since industrial operators and control system builders are not typically focused on security aspects during design, construction and testing. The types of vulnerabilities can become extremely diverse as a plant converts process elements to uniquely manufactured automated devices customized for that particular process element. Software and firmware vulnerabilities grow to offer a much greater attack surface than is currently available to the dedicated adversary. Plant operators and owners will need to increase their security staff or hire specialized security analysts to accommodate the deteriorating security of their systems. Alternatively, vendors could offer more secure hardware, firmware, and interconnections. This is less likely to occur in the short term.

16.2.3   The Internet of Things (IoT)

The term "Internet of Things" (IoT) and "Industrial Internet of Things" (IIoT) describe a vast number of connected industrial systems that are communicating and coordinating their data analytics and actions. As ICSs evolve, IIoT devices and methods will be introduced to improve industrial performance. Industrial systems that interface the digital world to the physical world through sensors and actuators that solve complex control problems fall under a much broader category of "Cyber-Physical Systems" (Monostoria 2014). The term "Cloud Manufacturing" (Wu et al. 2013) describes the distributed or remote infrastructure that will likely be needed to handle the growing amounts of information and demands on computer processing speeds in the manufacturing facilities of the future.

Although these advances were forecasted by several authors in the early 1990s, notably by Mark Weiser (1991), interest in the integration of advanced digital technologies into industrial production systems did not spread until the following decade, when related industrial consortia and governmental initiatives were started in several countries.

16.2.3.1   Global Development of the IIoT

A non-profit registered association named "Technology Initiative SmartFactory" was established in Germany in 2005 to develop, apply and distribute innovative, industrial plant technologies, and to create the foundation for their widespread use in research and practice (Zuehlke 2010). The partner circle grew rapidly, including producers and users of factory equipment as well as universities and research centers. Support was provided by industry and political organizations and eventually became national German policy as part of the "Industrie 4.0" plan, first discussed in 2011 and later adopted in 2013. The heart of the Industry 4.0 idea is intelligent manufacturing, *i.e.* applying the tools of information technology to production. In the German context, this primarily means using the IIoT to connect small and medium-sized companies more efficiently in global production and innovation networks so that they could more efficiently engage in mass production and more easily and efficiently customize products (Krueger et al. 2014).

The IIoT development efforts in Europe are being monitored by The Internet of Things European Research Cluster, which maintains its Strategic Research and Innovation Agenda (SRIA) taking into account its experiences and the results from the on-going exchange among European and international experts. The SRIA is updated every year with expert input from projects financed by the European Commission (Vermesan and Friess 2013).

In the United States, several private-industry consortia were formed starting with the "Object Management Group" in 1989 and have taken a leading role in developing standards for the IIoT. Relevant consortia include the "Data Distribution Service," the "Smart Grid Interoperability Panel" and "Open Interconnect." Particularly important is IIC, the "Industrial Internet Consortium," started in March 2014 by AT&T, Cisco, General Electric, IBM and Intel. IIC now has more than 200 member companies from 25 countries and recently released its reference architecture for the industrial Internet (Industrial Internet Consortium 2015). Through the National Institute of Standards and Technology, the Federal government started an Advanced Manufacturing program that includes many technologies related to IIoT. One of the program objectives is to create several linked institutes for manufacturing innovation, with common goals but unique concentrations (NIST 2015). For example a new 94,000 square feet Digital Manufacturing and Design Innovation Institute/UI Labs opened on May 22, 2015 in Chicago, Illinois.

"Made in China 2025" is a plan released in May 2015 to comprehensively upgrade Chinese industry (Kennedy 2015). The initiative draws direct inspiration from Germany's Industry 4.0 plan, but the Chinese effort is far broader. Its guiding principles are for manufacturing to be innovation-driven, to emphasize quality over quantity, achieve green development, optimize the structure of Chinese industry, and nurture human talent. The goal is to comprehensively upgrade Chinese industry, making it more efficient and integrated so that it can occupy the highest levels of global production chains.

16.2.3.2 Expected Impact

It is widely expected that the IIoT will have an enormous impact. Its global economic added value has been variously estimated between $1-trillion and $20-trillion of GDP growth in 15 years (Press 2014). However, the introduction of the IIoT is expected to occur more gradually and be less disruptive than previous industrial revolutions. According to a report by McKinsey & Co (2015). Fourth industrial revolution analyzed in new report [Online] May 5 2015), the implementation of the IIoT will require the replacement of 40 to 50% of the current equipment in traditional industries. Those figures compare favorably with the introduction of industrial automation, which required an 80 to 90% rate of replacement.

As mentioned in the previous section, the increase in automation will cause a major increase in system vulnerability until security measures are included with the new hardware and software, and security staff is increased appropriately to monitor the new "things," services, and methods in the IIoT. Automated security monitoring will be essential as control systems grow to exceed the capacity of humans to identify and process security logs and other security information.

16.3   Game Changers in the Future ICS and IoT Security

In this section we explore specific aspects of present and future control systems that we believe will greatly affect the design and security of future ICSs and the IoT as a whole As shown in Fig. 16.1, we group the relevant aspects into three general areas:

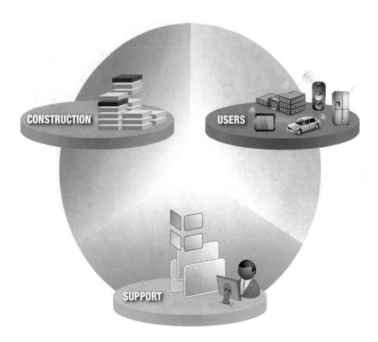

Fig. 16.1 Focus areas for secure future IoT

1. Construction of the Future IoT—commercial and academic efforts to design and build innovative new "things" that other will use
2. Users of the Future IoT—industrial users and consumers who use these "things"
3. Support for the Future IoT—services and collaborative efforts to support the ability of users to use the new "things"

We identify aspects in each of these general areas that will contribute significantly to the future security of ICSs. As mentioned, industrial control is not limited to manufacturing and other industrial processes. Devices and controllers are used by consumers worldwide for controlling home lighting, security cameras, automobiles, and many more home-based sensors. One difference is that home-based devices and controllers are cheaper, are mass-manufactured with generally poor software and firmware security, and are usually connected to the Internet. ICSs were designed with the general understanding that they would have no network connectivity to the outside world. However, this is changing as industry wishes to exploit the advantages in convenience provided by expanding network connectivity.

As shown in Fig. 16.2, we break our three general areas into eight categories. In the following sections, we elaborate on specific aspects of these eight categories.

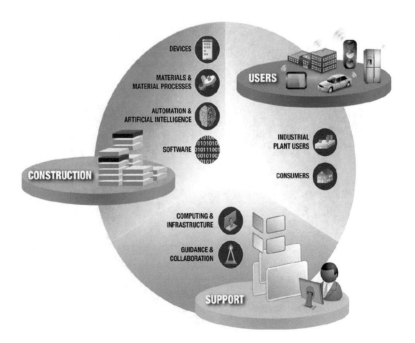

Fig. 16.2 Categories within three focus areas for a secure future IoT

Eight Categories within IoT Focus Areas:

- Focus Area 1: Construction of the Future IoT

  - Devices
  - Materials and Material Processes
  - Automation and Artificial Intelligence
  - Software

- Focus Area 2: Users of the Future IoT

  - Industrial Plant Users
  - Consumers

- Focus Area 3: Support for the Future IoT

  - Computing and Infrastructure
  - Government and Industry Guidance and Collaboration

16.3.1 Construction of the Future IoT

16.3.1.1 Devices

Miniaturization of End Devices and Sensors

As transistor density on silicon-based chips continues to follow Moore's law and doubles every 1.5–2 years, not only does overall computing ability increase, but computing ability per unit volume increases. Hand-held devices of today have the computing power of "supercomputers" of yesteryear. For the future IoT, this has a number of important implications.

Miniaturized computing devices will be more ubiquitous due to mass manufacturing at relatively low cost. This includes not only CPU and memory chips, but RF and other sensor-based technologies integrated into System-on-a-Chip technologies. Innovative packaging methods for chips (e.g., Charles 2005) will allow considerable flexibility for future manufacturers and integrators.

With more computing power in miniature computing devices comes a requirement to process and condense larger amounts of sensor and other data being processed by the end devices. Proxy communication by cellular phones is currently being used between miniature end devices (such as wearable fitness devices) and the Internet and cloud storage, as there is no possibility to store all of the sensor data in the cloud (e.g. Want et al. 2015). Endpoint devices must be able to pre-process raw data and forward a useful subset of the information to the proxy or directly to the Internet. Proxy devices must be able to handle the volume of the network traffic and communicate safely and reliably to the end devices. Browser protocols such as HTML for human-to-machine (H2M) interaction will need to be updated with machine-to-machine (M2M) protocols for increased efficiency (Want et al. 2015).

In order to accommodate local network traffic, cloud storage models may favor increased amounts of storage and processing in local servers such as cloudlet servers, which could run as virtual machines on desktops or even dedicated embedded servers.

Securing the array of miniaturized devices will be challenging initially (cf. Green 2015). This is mostly due to the fact that the driving force in the IoT is marketing of the new technologies, not the security of the new devices. Inexpensive devices that can increase profits of a company are highly attractive to corporate decision makers, even if a security risk is implied.

The number of embedded devices and sensors will increase, by a factor of ten, and even higher. Some will have IP addresses and will communicate with secure TCP protocols via secure applications, but many will use proprietary or ad-hoc communication methods, such as insecure 802.11 or Bluetooth wireless. The data from the sensors and devices will be accessible from the proxy server, which may be a cellphone or a small dedicated embedded device in an industrial setting. Access to that proxy server can provide an adversary with the ability to inspect or modify a much larger amount of information than before. To preserve confidentiality and availability, system owners should analyze the information being recorded and communicated by the end devices and sensors, and protect access as needed. At some point, as with the Internet, the amount of information will be too large for a human to monitor, and security tools will need to be developed to validate secure data flow from end devices and sensors.

As the number of end devices and sensor, and proxy devices increases, so does the volume of software that controls those devices. Software is developed by humans and always has vulnerabilities than can be exploited, especially if innovative end devices are pushed to market quickly with little security engineering. Unauthorized access to information in proxy servers or end devices themselves will need to be analyzed and vulnerabilities will need to be mitigated. While it would make sense for this activity to be performed before or during installation of IoT devices, it is often neglected until after an incident is reported.

Mobility and Wearable Devices

Recent advances in battery life, miniaturization, energy harvesting, communication protocols, and lower hardware costs are bringing the vision and utility of the IoT closer to reality (Zorzi et al. 2010). Mobile devices and wireless devices connected to mobile networks are key aspects of this development process. The number of Internet connected devices has already exceeded 1.0 per person on the planet, and is expected to be 4.3 per person by 2020 (Waring 2014). The wearable technology market is expected to grow by a remarkable factor of three in the next 3 years (2015–2018, Rizzo 2013). By 2020, there is expected to be an additional two devices per person on the planet, including end devices, sensors, and wearable devices. How will the current communication infrastructure handle this additional burden?

Mobile devices will impact the IoT infrastructure in a number of ways. Many personal-based wearable devices do not connect directly to the Internet or to a corporate network, but connect to a mobile device such as a cellular phone that serves as a communication hub for the wearables. In addition, the lack of a direct connection to the wearable devices offers some privacy security to potentially sensitive information. While RFID devices such as identification badges, credit cards, and passports may not currently be integrated into the consumer-based IoT, their utility as authentication of identity and location in the workplace can easily fit into the future global IoT. For example, as one maneuvers through a physical plant or one's home, it may be desirable for the lighting, HVAC system, audio-visual systems, or other "things" in the workplace or home, to recognize one's presence and adjust accordingly. For a home setting, one might always want the television to resume a video series with the window shades and lighting adjusted accordingly.

For third-world countries (Glickman 2015), mobile phones provide crucial news and agricultural information so that small-scale farmers can plant and harvest food more effectively based on weather information, seed prices, and market demand. Many countries have poor or non-existent wired infrastructure, so inexpensive mobile connectivity offers a great utility for improving agricultural efficiency.

First-world country industry and health-care are not entirely dissimilar. Manufacturing plants save tremendous costs if remote sensing data from "things" can be placed anywhere in the plant and the data fed back wirelessly. Plant operators with wearable technology will provide crucial feedback about the plant environment as they visit locations within the plant during the day. Wearable devices have the potential to make operators more mobile and effective. Devices like the virtual reality headsets allow operators to have a more global view of plant operations and are invaluable for training exercises. Augmentation of the human body can increase human strength for lifting heavy objects (Hirukawa 2015).

Hospital workers already use IoT methodologies. Sensors in rooms identify humans and material assets for inventory and emergency purposes. Medical sensors for blood pressure, pulse, oxygen level, and other vital statistics can report the information directly to a central database, which is readily accessible by clinicians by laptop or tablet via wireless communication. Privacy concerns are significant, as HIPAA laws strictly protect personal information.

This privacy concern also applies to health-related wearables in the consumer market. The consumer will want to share vital health statistics with health-care providers, friends, and family, but not with general public who may have physical proximity to the wearable. In addition, wearables with cameras or microphones, such as Google Glass, have the potential of violating the privacy of others by recording audio or video. While this is not a new problem, broad use of the Glass has resurfaced the issue.

Consumer-based smart watches and fitness trackers are increasingly becoming fashion accessories. Wearable device use will soar. Aesthetics of smart phones and miniature mobile devices have always been important in the consumer market.

How will the global IoT accommodate the expected exponential growth of mobile device connectivity? Adaptation of heterogeneous access network and efficient use of available resources are important. Large numbers of mobile devices with multiple tethered wearable (or local) devices will be roaming in and out of mobility cells in automobiles, trains, airplanes, and drones. Machine-to-Machine

(M2M) communication is an important facilitating technology for the IoT, and future M2M communication methods need to accommodate this expanding demand for connectivity. Methods from Heterogeneous MANET (Mobile Ad Hoc Network) (Ahmad et al. 2015) may be useful in this regard.

Until there is better guidance on privacy of personal information (not just healthcare related information), and better security guidelines on wireless communication methods and data/cloud storage, security of wearable and other mobility devices will remain poor. Eventually many of the wearable devices that are tethered to cellular and mobile phones will be released with automated Internet connectivity to IPv4 and/or IPv6 networks, which will allow them to be publicly accessible. Within an industrial setting, this would mean that access and authentication vulnerabilities would be available to any adversary that gains physical access to the wireless signal. Since many of the end devices would have automatic authentication to the network (or to the operator mobile phone), adversaries would have a much larger number of attack vectors than before. Most likely, the end devices would not have been hardened. Initially, the mobility-based IoT will be very vulnerable to attack. Careful analyses of the control system networks and devices should be done, and appropriate mitigations should be put in place.

16.3.1.2 Materials and Material Processes

Advances in Materials

Materials are the building blocks of every physical product. Improvements to materials such as steels, metals, plastics, and ceramics have been vital to many of significant technological developments. The newer nanoscale, biological, smart, and composite materials will enable future technological breakthroughs. Some of these breakthroughs will transform existing industries while others will spawn entirely new ones. (Holdren et al. 2012) The advances in material science are co-evolving with advances in 3D-Printing. The demand for new material properties is partly driven by what is feasible with a 3-D Printer. However, imagine a scenario where a malicious actor "hacks" into your 3-D printer and steals critical design plans? What if the hacker tampers with the design just enough to impose a flaw to the structural integrity to a printed component for an aircraft? We explore security concerns with 3D-printers below.

Advanced materials offer the potential to make vehicles much lighter, dramatically increase the energy density of batteries, or allow a much lighter alternative to glass in space based systems. Consider concrete as one example. It is difficult to imagine just how much concrete exists in our manufacturing facilities and roadways worldwide, but it is undeniable that Concrete is a very prevalent material in manufacturing facilities and roadways worldwide. Its use, however, is limited by its inherent susceptibility to cracks, and leaks due to the fact that concrete often develops micro-cracks during the construction process. Although these tiny cracks may not immediately affect the building's structural integrity, they eventually can lead to leakage problems. Leakage can eventually corrode the concrete's steel reinforcements, which can ultimately cause a collapse. With the emerging self-healing technology, cracks can be sealed immediately, preventing future leakage and the high cost of repair. (Matchar 2015).

Self-healing materials are inspired by the healing mechanisms of the human body. Self-healing concrete works by embedding capsules of limestone-producing bacteria and calcium lactate within concrete. When the concrete cracks, air and moisture cause the bacteria to begin consuming the calcium lactate. They convert the calcium lactate to calcite, an ingredient in limestone, thus sealing off the cracks (Matchar 2015). The bacteria can lie dormant for as long as 200 years, well beyond the lifespan of most modern buildings.

So how could something like this be a cyber security concern? Here the supply chain vulnerability is a major component of security. It is becoming an increasingly greater concern as the logistic chains for even some of less noteworthy components of manufacturing processes often cross international boundaries.

Imagine a scenario where a hacker interferes with the supply chain of this "self-healing" concrete. What if the supply chain is contaminated in a manner to allow the bacteria to continue after consumption of the calcium lactate? How much security do we need to consider, not only in our own manufacturing facilities, but also in the facilities which supply raw materials to us?

3D Manufacturing

3D Manufacturing is very much connected to advances in material science. Advances in printing technologies have opened the potential for conformable electronics and physical components and even for subsystems and components embedded in 3D structures. Over the past 20 years, 3D additive manufacturing technologies have been advancing at a rapid pace. These systems have been used in a variety of applications ranging from conventional prototyping and rapid tooling to more advanced applications such as medical implants, aerospace and automotive manufacturing, 3D electronic devices, and micro-systems (Melchels et al. 2012; Pique et al. 2006). The technologies are becoming more accurate with features ranging from micron-sized to building sized (Joshi et al. 2012). The process removes the traditional limits on part geometry, and leads to components that can be produced faster while consuming less material and using less energy.

Precision modeling and simulation may be combined with additive manufacturing to create complex parts that are impossible to manufacture today. Features like durable lattice work, intricate textures and organic shapes are all possible, and even extensions and optimization of existing component parts have been made possible with 3D printing technology. The reduction of mass of printed devices can lead to vast improvements. For example, 3D printing reduced the mass of an antenna-reflector from 395 g to around 80 g (Williamson 2015).

In spite of its benefits, 3D printing raises concerns from the security perspective. Indeed, engineers of the future will need to have knowledge of cyber security.

Advances in software tools that provide automatic correction for 3-D printing does offer some potential to protect 3D printing processes from hacks and from model corruption. However, with every "auto-correction" software tool, there is the potential for an "auto-corruption" tool. Also, as previously mentioned, there is potential for a malicious actor to reside on your system or network, learning about what you printing, or what blueprints a supplier may be transmitting to the end user or customer. The 3D printing technologies are susceptible to all the "D5 effects" (deception, denial of service, disruption, degradation, and destruction).

16.3.1.3   Automation and Robotics

Automation and Artificial Intelligence

As the number of end devices and sensors increases in the IoT, these will be utilized to reduce operating costs or to increase process efficiency. A reduction of manual processes and an increase in automated processes will be a significant benefit to the consumer and to industrial IoT. A goal is for the industrial IoT be "self-organizing, self-configuring, self-healing, scalable to large sizes, with very low energy consumption, low cost, simple to install and based on global standards." (Pinto 2012). In this vision, vendors will work together so that addition of new sensors or new software or networks will be handled automatically, with no manual effort required. The current lack of hardware and communication interoperability presents a significant challenge to overcome before such advanced automation can be realized.

Increased automated feedback from the increased number of sensors and higher fidelity of those sensor readings can provide great value in an industrial setting. Automatic analysis of the data and dynamic adjustments in the process can lead to major reductions in waste, energy costs, and human intervention (Chui et al. 2010). In a consumer setting, home gas, electric, and solar energy usage and production can be monitored and adjusted automatically for significant energy and cost savings, for example to avoid peak gas and electric rates. HVAC, lights, and refrigeration units can be set for lower power usage or turned off when no human presence is detected or expected. Electric vehicles can be charged when electric power is most cheaply available. The efficiency of automatic braking or collision avoidance systems in automobiles can be improved as sensors and feedback become more advanced.

The most demanding use of the IoT involves rapid, real-time sensing of unpredictable conditions and instantaneous responses guided by automated systems mimicking human reactions (Chui et al. 2010). For comparison, one might consider the rate of data the human eye sensors record (perhaps megabits per second), transmission of an appropriately reduced amount of optical information to the human brain, and the complex function and processing utility of the human brain in this automated process. All aspects (sensing, data reduction, process, archival storage) of the complex process of the human process of seeing will need to be better understood in the new era of the future IoT. Advances in robotics and artificial intelligence will be as important as efficient interoperability needed for a self-organizing IoT.

With automation comes the necessity of minimizing manual interventions, which is a security issue. How can one monitor all of these automated processes if they are being performed automatically without human intervention? The amount of software that will be needed to accomplish these security goals is exponentially larger than presently, also implying an exponential increase in software vulnerabilities. Will all automated systems be tested fully before they are released for public use? Since the systems will likely be dynamically created by a plant operator or home user, the answer is probably negative. Systems for highly critical processes may be better tested for vulnerabilities, but the general mode of vendors has been to release when functional requirements of a product are met, and worry about security later. This implies that our original automated IoT will be severely insecure (cf. Green 2015).

Robotics

Industrial robots have the potential to change production processes as much as computers have changed the office work environment. Robots can be designed for performing operations quickly, repeatedly, and accurately. They have applicability across many different domains in the manufacturing industry and have added tremendous value to various manufacturing processes. Petro chemical industry, for example, has used robotic systems to improve safety and efficiency, and to reduce environmental impact. In regions where it is difficult or dangerous for humans to work, robots may be enabled to carry out such tasks as maintenance, inspection and repairs (Heyer 2010). As robots are introduced to these types of environments, however, issues of trust and accountability come into consideration. One must also consider how the robots will fit into the organizational structure. Finally, any distributed system introduces vulnerabilities in the network layer. These vulnerabilities can be compromised in such a way as to sever or corrupt communications. They are also susceptible to all the D5 effects noted in the previous section.

Some robots are built to operate autonomously, with little to no human intervention, and some are remotely controlled. In order for the next generations of users and operators to trust autonomy, however, it must be predictable enough to operate under complex and dynamic conditions with high confidence levels and still be able to be tightly controlled or potentially instantly interrupted by the human operator (Murphy and Shields 2012). Maintaining this flexibility in future system will allow for sufficient levels of confidence in the actions performed by our robotic counterparts.

The human response to increased levels of autonomy also needs to be considered. If robots have too little autonomy, human operators will waste time attending to robots instead of attending to their work tasks. Also, a new skill set will need to evolve for future human operators if they are going to be skilled enough to fix or maintain robots in their manufacturing environments.

The main benefits of autonomous capabilities are to extend and complement human performance, not provide a direct replacement of humans. If robots are highly autonomous, situational awareness of plant activity may start to diminish (Kott et al. 2014b). Robots can augment human perception, action, speed, persistence, resistance to fatigue. They can permit delegation and reduction of cognitive load. Some robots will be equipped with the ability to perform inspection and sample taking, while others will carry out more sophisticated operations like maintenance and repairs. Together, they can enable operation in areas too hazardous for humans to work in (Heyer 2010).

Some experts advocate that no matter how much we depend on robots and autonomy, we should ensure humans have ultimate control. Humans need to oversee, and have the ability to modify behavior as needed. As our trust in robots and autonomous systems increases, the range of levels of autonomy available can shift over time as needed (Endsley 2014)

In situations where the work space is dangerous for humans, robots can be used to improve safety in the workplace. Robots are not as vulnerable to workplace hazards including high temperatures, hazardous chemicals, radiation, and reaching difficult physical access points in manufacturing environments. Mobile robots including unmanned aerial vehicles have been developed to work in disaster response, inspections of infrastructure and decommissioning of nuclear plants. A key technology for the robots is teleoperation that enables humans to control robots remotely (Hirukawa 2015).

Autonomously guided vehicles have been widely used for manufacturing, mainly for carrying parts in factories, and in other applications of robotics for logistics. Robots are also used in manufacturing facilities today to unload and move parts from trucks to the plant supply rooms while simultaneously maintaining inventory accountability and control. This role of robot systems is likely to increase in years to come.

There are other noteworthy types of robotic systems that are gaining popularity in manufacturing; robotic human augmentation and nano-bots. These are two areas are worth discussing because there are being extensively researched in the defense and security fields today.

Nanobots

Nanobots are a type of microscopic robot. A nanorobot is any artificial machine with overall size on the order of a few micrometers or less in all spatial directions and constituted by nanoscopic components with individual dimensions in the interval between 1 and 100 nm (Requicha 2003). A nanobot device has shown to have the capability to move quite freely through the entire human body circulatory system. One can envision a future where these nanobot technologies could be used in a manufacturing process, for example, to provide a microscopic view into the process conditions critical to certain bio-pharmaceutical or nuclear facilities.

The idea of surveying the state of fluid suspension with swarms of nanobots could be demonstrated in the bloodstream. A nanobot in a capillary has demonstrated the ability to feel the metabolic pattern of the family of cells fed by the capillary itself, thus surveying the cells contained within a given length of the tube. Each nanobot is a self-propelled machine, obtaining energy from the environment, and is able to recognize and dock to the components within their process (Cavalcanti et al. 2006). They can sense membranes and subsequently recognize the state of health of its environment. They also may be used to store the information, to transfer it to the central unit, and eventually take actions which may have an effect on the overall process conditions. Within a swarm of nanobots, each bot stores specific chemicals to be released for detection by other nanobots (Cavalcanti et al. 2006). This could also be used in a manufacturing setting to transfer information from one location in the process to the other.

Ensuring that nanobots and nanobot swarms are operating securely is a complicated matter. Nanobots are by definition extremely small and are therefore very difficult to monitor for individual malicious behaviors, especially if a large swarm of nanobots is deployed. If individual nanobots are programmed with software, how might one scan the nanobot operating code for infections? If nanobot swarms are programmed with chemical means, would there be a means to ensure that the function and control of the swarm not be overtaken by a malicious actor, in the same manner that viri and bacteria affect human biological receptors? How will the health monitoring and maintenance of the nanobot swarm be performed? When nanobots reach the end of life, how are they disposed? As with other aspects of innovative IoT devices, nanobot systems offer incredible utility but have not been yet designed or analyzed for safety and security.

16.3.1.4 Software

Software and Applications

Getting all segments of the IoT to communicate and work together is key to its success. This means deploying significant volumes of the software and middleware that will enable the diverse hardware devices to talk to other hardware and the IoT infrastructure (Karimi and Atkinson 2015). Much of the software will be local to the devices and will be provided by the vendors of the hardware devices. Because the devices are inexpensive and easily replaced or upgraded, software patching for security or other purposes will likely be neglected or ignored, especially by consumers.

IoT solutions do not follow a unified business model (cf. Schartel 2015), and over time software engineers and architects will need to accommodate the requirements of additional diverse stakeholders. Currently, security guidance and technical guidelines for global interconnectivity are poor and incomplete. There is not a clear understanding of preferred methods for how devices will identify and automatically interconnect to local networks and cloud data services, let alone how they will do this in a secure fashion. Since the IoT market is driven by vendor markets, cooperation will be needed by major vendors to establish guidelines and requirements for software engineers who write code for vendor devices. Consumers and industry owners will need to demand increased authentication security and reliability, especially for IoT components of critical control systems.

The software that makes IoT devices "smart" will have varying levels of "smartness." Efforts to add "smartness" to devices will be popular for some things with IoT connectivity, specifically, things with longer life cycles. Examples, include local networks in automobiles, large home appliances such as refrigerators and televisions, home lighting and home security systems, and most industrial control system components that were never designed for the IoT. As the IoT matures, software engineers will be able to accommodate requirements for security and interconnectivity between multiple vendors' things. Currently, however, most vendor business models seem to focus on producing products quickly for maximum profit, and to neglect security features until they are demanded.

The future IoT will also generate tremendous amounts of new sensor data and information. Markets for software for data management, data formatting, data storage, and secure data transfer will boom as the size of the IoT grows. Methods for ensuring data privacy will be demanded by the consumer, but methods for data mining will also generate an increased software demand as corporations realize the potential for profit optimization from the new IoT information. Network infrastructure usage patterns and personal information not protected by privacy laws will be harvested and offered for sale by those providers with the most intelligent software products. A new layer of compliance software may be needed to ensure that government privacy laws are enforced. Software analysts working for financial firms will turn their attention toward the new IoT data and will develop tools for market prediction.

System automation, artificial intelligence, and automatic network and device authentication are integral to the IoT, yet they are non-trivial problems solutions to which are not yet fully developed. Ensuring that automation occurs is vital to the development of the IoT. Ensuring that automation is secure is vital to sustainment of the IoT. The level of software effort needed for automation is tremendous, not only because the number of devices is increasing exponentially, but because there will be a continuous need for requirement definition and redefinition as the IoT architecture begins to be affected by all of the stakeholders. Software will need to be continually revised, rewritten, and reused to accommodate the changing requirements. Lack of attention to changes in the software will create software vulnerabilities in device and network access, cloud and data storage, and any other IoT component.

Software apps will take a different approach in the IoT context. In the current approach, users use a few apps every day for everyday tasks. IoT device manufacturers will not be able to provide a single app for controlling their unique function, since users will not be able to accommodate a huge number of these simple apps. There will need to be a consolidated effort to provide the consumer (e.g., cell phone user) or industrial control system operator with apps or software that monitor and control a large number of device functions. Such an app will need to condense the information and provide some level of security alerting when device values need attention. This software will need to be universal in the sense that it can accommodate a new type of IoT device to which the consumer or operator would like to connect. The software needs to accommodate the device in an automated fashion, since from a practical standpoint, the user will not be able to download vendor software each time a new device connects. Semantic middleware for the IoT (cf. Whitmore et al. 2014) may offer a solution for this problem.

As with most of the IoT, functionality of these software systems will be the initial focus, and security will be a secondary consideration. What is important, however, is to realize that as any system (such as the IoT) grows in complexity and intelligence, the dependence on software increases, and software, being a human product, has imperfections. Incorporation of greater automation into the system also means there is less inspection by humans. Computer-aided tools will need to allow reliable security monitoring of this complex system. If the future IoT is to be safe for the consumer and industry, improved security methods will be needed. The attack surface presented to an adversary will be exceedingly large if one scales current interconnected devices to IoT scales and makes them all Internet accessible. Network isolation and segmentation with virtualization and hardware-based security methods (e.g. Ukil et al. 2011) may help.

16.3.2   Users of the Future IoT

We discuss two distinct groups of users of the future IoT: users of future industrial plant control systems (i.e., the IIoT), and consumers who will use the larger scale IoT.

16.3.2.1   Industrial Plant Users

Cyber-attacks in manufacturing environments are becoming more sophisticated, leveraging remote access vulnerabilities, supply chain interdiction, and insider threats. In the next three sub-sections, we discuss key aspects of the IIoT that will be affected by its ongoing evolution.

Plant Control Methods

The first control systems were mechanical and integrated in one mechanism the sensor, the actuator and the controller. For example, in the speed regulator invented by James Watt the centrifugal force exerted on two spinning masses moved the lever that controlled the flow of steam to the engine. That enabled a proportional-only control.

Pneumatic and hydraulic control systems were first developed for ship steering in the 1890's and soon after were applied to manufacturing (Bennett 1996). Through various types of physical devices operated by compressed air or hydraulic fluid, it was soon possible to perform proportional, integral and derivative control (PID). Until the introduction of electronic controls in the second half of the 20th Century, most manufacturing automation used stand-alone single loop pneumatic and hydraulic controllers. Multi-variable control required complex assemblies of physical devices and tubing and a change in control strategy necessitated changes in the tubing and often new devices. Tuning was done in the field controller with knobs.

Much simpler solid-state analog electronic sensors and controllers were introduced in 1959 and spread rapidly, while the motive force for actuators generally remained pneumatic or hydraulic. At that point, changes in control strategy required only rewiring and installing inexpensive components. The first digital and freely programmable control systems were introduced in 1969, replacing the traditional hardwiring of analog logic and control programs (Krueger et al. 2014). However, the functionality remained mostly the same PID control as in the original pneumatic and hydraulic devices due to the tendency towards one-to-one replacement and the availability of well-established methods for PID loop tuning and troubleshooting (Bennett 1996).

There is no particular reason to use only PID control, as other control strategies can be programmed, such as RST (Discrete-time linear MISO controllers), SFO (State Feedback and Observers), MPC (Model Predictive Control) and Fuzzy Logic Control. Of those, the most successful has been MPC, typically used in supervisory mode with PID controllers at the base level. MPC offers drastic improvements in set point responses for multivariable systems because of the coordination it provides (Astrom and Hagglund 2001).

Yet, the bulk of the industrial control systems are single PID loops. Often they are not performing as well as they could. In a typical plant 50 out of 100 PID loops will show degraded performance after six months. Typically, 30 % of the loops are run in manual mode, 15 % have an output out of range, 30 % are increasing process variability instead of reducing it, and only 25 % are actually improving the process (Starr 2015). The increased automation and optimization promised in the IIoT will help improve the efficiency of these control loop processes. Since the automation will be under software control, it will be necessary to analyze and monitor access and use of that code in order to maintain secure and safe operability of the added automation.

Data Transfer Media in Plants

Data transfer media is also evolving. Older process plants were built with 2-wire twisted-pair cable networks, connecting all the process units and measuring instruments together in an overall plant control scheme. These relatively unsophisticated instruments convert their measurement by various means into a 4–20 mA output or pulse signal to the control system. The more advanced technologies, such as Coriolis, ultrasonic or electromagnetic flowmeters have, until 2006, required a dedicated power supply for their functions, in addition to the output loop, and thus a 4-wire infrastructure was required as a minimum. Newer flowmeters can also be installed with a single 2-wire connection, and the low energy levels supported by these 2-wire loops are more easily rendered safe, in terms of explosive risk in hazardous areas containing flammable materials. However, the amount of information that can be passed back and forth is very limited.

Smart Sensors

Many new sensors are revolutionizing the manufacturing process already. A smart sensor often contains a microprocessor that conditions the signals before transmission to the control network. It filters out unwanted noise and compensates for errors before sending the data. Some sensors can be custom programmed to produce alerts on their own when critical limits are reached. Caution needs to be taken, however, to ensure such sensors have the proper security protocols in place to prevent a cyber intruder from tampering with the controls.

In contrast, the soft sensor, or virtual sensor, is a piece of software which represents a "sensor" that is not actually there. Often this sensor "output" considers several physical sensor values and fuses the data together to provide a new sensor value. The soft sensor may represent dozens or even hundreds of measurements. Soft sensors are especially useful in situations when the insertion of a physical sensor is not feasible. Software algorithms that are used to generate the output values of soft sensors include Kalman filters and Artificial Neural Networks. As with other new software-based features in the IIoT, one must be aware that additional software control introduces additional avenues for malicious manipulation of system control processes, and appropriate security measures need to be taken to ensure that unauthorized remote access and other vulnerabilities are mitigated.

The Network Layer

EtherNet/IP Standard IEC 61784–2 is open, manufacturer-independent and stable, and is supported by more than 300 member companies and hundreds of products. Using EtherNet/IP allows the user to access to the smartness of multivariable devices (Endress + Hauser 2014). For example, data regarding mass flow, density, temperature, totalizer settings as well as diagnostics can be delivered over a single cable. In addition, savings of 40 % can be made through reduced commissioning time. The time spent on loop identification, device integration and process-loop tuning can also be reduced by 25 %.

The connected factory provides a clear set of architectural guidelines and products that tie together factory automation systems, enterprise applications, and the wider ecosystem of supplier and partner solution. The common architecture will be more scalable for ruggedized Industrial Ethernet and enterprise networks. It will offer a standards-based Industrial IP Ethernet switching and security service.

However, as things become more connected, the cyber-attack surface and the vulnerabilities opened up through the increasing number of access points becomes a greater concern. Monitoring systems which employ behavior based analysis in industrial control systems are gaining more popularity as it is becoming more difficult to rely on threshold based or single- point of failure based alerting (Blowers 2014). There will be a need in future systems to have an autonomous supervisory system to monitor the overall process behaviors of the manufacturing processes.

As shown in past cyber-attacks on industrial systems, like STUXNET, it is becoming quite common to target single control loops or spoof specific sensor outputs. Monitoring systems which employ behavior based analysis of events occurring in the industrial process will need to be integrated with the network layer so that correlations and dependencies may be baselined, and anomalies can be quickly detected (Blowers 2014).

16.3.2.2 Consumers

Arguably, the most important long-term influence on the construction, security, and support for the future IoT is the consumer. Wearable devices and home controllers are built by vendors at the demand of consumers. New innovative connectivity devices and entertainment features for automobiles and home are created due to consumer interest and demand. Wireless connectivity and other convenience technology eventually migrates into industrial settings as plant owners realize lower costs and easier (but often less secure) operations. Consumer cell phones are no longer only portable communication devices—they are now centralized access points for much of information. The philosophy of interconnected apps used on a cellphone is a primary inspiration and basis for the IoT.

The security issues associated with consumer demand for innovative IoT are enormous. They are also unknown. Vendors will continue to develop and market new devices and sensors that they believe consumers will want. They will not generally be designed for security, although current concern about data privacy may be addressed at some level. The ability to create secure IoT devices and services depends upon the definition and agreement of security standards for the anticipated interconnectivity methods. Until the methods are defined and the security issues are addressed by all vendors, new devices and sensors for consumers will seriously increase the vulnerability of the IoT as it develops (e.g. Green 2015).

Unlike IoT, the future IIoT will benefit from the fact that adoption of new devices and methods will come slower since control engineers will be resistant to potentially dangerous new technologies. Some security issues that will be adopted by consumers in the larger scale IoT may be resolved by the time they are adopted in industrial control settings. However, it may be impossible for control engineers to have enough time to adequately evaluate these new technologies before they have to be adopted.

16.3.3 Support for the Future IoT

In this subsection, we discuss services and collaborative efforts for supporting users of the IoT.

16.3.3.1 Computing and Infrastructure

Industrial Control Efficiency

Efficiencies are already being realized in manufacturing and even in our own homes with the inclusion of industrial control systems for everything from heating, ventilation, and air conditioning control to ambient light sensing and adjustment. These capabilities allow facility operating costs to be slashed by adjusting temperature and lighting based on occupancy. In addition, through data collection, trends for energy consumption can be developed and monitored to support problem diagnosis. However, this is just the beginning of the Internet of Things revolution in manufacturing. From a facility maintenance perspective, smart devices such as emergency lighting and smoke detectors can alert maintenance staff proactively when problems occur. Mundane tasks like monitoring soap levels in washrooms can also be automated to reduce staff levels and decrease response time. Other technologies such as smart elevators promise to more efficiently manage resource use and minimize wait times for users by predicting peak usage and positioning cars strategically for response.

A larger increase in efficiency will come when smart IoT products begin communicating between themselves automatically. For example, infrared and motion sensors could communicate to other systems that there has been no human activity in the home or office, and thus appliances such as water coolers, HVAC systems, and water heaters could be switched to a lower-power standby mode. This obviously happens with no human intervention and presents a security issue. Automatic authorization and command of utilities and appliances can be dangerous if it is possible that they can be set to unsafe ranges. The communication method between smart devices must be secure so that outsiders will not have access to information such as when humans are present or not.

Networks and Infrastructure

The future IoT will require significant changes in supporting infrastructure to accommodate the increased number of addressable sensors and devices, and the diversity in how those devices communicate. It is however unclear what architectural changes will occur, since relevant interoperability guidelines, communication standards, and vendor designs are still immature.

IoT end devices and sensors currently use a large number of communication methods, such as Bluetooth, NFC, RFID, ZibBee, WiFi, Ethernet, and cellular protocols. The TCP/IP 3-way handshake produces unwanted overhead network traffic for some inter-device packet communications, and may need to be replaced for some communication links in the future IoT. Requirements for global addressability of things for IoT automation may be satisfied by using IPv6 addressing. An alternative may be to abandon global addressability using NAT or local-only addressing such as private IPv4 addressing. This may provide an additional layer of security over a globally-accessible IoT model using IPv6. IP addressing is not ubiquitous among IoT devices—many use RFID, Bluetooth, or proprietary addressing methods. Some researchers in the field of future IoT network architecture propose integrating technology from IEEE 802.15.4 wireless sensor networks (WSN) with that of RFID systems and IP networks (e.g. Atzori et al. 2010; Castellani et al. 2010; Gubbi et al. 2013). This may allow use of small packet frames compared to what is needed for the IP protocol. Most wireless sensors using WSN spend most of their time "sleeping" so that they are not responsive.

Clearly the initial IoT will be a blend of many different types of hardware using diverse communication methods. This will increase the attack surface for malicious outsiders, and is likely to create a privacy issue for new systems designed without security in mind.

In time, the future IoT networks will be self-aware and self-adapting, so that they can accommodate the bandwith and global connectivity requirements of new subnets of things when they connect. This will require better standardization and interoperability guidelines between vendors so that the networks can accomplish efficient transport and maintain network security of the data on the subnet devices. Research in network management methods and secure software-defined networking is needed.

A careful accounting of the IoT devices should be accommodated by the infrastructure, similar to mobile technology. As proposed by Zorzi et al. (2010), the infrastructure should:

- Discover entities based on identifier, location, type, provider, etc.
- Provide a lookup service for entity properties, which would allow interaction with the device
- Monitor the state of the entities, and keep the lookup information and links up to date

It is obvious that the desired state of the future IoT infrastructure is quite different from the present state, and that much research and development is needed. Security must be considered and tested as part of that effort.

New Territories for Network Complexity

As the IoT network infrastructure grows, as expected, in the exponential manner, an even more fundamental environmental game changer may occur. We will eventually cross a network complexity threshold and enter new territories beyond the limits of conventional system manageability, perhaps even stretching human comprehension. Qualitative increases in technological complexity—enormous in size, connectivity, interdependence, heterogeneity, and dynamic capabilities— coupled with the exploding network growth occurring now in under-served communities worldwide might defeat conventional scientific and engineering approaches to cybersecurity.

Right now, the cyber-research community offers few insights to help us observe, stabilize, and control very-large-scale and multidimensional networks. There is still much for us to understand about how social-cognitive and cyber-physical links will govern overall network complexity. Even single vendors have problems keeping up with all of the items in their product line. We expect vendors to produce large numbers of inexpensive devices with short lifetimes on the order of less than a year. Those devices will be present on the IoT long after they are no longer supported by the vendor. Nobody will fully understand the devices in their network. This increased system complexity enhances opportunities for adversarial attack.

Computing and Cloud Services

Computing and data storage methods have changed drastically from centrally located large single mainframes in the middle of the century to powerful desktop computers and servers in the later part of the century. Further, a client–server service model has emerged so that much of the computing and storage is done remotely and a thin client interacts with the remote service over the Internet, or "the cloud." The current cloud model will necessarily support initial IoT devices since this is the model in place, but some changes will be needed to accommodate the expected architecture of the IoT.

As mentioned, devices in the IoT may not be globally addressable via an IP address and may not be directly connected to cloud storage and processing. In addition, one need not keep all of the data coming from a sensor device. The data needs to be processed locally into useful, intelligent information, which can then be forwarded to a proxy device such as a cellphone or dedicated server. The proxy device can then store the data locally or push it to the cloud for further processing. Privacy concerns can be a factor in protecting the sensor data. There is no doubt that cloud services will need to scale with the growth of the IoT, but it should not scale exactly to the size of the data collected by the sensors. Some of the sensor data will be thrown away, and some will be sent to a central cloud for storage and further processing. Restricted-access local cloud storage and processing may be useful for temporary or permanent sensor data, especially when sensor data or cloud service traffic becomes prohibitively high to push to a globally-accessible public cloud. Gubbi et al. (2013) propose a scalable cloud framework which allows networking, computation, storage and visualization themes to scale separately, accommodating the indeterminate growth of the future IoT.

Context-aware computing (e.g. Perera et al. 2014) will be important as IoT sensor data volume becomes large and data owners wish to better harvest the value of the information. The data collected by the sensors will not have high value unless it is properly understood by storing context-related information with the raw sensor data so that data interpretation is more meaningful. Cloud storage and processing techniques can then be used to analyze additional contextual meta-data together with the sensor data. Examples of context-oriented meta-data are location and time information, data owner, digital chain of custody, access information, and medical history (for health care data).

An important aspect of future IoT cloud storage and computing is that ISPs and telecommunication companies control access to the data, and may even have preferential rights to data the customers store on their platforms. Once your data leaves your globally-connected IoT sensor or IP-connected proxy server for the cloud, you no longer have the ability to secure the data. You must encrypt the data or rely on provider security. While the providers may mean well and may have very high security standards, they cannot provide 100 % protection against unauthorized access.

New Computing Paradigms

While standard silicon-wafer CPU computing methods are commonplace today, emerging computing paradigms — nanocomputing, quantum computing, biologically or genome-based computing—might develop soon enough to make most current cybersecurity technologies obsolete, thus drastically changing the related markets.

Quantum computing and networking are already fueling lively debate, with one side making claims for the technologies' inherent security while the other side highlights the opportunities it presents for hacking. Biologically inspired computation and communication paradigms—for example, the Gaian dynamic distributed federated database (Toth et al. 2013) and related cybersecurity applications, such as artificial immune systems—will attract growing interest, especially as they offer promises for autonomous adaptation to previously unknown threats and even self-healing (Kott 2014).

If implemented, these emerging computing methods would bring an exponential layer of complexity to the IoT. Security and privacy of data would be unpredictable for systems that rely on strong encryption. Depending on the cost of the computing methods, centralized processing with cloud systems could become obsolete, especially if IoT sensor processing power both increased dramatically in capability and remained low cost.

16.3.3.2   Government and Industry Guidance and Collaboration

The exact functional nature of the future IoT for both industry and consumer cannot currently be defined. Regulators and interoperability collaborations will drive the development of future cross-industry standards (McDonald 2014). While the development of IoT standards is underway, larger organizations may not have an interest in participating if their IoT market share does not seem threatened. Gartner estimates five billion smart devices will be in use by the end of this year (2015), and yet no central IoT standards are in use, and there is no real oversight of IoT development methods (Null 2015). It is clear that a lot of work will be needed to develop a large number of standards to make the IoT function efficiently and safely, but as asserted by Schneier (Green 2015) at the moment "it's all really, really bad and it's going to come crashing down."

Some examples of current IoT standards groups are Thread, AllSeen Alliance, Open Interconnect Consortium, Industrial Internet Consortium, the ITU SG20 standards group, the IEEE P2413 project, the Apple HomeKit, the IETF RPL, CoAP, and 6LoWPAN protocol standards groups (Null 2015; Sheng et al. 2013). These cover a wide range of technical issues, such as M2M communication, interoperability between large vendors, wireless communication standards, home and user based technical IoT issues, addressability and routing issues. It is a good start, but it is only a start.

Better solutions will need to be developed as the IoT builds out and more vendor devices and functions need to be accommodated. There seems to be a lack of standardization effort related to data models, ontologies, and data formats to be used in IoT applications; this may present a barrier to innovative development of key IoT technologies (Miorandi et al. 2012). The rapid growth of the IoT makes efficient standardization difficult if not impossible. Specific issues in IoT standardization include vendor interoperability, radio/wireless access, security and privacy, addressing and networking, and guidelines for industrial environments (Atzori et al. 2010; Da Xu et al. 2014). Efficient allocation of the wireless spectrum by the FCC and similar organizations will be needed if the future IoT is to have the envisioned wireless interconnectivity. Interoperability agreements and standards and vendor collaboration will take some time as IoT market leaders engage with each other and IoT users. Since IoT development is market-driven, there is no single architect to organize this effort. Governments can provide some guidance, but cannot regulate the future IoT any more than they can regulate the global Internet.

The importance of governance in ICSs is discussed in an earlier chapter of this volume which mentions that while unstructured short—term successes are vital, long-term success requires a more structured approach. Stakeholders are less interested in making informed decisions toward an overarching plan when environments are increasingly connected (Westby 2003). Governing for security means viewing adequate security as a nonnegotiable requirement of being in business (Allen 2005). The governing body must have the authority, accountability and resources to act and enforce compliance. Among the governing documents within an organization, the most powerful to enable resource decisions and revealing to make security modifications are assessments. Four examples of current assessment methods for control systems security are NIST Cybersecurity Framework, DoE C2M2, RIPE Framework, and the DHS CSET framework. Each approach is based on years of subject matter experience and community best practices. The amount of experience securing the IoT (and future IoT) is obviously significantly less than that for current control systems, which explains in part the current inability to propose useful governance for the IoT. Not only is there no functional architect, there is also no security architect, or governing body.

16.4   Predictions and Potential Solutions

The future manufacturing will evolve to accommodate many global changes. There will be limitations on resources such as energy, population, special metals, etc. The population will demand more products. In the US there is a strong decline in the number of students pursuing education in science, technology and math, and a decline in the number who are willing to pursue career fields in manufacturing. This may significantly increase the demands for autonomous systems and robotics.

The interconnectivity of things is creating a world of unknown potential. Through distributed systems, information sharing is greatly improved. Information can reach a wider population, and products and services can be made more readily available. However, it also makes us significantly more vulnerable than we ever could have imagined in the recent world of isolated systems.

In the following subsections, we envision some potential solutions to the anticipated security challenges in the future IoT (Kott et al. 2014a).

16.4.1   Resilient Self-Adaption

Potential innovations based on resilient self-adaptation could be very important for the security of the future IoT. Cybersecurity in this case will derive largely from system agility, moving-target defenses, cybermaneuvering, and other autonomous or semi-autonomous behaviors (Jajodia et al. 2011). Exploiting such self-adaptation might mean shifting a significant fraction of design resources from reducing vulnerabilities to increasing resiliency.

A truly resilient system could experience a major capability loss due to cyberattack, but recover sufficiently rapidly and fully so that its overall mission proceeds successfully. For example, promising results have been shown for software residing on a mobile phone to perform self-healing—by applying patches or self-rewriting code—in response to abnormal behaviors it detects (Azim et al. 2014).

However, effective autonomous self-adaptation calls for a degree of machine intelligence far ahead of what's now imaginable and would also increase system complexity, thus multiplying vulnerability risks. Given that complex attacks, along with their circumstances, are both diverse and unpredictable, achieving practical resiliency is no more than probabilistic—not a comforting thought for future systems operators.

16.4.2   Mixed-Trust Systems

New design methods for mixed-trusted systems may also be important for future IoT security. We see these as security-minded, flexible, modifiable systems that combine and accommodate untrusted hardware and software—resulting from dubious supply chains, legacy elements, accreted complexity, and numerous other sources—with clean-slate components. Related ideas include a management protocol that applies trust-based intrusion detection to assess degrees of sensor-node trustworthiness and maliciousness (Bao et al. 2011).

Success depends on qualitatively significant changes in the design methodologies and tools that enable complex systems to be synthesized--for example, reinforcing untrusted components with clean-slate, highly trusted "braces." Such designs would also have to include components that could be rapidly and inexpensively modified to defend against new threats as they are discovered. A breakthrough in current formal methods or the emergence of as yet unknown but highly reliable semiformal methods would thus be required.

16.4.3   Big Data Analytics

Though still immature from a cybersecurity perspective, big data analytics—predictive and autonomous—is an area already exerting a noticeable influence. Potentially reaching global scale, able to anticipate multiple new cyberthreats within actionable timeframes, and requiring little or no human cyberanalysis (Gil et al. 2014), big data analytics is a game changer that could bring new potency to cyberdefense.

Much of this power will likely derive from aggregating and correlating a broad range of highly heterogeneous data, which is challenging in itself. Add to this heterogeneity the noise, incompleteness, and massive scale characteristic of cyber-data, and the challenges only increase (Kott and Arnold 2013). Much work remains for developing algorithms that can ferret out deeply hidden, possibly detection-protected information from so heterogeneous a mass.

16.4.4   Proactive Threat Responsiveness

Finally, IoT security may be improved through the possible emergence of proactive threat-source responses: strategy-oriented approaches, offense-based techniques, alternative security postures, and deception- and psychology-aware mechanisms. Currently, little is understood about the shape such methods might take, especially in view of the legal and policy uncertainties surrounding cybersecurity in general, and proactive cyberthreat responses in particular.

Extensive strategic and tactical knowledge developed through our long experience with conventional conflicts might offer important insights about anticipating adversaries' actions (Ownby and Kott 2006), holding adversaries at bay and defeating their will to attack. But focus on the past might also mislead and limit our thinking.

Whatever the details, any such approaches will benefit from greater situational awareness and require understanding our adversaries' architectures, infrastructure, and sensing capabilities, as well as we do our own. We will also need languages to help clearly and precisely articulate the specific defensive and offensive circumstances, cultural intelligence and adversary modeling, and deep insights into individual and collective cognitive processes.

16.5   Summary and Conclusions

IT and control systems manufacturers are seizing the opportunity of having new novel hardware devices as the "Internet of Things" begins to scale up. As the number of devices continues to increase, more automation will be required for both the consumer (e.g. home and car) and industrial environments. As automation increases in IoT control systems, software and hardware vulnerabilities will also increase.

In the near term, data from IoT hardware sensors and devices will be handled by proxy network servers (such as a cellphone) since current end devices and wearables have little or no built-in security. The security of that proxy device will be critical if sensor information needs to be safeguarded. The number of sensors per proxy will eventually become large enough so that it will be inconvenient for users to manage using one separate app per sensor. This implies single apps with control many "things," creating a data management (and vendor collaboration) problem that may be difficult to resolve. An exponentially larger volume of software will be needed to support the future IoT. The average number of software bugs per line of code has not changed, which means there will also be an exponentially larger volume of exploitable bugs for adversaries.

Until there are better standards for privacy protection of personal information and better security guidelines on communication methods and data/cloud storage, security of wearable and other mobility devices will remain poor. More work needs to be spent on designing IoT devices before too many devices are built with default (little or no) security.

Physical security will change as well. As self-healing materials and 3D printers gain use in industry, supply-chain attacks could introduce malicious effects, especially if new materials and parts are not inspected or tested before use.

The main benefits of autonomous capabilities in the future IoT is to extend and complement human performance. Robotic manufacturing and medical nanobots may be useful; however, devices (including robots) run software created by human. The danger of the increased vulnerabilities is not being addressed by security workers at the same rate that vendors are devoting time to innovation. Consider how one might perform security monitoring of thousands of medical nanobots in a human body.

The ability to create secure IoT devices and services depends upon the definition of security standards and agreements between vendors. ISPs and telecommunication companies will control access to sensor data "in the cloud" and they cannot provide 100 % protection against unauthorized access. IoT user data will be at risk.

Diversity of the hardware and software in the future IoT provides strong market competition, but this diversity is also a security issue in that there is no single security architect overseeing the entire "system" of the IoT. The "mission" of the entire IoT "system" was not pre-defined; it is dynamically defined by the demand of the consumer and the response of vendors. Little or no governance exists and current standards are weak. Cooperation and collaboration between vendors is essential for a secure future IoT, and there is no guarantee of success.

References

Ahmad, A., Paul, A., Rathore, M. M., & Rho, S. (2015). Power aware mobility management of M2M for IoT communications. *Mobile Information Systems, 501,* 14.

Allen, J. (2005). *Governing for enterprise security (CMU/SEI-2005-TN-023).* Pittsburgh, PA: Software Engineering Institute, Carnegie Mellon University.

Astrom, K. J., & Hagglund, T. (2001). The future of PID control. *Control Engineering Practice, 9,* 1163–1175.

Atzori, L., Iera, A., & Morabito, G. (2010). The Internet of Things: A survey. *Computer Networks, 54*(15), 2787–2805.

Azim, T., Neamtiu, I., & Marvel, L. (2014). Towards self-healing smartphone software via automated patching, *Proceedings 29th IEEE/ACM International Conference Automated Software Eng. (ASE 14),* (pp. 623–628), ACM

Bao, F., Chen, I., Chang, M., & Cho, J. (2011). Trust-based intrusion detection in wireless sensor networks. *Proceedings 2011 IEEE International Conference Communications (ICC 11)* (pp. 1–6). DOI: 10.1109/icc.2011.5963250.

Bennett, S. (1996). A brief history of automatic control. *IEEE Control Systems, 96*, 17–25.

Blowers, M. (2014). *Know thy operator; Establishing ground truth in industrial control systems (ICS).* Las Vegas, NV: BSIDES.

Castellani, A., Bui, N., Casari, P., Rossi, M., Shelby, Z., & Zorzi, M. (2010, March). Architecture and protocols for the Internet of Things: A case study. *Pervasive Computing and Communications Workshops (PERCOM Workshops), 2010 8th IEEE International Conference on* (pp. 678–683). IEEE.

Cavalcanti, A., Hogg, T., Shirinzadeh, B., & Liaw, H.C. (2006). Nanobot communication techniques: A comprehensive tutorial. *International Conference Control, Automation, Robotics and Vision, ICCARV, 2006, Singapore.*

Cavallaro, F. (2015). *Changing minds: The first step to closing the manufacturing skills gap.* EBN Online [Online]. Retrieved July 31, 2015, from http://www.ebnonline.com/author.asp?section_id=2171&doc_id=278288.

Charles, H. K., Jr. (2005). Miniaturized electronics. *Johns Hopkins APL Technical Digest, 26*(4), 402–413.

Chui, M., Loffler, M., & Roberts, R. (2010). The Internet of Things. *McKinsey Quarterly, 2*(2010), 1–9.

Da Xu, L., He, W., & Li, S. (2014). Internet of Things in industries: A survey. *IEEE Transactions on Industrial Informatics, 10*(4), 2233–2243.

Endress + Hauser. (2014). *Brochure. EtherNet/IP: Leveraging instrument information to enterprise level.* Reinach: Endress + Hauser.

Endsley, M. (2014). *Integrating Humans & Autonomy* [Online] March 2014. Retrieved September 1, 2015, from https://s3.amazonaws.com/edas.assets/cogsima2014/CogSIMA_2014_Endsley.pdf.

Forrest, C. (2015). *Chinese factory replaces 90% of humans with robots, production soars.* Tech Republic [Online] July 30, 2015. Retrieved August 6, 2015, from http://www.techrepublic.com/article/chinese-factory-replaces-90-of-humans-with-robots-pr.

Gil, S., Kott, A., & Barabási, A.-L. (2014). A genetic epidemiology approach to cyber-security. *Scientific Reports, 4*, 5659.

Glickman, D. (2015). *How cell phones can help end world hunger*, National Geographic (June 10, 2015).Retrievedfromhttp://news.nationalgeographic.com/2015/06/150610-hunger-nutrition-cell-phone-farming-agriculture-africa-world/.

Green, T. (2015). Schneier on 'really bad' IoT security: 'It's going to come crashing down', Network World (April 13, 2015). Retrieved from http://www.networkworld.com/article/2909212/security0/schneier-on-really-bad-iot-security-it-s-going-to-come-crashing-down.html.

Gubbi, J., Buyya, R., Marusic, S., & Palaniswami, M. (2013). Internet of Things (IoT): A vision, architectural elements, and future directions. *Future Generation Computer Systems, 29*(7), 1645–1660.

Heyer, C. (2010). Human-robot interaction and future industrial robotics applications. *International Conference on Intelligent Robots and Systems, 18–22 October 2010* (pp. 4749–4754). IEEE/RSJ.

Higgins, K.T. (2015). *Working with the next generation of plant pros.* Food Processing [Online]. Retrieved July 31, 2015, from http://www.foodprocessing.com/articles/2015/next-generation-of-plant-pros/?show=all.

Hirukawa, H. (2015). Robotics for innovation. *2015 Symposium on VLSI Technology (VLSI Technology) (Vol. June).*

Holdren, J. P., et al. (2012). *A national strategic plan for advanced manufacturing* (p. 2012). Washington, DC: US National Science and Technology Council.

Industrial Internet Consortium. (2015). *Industrial Internet reference architecture* (p. 2015). Needham, MA: Industrial Internet Consortium.

Jajodia, S., Ghosh, A., Swarup, V., Wang, C., & Wang, X. (2011). *Moving target defense: Creating asymmetric uncertainty for cyber threats* (Vol. 54). New York: Springer.

Joshi, P.C., et al. (2012). Direct digital additive manufacturing technologies: Path towards hybrid integration. *Future of Instrumentation International Workshop (FIIW), 2012.*

Karimi, K., & Atkinson, G. (2015). *What Internet of Things needs to become a reality.* EE Times July, 19.

Kennedy, S. (2015). *Made in China 2025.* Center for strategic and international studies [Online] June 2015. Retrieved August 11, 2015, from http://csis.org/publication/made-china-2025.

Kletz, T.A. (2009). *Bhopal leaves a lasting legacy.* Chemical Processing [Online] November 23, 2009. Retrieved August 28, 2015, from http://www.chemicalprocessing.com/articles/2009/23 8/?show=all.

Kott, A. (2014). *Towards fundamental science of cyber security* (Network Science and Cybersecurity, pp. 1–13). New York: Springer.

Kott, A., & Arnold, C. (2013). The promises and challenges of continuous monitoring and risk scoring. *IEEE Security and Privacy, 11*(1), 90–93.

Kott, A., Swami, A., & McDaniel, P. (2014a). Six potential game-changers in cyber security. *Computer, 47*(12), 104–106.

Kott, A., Wang, C., & Erbacher, R. F. (Eds.). (2014b). *Cyber defense and situational awareness.* New York: Springer.

Krueger, M., et al. (2014). A new era. *ABB Review, 4*, 70–75.

Matchar, E. (2015). *With this self-healing concrete, buildings repair themselves.* Smithsonian Magazine [Online] June 5, 2015. Retrieved July 22, 2015, from http://www.smithsonianmag. com/innovation/with-this-self-healing-concrete-buildings-repair-themselves-180955474/?no-ist.

McDonald, C. (2014). *How the developments of standards will affect the Internet of Things, Computer Weekly.com (November 2014).* Retrieved from http://www.computerweekly.com/feature/How-the-development-of-standards-will-affect-the-internet-of-things.

Meister, J.(2015). *Fourth industrial revolution analyzed in new report* [Online] May 5, 2015. Retrieved July 8, 2015, from http://www.pddnet.com/news/2015/05/fourth-industrial-revolution-analyzed-new-report.

Melchels, F. P. W., Domingos, M., Klein, T. J., Malda, J., & Bartolo, P. J. (2012). Additive manufacturing of tissues and organs. *Progress in Polymer Science, 37*(8), 1079–1104.

Miorandi, D., Sicari, S., De Pellegrini, F., & Chlamtac, I. (2012). Internet of Things: Vision, applications and research challenges. *Ad Hoc Networks, 10*(7), 1497–1516.

Monostoria, L. (2014). Cyber-physical production systems: Roots, expectations and R&D challenges. *The 47th CIRP Conference on Manufacturing Systems* (Vol. 17, pp. 9–13).

Moore, D. A. (2006). *Inherently safer technology in the context of chemical site security.* Alexandria, VA: AcuTech. Testimony before the U.S. Senate Environment and Public Works Committee.

Murphy, R., & Shields, J. (2012). *The role of autonomy in DoD systems.* Federation of American Scientists [Online] 2012. Retrieved from http://fas.org/irp/agency/dod/dsb/autonomy.pdf.

NIST (2015). *About Manufacturing.gov! Manufacturing.org* [Online]. Retrieved August 21, 2015, from http://www.manufacturing.gov/about_adv_mfg.html.

Null, C. (2015). *The state of IoT standards: Stand by for the big shakeout*, TechBeacon (September 2, 2015). Retrieved from http://techbeacon.com/state-iot-standards-stand-big-shakeout.

Ownby, M., & Kott, A. (2006). Reading the mind of the enemy: predictive analysis and command effectiveness. *CCRTS 2006.*

Perera, C., Zaslavsky, A., Christen, P., & Georgakopoulos, D. (2014). Context aware computing for the Internet of Things: A survey. *IEEE Communications Surveys and Tutorials, 16*(1), 414–454.

Pinto, J. (2012). *The Automation Internet of Things, Automation World* (September 25, 2012). Retrieved from http://www.automationworld.com/sensors-discrete/automation-internet-things.

Pique, A., Mathews, S. A., Pratap, B., Auyeung, R. C. Y., & Karns, B. J. (2006). Embedding electronic circuits by laser direct-write. *Microelectronic Engineering, 83*, 2527–2533.

Press, G. (2014). *Internet of Things by the numbers: Market estimates and forecasts.* Forbes [Online] August 22, 2014. Retrieved July 22, 2015, from http://www.forbes.com/sites/gilpress/2014/08/22/internet-of-things-by-the-numbers-marke.

Requicha, A. A. G. (2003). Nanobots, NEMS, and nanoassembly. *Proceedings of the IEEE, 91*, 1922.

Rizzo, T. (2013). *Wearable tech news* (January 22, 2013). Retrieved from http://www.wearabletechworld.com/topics/from-the-experts/articles/323855-wearable-technology-next-mobility-market-booming.htm.

Schartel, M. (2015). *Software architects in the IoT, Bosch ConnectedWorld Blog* (11 March 2015). Retrieved from http://blog.bosch-si.com/categories/technology/2015/11/software-architects-iot/.

Sheng, Z., Yang, S., Yu, Y., Vasilakos, A., Mccann, J., & Leung, K. (2013). A survey on the IETF protocol suite for the Internet of Things: Standards, challenges, and opportunities. *IEEE Wireless Communications, 20*(6), 91–98.

Starr, K. (2015). *Tuning in to customer controls.* Westerville, OH: ABB Advanced Services.

The Economist, Editorial. *The third industrial revolution.* The Economist [Online] April 2012. Retrieved June 24, 2015, from http://www.economist.com/node/21553017/print.

Toth, A., et al. (2013). Coalition warfare program (CWP): Secure policy controlled information query and dissemination over a BICES network. In T. Pham et al. (Eds.), *Ground/air multisensor interoperability, integration, and networking for persistent ISR IV.* Baltimore, MD: SPIE Digital Library. http://proceedings.spiedigitallibrary.org/proceeding.aspx?articleid=1691136.

Ukil, A., Sen, J., & Koilakonda, S. (2011, March). Embedded security for Internet of Things. *Emerging Trends and Applications in Computer Science (NCETACS), 2011 2nd National Conference on* (pp. 1–6). IEEE.

Vermesan, O., & Friess, P. (Eds.). (2013). *Internet of Things: Converging technologies for smart environments and integrated ecosystems.* Aalborg, Denmark: River Publishers. E-Book. ISBN 978-87-92982-96-4.

Want, R., Schilit, B. N., & Jenson, S. (2015). Enabling the Internet of Things. *IEEE Computer Society, 1*, 28–35.

Waring, J. (2014). *Mobile World Live* (October 16, 2014). Retrieved from http://www.mobileworldlive.com/featured-content/home-banner/connected-devices-to-hit-4-3-per-person-by-2020-report/.

Weiser, M. (1991). The computer of the 21st century, Special issue on communications, computers, and networks. *Scientific American, 3*(3), 3–11.

Westby, J.R. (2003). *Information Security Governance: Toward a Framework for Action*, Business Software Alliance. Retrieved from http://www.bsa.org/country/Research%20and%20Statistics/~/media/BD05BC8FF0F04CBD9D76460B4BED0E67.ashx.

Whitmore, A., Agarwal, A., & Da Xu, L. (2014). The Internet of Things — A survey of topics and trends. *Information Systems Frontiers, 17*(2), 261–274.

Williamson, M. (2015). 3D printing space exploration. *Engineering and Technology, 10*(2), 40–43.

Wu, D., Greer, M.J., Rosen, D.W., & Schaefer, D. (2013). Cloud manufacturing: Drivers, current status and future trends. *ASME 2013 International Manufacturing Science and Engineering Conference, Madison, Wisconsin (Vols. MSEC2013-1106).*

Young, S. (2015). *The automation dilemma: Job shifts or eliminations?* Argus Leader [Online] August 10, 2015. Retrieved August 15, 2015, from http://www.argusleader.com/story/news/2015/08/10/automation-dilemma-job-shifts-eliminations/31441.

Zorzi, M., Gluhak, A., Lange, S., & Bassi, A. (2010). From today's intranet of things to a future Internet of things: a wireless-and mobility-related view. *IEEE Wireless Communications, 17*(6), 44–51.

Zuehlke, D. (2010). SmartFactory — Towards a factory-of-things. *Annual Reviews in Control, 34*, 129–138. doi:10.1016/j.arcontrol.2010.02.008.

Printed in the United States
By Bookmasters